VERIFICATION OF COMMUNICATION PROTOCOLS IN WEB SERVICES

WILEY SERIES ON PARALLEL AND DISTRIBUTED COMPUTING

Editor: Albert Y. Zomaya

A complete list of titles in this series appears at the end of this volume.

VERIFICATION OF COMMUNICATION PROTOCOLS IN WEB SERVICES

Model-Checking Service Compositions

ZAHIR TARI
PETER BERTOK
ANSHUMAN MUKHERJEE
RMIT University

Published by John Wiley & Sons, Inc., Hoboken, New Jersey.
Published simultaneously in Canada.

Library of Congress Cataloging-in-Publication Data:

Tari, Zahir.
Verification of communication protocols in web services : model-checking service compositions / Zahir Tari, Peter Bertok, Anshuman Mukherjee.
pages cm – (Wiley series on parallel and distributed computing ; 83)
ISBN 978-0-470-90539-5 (hardback)
1. Web services–Testing. 2. Computer network protocols. I. Bertok, Peter, 1952–. II. Mukherjee, Anushuman. III. Title.
TK5105.88813.M85 2013
004.6′2–dc23

2013011613

Printed in Singapore.

10 9 8 7 6 5 4 3 2 1

We would like to thank
our families for all their support
during both good and difficult times

CONTENTS

PREFACE

The last decade has seen a major shift toward a service-oriented paradigm. Companies have been promoting their software as services to be used by other applications over the web, and the ubiquity of the Internet has allowed these services to be used from across the globe. The major results of this shift include resolving software interoperability issues, increased reusability of code, easy interapplication communications, and significant cost reduction, which have created significant business opportunities for companies offering webservices.

However, individual webservices seldom meet all the business requirements of an application. Usually, an application interacts with several web services, as required by its workflow. Considering that this might require a number of activities, including sharing data with multiple services, tracking the response for each service request, and detecting and compensating service failures, a domain-specific language is generally used for service composition. Each service's offerings are outlined by interfaces that also serve as a basis for service composition.

Nevertheless, any error or omission in these published interfaces could result in a number of glitches in the composition and the overlying application. This is exacerbated further by dynamic service composition techniques wherein services could be added, removed, or updated at runtime. Consequently, service-consuming applications depend heavily on verification techniques for reliability and usability assertion.

Traditionally, software systems were verified by rigorous testing under a variety of circumstances. The success of such approaches depends entirely on the methods used to choose the test cases. Given the complexity of contemporary systems, comprehensive knowledge of an entire system is difficult to obtain, and test cases are often based on educated guesses.

The scope of applications based on service composition is expanding rapidly into critical domains in which the stakes are high, such as stock markets and financial transactions. To achieve dependability, verification cannot be based solely on educated guesses—more reliable techniques are needed. Model checking is a formal method that has the ability to endorse the correctness of a system. Model-checking techniques offer a solution, as they can verify a system exhaustively and can be used in conjunction with testing techniques to further enhance reliability. The process involves modeling a system before verifying it for a set of properties by using a model-checking tool. However, this approach has hitherto been used sparingly because of the associated time and memory costs, and the use of model-checking techniques in verifying service compositions has not been very common. This has been exacerbated further by the size of formal representations, which are often too large for human comprehension.

In this book we describe new solutions to deal with these limitations in verifying a service composition. A technique is presented for modeling a service composition prior to verifying it using a model-checking tool. Compared to techniques that are ad hoc and temporary, this solution streamlines the transformation by introducing a generic framework that transforms the composition into intermediate data transfer objects (DTOs) before actual modeling. The DTOs help in automating the transformation by allowing access programmatically to the information required. The experimental results indicate that the framework takes less than a second (on average) to transform BPEL specifications. Memory requirements are lowered by storing the states as the difference from an adjoining state. An additional reduction in time is realized by concurrent exploration of the modules of a hierarchical model. These techniques reduce memory requirements by up to 95% and processing time by up to 86%. The time-reduction technique is also extended to nonhierarchical models. This involves introducing hierarchy into a flat model in linear time before applying time-reduction techniques. At the same time, the method ensures that the transformed model is equivalent to the original model.

Zahir Tari
Peter Bertok
Anshuman Mukherjee

CHAPTER 1

INTRODUCTION: SERVICE RELIABILITY

Service-oriented architecture (SOA)–based applications are built as an assembly of existing web services wherein the component services can span across several organizations and have any underlying implementations. These services are invoked in a sequence based on the business logic and on the workflow of the application. They have alleviated software interoperability problems and catapulted SOA into the forefront of software-development architectures. The rapid inroads made by such applications can be attributed to their agility, maintainability, and modularity.

SOA-based applications require software components to be exposed as *services*. Each service has an *interface* that outlines the functionality exposed. Ideally, an application is designed by discovering appropriate services, using their interfaces, and composing them. Such static compositions require the services involved to be perpetual and consistent throughout the lifetime of the application. Microsoft Biztalk [52] and Oracle WebLogic [38] are among popular static composition engines.

However, existing web services can break, and newer (and probably better) services can surface. Furthermore, a change in the business logic of an application during its lifetime might necessitate that additional web services be composed dynamically. Such a state of events has culminated in dynamic web service composition. Compared to their static counterparts, an application based on dynamic

Verification of Communication Protocols in Web Services: Model-Checking Service Compositions, First Edition. Zahir Tari, Peter Bertok, Anshuman Mukherjee.

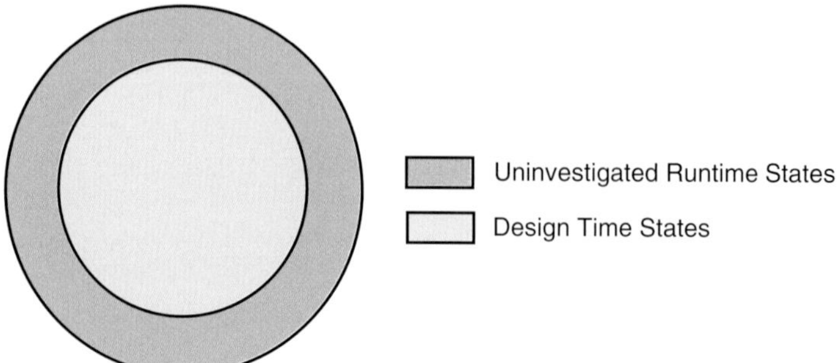

FIGURE 1.1 Additional states for runtime verification.

composition is open to modification, extension, and adaptation at runtime. Stanford's Sword [44] and HP's eFlow [7] are among the popular dynamic service composition platforms.

Nevertheless, dynamic composition [9,57] presents immense challenges. An enterprise application is expected to be void of deadlocks, live-locks, and conflicts. A static composition can be *verified* for these behavioral properties at design time. However, the verification of dynamically composed applications can be done only at runtime. This is exacerbated further by services that do not conform to their published interfaces at runtime. Considering the remarkable ingenuity of formal methods in runtime verification of traditional systems, they ought to be used for SOA-based applications [5,28].

The reliability and usability of SOA-based applications require lifelong verification of the corresponding service composition. This includes verifying a composition at design time and monitoring its behavior at runtime. Verification at the design stage involves generating and scrutinizing the entire state space of the composition for behavioral properties. Unless the underlying composition is altered at runtime, the application would always be in one of the states scrutinized. However, as shown in Figure 1.1, the application might reach uninvestigated states at runtime, owing to the dynamic nature of the composition. These states could be reached if services in the target application are added, removed, or updated. To verify the behavioral properties for runtime states, the model checking should not terminate with design-time verification. Instead, it should continue at runtime to determine the uninvestigated states reached by the application and to scrutinize them to verify the behavioral properties.

Conventional techniques [1,42] cannot be used to verify SOA-based applications, for several reasons. First, most faults are related to the business logic of the service composition rather than to the source code or implementation of underlying services; second, even if an issue has been found with the implementation of a service, the source code is usually not available for rectification; and third, even if the source code is available, it cannot be rectified immediately, as this might break many other applications using this service. Furthermore, the reliability of conventional verification methods were seriously undermined by the *Ariane 5* rocket launch failure [15] and the deaths due to malfunctioning of a Therac-25 radiation therapy machine [45] despite rigorous software testing. The teams investigating these disasters recommended using formal methods to complement testing, as the former assures exhaustive verification of a system [15,45].

Formal methods have remarkable ingenuity in warranting the safety and usability of a system. They involve writing a formal description of the system that is under deliberation and analyzing it to discover faults and inconsistencies. The formal description of a system is abstract, precise, and complete [33]. Although the abstractness allows a high-level understanding of the system, all inconsistencies and ambiguities in it are resolved in formulating a precise and complete description. Furthermore, the abstractness makes it possible to ignore the underlying architectural differences in SOA-based applications and to analyze them like any other software application. At the early stages of application development, formal methods are often employed that involve requirement analysis, specification, and high-level design.

The formal description of SOA-based applications should comprise the business logic for underlying service composition. Among all the domain-specific languages that were proposed for specifying web service composition, the Business Process Execution Language for web services (BPEL4WS or simply BPEL) [2,4,17] stands out as the de facto industry standard. Unfortunately, the overlapping constructs [54] and the lack of sound formal or mathematical semantics [46,51] in BPEL do not allow it to be used as a formal description. These inconsistencies are the outcome of two conceptually contrasting languages (Web Services Flow Language (WSFL) [37] of IBM and XLANG [50] of Microsoft) that were amalgamated to constitute BPEL [46]. This necessitates transforming the textual specification of BPEL into a formal description prior to formal analysis.

Unfortunately, existing solutions for formalizing a BPEL specification are ad hoc and temporary [26,40,55,56]. Despite the many modeling languages available (e.g., Promela, petri nets, automata, process algebras), these solutions specifically target a particular language. In pursuit of a generic solution, we transform a BPEL specification into an intermediate specification before the actual formalization. In software engineering, data transfer objects (DTOs) constitute a commonly used design pattern for storing and transferring data [16], and we use DTOs to store the generic intermediate specification, wherein each BPEL activity is mapped to a separate DTO. These DTOs can then be transformed into any modeling language.

However, model-checking techniques often have associated time and memory requirements that exceed the resources available, and software developers often skip formal methods because of budget and deadline constraints. Consequently, it is necessary to address these issues before we can use the method to verify SOA-based applications. A BPEL specification verification is preceded by memory- and time-reduction procedures for model checking [15]. The time and memory costs for model checking are linked—any reduction in memory requirements entails an increase in execution time [22].

Although it is possible to check a system model irrespective of its size and orientation (i.e., flat or hierarchical), it is important to recognize the advantages of a hierarchical and succinct system representation. A hierarchical model is easy to draw, analyze, and maintain [39]. Analyzing a system model might also assist in

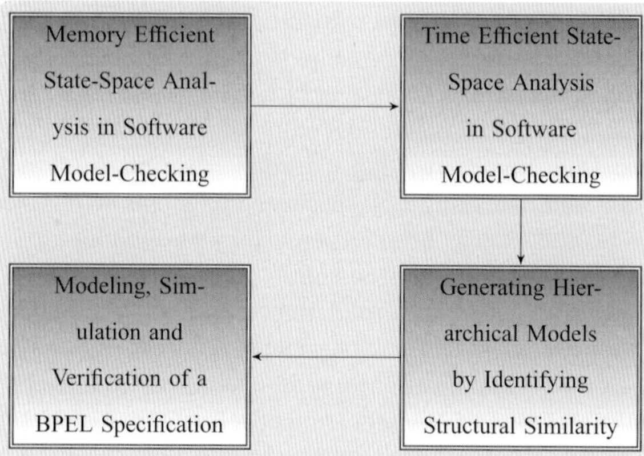

FIGURE 1.2 Verification steps.

accomplishing additional objectives, such as identifying the overall architecture of the system, understanding its dependencies, visualizing the flow of information through it, identifying its capabilities and limitations, and calculating its complexity [13]. Having recognized the importance of concise and modular system representation, we present techniques to introduce hierarchy into a flat model. As illustrated in Figure 1.2, this technique immediately precedes the procedure for model checking an SOA-based application.

1.1 MOTIVATION

SOA-based applications are prone to failures and inconsistencies, owing to multiple *single points of failure* (SPOFs) [8,36]. An SPOF is an element or part of a system whose failure leads to a system crash and eventually to the termination of service or to erroneous behavior. Typical SPOFs in a service composition could be (1) the composition itself, and (2) any component service that is also created by composing services. This is essentially because the reliability of the constituent services does not guarantee the reliability of the composition. Consequently, irrespective of efforts to validate the individual services, their composition remains an SPOF. The problem is further exacerbated by dynamic service compositions wherein services can be added to, removed from, or replaced in the composition at runtime. Considering that an SOA-based application constitutes a hierarchy of services, a failure at any level can break the application. This is illustrated in Figure 1.3.

Although model-checking techniques can be used to verify a service composition exhaustively and determine the SPOFs, they are used sparingly, due to the associated time and memory requirements. Model checking involves scrutinizing the reachable states of a system to identify predefined undesirable properties. However, modern software systems have very large state spaces, owing to their complex and concurrent components. Consequently, the time required to examine each of these

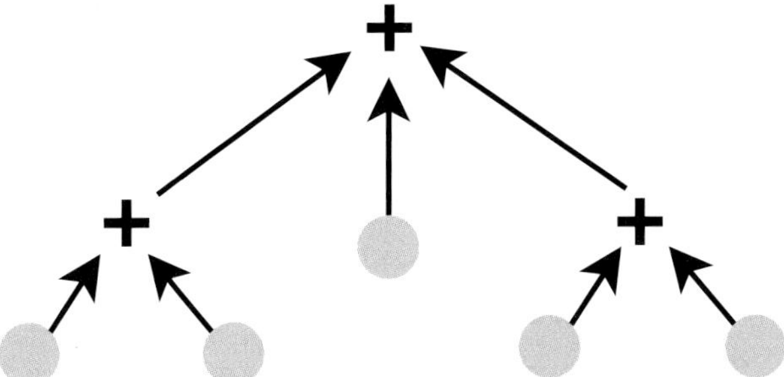

FIGURE 1.3 An SOA-based application constitutes a hierarchy of services.

states is substantial. This is aggravated further by systems that reach one or more states repeatedly during their course of execution. Without detecting duplicate states, model checking can take a very long time. By storing the states generated hitherto in memory and comparing them to any state reached subsequently, we can reduce model-checking time significantly. However, storing the large state space of a system has significant memory requirements.

The formal representation (or model) of a service composition can also be used to determine the SPOFs, because a formal model is unambiguous, owing to its mathematical semantics. However, the representation can be huge for a complex composition, and it might be impossible for a human modeler to analyze and identify the SPOFs.

The last three decades have seen extensive research on model-checking techniques [31]. Most of the work has focused on state-space explosion [11], wherein an overwhelmingly large number of states need to be checked to verify a system. Although numerous techniques have been proposed [11,22,34,53], further improvements are still needed.

1.2 TECHNICAL CHALLENGES

The proliferation of web services over the last decade has called for improved reliability of service compositions, and addressing this with formal methods is a promising approach. The first two major challenges addressed in this book relate to a twofold problem: (1) the memory costs for storing states increase with the size of the state space; and (2) the delay in generating state space increases with the size of the state space. The remaining issues relate to the installation of hierarchy into a model and to the verification of a BPEL specification.

- *How can the memory costs of model-checking a service composition be reduced?* For verification, a composition needs to be formalized and then evaluated by a model-checking tool. The tool generates the state space of the system and scrutinizes it for undesirable properties. During state-space exploration, a state can be generated more than once. To avoid analyzing the same states repeatedly, it is necessary to remember the states already explored by storing them in memory. This also ensures termination, a condition in which no new states could be generated. However, this can lead to storing a vast number of states and eventually to state-space explosion. This results in huge memory costs, as each new state has to be stored. We look into ways of reducing this memory requirement.

- *How can the time taken by model-checking a service composition be reduced?* State-space analysis of a service composition is performed by generating a reachability graph wherein each node corresponds to a state of the composition. However, the ever-increasing intricacies in contemporary SOA-based systems make the reachability graph contain a vast number of states. The resulting state-space explosion [11] leads to huge delays in producing and analyzing the state space. This is exacerbated further by having to store states that have been generated so far and compare each of them to all states produced previously. Regardless of the numerous algorithms proposed for efficient storage and comparison of states, there is always an associated time overhead. We look at various ways of reducing the delay.
- *How can we install hierarchy into a flat model to make it exponentially more succinct?* A service composition needs to be modeled prior to generating its reachability graph using one of several modeling languages available. This is a tedious and error-prone activity, and several techniques have been proposed to autogenerate a formal representation of the software system under consideration [10,27]. The primary objective of autogenerating a model is to produce the input for a model-checking tool; enhancing human understandability of the model rendered (e.g., by introducing modularity and hierarchy) is considered less important. However, the formal model for service composition might assist a human modeler in accomplishing additional objectives such as identifying the overall architecture of the composition, understanding its dependencies, visualizing the flow of information through it, identifying its capabilities and limitations, and calculating its complexity [13]. The flat models produced by autogenerating techniques provide little help in accomplishing these objectives. We examine various ways of introducing hierarchy into a flat model and making it exponentially more succinct.
- *How can we model, simulate, and verify a BPEL specification?* Being loosely coupled systems, the safety and reliability of SOA-based applications depend on the precision of service descriptions. Any implicit assumption or unforeseen usage scenarios can lead to undesirable consequences, such as deadlocks or race conditions [48]. Further complexities can be added by dynamic service composition, wherein services could be added, removed, or updated at runtime. The business process execution language (BPEL) is the de facto industry standard for service composition. Any inconsistencies or ambiguities in it will affect the reliability and hence the usability of the system produced. We look into ways of modeling, simulating, and verifying a BPEL specification.

1.3 SUMMARY OF EARLIER SOLUTIONS

In this section we sum up earlier solutions and point out their main limitations. In later chapters we examine them in more detail.

- *Memory-efficient state-space analysis in software model checking.* Extensive research on memory-efficient state-space analysis techniques has produced good results over the last three decades, but there are still issues to be solved. Most existing solutions can be classified as either (1) exhaustive storage [22,34,47], (2) partial storage [11], or (3) lossy storage [35,53] techniques. Exhaustive storage techniques compress and store each state in the state space, whereas partial storage techniques store only a subset of these states. Lossy storage techniques differ from exhaustive techniques in using compression algorithms that are not reversible. Exhaustive techniques are characterized by the compression algorithm used to encode a state (e.g., state collapsing [53], recursive indexing [34], very tight hashing [29], sharing trees [30], difference compression [43]). As indicated previously, each of these techniques has an associated time delay. One solution proposed [22] reduces the memory costs by 95% while only tripling the delay and is considered one of the best existing techniques. Partial techniques use specific algorithms (e.g., state-space caching) to determine states that could be safely deleted from memory. Exhaustive techniques are by far the most generic and are widely used. However, all these techniques are open to improvement, such as further reduction in the memory requirements for model checking and reduction in the associated time overhead.
- *Time-efficient state-space analysis in software model checking.* Time-efficient state-space analysis techniques have received less attention than have memory-efficient techniques. This possibly indicates a greater tolerance to delays in model checking. All existing solutions for reducing the time requirement for model checking can be categorized as either (1) partial order reduction [21,41], (2) symmetry-based reduction [18], or (3) modular state-space generation [12]. Partial order techniques involve determining *stubborn sets* (i.e., sets of transitions in which a transition outside a set cannot affect the set's behavior) and executing only the transitions enabled in each set. However, the problem of deciding if a set of transitions is stubborn is at least as difficult as the reachability problem [15]. The symmetry method exploits the presence of any symmetrical components in a system that exhibit identical behavior and have identical state graphs. The subgraphs of these components in the reachability graph of the entire system are usually interchangeable with some permutation of states. However, it is difficult to determine a subgraph whose permutations would produce other subgraphs (known as the *orbit problem* [14,19]). Furthermore, these techniques are void for models that lack symmetry. Modular state-space generation involves generating the reachability graph of each module independently and then composing them to generate the reachability graph

for an entire model. Although modular techniques look more promising, most existing solutions are dated [12].

- *Reducing the size of a formal model.* Most existing solutions decrease the size of a model by transforming it based on a set of proposed postulates. The transformations proposed by Berthelot [6] aim to reduce the size of a petri net model by merging two or more of its places or transitions based on certain conditions. The transformations used most frequently are implicit place simplification and pre- and post-agglomeration of transitions. These transformations have been extended for colored petri nets [20,32]. Although these transformations preserve several classical properties of nets (e.g., boundedness, safety, liveness) and reduce the number of reachable states when performing state-space analysis, the transformed model may not be equivalent to the original model. Consequently, an analysis of the reduced model would be incomplete.
- *Verification of a BPEL specification.* The existing solutions for formalizing a BPEL specification involve a transformation into (1) petri nets or colored petri nets [40,48,49,55], (2) process algebras [25], (3) an abstract state machine [23,24] or (4) an automaton [3,27]. The problem is addressed by generating a model for each BPEL activity using one of the aforementioned modeling languages. Thereafter, users are required to scan the BPEL specification and replace each activity with its corresponding formal model. Apart from being a cumbersome process, such an exercise is error-prone and time consuming. Although there are solutions that automate this translation, they do not consider BPEL's most interesting and complicated activities, such as *eventHandler* and *links* [27]. Despite being feature complete, the models obtained using Stahl's report [49] are bulky and error-prone, owing to the plain petri nets used. The abstract state-machine-based solutions are also feature-complete. However, they lack adequate tool support for simulation and verification.

1.4 SUMMARY OF NEW WAYS TO VERIFY WEB SERVICES

In this section we highlight the new techniques, models, and algorithms presented in this book to address the various problems described earlier.

- *Memory-efficient state-space analysis technique.* A technique is described to reduce the memory costs otherwise involved in model-checking a service composition by storing states as the difference from one of the neighboring states. Asserting that "the change in a state is always smaller than the state itself," storing the states in difference form results in a reduction in memory costs of up to 95%. Based on the neighboring state used to calculate the difference, the technique is divided further into two related models: (1) a *sequential model* stores a state as to how different it is from its immediately preceding state; and (2) a *tree model* stores a state as to how different it is from its nearest state in explicit form. The solution is based on the exhaustive storage technique discussed earlier. The 95% reduction noted above allows model checking in a machine with only 5% of the memory needed otherwise. The advantage is thus twofold: (1) only 5% of the physical memory is required to validate the composition, and (2) as more states can now be stored in a memory of the same size, the chance of a complete state-space composition analysis is high. The compression algorithm achieves a 95% reduction in memory requirements with only twice the delay. Other solutions [22,34] incur considerably larger delays and offer significantly less memory reduction.

- *Time-efficient state-space analysis technique.* A method is also presented to reduce the time requirement for model checking a service composition. It includes formalizing the composition as a hierarchical model that consists of a set of interdependent modules. The reduction in delay offered is attributed to the concurrent exploration of all such modules in a hierarchical model and exposing the outcome using special data structures. These structures, known as *parameterized reachability graphs* and *access tables*, act as a repository of corresponding module behavior, and a module can use these data structures to determine the behavior of any other module without actually executing the module. In addition to concurrency, exposing such module behavior repositories eliminates the need to execute a module more than once and thereby helps, to reduce the delay. The dependency on a module of other modules is injected into its repository by using parameters. Later, these parameters are assigned specific values to obtain the corresponding reachability graph for the hierarchical model. The technique offers a time reduction of 86% in generating the first 25,000 markings. Other solutions [21,41] offer significantly less reduction in delay. Furthermore, the solution prerequisites (i.e., a hierarchical model) are less stringent than those of techniques that necessitate stubborn sets or symmetry in the model.
- *Technique for reducing the size of a model exponentially.* This technique allows an exponentially more succinct representation of a service composition by embracing the notion of hierarchy. A hierarchical model consists of a set of modules wherein each module represents a system component. In such a setup, the module for a high-level component refers to its underlying components via their module names or references. This avoids "blow-up" in including the actual representation of underlying components. Furthermore, the benefits increase with each additional high-level component sharing an underlying component. Consequently, the model obtained would be exponentially more succinct, owing to the notion of the hierarchy introduced. The solution establishes hierarchy after identifying the set of structurally similar components in a model. The experimental results indicate that this takes linear time, and the time also depends on the number of identical components in the model. The solution is generic and can be applied to any modeling language that defines the semantics of hierarchy and structural similarity.
- *Technique for modeling, simulating, and verifying a BPEL specification.* A verification framework is described to formalize a BPEL specification by

transforming it into an XML-based formal model. Existing solutions utilize ad hoc techniques to formalize a BPEL specification into a specific modeling language. However, the fast growth of SOA-based applications in recent years has necessitated the streamlining of BPEL formalization. In pursuit of generalizing the transformation, initially the specification is transformed into intermediate DTOs. This is done by extending the *Spring framework* to represent each BPEL activity using a *Java bean*. Spring helps to significantly automate the creation of intermediate DTOs. The framework instantiates the beans corresponding to activities in a BPEL specification and injects the dependencies to yield a *bean factory*, which contains all the information required to construct a formal model.

As mentioned previously, the generic intermediate specification can be transformed into any modeling language. However, to demonstrate the actual formalization, these DTOs are transformed into an XML-based formal model (e.g., colored petri nets (CPNs) [39]). This is done using the *Java Architecture for XML Binding (JAXB) 2* application programming interface (API), which offers a practical, efficient, and standard way of mapping between XML and Java code. However, the JAXB 2 API requires XML mapping for each BPEL activity. It uses the corresponding schemas to transform the bean factory into a formal model. Consequently, a CPN-based template is applied to each BPEL activity. Templates are part of a formal model. Given that CPN models (1) offer hierarchical semantics, (2) are visually expressive, (3) can be both simulated and verified, (4) are XML documents like BPEL specification, (5) have extensive tool support, and (6) support a built-in and user-defined data type, they are selected as the target for transformation. Furthermore, an object model is used to determine the relationship between BPEL activities. This object model is used to create Java beans corresponding to BPEL activities. In addition, the CPN templates exploit any hierarchy in the object model to reuse a parent template for its child activities after any required customization. The solution is feature-complete and extensible.

1.5 STRUCTURE OF THE BOOK

The remainder of the book is organized as follows:

- In Chapters 2 to 4 we provide the necessary background knowledge to ensure a better understanding of the relevant concepts. This includes a run-through of model checking, colored petri nets, hashing, BPEL activities, the Spring framework, and the Java Architecture for XML Binding 2 API.
- In Chapter 5 we present two techniques for reducing the memory costs otherwise involved in model checking, which involve storing states as the difference from one of the neighboring states. Theoretical evaluation and experimental results indicate a significant reduction in memory requirements.

- In Chapter 6 we describe a novel method to reduce the time requirement for model checking a hierarchical model by exploring its inter dependent modules in parallel. These dependencies are stored as parameters in special data structures. On assigning specific values to these parameters, these dependencies are resolved and the reachability graph envisioned is obtained. The experimental results indicate a significant reduction in the time requirement.
- In Chapter 7 we introduce a technique to install hierarchy into a flat model by identifying the structural similarity. The technique is based on the decrease-and-conquer approach, wherein the bigger problem is broken into smaller problems and the solutions to the smaller problems are combined to solve the original problem. Compared to existing techniques, the model rendered is equivalent to the original model.
- In Chapter 8 we portray a verification framework to formalize a BPEL specification by transforming it into an XML-based formal model. This is done by extending the Spring framework and using JAXB 2 APIs. In addition, we determine a hierarchical relationship among BPEL activities to enhance the efficiency of this transformation. This framework (1) is extensible, (2) has a small amount of transformation time, and (3) can be used in combination with existing techniques.
- We conclude in Chapter 9 by summarizing the main achievements reported and listing possible directions for future research.

REFERENCES

1. P. Ammann and J. Offutt. *Introduction to Software Testing*. Cambridge University Press, New York, 2008.
2. T. Andrews, F. Curbera, H. Dholakia, Y. Goland, J. Klein, F. Leymann, K. Liu, D. Roller, D. Smith, S. Thatte, I. Trickovic, and S. Weerawarana. *Business Process Execution Language for Web Services, Version 1.1*, May 2003.
3. J. A. Fisteus, L. S. Fernández, and C. D. Kloos. Formal verification of BPEL4WS business collaborations. In *E-Commerce and Web Technologies*, pages 76–85, 2004.
4. A. Arkin, S. Askary, B. Bloch, F. Curbera, Y. Goland, N. Kartha, C. K. Liu, V. Mehta, S. Thatte, P. Yendluri, A. Yiu, and A. Alves. *Web Services Business Process Execution Language, Version 2.0*, December 2005.
5. A. A. Bayazit and S. Malik. Complementary use of runtime validation and model checking. In *Proceedings of the 2005 IEEE/ACM International Conference on Computer-Aided Design*, ICCAD '05, pages 1052–1059. IEEE Computer Society, Washington, DC, 2005.
6. G. Berthelot. Checking properties of nets using transformation. In *Advances in Petri Nets 1985, covers the 6th European Workshop on Applications and Theory in Petri Nets—Selected Papers*, pages 19–40. Springer-Verlag, Berlin, 1986.
7. F. Casati, S. Ilnicki, L.-J. Jin, V. Krishnamoorthy, and M.-C. Shan. eflow: a platform for developing and managing composite e-services. In *Proceedings of the Academia/Industry*

Working Conference on Research Challenges, AIWORC '00, pages 341–348. IEEE Computer Society. Washington, DC, 2000.

8. D. Chakraborty, F. Perich, A. Joshi, T. W. Finin, and Y. Yesha. A reactive service composition architecture for pervasive computing environments. In *Proceedings of the IFIP TC6/WG6.8 Working Conference on Personal Wireless Communications*, PWC '02, pages 53–62, 2002.
9. P. P.-W. Chan and M. R. Lyu. Dynamic web service composition: a new approach in building reliable web service. In *Advanced Information Networking and Applications*, pages 20–25, 2008.
10. J. Chen and H. Cui. Translation from adapted UML to Promela for Corba-based applications. In *Proceedings of the 11th International SPIN Workshop*, pages 234–251, 2004.
11. S. Christensen, L. M. Kristensen, and T. Mailund. A sweep-line method for state space exploration. In *Proceedings of the 7th International Conference on Tools and Algorithms for the Construction and Analysis of Systems, TACAS 2001*, pages 450–464, 2001.
12. S. Christensen and L. Petrucci. Modular state space analysis of colored petri nets. In *Proceedings of the 16th International Conference on Application and Theory of Petri Nets ICATPN '95*, pages 201–217. Springer-Verlag, Berlin, 1995.
13. C. Z. Garrett. Software modeling introduction. *Borland White Paper*. Borland Software Corporation, Austin, TX, March 2003.
14. E. M. Clarke, E. A. Emerson, S. Jha, and A. P. Sistla. Symmetry reductions in model checking. In *Computer Aided Verification*, volume 1427 of *Lecture Notes in Computer Science*, pages 147–158. Springer-Verlag, Berlin, 1998.
15. E. Clarke, O. Grumberg, and D. Peled. *Model Checking*. MIT Press, Cambridge, MA, 2000.
16. W. Crawford and J. Kaplan. *J2EE Design Patterns*. O'Reilly & Associates, Sebastopol, CA, 2003.
17. F. Curbera, Y. Goland, J. Klein, F. Leymann, D. Roller, S. Thatte, and S. Weerawarana. *Business Process Execution Language for Web Services, Version 1.0*. IBM, Microsoft, BEA Systems, July 2002.
18. L. Elgaard. *The Symmetry Method for Colored Petri Nets: Theory, Tools and Practical Use*. Ph.D. dissertation, University of Aarhus, Denmark, 2002.
19. E. A. Emerson and A. P. Sistla. Symmetry and model checking. *Formal Methods in System Design*, 9(1–2):105–131, 1996.
20. S. Evangelista, S. Haddad, and J.-F. Pradat-Peyre. Syntactical colored petri nets reductions. In *Proceedings of the 3rd International Symposium on Automated Technology for Verification and Analysis, ATVA 2005*, volume 3707 of *Lecture Notes in Computer Science*, pages 202–216. Springer-Verlag, Berlin, 2005.
21. S. Evangelista and J.-F. Pradat-Peyre. On the computation of stubborn sets of colored petri nets. In *Proceedings of the 27th International Conference on Application and Theory of Petri Nets, ICATPN '06*, pages 146–165. Springer-Verlag, Berlin, 2006.
22. S. Evangelista and J.-F. Pradat-Peyre. Memory efficient state space storage in explicit software model checking. In *Proceedings of the 12th International SPIN Workshop on Model Checking of Software*, volume 3639 of *Lecture Notes in Computer Science*, pages 43–57. Springer-Verlag, Berlin, 2005.

23. D. Fahland, W. Reisig, and D. Fahland. ASM-based semantics for BPEL: the negative control flow. In *Proceedings of the 12th International Workshop on Abstract State Machines*, pages 131–151, 2005.
24. D. Fahland. Complete abstract operational semantics for the web service business process execution language. *Informatik-Berichte 190*. Humboldt-Universität zu Berlin, September 2005.
25. A. Ferrara. Web services: a process algebra approach. In *Proceedings of the 2nd International Conference on Service Oriented Computing, ICSOC '04*, pages 242–251, 2004.
26. H. Foster, S. Uchitel, J. Magee, and J. Kramer. Model-based verification of web service compositions. In *Proceedings of the 18th IEEE International Conference on Automated Software Engineering, 2003*, pages 152–161, October 2003.
27. X. Fu, T. Bultan, and J. Su. Analysis of interacting BPEL web services. In *Proceedings of the 13th World Wide Web Conference*, pages 621–630. ACM, New York, 2004.
28. Y. Gan, M. Chechik, S. Nejati, J. Bennett, B. O'Farrell, and J. Waterhouse. Runtime monitoring of web service conversations. In *Proceedings of the 2007 Conference of the Center for Advanced Studies on Collaborative Research*, CASCON '07, pages 42–57. ACM, New York, 2007.
29. J. Geldenhuys and A. Valmari. A nearly memory-optimal data structure for sets and mappings. In *Proceedings of the 10th International SPIN Conference on Model Checking Software*, pages 136–150. Springer-Verlag, Berlin, 2003.
30. J.-C. Grégoire. State space compression in spin with GETSs. In *Proceedings of the 2nd SPIN Workshop*, pages 3–19. American Mathematical Society, Providence, RI, 1996.
31. O. Grumberg and H. Veith, Eds. *25 Years of Model Checking: History, Achievements, Perspectives*, volume 5000 of *Lecture Notes in Computer Science*. Springer-Verlag, Berlin, 2008.
32. S. Haddad. A reduction theory for colored nets. In *Advances in Petri Nets 1989, covers the 9th European Workshop on Applications and Theory in Petri Nets—Selected Papers*, pages 209–235. Springer-Verlag, Berlin, 1990.
33. A. Hall. Realising the benefits of formal methods. In *Proceedings of the 7th International Conference on Formal Engineering Methods*, pages 1–4, 2005.
34. G. J. Holzmann. State compression in spin: recursive indexing and compression training runs. In *Proceedings of the 3rd International SPIN Workshop*, 1997.
35. G. J. Holzmann and A. Puri. A minimized automaton representation of reachable states. *Software Tools for Technology Transfer*, 2:270–278, 1999.
36. J. Hu, C. Guo, H. Wang, and P. Zou. Web services peer-to-peer discovery service for automated web service composition. In *Proceedings of the 3rd International Conference on Network and Mobile Computing, ICCNMC '05*, pages 509–518, 2005.
37. F. Leyman. *Web Services Flow Language, Version 1.0*. IBM, Armonk, NY, May 2001.
38. D. Jacobs. Distributed computing with bea weblogic server. In *Proceedings of the 2003 CIDR Conference*, 2003.
39. K. Jensen and L. M. Kristensen. *Colored Petri Nets: Modelling and Validation of Concurrent Systems*. Springer-Verlag, Berlin, 2009.
40. H. Kang, X. Yang, and S. Yuan. Modeling and verification of web services composition based on cpn. In *Proceedings of the 2007 IFIP International Conference on Network and*

Parallel Computing Workshops, pages 613–617. IEEE Computer Society, Washington, DC, 2007.

41. L. M. Kristensen and A. Valmari. Finding stubborn sets of colored petri nets without unfolding. In *Proceedings of the 19th International Conference on Application and Theory of Petri Nets, ICATPN '98*; pages 104–123. Springer-Verlag, Berlin, 1998.
42. G. J. Myers. *Art of Software Testing*. J. Wiley, New York, 1979.
43. B. Parreaux. Difference compression in spin. In *Proceedings of the 4th SPIN Workshop*, 1998.
44. S. R. Ponnekanti and A. Fox. Sword: a developer toolkit for web service composition. In *Proceedings of the 11th International World Wide Web Conference*, Honolulu, HI, 2002.
45. J. Rushby. Formal methods and critical systems in the real world. In *Formal Methods for Trustworthy Computer Systems, FM '89*, pages 121–125, 1989.
46. K. Schmidt and C. Stahl. A petri net semantic for BPEL4WS validation and application. In *Proceedings of the 11th Workshop on Algorithms and Tools for Petri Nets, AWPN '04*, pages 1–6, 2004.
47. K. Schmidt. Using petri net invariants in state space construction. In *Proceedings of the 9th International Conference on Tools and Algorithms for the Construction and Analysis of Systems, TACAS 2003*, pages 473–488. Springer-Verlag, Berlin, 2003.
48. J. C. Sloan and T. M. Khoshgoftaar. From web service artifact to a readable and verifiable model. *IEEE Transactions on Services Computing*, 2:277–288, October 2009.
49. C. Stahl. A petri net semantics for BPEL. *Informatik-Berichte 188*. Humboldt-Universität zu Berlin, July 2005.
50. S. Thatte. *XLANG Web Services for Business Process Design*. Microsoft Corporation, Redmond, CA, May 2001.
51. W. M. P. van der Aalst. Don't go with the flow: web services composition standards exposed. *IEEE Intelligent Systems*, January–February 2003.
52. C. F. Vasters. *Biztalk Server 2000: A Beginner's Guide*. McGraw-Hill, New York, 2001.
53. W. Visser. Memory efficient state storage in spin. In *Proceedings of the 2nd SPIN Workshop*, pages 21–35. American Mathematical Society, Providence, RI, 1996.
54. P. Wohed, W. M. P. van der Aalst, M. Dumas, and A. H. M. ter Hofstede. Pattern-based analysis of BPEL4WS. *QUT Technical Report FIT-TR-2002-04*. Queensland University of Technology, Brisbane, Australia, 2002.
55. Y.-P. Yang, Q.-P. Tan, Y. Xiao, J.-Shan Yu, and F. Liu. Verifying web services composition: a transformation-based approach. In *Proceedings of the 6th International Conference on Parallel and Distributed Computing Applications and Technologies*, pages 546–548. IEEE Computer Society, Washington, DC, 2005.
56. X. Yi and K. J. Kochut. A cp-nets-based design and verification framework for web services composition. In *Proceedings of the IEEE International Conference on Web Services, ICWS '04*; page 756. IEEE Computer Society, Washington, DC, USA, 2004.
57. L. Zeng. *Dynamic Web Services Composition*. Ph.D. dissertation, University of New South Wales, Australia, 2003.

CHAPTER 2

MODEL CHECKING

It has been observed [18] that the industry average (1) is 15 to 50 errors per 1000 lines of code delivered, (2) is about 10 to 20 defects per 1000 lines of code in Microsoft applications, and that (3) formal development methods, peer reviews, and statistical testing have helped to reduce this to zero per 500,000 lines of code.

The world has recognized the advantages of using the proper software for a particular need. This is almost as important as using the proper hardware. For example, video-streaming software might significantly inflate the broadband bill unless the correct compression technology is used. Consequently, a significant amount of time is spent in testing software prior to releasing it. Based on the magnitude of failures and their consequences, this might involve a massive cost.

Software engineering is different from other engineering disciplines because the product envisioned has no physical existence. It needs appropriate hardware to exhibit its presence and abilities. Furthermore, it was observed in 1997 that (1) software systems are discontinuous compared to physical systems, which are continuous, and (2) modern systems require that most functionalities be provided by software, thereby increasing their complexity. Continuous systems exhibit smooth

Verification of Communication Protocols in Web Services: Model-Checking Service Compositions, First Edition. Zahir Tari, Peter Bertok, Anshuman Mukherjee.

changes in output in response to a smooth change in input, whereas the output for a discontinuous system can change significantly even for a small change in input.

In recent years, the software and application domains have increased significantly. For example, General Motors began the "computer age" for automobiles by incorporating the first microcomputerized engine control in 1981 [2]. Today, a luxury car might contain up to 100 million lines of code, executing on 70 to 100 microprocessor-based electronic control units (ECUs) networked throughout the body of the car [6]. Consequently, the complexity of software has increased along with the associated cost of verification. Unfortunately, one-third of large-scale software systems end up as "failures" that do not operate as intended or are never used [11]. Other projects usually overshoot their schedule by half. This is essentially because the increased number of domains targeted for a system increases its complexity. Furthermore, any cross-domain knowledge needed in developing such intricate systems is rare among engineers. This often leads to errors in system design and development.

A range of techniques are available to resolve design errors. However, they can all be put into one of the following three categories: (1) testing, (2) design diversity, and (3) fault tolerance [4]. Traditionally, a rigorous testing phase established the reliability of software systems [1]. This involves executing a system with a set of inputs to verify that it behaves as expected. The success of such techniques depends entirely on the methods used to decide on test cases. Usually, thorough knowledge of the system is required to decide on such cases. However, considering the complexity of modern systems, this is often not the case. Consequently, most systems are tested based on *educated guesses* based on partial understanding of the system.

The discontinuous nature of software causes further problems for testing techniques. The behavior of a continuous system can be determined by testing only a few inputs and then extrapolating and interpolating them [4]. However, such techniques are not applicable to software systems, and they need to be tested extensively. This extensiveness depends on the reliability desired for the target software. Such a state of events increases the cost of high-integrity software significantly.

Design diversity has multiple teams producing multiple versions of the same software. The design errors arising from erroneous code and faulty specifications are countered by the mutually complementing products obtained. Assuming that the software developed by each team is independent, they are unlikely to share the same errors. Consequently, the fault tolerance envisioned is achieved by using them in a space- or time-redundant manner. However, the assumption of independence among different versions of the software is often not valid. Furthermore, the cost of developing multiple versions of the software acts as an impediment in using design diversity.

Fault avoidance techniques combat the aforementioned shortcomings of testing and design diversity methods. They involve removing the design flaws at an early phase of software development. Formal methods are rigorous mathematical fault-avoidance techniques that are used by system designers to specify and verify the properties desired for a system. Although they are generally employed in the early stages of system development, they can be used later to verify the correctness of system implementation [25].

Model checking [7] is a formal method for automatic verification of software systems, which offers distinct advantages over conventional testing and simulation techniques. It is a rigorous technique wherein all possible behaviors of a system are scrutinized exhaustively. Consequently, if there is a problem, model checking will detect it. It is being adopted increasingly as a standard procedure for quality assurance of software systems [19]. Contrary to traditional software systems that compute some result from the input values given, a modern software system maintains an ongoing interaction with its environment and is therefore known as a *reactive system* [13,17]. Because of the nondeterministic nature of such systems, any amount of testing is grossly inadequate to estimate their reliability [22]. Model checking is a progressively complementing standard testing procedure that is part of software development. It involves three basic steps: (1) modeling the system, (2) specifying the properties to be verified, and (3) verifying the properties in all possible states of the system. Initially, a model checker requires a formal design of the system and the properties to be verified. It then explores the state space of the system to find a state that violates the given properties, where the state space is the set of states reachable from the initial state. *Marking* is sometimes used synonymously with *state*. If a violating state is found, it is returned as a counterexample. Otherwise, the model checker returns "yes," implying that the properties are satisfied by all reachable states of the system.

Modeling in computer science is significantly different from modeling in the natural sciences. According to a recent article, computer science uses precise models wherein its properties map into the properties of the real system [3]. However, this requires some abstraction to handle any issues with the ancillary components of the model. Usually, a high-level abstract modeling language is used to model the system that is envisioned. Furthermore, it is common for a model to capture only certain specific aspects of a system. A model must not have any fundamental flaws and should not be trivial. Typically, a model checker verifies the model for the set of properties required. However, model-checking techniques are also applicable for concrete systems wherein the system description is available in detail.

It should be noted that model checking is limited to finite-state systems, but that does not reduce its importance. In most cases a system with an infinite state space could be reduced to a finite-state-space system. For example, a communication protocol without a buffer limit can be verified using a very large buffer limit. However, it turns out that most hardware controllers and communication protocols are finite-state systems [7].

Model checking requires the designer to specify system properties using a specification language. According to Biere, model checking is typically concerned with the temporal behaviors of a system, and they are described using temporal logic [3]. Pnueli first observed the benefits of using temporal logic to specify the properties of reactive systems [20]. Contrary to normal systems, a reactive system maintains ongoing interaction with its environment.

Figure 2.1 illustrates the process of *model checking*. As a prerequisite, it requires a formal model and the specification that is to be verified. Considering the time and memory constraints, the former is often an abstraction of the system to be verified.

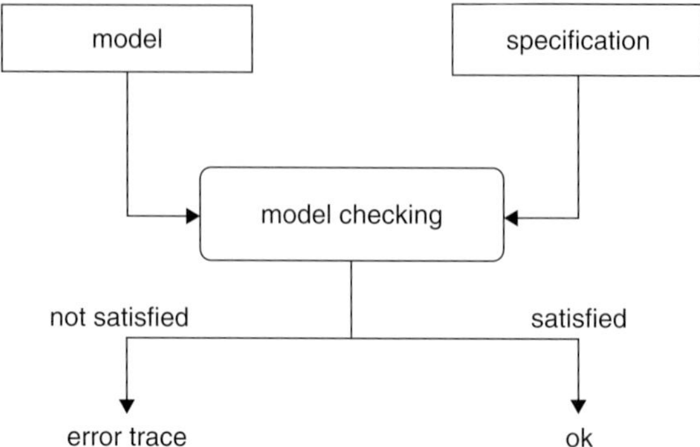

FIGURE 2.1 The model-checking process.

The specification states the properties that the target system must satisfy. This is often specified using temporal logic. The model checker verifies if the properties stated in the specification are satisfied for all possible execution paths of the system. In case the specification is not satisfied by the system, the model checker returns an error trace.

Unfortunately, the number of reachable states of any nontrivial system is extremely large. Since a model checker is required to explore and scrutinize each of these states for the set of desirable properties, model checking is time consuming. Furthermore the unique states explored earlier by the model checker need to be stored in memory to prevent exploring the same state repeatedly. Regardless of the space occupied by each state, model checking also has a large memory requirement.

2.1 ADVANTAGES AND DISADVANTAGES OF MODEL CHECKING

Model checking has several advantages [12]:

- It does not involve proofs, as opposed to *theorem proving*, which involves stating the requirement as a theorem and using the system properties to verify it.
- It is automatic and therefore fast. Automation is possible in model checking because the job of a model checker is repetitive once defined.
- The Model checker provides a counterexample if a particular state does not satisfy the requirement specified. The counterexample provided helps immensely in debugging the system.
- Model checking can be done with partial system specifications. Consequently, the verification can be started even before the design phase is complete.
- The properties that must be verified for a concurrent system can easily be specified using temporal logics.

There are, however, a few limitations in using model-checking techniques:

- Theorem proving often helps in better understanding of a system. This is essentially because model checking is mostly automatic and, unlike theorem proving, does not require a thorough understanding of the system.
- A specification using temporal logic is often difficult to understand.
- Writing the specification itself is a difficult problem.
- There is a state-space explosion problem, as discussed below.

2.2 STATE-SPACE EXPLOSION

Model checking involves scrutinizing the reachable states of a system for the undesirable or desirable properties specified. Typically, a model with a few hundred thousand states can be verified using a model-checking tool. However, considering the intricacies of modern software systems, larger models are often required, to include all the system properties required. This in turn strains the capabilities of a model-checking tool in verifying these properties. Usually, a model-checking tool remembers all the states explored by storing them in memory. This prevents losing time by checking the same state over and over. However, the enlarged state space also demands more memory for model checking.

An increase in state space also requires that the model checker scrutinize more states. This, in turn, increases the delay in model checking. This is exacerbated further by the strict time constraints of software projects.

All solutions proposed to reduce the memory requirements of the state space are classified as either (1) partial storage, (2) lossy storage, or (3) exhaustive storage. *Partial storage* techniques store in memory only a subset of the states explored. However, it is difficult to decide on the states that need to be stored. *Lossy storage* techniques produce the entire state space wherein each state explored is compressed and stored in a suitable data structure (e.g., a hash table) to ensure constant time lookup. However, the compression algorithm used is not reversible. To determine if a state is new, it is also compressed and compared with stored states. As we point out in Chapter 5, this often results in falsely identifying a state as a duplicate. There are several interesting solutions based on lossy storage:

1. *An ordered binary decision diagram* (OBDD) *with compression* uses a decision tree to store a state visited [23]. Figure 2.2 shows an acyclic graph that can store eight possible states. These states are represented using 3 bits, from 000 to 111. Each left arm of the acyclic graph represents a 0, and each right arm represents a 1. For example, starting at the root, a state 100 would use the right arm at the first level and the left arm at the remaining two levels. Finally, after traversing all the arms based on bit values, a terminal node is encountered that stores either *true* or *false*. A terminal node with *true* denotes that the marking that leads to it has been visited. Consequently, the terminal nodes for an acyclic

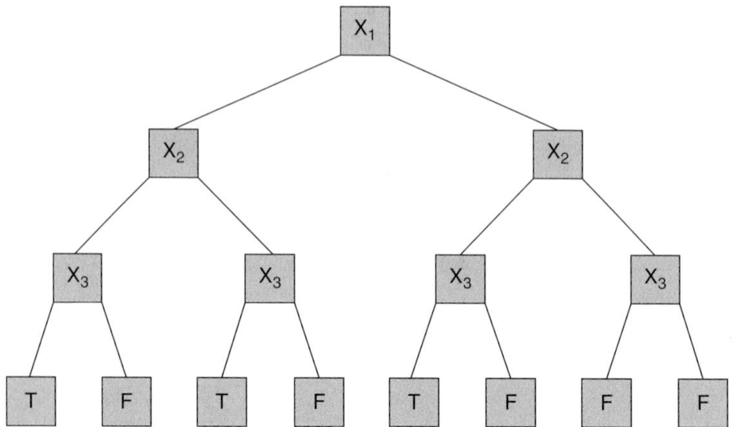

FIGURE 2.2 Decision tree for boolean function $f(x_1, x_2, x_3) = \overline{x_1} \cdot \overline{x_2} \cdot \overline{x_3} + \overline{x_1} \cdot x_2 \cdot \overline{x_3} + x_1 \cdot \overline{x_2} \cdot \overline{x_3}$

graph need to be updated whenever a new state is generated. The compression algorithm divides the bits representing a state into $p + 1$ parts such that part d has n_d bits. Each of these bit pieces has a table, and the table for the dth bit piece has k_d entries such that $m_d = \log_2 k_d << n_d$. This reduces the size of the graph by ensuring that a state is represented using fewer bits. Figure 2.3 illustrates the compression technique.

2. *An automaton representation of reachable states* stores states as a sequence of bits [16]. This is similar to an OBDD, where x bits were used to represent 2^x states. However, instead of an acyclic graph, an automaton is used to store the states. Its edges are inscribed with bit values *0* and *1*. Starting from the root node, the edges are followed based on the bits representing a state. If the terminal node has a *1*, the state is established to be a duplicate. Figure 2.4 shows an automaton that leads to a *1* node for the set of states represented by {000, 001, 101}. The automaton is modified whenever a new marking is generated, to ensure that its corresponding bit sequence leads to a *1* node.
3. *A graph-encoded tuple set* (GETS) enables compact representation of states wherein the common prefix and suffix for a set of states are used to reduce the graph size (see Figure 2.5). The reduction is obtained only when the state space is large. Otherwise, there might be an expansion of the storage required instead of the reduction envisioned. Results indicate that a GETS can decrease the memory requirements up to sevenfold, with a tripling of processing time.

Exhaustive storage techniques also produce the entire state space in which each state explored is compressed and stored in a suitable data structure (e.g., a hash table) to ensure constant time lookup. However, unlike lossy storage, the compression algorithm needs to be reversible, as otherwise the states cannot be regenerated for comparison.

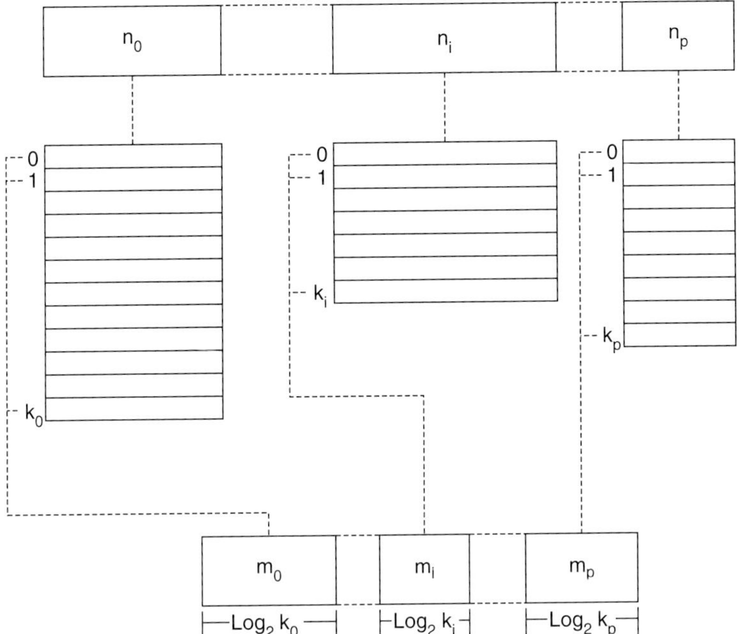

FIGURE 2.3 Compression of states represented by bits.

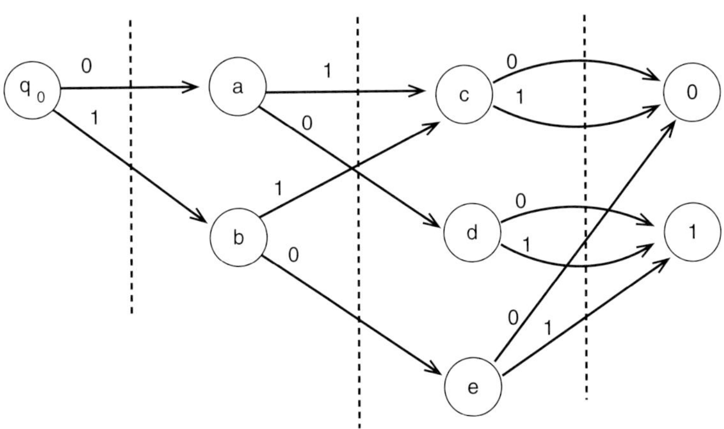

FIGURE 2.4 Storing states visited using an automaton.

When the aforementioned techniques do not work, additional techniques can be used, such as those listed below [12].

- *Compositional reasoning*. These techniques are used for concurrent systems that have multiple component processes running in parallel. Such a state of affairs makes it possible to divide a system into smaller modules and verify their

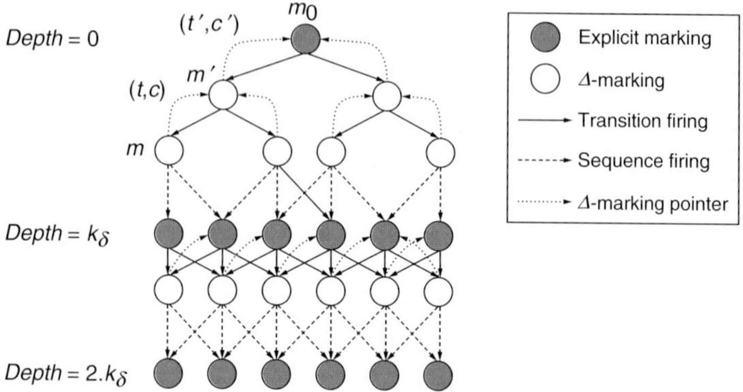

FIGURE 2.5 Generating state space with △-mappings [10].

behavior. Furthermore, if a property to be verified depends on the correctness of a particular module, it saves the effort in checking the other modules for this property. The conjunction of correctness for each of these local modules would ensure the correctness of the overlying system. However, such techniques assume mutual exclusiveness among modules and cannot be used in cases where mutual dependencies exist among the modules. Several extensions of this technique have been proposed wherein a module is verified by assuming the behavior of other modules [5]. Later, the other modules are verified to establish that their assumed behavior is correct. However, drafting the assumptions for other components is often not easy and has hitherto been done manually. Only recently has a method for automatic generation of assumption been proposed [8].

- *Symmetry reduction.* Symmetry reduction is used for finite-state systems that have replicated components. Consequently, the size of the model can be reduced and any additional execution traces can be eliminated to reduce the state space.

2.3 MODEL-CHECKING TOOLS

In this section we provide an overview of selected model-checking tools and their features.

- The SPIN model checker is used to verify asynchronous and concurrent systems. Its structure is illustrated in Figure 2.6. Initially, the graphical front end of SPIN, known as XSpin, is used to specify the high-level model of the system or protocol being scrutinized. Any syntax errors encountered in the course of generating the model are fixed. Then the model obtained is simulated to ensure a certain degree of correctness. Finally, SPIN generates an optimized

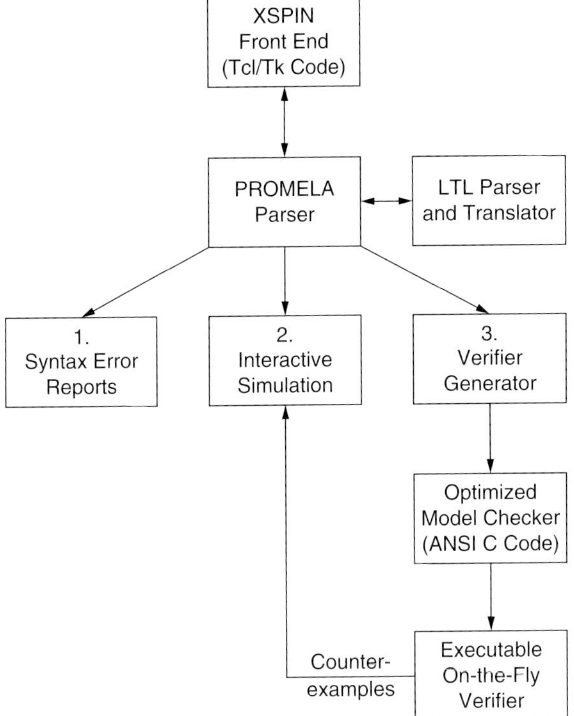

FIGURE 2.6 SPIN model checker [14].

program from the high-level specification. This program is compiled to detect any counterexamples corresponding to the properties required. SPIN allows any reduction algorithm to be used; the choice has to be made at compilation time. Any counterexamples found are sent to the simulator for further analysis.

- Colored petri nets (CPN) tools are used to create, simulate, and model-check CPN models. They are useful in verifying concurrent systems much as network protocols and workflows [24]. As shown in Figure 2.7 (top), the models are stored as XML documents. These are loaded using a graphical editor, which also makes it possible to construct the model interactively. Syntactical errors in the model are identified using the simulator, and any error detected is displayed by the editor. The editor can also be replaced using Access/CPN, as shown in Figure 2.7. This makes it possible to transform an XML-based model into Java objects. These objects are then sent to the simulator for error checking and simulating. This offers more flexibility in allowing external applications to integrate with the CPN simulator.
- The working of a Bandera tool [9] is shown in Figure 2.8. It accepts a Java program that needs to be checked against the requirements specified. The requirements are formalized using temporal logic formulas. Bandera provides

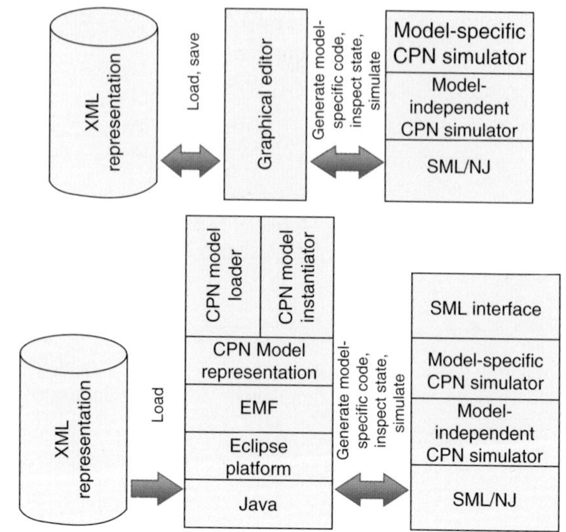

FIGURE 2.7 Architecture of CPN Tools and Access/CPN [24].

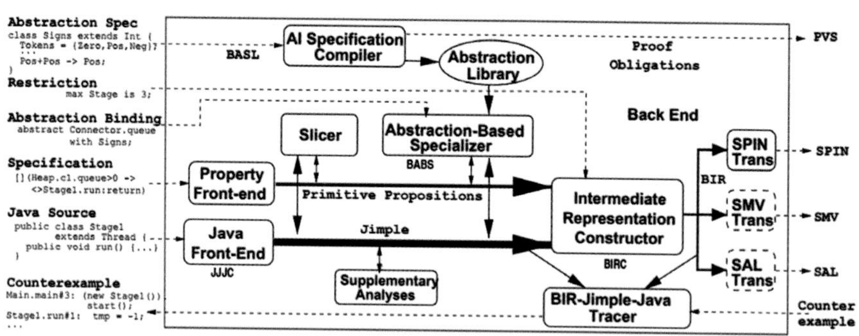

FIGURE 2.8 Bandera's internal architecture [9].

a set of specification templates that help the user to specify the requirements. When using these templates, the specification can be completed by filling in the template parameters. The transformation from Java to model-checker input language is done using multiple intermediate languages.

Model checking has been used in this book to verify service compositions because:

- It offers exhaustive verification of the system under deliberation. Consequently the enhancements in reliability and usability offered outweigh those of any alternative techniques.

- As discussed in Chapter 1, it allows lifelong verification of service compositions. This is done by verifying a composition at design time and monitoring its behavior at runtime.
- It requires creating an abstract representation of the system before verifying it. The experience in generating this representation leads to a better understanding of the system.
- It has excellent tool support [15,21], which ensures automatic verification.
- It does not require proving theorems.

REFERENCES

1. B. Beizer. *Software Testing Techniques*. Van Nostrand Reinhold, New York, 1990.
2. J. Bereisa. Applications of microcomputers in automotive electronics. *IEEE Transactions on Industrial Electronics*, 30(2):87–96, 1983.
3. A. Biere. Tutorial on model checking: modelling and verification in computer science. In *Proceedings of the 3rd International Conference on Algebraic Biology*, AB '08, pages 16–21. Springer-Verlag, Berlin, 2008.
4. C. M. Holloway. Why engineers should consider formal methods. In *AIAA/IEEE 16th Digital Avionics Systems Conference, Technical Report 01.03.* pages 16–22. Piscataway, New Jersey, 1997.
5. S. Chaki, E. Clarke, D. Giannakopoulou, and C. S. Pasareanu. Abstraction and assume-guarantee reasoning for automated software verification. *Technical Report 05.02*. Research Institute for Advanced Computer Science, Mountain View, CA, 2004.
6. R. N. Charette. This car runs on code. *IEEE Spectrum*, February 2009.
7. E. Clarke, O. Grumberg, and D. Peled. *Model Checking*. MIT Press, Cambridge, MA, 2000.
8. J. M. Cobleigh, D. Giannakopoulou, and C. S. Pasareanu. Learning assumptions for compositional verification. In *Proceedings of the 9th International Conference on Tools and Algorithms for the Construct and Analysis of Systems, TACAS 2003*, pages 331–346. Springer-Verlag, Berlin, 2003.
9. J. C. Corbett, M. B. Dwyer, J. Hatcliff, S. Laubach, C. S. Păsăreanu, and H. Zheng. Bandera: extracting finite-state models from Java source code. In *Proceedings of the 22nd International Conference on Software Engineering*, ICSE '00, pages 439–448. ACM, New York, 2000.
10. S. Evangelista and J.-F. Pradat-Peyre. Memory efficient state space storage in explicit software model checking. In *Proceedings of the 12th International SPIN Workshop on Model Checking Software*, volume 3639 of *Lecture Notes in Computer Science*, pages 43–57. Springer-Verlag, Berlin, 2005.
11. W. W. Gibbs. Software's chronic crisis. *Scientific American*, September 1994.
12. O. Grumberg and H. Veith, editors. *25 Years of Model Checking: History, Achievements, Perspectives*, volume 5000 of *Lecture Notes in Computer Science*. Springer-Verlag, Berlin, 2008.
13. D. Harel and A. Pnueli. On the development of reactive systems. In *Logics and Models of Concurrent Systems*, pages 477–498. Springer-Verlag, New York, 1985.

14. G. J. Holzmann. The model checker spin. *IEEE Transaction on Software Engineering*, 23(5):279–295, May 1997.

15. G. J. Holzmann. *The SPIN Model Checker: Primer and Reference Manual*. Addison-Wesley, Reading, MA, 2003.

16. G. J. Holzmann and A. Puri. A minimized automaton representation of reachable states. *Software Tools for Technology Transfer*, 2:270–278, 1999.

17. Z. Manna and A. Pnueli. *The Temporal Logic of Reactive and Concurrent Systems*. Springer-Verlag, New York, 1992.

18. S. McConnell. *Code Complete, 2nd edn*. Microsoft Press, Redmond, WA, 2004.

19. S. Merz. Model checking: a tutorial overview. In *Modeling and Verification of Parallel Processes*, pages 3–38. Springer-Verlag, Berlin, 2001.

20. A. Pnueli. The temporal logic of programs. In *Proceedings of the 18th Annual Symposium on Foundations of Computer Science*, SFCS '77, pages 46–57. IEEE Computer Society, Washington, DC, 1977.

21. A. V. Ratzer, L. Wells, H. M. Lassen, M. Laursen, J. F. Qvortrup, M. S. Stissing, M. Westergaard, S. Christensen, and K. Jensen. CPN tools for editing, simulating, and analysing colored petri nets. In *Proceedings of the 24th International Conference on Applications and Theory of Petri Nets, ICATPN 2003*, volume 2679 of *Lecture Notes in Computer Science*, pages 450–462. Springer-Verlag, Berlin, 2003.

22. K. Schneider. *Verification of Reactive Systems: Formal Methods and Algorithms*. Springer-Verlag, Berlin, 2004.

23. W. Visser. Memory efficient state storage in spin. In *Proceedings of the 2nd SPIN Workshop*, pages 21–35. American Mathematical Society, Providence, RI, 1996.

24. M. Westergaard and L. M. Kristensen. The access/CPN framework: A tool for interacting with the CPN tools simulator. In *Proceedings of the 30th International Conference on Applications and Theory of Petri Nets*, PETRI NETS '09, pages 313–322. Springer-Verlag, Berlin, 2009.

25. J. M. Wing. A specifier's introduction to formal methods. *Computer*, 23:8–23, September 1990.

CHAPTER 3

PETRI NETS

As discussed in Chapter 2, model checking necessitates a formal representation of a system prior to verifying it. Essentially, this involves creating a formal model of the system using any of the modeling languages available (e.g., Promela, petrinets, a process algebra, an automaton) [3]. However, the modeling language used significantly influences the properties of the model rendered. For example, the concurrent constructs of a system cannot be mapped into its model using an automaton.

A *petri net* (PN) is a mathematical modeling language and a graphical tool for the description and analysis of concurrent, asynchronous, parallel, distributed, nondeterministic, and stochastic systems [12]. As a graphical tool, it offers elements to create the formal representation of a system. Then mathematical analysis techniques can be used to render the behavior and properties of the system represented. Such analysis usually involves a computer-based tool for automation.

Petri nets are directed bipartite graphs that consist of places (circles) and transitions (rectangles) connected by arcs. The tokens (black dots) in the places define the state of a petri net. Events associated with a transition move the tokens between adjoining places along the arcs. Petri nets have been widely used as a design language for the specification of intricate workflows [16], owing to their graphical nature, expressiveness, formal semantics, and analysis techniques.

Verification of Communication Protocols in Web Services: Model-Checking Service Compositions, First Edition. Zahir Tari, Peter Bertok, Anshuman Mukherjee.

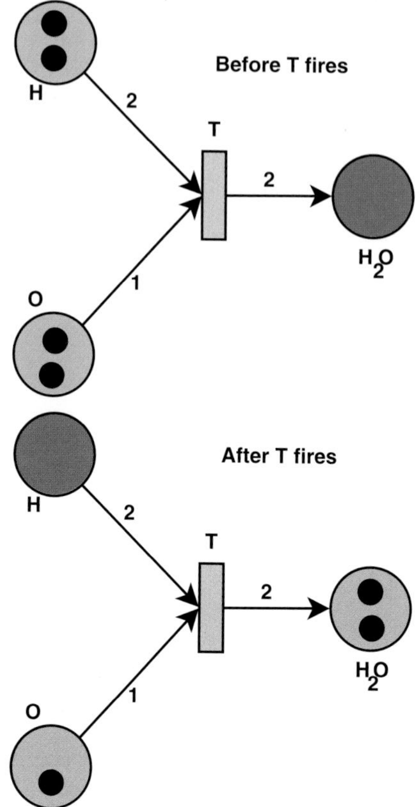

FIGURE 3.1 Petri net model [12].

Figure 3.1 illustrates a petri net model and its execution. The circles are known as *places* and the rectangles are known as *transitions*. A transition T is enabled if each of its input places P contains Z tokens, where Z is the weight on the arc connecting P to T. Consequently, the transition T is enabled. When it fires, it removes the Z_{in} tokens from their respective input places P_{in} and adds Z_{out} tokens to their output places P_{out}, where (1) Z_{in} is the weight on the arc connecting P_{in} and T, and (2) Z_{out} is the weight on the arc connecting T and P_{out}.

A petri net is defined formally as a 5-tuple PN = (P, T, F, W, M_0) [12], where

- $P = \{p_1, p_2, \ldots, p_n\}$ is a finite set of places.
- $T = \{t_1, t_2, \ldots, t_n\}$ is a finite set of transitions.
- $F \subseteq (P \times T) \cup (T \times P)$ is a set of arcs.
- $W: F \rightarrow \{1, 2, \ldots\}$ is a weight function that assigns a weight to each arc. The weight on an arc determines the number of tokens to be removed from (or added to) a place when a transition fires.

TABLE 3.1 Typical Interpretations of Transition and Places

Input Place	Transition	Output Place
Preconditions	Event	Postconditions
Input data	Computation step	Output data
Input signal	Signal processor	Output signal
Resources needed	Job	Resources released
Conditions	Clause in logic	Conclusion
Buffers	Processor	Buffers

Source: [12].

- $M_0: P \to \{0, 1, 2, \ldots\}$ is the initial marking that determines the initial number of tokens in each place.
- $P \cap T = \phi$ and $P \cup T \neq \phi$.

The behavior of a petri net is determined by the initial state and the transitions (or events) that bring system changes. Table 3.1 illustrates some typical interpretations of transitions and places.

Petri nets offer several advantages over other modeling languages:

- They have a graphical representation that is intuitive and easy to understand.
- They can model both states and events. Places and tokens are used to model states, and transitions are used to model events.
- They can be both simulated and verified.
- Model checking using petri nets and its extensions has been researched extensively in the last three decades. This has led to the development of a wide array of tools and techniques [4,6,13,14].
- Petri nets have a strong mathematical basis [12].

Petri nets are widely used, owing to their ability to model parallel and concurrent activities. This is essentially because a transition can have any number of input and output places. As shown in Figure 3.2, the execution of transition $T1$ simultaneously populates its output places, thereby, enabling transitions $T2$ and $T3$ concurrently.

Definition 3.1 *The set of transitions in $T = \{t_1, t_2, \ldots, t_m\}$ in a petri net M are concurrent if $\forall t_x \in T$, $\forall t_y \in T$, and t_x and t_y can fire in any order.*

Transitions $T2$ and $T3$ in Figure 3.2 are concurrent. However, transition $T4$ can fire only after both $T2$ and $T3$ have finished execution. Considering that these are concurrent transitions, $T4$ synchronizes the parallel components of the model.

As noted previously, at first a petri net is in its initial state, M_0. Then, if the firing of any enabled transition t_1 changes its state to M_1, state M_1 is said to be *reachable* from M_0, which is shown as $M_0[t_1 > M_1$. In general, if the ordered set of transitions $T = \{t_1, t_2, \ldots, t_m\}$ change the state of a petri net from M_0 to M_n, state M_n is said to

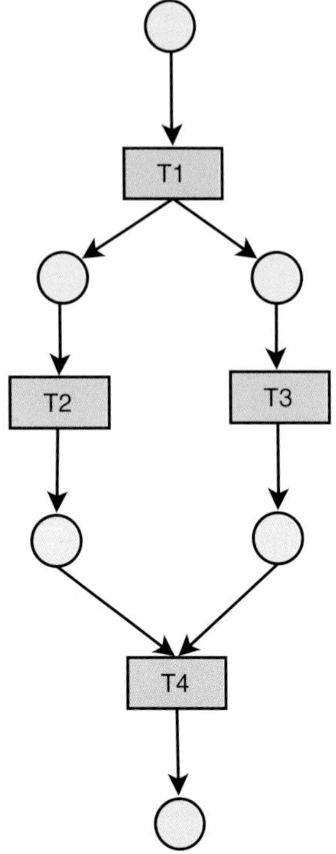

FIGURE 3.2 Concurrency and synchronization in a petri net model.

be reachable from M_0, which is shown as $M_0[T > M_n$. The set of all states that are reachable from the initial state M_0 of a petri net (N, M_0) is denoted as $R(M_0)$. The ordered set of transitions T that brought in this change is known as a *firing sequence*. The set of all firing sequences from the initial state M_0 of a petri net (N, M_0) is denoted as $L(M_0)$.

A petri net N is considered to be *live* if all the states that are reachable from its initial state M_0 have at least one enabled transition. Otherwise, it is considered to have a deadlock. Murata lists the various levels of liveness for a transition t in a petri net N with initial marking M_0 [12] as follows.

1. If t is not enabled for any of the firing sequences in $L(M_0)$, it is dead or L0-live.
2. If t can be fired at least once in some firing sequence in $L(M_0)$, it is L1-live.
3. If t can be fired at least k times in some firing sequence in $L(M_0)$, where k is a positive integer, it is L2-live.
4. If t appears infinitely often in some firing sequence in $L(M_0)$, it is L3-live.
5. If t is enabled for all states in $R(M_0)$, it is L4-live.

However, the complex and concurrent components in modern software systems have led to an exorbitant increase in the size of petri net representations.

Consequently, a range of extensions have been proposed that allow the convenient representation of petri nets [5,8,10]. These are known as *high-level* petri nets and are widely used.

3.1 COLORED PETRI NETS

Formal representations using plain petri nets are often very large. Consequently, they are difficult to draw and impractical to analyze and maintain. As noted previously, a range of extensions have been proposed to allow a convenient representation of petri nets [5,8,10]. These extensions offer all the advantages of petri nets discussed earlier. Furthermore, a formal representation using any of these extensions can be transformed into an equivalent petri net.

A colored petri net (CPN) [7] is a petri net extended with programming constructs. The concurrent constructs of the latter are supplemented with data definition and data manipulation constructs of programming languages. A CPN is used for design, specification, simulation, and verification of systems. In contrast to a PN, each token in a CPN has a data value attached. The data type of this value determines the color of the token. All tokens in a place must be of the color specified by the color set of that place. The CPN modeling language (CPN ML) is used to declare variables, functions, color sets, and so on, for CPN models.

3.1.1 CPN ML

CPN ML is a functional programming language that is based on standard ML [11]. A functional language is significantly different from object-oriented and procedural programming languages in the following ways:

- It does not maintain a state. Functions control program execution by actioning on the data they receive and returning the result. However, they (1) cannot keep a reference to the data, (2) cannot have fields or attributes, and (3) can act only on the data passed to them.
- It does not cause side effects. A function cannot (1) modify the data passed to it and (2) act on data that are not passed to it.
- It is thread-safe, as two or more functions cannot refer to the same data to operate on.
- There are no objects, and no instantiations are required.
- Data are always passed by value.
- There is no iteration or looping in functional programming, and therefore such operations are performed using recursion.
- Functions can be passed as arguments to other functions. A function can also return another function as a result.
- A function must always return a result.

In addition to being a functional language, CPN ML supports polymorphism and is strongly typed. A CPN extends standard ML with color sets, variables, multisets, and functions for manipulation of multisets [8]. The CPN ML programming language is discussed below in further detail. We refer the reader to a book by Jensen and Kristensen [8] for more comprehensive coverage.

Color Sets. As noted earlier, the data type of a place is defined by its color set, and all tokens in a place must correspond to its data type. CPN ML inherits a set of *simple color sets* from standard ML which could be used by themselves or combined to produce *compound color sets*. The simple color sets in CPN ML are:

- *Unit color set.* This set consists of a single element that is declared as ( ) (e.g., *colset C = unit*).
- *Boolean color set.* A place with a boolean color set requires that it contain tokens having *true* or *false* values (e.g., *colset C = bool*).
- *Integer color set.* A place with an integer color set requires that it contain tokens having any integer value (e.g., *colset C = int*). An integer color set does not have any restriction on the minimum and maximum values of the integers allowed. However, such restrictions can be imposed by using a *with* clause (e.g., *colset CR = int with 5 · · · 12*). A place with integer color set CR would requires that it contain tokens having any integer value between 5 and 12, both inclusive.
- *String color set.* A place with a boolean color set requires that it contain tokens having any string value (e.g., *colset C = string*). In addition, the character set of the strings allowed could be specified using a *with* clause (e.g., *colset C = string with "a" · · · "z"*). This would only allow tokens with lower case alphabetical strings. It is also possible to restrict the length of string using an *and* clause (e.g., *colset C = string with "a" · · · "z" and 6-9*). This would only allow tokens with lower case alphabetical strings, with length between 6 and 9.
- *Enumerated color set.* A place with a boolean color set requires that it contain tokens having any of the alphanumeric values specified in the enumeration (e.g., *colset C = with two/three/four/five*).
- *Index color set.* Index values are a sequence of values that are specified using an identifier and an index (e.g., *colset C = index ind with 1 · · · 10*).

These simple color sets can be used to create compound color sets using any of the following operations:

- *Product color set.* A product color set is an ordered set of simple or complex color sets (e.g., *colset C1 = int; colset C2 = string; colset C = product C1*C2*). A place with color set C can have tokens of value in the order required.
- *Record color set.* A record color set is a cartesian product of a set of simple or compound color sets. The simple color sets are identified by unique

labels to ensure that they are position independent (e.g., *colset C1 = int; colset C2 = string; colset C = record r1:C1*r2:C2*).

- *List color set.* A list color set is a list of similar or compound color set items (e.g., *colset C = list int.*)
  The minimum and maximum number of items in a list can be specified using a *with* clause (e.g., *colset C = list int with 3 ⋯ 7.*)
- *Union color set.* A union color set is a disjoint set of simple or compound color sets (e.g., *color C1 = string; color C2 = int; color C = union C1:u1 + C2:u2*).
- *Subset color set.* A subset color set is used to declare a subset of colored set declared previously. It is declared using either *by* or *with* clauses. A *by* clause is used to specify a function that returns a boolean value, and a subset color set contains only those values for which the function returns *true* [e.g., *fun even i = (i mod 2) = 0; colset even = subset int by even.*] A *with* clause is used to specify a list of values that are to be chosen from the original color set (e.g., *colset C = subset int with [3,4,5]*).
- *Alias color set.* An alias is used to declare a color set that has its properties and values similar to those of an existing color set. (e.g., *colset C1 = int; colset C = C1.*)

Color Set Functions. A set of functions are available that might be applicable either to all color sets or to a selected set of color sets. The equality (=) and inequality (< >) operators can be used on elements of all color sets to determine their equality or inequality. Other functions that are applicable for all color sets are less-than (*lt*), *legal*, and *mkstr*. The *lt* function is used to determine the order of elements in a color set.

```
colset INT = int;
INT.lt(8,10); // returns true
```

The *legal* function is used to determine if an item belongs to a color set, to its alias, or to its superset color set.

```
colset INT = int;
INT.legal(s); // returns false
```

The *mkstr* function is used to create the string representation of a color.

```
colset INT = int;
INT.mkstr(23); // returns "23"
```

A color set is said to be small if it has fewer than 100 elements. The following functions are applicable for small color sets: *all*, *ran*, *col*, and *size*. The function *all* returns a multiset containing all the elements of the color set.

```
colset C = with A | B;
c.all;// returns {A, B}
```

The function *ran* returns a random color from a color set.

```
colset INT = int;
INT.ran( ); // returns random integer
```

The function *col* returns the color at a particular position of a color set.

```
colset C = with A | B;
C.col(0); // returns A
```

The function *size* returns the size of a color set.

```
colset C = with A | B;
C.size( ); // returns 2;
```

The *list* color set has an extensive set of functions [1]:

- *e::l* is used to prepend an item *e* to list l.
- *hd l* fetches the first element of list l.
- *tl l* returns the list without the first element.
- *length l* returns the length of list l.
- *rev l* reverses list l.
- *map f l* returns the resulting list after applying function *f* to each element in list l.
- *app f l* applies function *f* to each element of list l.
- *List.nth(l,n)* returns the *n*th element in list l.
- *List.drop(l,n)* returns the list after removing the first *n* elements from list l.
- *List.take(l,n)* returns the first *n* elements of list l.
- *List.exists p l* returns *true* if *p* is true for at least one element in list l.
- *List.null l* returns *false* unless the list is empty.
- *l1^^l2* concatenate two lists, l1 and l2.
- *mem l x* returns *false* unless element *x* is in list l.
- *remdupl l* removes the duplicate elements from list l.
- *rm x l* looks for element *x* in list l and removes its first appearance.
- *rmall x l* looks for element *x* in list l and removes all occurrences of it.
- *contains l1 l2* searches list l1 for the elements in l2 and returns *true* if all elements in l2 exist in l1, regardless of their multiplicity.
- *intersect l1 l2* returns the intersection of elements in lists l1 and l2.
- *union l1 l2* returns the union of elements in lists l1 and l2.

Control Structures. CPN ML has two control structures: *if-then-else* and *case*. The former is a *multiple decision* statement, and the latter is a *multi way decision* statement. The syntax for these statements is as follows [1]:

if boolean-expression then exp1 else exp2

where the expressions *exp1* and *exp2* must be of the same type:

case exp of pattern1 => expression1
| pattern2 => expression2
| pattern3 => expression3
⋮
| patternN => expressionN

where all the expressions must be of the same type. These control structures are illustrated further using example nets in Figures 3.3 to 3.6.

3.1.2 CPN Syntax and Semantics

Figure 3.7 shows a CPN model with three places (the circles) and two transitions (the rectangles). Place *A* has two tokens (indicated by a 2 in the circle next to it), 1`5 and 1`7, where 1`5 implies that there is one token with integer value 5. The tokens

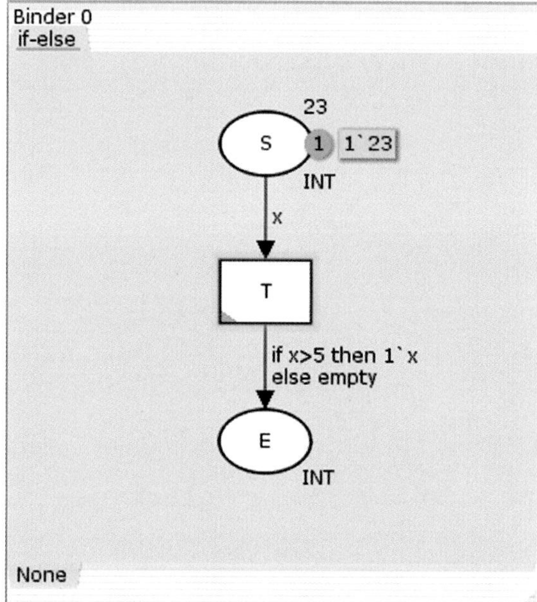

FIGURE 3.3 CPN model with an *if* control structure.

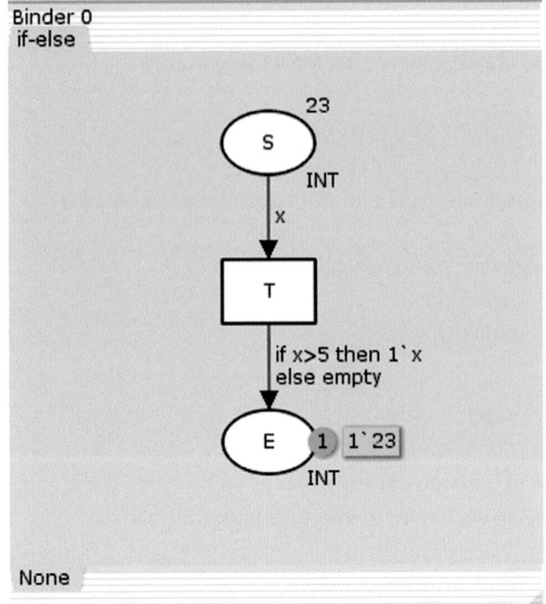

FIGURE 3.4 Model in Figure 3.3 after transition execution.

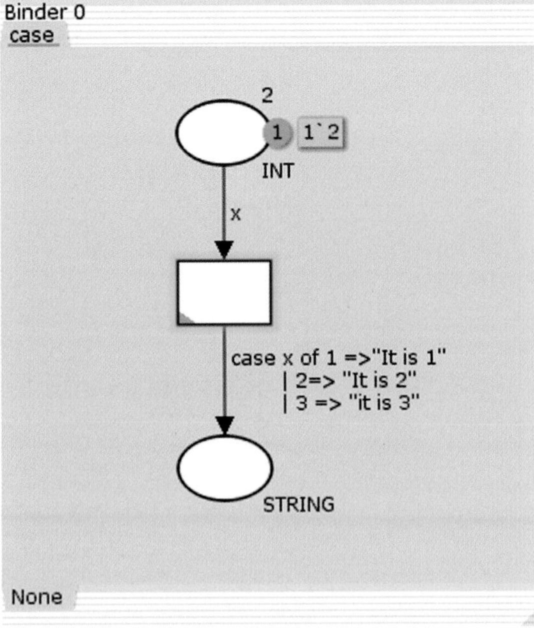

FIGURE 3.5 CPN model with a case control structure.

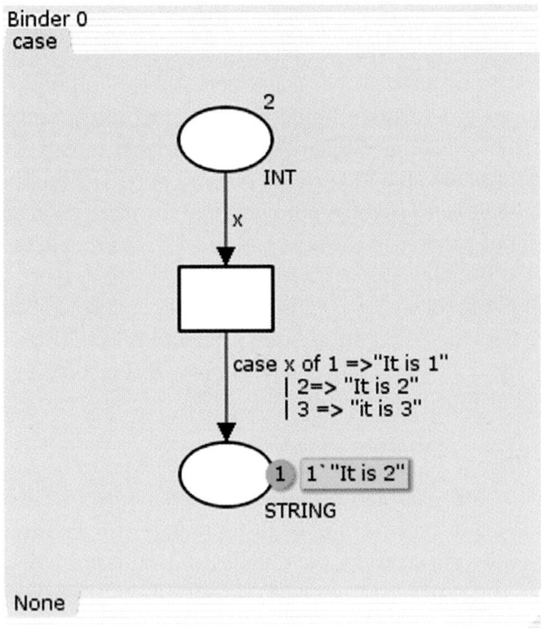

FIGURE 3.6 Model in Figure 3.5 after transition execution.

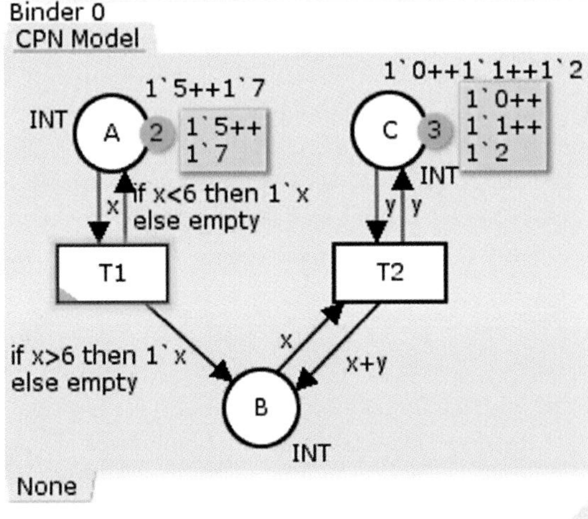

FIGURE 3.7 Colored petri net model. Variables x and y are of type INT.

in a place are listed next to it and they are separated by the "++" symbol. The text "1`0++1`1++1`2" near place C implies that it has one token with value 0, one token with value 1 and one token with value 2. Each place also has its color (or data type) inscribed next to it. In this model, all places have color INT; hence, they can only have integer tokens.

A place and a transition are connected by an arc. Transition $T1$ in Figure 3.7 has an input arc from place A and two output arcs to places A and B. When $T1$ executes, it removes tokens from input place A and adds tokens to output places A and B. The tokens removed or added are found by evaluating the arc inscription. As all of these arc inscriptions are defined in terms of the variable x, they can be evaluated by assigning an appropriate value to x, called *binding of x*. The binding of x is decided after considering the tokens in the input place and the inscription of the input arc. In the case of $T1$, input place A has tokens 1`5 and 1`7 and the input arc inscription is x. Hence, the only possible values of x for which $T1$ is enabled are 5 and 7. When T_1 fires with x bound to 5, token 1`5 is removed from $A$ and added back to $A$. No token is added to place $B$ as the *if* condition is not satisfied. When $T1$ fires with $x$ bound to 7, token 1`7 is removed from A and added to place B. The bindings for which $T2$ is enabled can be determined identically.

CPN ML Identifiers. Identifiers are used in CPN ML to declare variables, constants, functions, color sets, and so on. Any alphanumerical sequence of letters, digits, apostrophes, and underscores is an identifier, provided that it starts with a letter [1]. In the following sections, the CPN ML identifiers are discussed further.

Variables. Variables are identifiers that can be assigned any value while executing the model. As illustrated earlier, they are used in the arc expressions of a CPN model. The scope of a variable is local to the transition. Therefore, each occurrence of the variable x in the input and output arcs of transition T1 in Figure 3.7 refers to the same variable. To enable a transition, the transition's variables must be appropriate values. Assigning values to a transition variable is called *binding*. It is possible for a transition to be enabled for more than one binding. However, a transition can execute based on any single binding at any time.

Variables are declared using the *var* keyword. Each variable is defined using a previously declared color set. Multiple variables can be declared using a comma-separated list. This is illustrated in the example

```
colset INT = int;
var x, y, z : INT;
```

CPN ML also provides reference variables that have a global scope. However, considering the fact that functional programming languages (1) should not maintain the state and (2) should not have side effects, they should be used sparingly. The reference variables are declared using *globref*:

```
globref x = 20;
```

Constants. Constants are defined in CPN ML using the value declaration. This is done using the *val* keyword:

```
val id = exp;
```

Value declaration does not need any colored-sets declared previously.

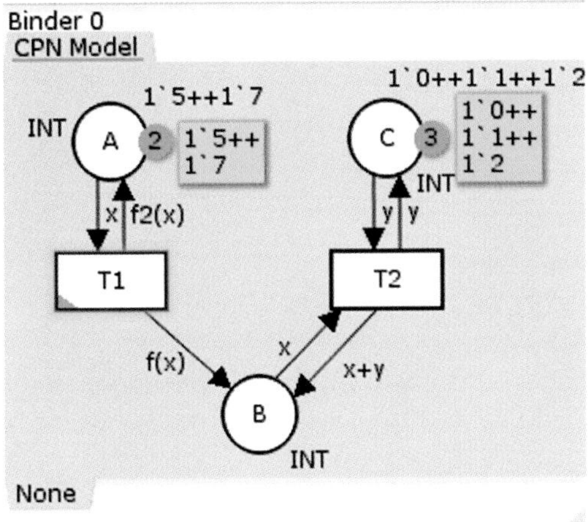

FIGURE 3.8 Model in Figure 3.7 using functions. Variables x and y are of type INT.

Functions. Functions in CPN ML are similar to functions in procedural and object-oriented languages. However, as mentioned earlier, the functions can only access data that are passed to them. Furthermore, they cannot change these data or store a reference to them. Functions are often used to express arc expressions and guard conditions of a transition. A *guard condition* is a boolean expression attached to a transition. A transition cannot be enabled unless the guard condition evaluates as *true*. It often uses the transition variables and is evaluated for each of their bindings. Using functions to express arc expressions and guard conditions saves space and prevents a model from getting cluttered. It also allows the reuse of a complex expression by using the function name. This is shown in Figure 3.8, where the bulky arc expressions in Figure 3.7 are replaced by functions.

Functions in CPN ML are defined using the keyword *fun* followed by the function name and comma-delimited parameters.

```
fun name pattern1 => expression1
| pattern2 => expression2
| pattern3 => expression3
:
| patternN => expressionN
```

where all the expressions are of same type and the patterns could be a single parameter or an ordered list of parameters. The functions $f(x)$ and $f2(x)$ in Figure 3.8 are declared as follows:

```
fun f (x) = if x>6 then 1‘x else empty;
fun f2 x = if x<6 then 1‘x else empty;
```

Local variables can be declared inside a function using the *let* construct [1].

```
let pattern1 = expression1
| pattern2 = expression2
| pattern3 = expression3
⋮
| patternN = expressionN
in exp end
```

The scope of the variables declared is limited to the expression in the *in* section. A transition can also have an attached *code section* that is executed when the transition is fired. The code region is in the form

```
input pattern1;
output pattern2;
action exp;
```

A code region is similar to a function wherein the data are received by using *input*, the result is returned by using *output*, and the computation is performed by using *action*. Consequently, the parameters in *input* cannot be modified by the *action*. However, the *input* and *output* patterns are optional. The code region is illustrated in Figure 3.9 using the transition *condition*.

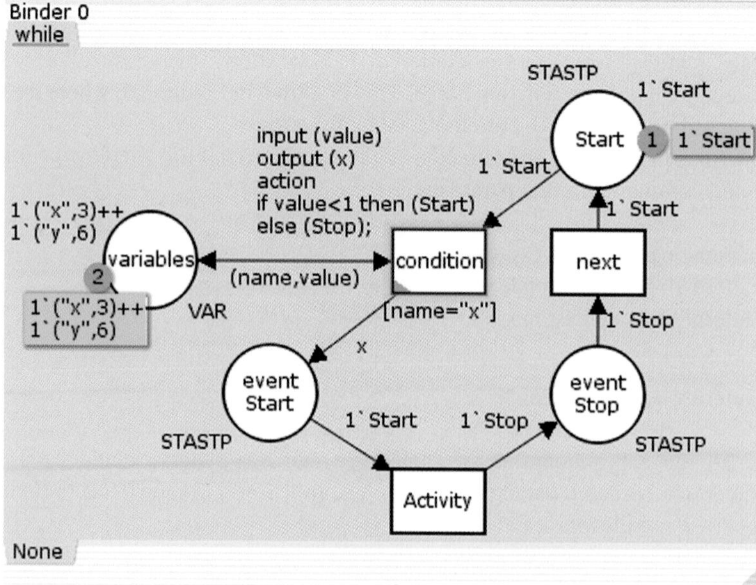

FIGURE 3.9 Code region for a transition.

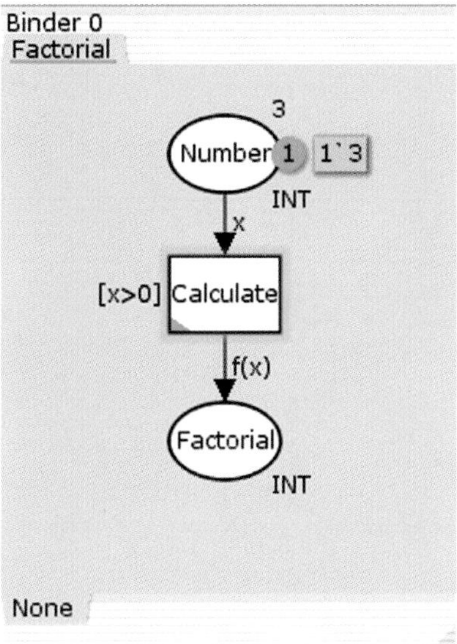

FIGURE 3.10 Model for finding the factorial for an integer.

Recursions. As noted earlier, functional programming languages do not support looping and iteration; such problems are solved using recursion instead. This is illustrated in Figure 3.10, where the factorial for an integer is computed.

The recursive function used to calculate the factorial is

```
fun f x = if x¡1 then 1 else x*f(x-1);
```

This function uses the parameter without actually changing its value. At each step, the function calls itself with a reduced parameter value until it is reduced to 1. The factorial is calculated by multiplying all the results obtained.

3.1.3 Timed Colored Petri Nets

Timed colored petri nets are used to model and validate real-time systems wherein the timing of the events determines the correctness of the system. For example, the average turnaround time, processing time, or I/O time, for a system might determine its correctness. Such systems have deadlines, and meeting these deadlines is often as important as processing the result itself. Timed colored petri nets can be used to determine if a system meets certain deadlines.

However, prior to verifying a timed CPN model, it might be worth creating and verifying an untimed version of it. This would ensure the functional correctness of a system before verifying the timing aspects. This is shown in Figures 3.11 to 3.14, where the untimed model for a factorial is created (and verified) before creating the timed version.

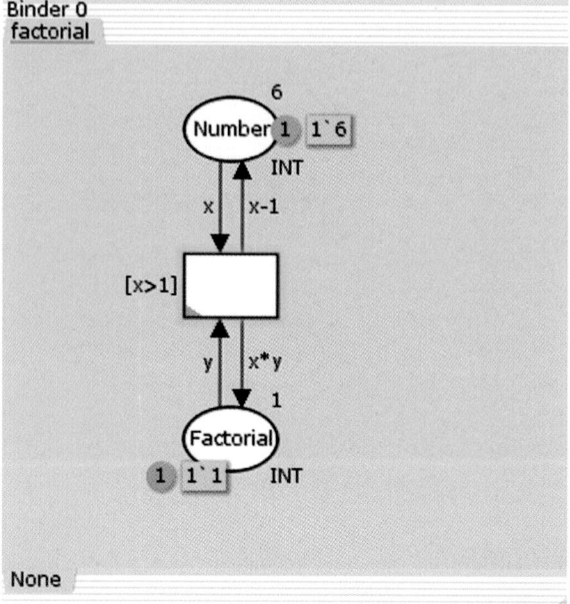

FIGURE 3.11 Colored petri net for a factorial initially.

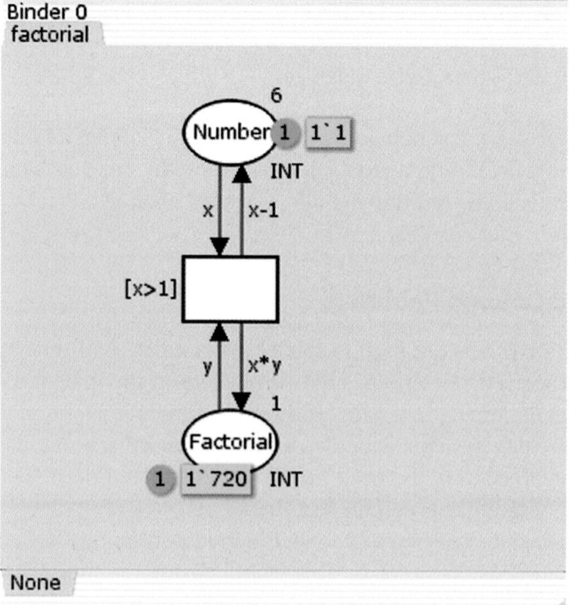

FIGURE 3.12 Colored petri net for a factorial after execution.

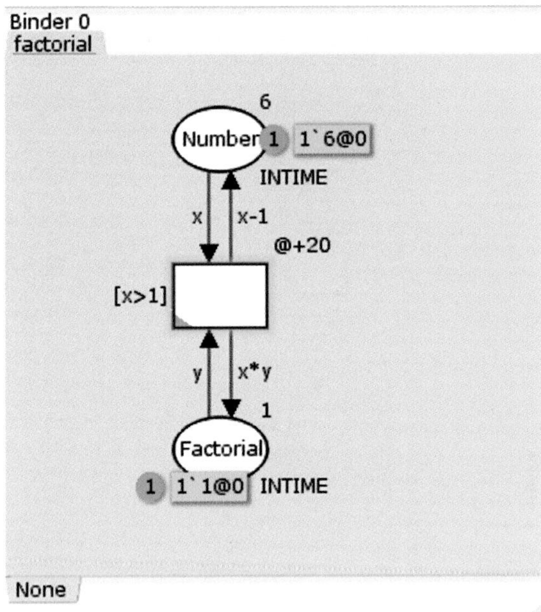

FIGURE 3.13 Timed colored petri net for a factorial initially.

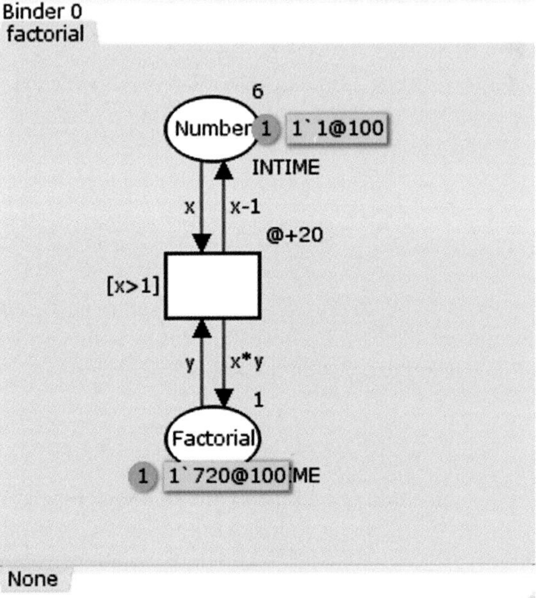

FIGURE 3.14 Timed colored petri net for a factorial after execution.

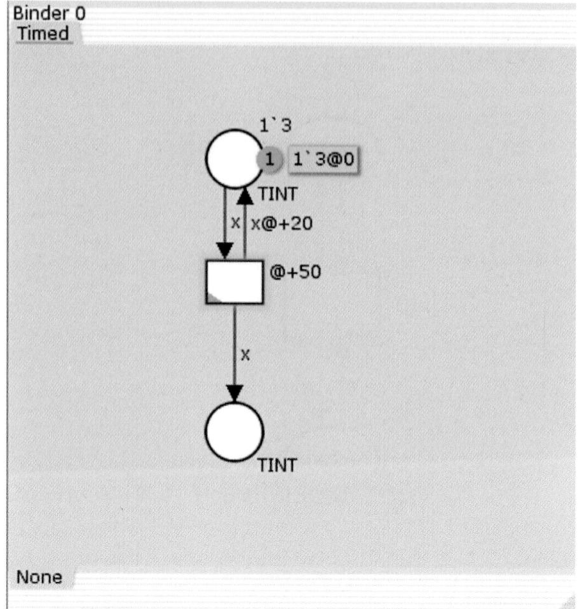

FIGURE 3.15 Timed colored petri net initially.

Such a state of affairs saves a lot of time, because we do not need to construct two totally independent models of the system. Instead, the model used to verify functionality can be modified slightly to obtain a timed model. Furthermore, the reverse process of transforming a timed CPN into an untimed CPN can be performed by (1) making the color sets untimed, and (2) removing any time expression attached to transitions, arcs, and initial marking. Figures 3.15 to 3.18 illustrate the execution of a timed colored petri net. A timed color set of type integer is declared as

```
colset TINT=int timed;
```

A timed color set is required for timed colored petri nets, and this is obtained using the *timed* keyword. Then any token in a place with a timed color set has a *delay expression*. The delay expression takes the form

@+ expression

where @ denotes the current time and the expression denotes the delay. In addition to a token, delay expressions can be added to output arc expressions and transitions. Although transitions are executed instantaneously, adding a delay simulates the situation where an event takes some time to complete. For example, the transition in Figures 3.13 and 3.14 illustrates the delays in operation. Consequently, the system modeled cannot be used to calculate a factorial of 6 if a delay of 100 is not acceptable.

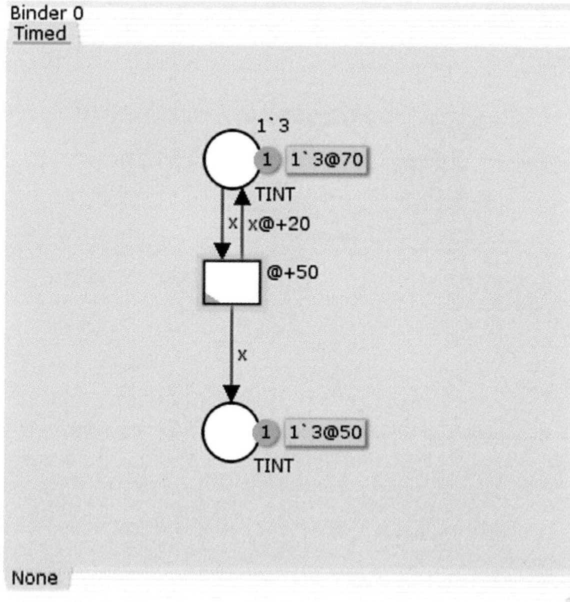

FIGURE 3.16 Timed colored petri net after the first transition execution.

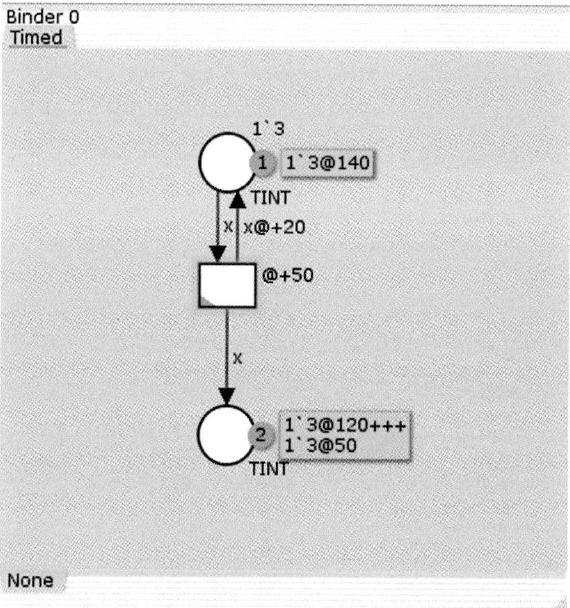

FIGURE 3.17 Timed colored petri net after the second transition execution.

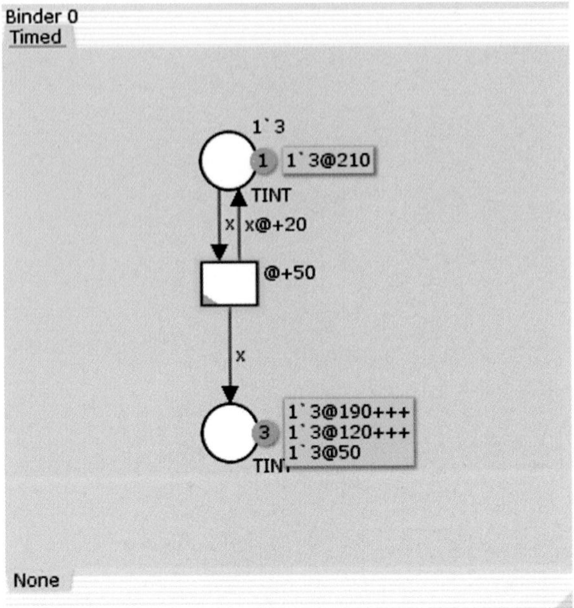

FIGURE 3.18 Timed colored petri net after the third transition execution.

As illustrated using the examples, using the delay expression adds a delay to the token time stamp.

Each time the transition in Figure 3.15 executes, it adds a delay to the tokens from input places. More delay is added based on the delay expressions on the output arcs. CPN ML provides a set of functions to add delay in a delay expression. These randomly distributed functions are listed in Table 3.2.

TABLE 3.2 Random Distribution Functions Offered by CPN Tools

Function	Conditions	Mean	Variance
bernoulli(p:real): int	$0.0 \leq p \leq 1.0$	p	$p(1-p)$
binomial(n:int, p:real): int	$n \geq 1, 0.0 \leq p \leq 1.0$	np	$np(1-p)$
chisq(n:int): real	$n \geq 1$	n	$2n$
discrete(a:int, b:int): int	$a \leq b$	$(a+b)/2$	$[(b-a+1)^2-1]/12$
erlang(n:int, r:real): real	$n \geq 1, r > 0.0$	n/r	n/r^2
exponential(r:real): real	$r > 0.0$	$1/r$	$1/r^2$
normal(n:real, v:real): real	—	n	v
poisson(m:real): int	$m > 0.0$	m	m
student(n:int): real	$n \geq 1$	0	$1/n-2$
uniform(a:real, b:real): real	$a \leq b$	$(a+b)/2$	$[(b-a)^2]/12$

Timed color sets have a set of built-in functions that extend the equivalent function for nontimed color sets. It was noted earlier that a function *fun* for a color set *cs* is invoked using

cs.fun( )

The same function for a timed color set is invoked using

cs‘timed.fun()

Furthermore, time stamps are added to the parameters of timed color set functions. Certain important functions for a timed color set are the following.

- *cs‘timed.lt(c1@ts1,c2@ts2):* compares $c1$ and $c2$ using $cs.lt(c1, c2)$ and returns the boolean result. However, if $c1 = c2$, the time stamps attached to these colors are compared to determine the result.
- *cs‘timed.legal(v@ts):* checks if v is a legitimate element of untimed color set *cs*, of any of its aliases or of its super color set.
- *cs‘timed.mkstr(c@ts):* returns a string value of the color c along with its time stamp.

3.1.4 Multisets

A *multiset* is a set that can have multiple instances of an element. In CPN ML, all color sets are multisets wherein an element and its number of appearances in a multiset is separated by a back quote.

(number of instances) ’ (the element)

The elements of a multiset are separated using the ++ symbol. This is shown in Figure 3.19, where the place *start* has one token of type $(SenA, 0)$, two tokens of type $(SenB, 0)$, four tokens of type $(SenC, 0)$, and one token of type $(Rec, 0)$.

3.1.5 CPN Definitions

A colored petri net is defined [7] as a 9-tuple, CPN $= (\Sigma, P, T, A, N, C, G, E, I)$, where:

- Σ is a finite set of nonempty types called *color sets*.
- P is a finite set of *places*.
- T is a finite set of *transitions*.
- A is a finite set of *arcs* such that

$$P \cap T = P \cap A = T \cap A = \emptyset$$

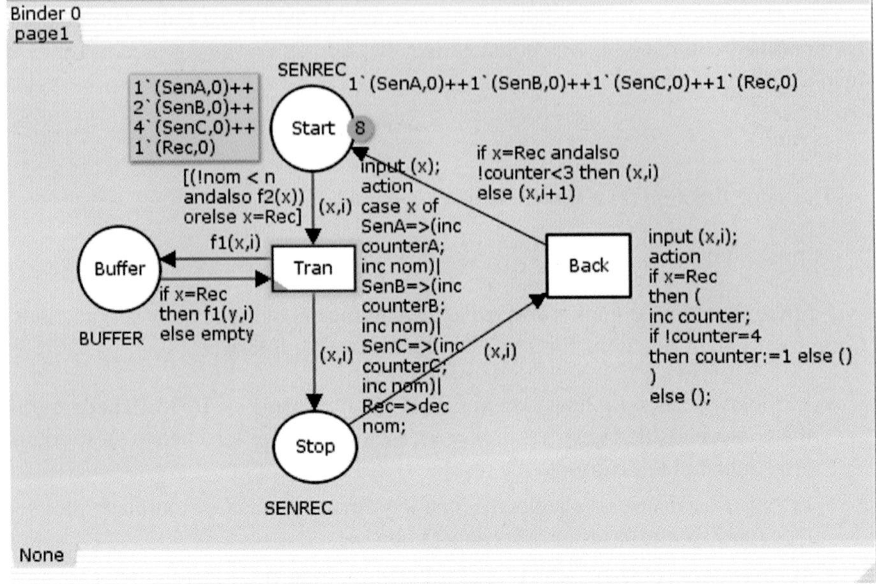

FIGURE 3.19 Multiset of tokens in the place start.

- N is a *node* function. It is defined from A into $P \times T \cup T \times P$.
- C is a *color* function. It is defined from P into Σ.
- G is a *guard* function. It is defined from T into expressions such that

$$\forall t \in T : [\text{Type}(G(t)) = B \wedge \text{Type}(\text{Var}(G(t))) \subseteq \Sigma]$$

- E is an *arc expression* function. It is defined from A into expressions such that

$$\forall a \in A : [\text{Type}(E(a)) = C(p(a))_{MS} \wedge \text{Type}(\text{Var}(E(a))) \subseteq \Sigma]$$

- I is an *initialization* function. It is defined from P into expressions such that

$$\forall p \in P : [\text{Type}(I(p)) = C(p(a))_{MS}]$$

A timed nonhierarchical colored petri net is a 9-tuple, $\text{CPN}_T = (p, T, A, \Sigma, V, C, G, E, I)$, where:

- P is a finite set of places.
- T is a finite set of transitions such that $P \cap T = \emptyset$.
- $A \subseteq PxT \cup TxP$ is a set of directed arcs.

- Σ is a finite set of nonempty color sets. Each color set is either untimed or timed.
- V is a finite set of typed variables such that Type$[v] \in \Sigma$ for all variables $v \in V$.
- $C : P \rightarrow \Sigma$ is a color set function that assigns a color set to each place. A place p is timed if $C(p)$ is timed; otherwise, p is untimed.
- $G : T \rightarrow EXPR_V$ is a guard function that assigns a guard to each transition t such that Type$[G(t)]$ = bool.
- $E : A \rightarrow \text{EXPR}_V$ is an arc expression function that assigns an arc expression to each arc a such that
  - Type$[E(a)] = C(p)_{MS}$ if p is untimed;
  - Type$[E(a)] = C(p)_{TMS}$ if p is timed.

  Here, p is the place connected to the arc a.
- $I : P \rightarrow \text{EXPR}_\phi$ is an initialization function that assigns an initialization expression to each place p such that
  - Type$[I(p)] = C(p)_{MS}$ if p is untimed;
  - Type$[I(p)] = C(p)_{TMS}$ if p is timed.

3.2 HIERARCHICAL COLORED PETRI NETS

A *hierarchical colored petri net* (HCPN) [7] model consists of a finite set of nonhierarchical CPN models, also known as *modules*. Figures 3.20 and 3.21 show a collection of modules that together constitute an HCPN model. The modules depict a simple stop-and-wait *Protocol* [15] for transferring a number of data packets from *Sender* to *Receiver* over an unreliable *Network* (module names in italic). For multiple receivers, as is the case here, a copy of the packet is delivered to each receiver independently. The three receivers here are identified as *Recv*(1), *Recv*(2), and *Recv*(3). The technique for time-efficient state-space analysis, presented later, is discussed in reference to this example net.

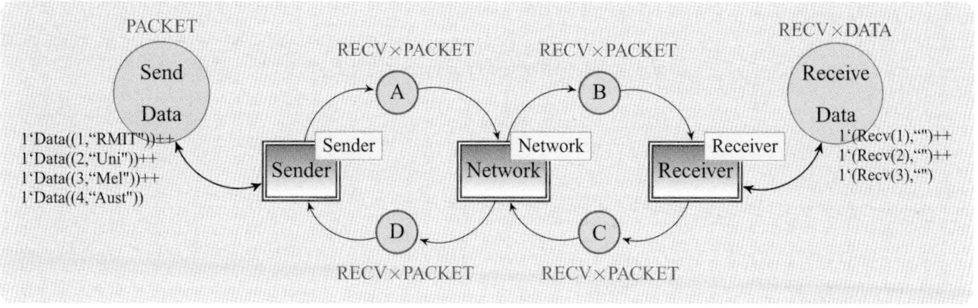

FIGURE 3.20 Module for *Protocol*.

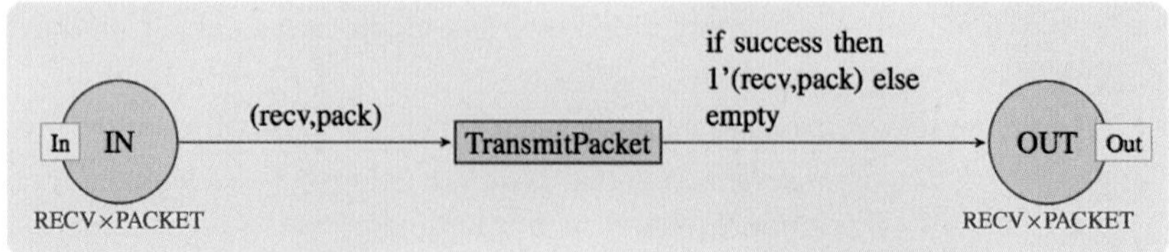

FIGURE 3.21 Module for *Transmit* in Figure 3.23.

Definition 3.2 *A module [8] $s \in S$ is a four-tuple $s=(CPN^s, T^s_{sub}, P^s_{port}, PT^s)$, where*

(a) $CPN^s = (p^s, T^s, A^s, \sum^s, V^s, C^s, G^s, E^s, I^s)$ *is a nonhierarchical colored petri net.*
(b) $T^s_{sub} \subseteq T^s$ *is a set of substitution transitions.*
(c) $P^s_{port} \subseteq P^s$ *is a set of port places.*
(d) $PT{:}P^s_{port} \rightarrow \{IN, OUT, I/O\}$ *is a port-type function that specifies the port type for each port place.*

For all $s_1,s_2 \in S$: $s_1 \neq s_2$, we have $(p^{s1} \bigcup T^{s1}) \bigcap (p^{s2} \bigcup T^{s2}) = \emptyset$. This implies that no two modules should share their places and/or transitions.

Corollary 3.1 *A module containing a substitution transition is known as a super-module; the module it substitutes is known as a submodule.*

Figure 3.20 shows the module *Protocol*, containing six places (the ellipses) and three substitution transitions (bordered rectangles) connected by arcs (arrows). As the name emphasizes, a *substitution transition* acts as a substitute for another module that executes whenever it fires. The module substituted is indicated by an associated tag. For example, the substitution transition *Sender* replaces a module by the same name that is shown in Figure 3.22. Similarly, the module *Network* in Figure 3.23 has two substitution transitions, each with an associated tag *Transmit*. However, it is important to point out that they replace different copies (or instances) of the module *Transmit*. The real power of HCPN lies in the fact that a module can have multiple instances, one for each substitution transition.

Definition 3.3 *A substitution transition $t \in T^s_{sub}$ is defined as the 3-tuple $t = \{SM^s, P^t_{sock}, PS^s\}$ where*

(a) SM^s: $T^s_{sub} \rightarrow S\text{-}s$ *is the submodule function for module s and associates a module (other than s) with each substitution transition $t \in T^s_{sub}$. If $s' = SM^s(t)$, then $s,s' \in S$: $s \neq s'$ and there exists a nontrivial path $s \xrightarrow{t} s'$. The module s' is denoted as the submodule of s.*
(b) $P^t_{sock} \subseteq P^s$ *is the set of adjoining places of t, referred to as its socket.*

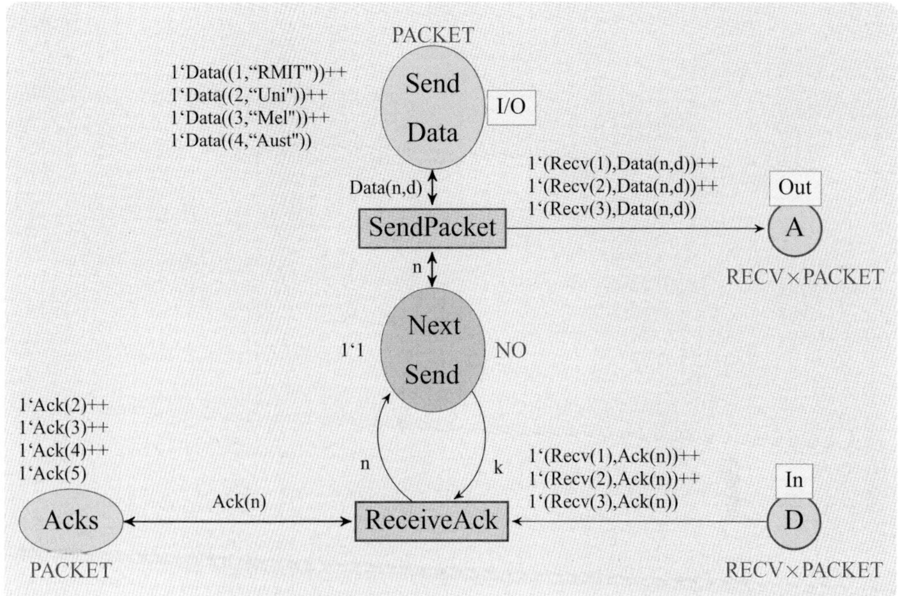

FIGURE 3.22 Module for *Sender* in Figure 3.20.

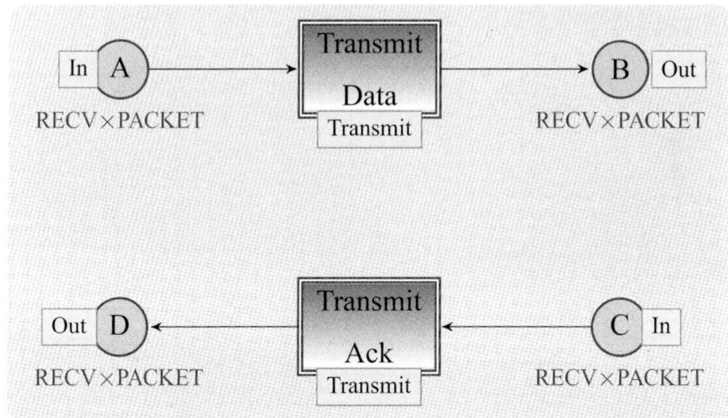

FIGURE 3.23 Module for *Network*.

(c) $PS^s(t) \subseteq P^t_{\text{sock}} \times P^{SM^s(t)}_{\text{port}}$ *is a port–socket function that is used to "glue" a module and its submodule. This is accomplished by mapping each port in a submodule with a socket in a corresponding module.*

A supermodule and its submodules are glued by defining a one-to-one relationship between a subset of their places. Each place adjacent to a substitution transition is known as a *socket* and has a counterpart in the associated submodule known as a *port*. Although not necessary, the port–socket pairs in our example net have the same name. Furthermore, considering that a socket could be either an input, an

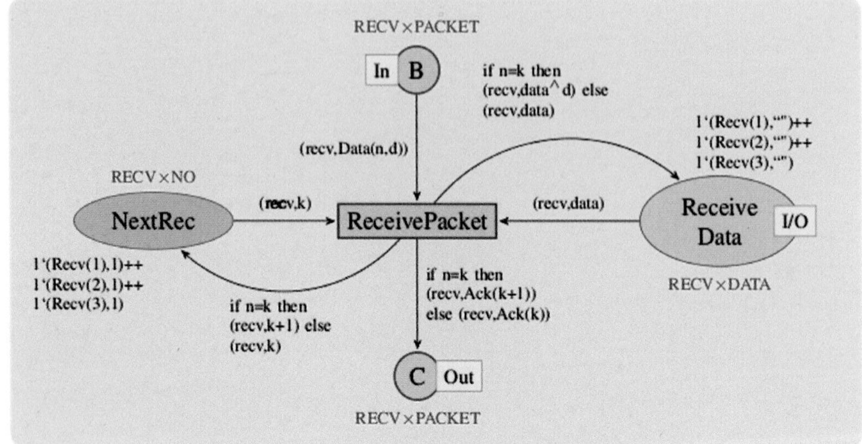

FIGURE 3.24 Module for *Receiver* in Figure 3.20.

```
colset NO = int;
colset DATA = string;
colset NOxDATA = product NO * DATA;
colset PACKET = union Data:NOxDATA + Ack:NO;
val NoRecvs = 3;
colset RECV = index Recv with 1..NoRecvs;
colset RECVxPACKET = product RECV * PACKET;
colset RECVxDATA = product RECV * DATA;
colset RECVxNO = product RECV * NO;
var n, k : NO;
var d : DATA;
var pack : PACKET;
```

FIGURE 3.25 Declarations for modules in Figures 3.20 and 3.21.

output, or an I/O place of substitution transition, an equivalent tag is attached to the corresponding port to indicate its permitted type.

If each module is linked to its submodules using directed arcs, the resulting graph is known as a *module hierarchy*. Figure 3.26 illustrates the module hierarchy of our example HCPN model. Each directed arc is labeled with the name of a substitution transition that represents its target module. Considering that a module cannot be its own submodule, the module hierarchy is essentially an acyclic directed graph [2]. Roots of the module hierarchy with no incoming arcs are known as *prime modules* [8] and are denoted by S_{PM}. A module hierarchy can have multiple prime modules.

Each place in a module has an affiliated data type (known as its color) and all data values (known as *tokens*) in it must conform to this type. For example, the token 1'*Data* ((1, "*RMIT*")) in the place *Send Data* is of type *PACKET*. The preceding

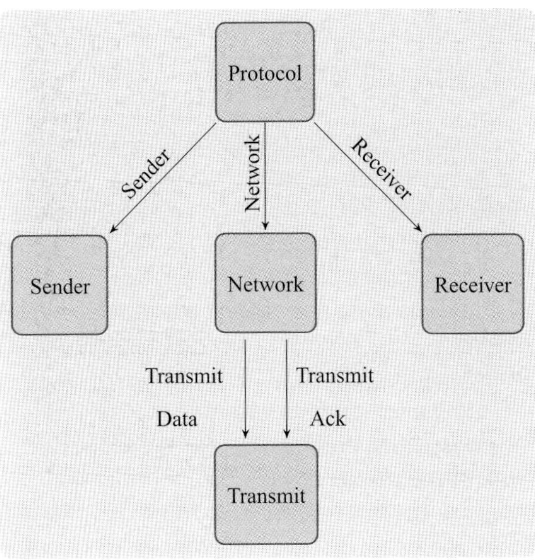

FIGURE 3.26 Module hierarchy for the example HCPN model.

number followed by a back quote (e.g., 1') indicates the count of a token, and a "++" separates two tokens.

A module might also have nonhierarchical transitions (rectangles with no border) that can manipulate these data values when *enabled* and move them between places through an arc. To enable a transition, an appropriate value needs to be assigned to each variable associated with it, a process known as *binding*. A binding enables a transition iff (1) each arc expression on an input arc evaluates to a subset of markings (see below) of the corresponding input place, and (2) the guard condition (if one exists) is satisfied. Accordingly, a binding b enables a transition t if the following holds:

$$\forall p \in P_{\text{In}}(t): (E(p,t)\langle b\rangle \subseteq M(p)) \wedge G(t)\langle b\rangle \tag{3.1}$$

where $P_{\text{In}}(t)$ is the set of input places of t, $E(p,t)$ is the expression on an arc connecting p to t, $M(p)$ denotes the set of tokens in p (known as its *marking*), and $G(t)$ denotes the guard, which is nothing but a boolean expression attached to t. For example, the transition *ReceiveAck* in Figure 6.3 has two variables, n and k, and a binding $\langle n = 3, k = 2\rangle$ would enable it only when $2 \in M(\textit{Next Send})$ and $\textit{Ack}(3) \in M(D)$. None of the transitions in the example net have an associated guard condition.

It is worth mentioning that a substitution transition has no associated variables. Consequently, it cannot be "bound" and cannot get "enabled." For a particular substitution transition, the tokens in its adjoining places (i.e., sockets) are concurrently available to their associated ports in the submodule, and vice versa. For example, the socket *Send Data* in Figure 6.1 and its port in Figure 6.3 have the same marking.

This allows one or more nonhierarchical transitions in the submodule to get become enabled and consume these tokens. After the submodule finishes execution, the leftover tokens at its ports can be claimed back by the sockets.

Reachability Graph for HCPN. Prior to generating the reachability graph for a HCPN model, all its modules are joined to constitute a single large module. This is accomplished by overlapping each port–socket pair, rendering the substitution transitions useless. Each place in the newly constituted module is known as a *compound place*. However, only a subset of compound places is an outcome of the aforementioned port–socket fusion.

Table 3.3 lists the initial marking for each compound place that is constituted from the example HCPN model. Each port–socket pair in the HCPN model would join to constitute a compound place for the new module. Furthermore, a place in an HCPN model that is neither a port nor a socket (e.g., *Next Send*) would be a compound place by itself. The compound place corresponding to a place p in an HCPN model is denoted as $[p^*]$. Furthermore, $[p^*] \sim_{cp} [q^*]$ denotes that p and q belong to the same compound place. Any conflict in place names is resolved by including the module name as a subscript. Our new module has eight compound places, corresponding to the eight rows in Table 3.3. The multiple entries of the compound places $[IN^*]$ and $[OUT^*]$ correspond to separate instances of module *Transmit*. whereas the place *IN* from the first instance forms a compound place with A, the same place from another instance forms a compound place with C. Similarly, the two instances of *OUT* form compound places with B and D.

TABLE 3.3 The Compound Places in an HCPN Model and with Their Initial Markings

Compound Place	Initial Marking M_0
$[SendData^*_{Protocol}] \sim_{cp} [SendData^*_{Sender}]$	$1`Data((1, \text{"}RMIT\text{"}))$ ++ $1`Data((2, \text{"}Uni\text{"}))$ ++ $1`Data((3, \text{"}Mel\text{"}))$ ++ $1`Data((4, \text{"}Aust\text{"}))$
$[A^*_{Protocol}] \sim_{cp} [A^*_{Sender}] \sim_{cp} [A^*_{Network}] \sim_{cp} [IN^*]$	$\emptyset$
$[D^*_{Protocol}] \sim_{cp} [D^*_{Sender}] \sim_{cp} [D^*_{Network}] \sim_{cp} [OUT^*]$	$\emptyset$
$[B^*_{Protocol}] \sim_{cp} [B^*_{Network}] \sim_{cp} [B^*_{Receiver}] \sim_{cp} [OUT^*]$	$\emptyset$
$[C^*_{Protocol}] \sim_{cp} [C^*_{Network}] \sim_{cp} [C^*_{Receiver}] \sim_{cp} [IN^*]$	$\emptyset$
$[ReceiveData^*_{Protocol}] \sim_{cp} [ReceiveData^*_{Receiver}]$	$1`(Recv(1), \text{""})$ ++ $1`(Recv(2), \text{""})$ ++ $1`(Recv(3), \text{""})$
$[NextSend^*]$	$1`1$
$[Acks^*]$	$1`Ack(2)$ ++ $1`Ack(3)$ ++ $1`Ack(4)$ ++ $1`Ack(5)$
$[NextRec^*]$	$1`(Recv(1), 1)$ ++ $1`(Recv(2), 1)$ ++ $1`(Recv(3), 1)$

The initial marking constitutes the root node of the reachability graph. The events enabled at this marking can bring about a change in state. The root node has an outgoing edge for each enabled marking, leading to a new node. The markings that correspond to these new nodes are then analyzed to find the next set of enabled events that would lead to another set of new nodes. The analysis continues until there are no enabled events.

However, if there exists a nonempty sequence of events that causes no net change in a marking M (i.e., $M[e_1\rangle M_1[e_2\rangle M_2 \ldots M_{r-1}[e_r\rangle M : r > 0$), the analysis of states $\{M, M_1 \ldots, M_{r-1}\}$ would never end. To ensure termination, all the unique markings encountered hitherto are stored and compared with the markings generated hereafter.

The extensive use of colored petri nets in this book can be attributed to the following benefits [7]:

- All the aforementioned advantages for petri nets are applicable for CPNs.
- CPN models natively define hierarchical semantics for better representation.
- CPN models have extensive tool support for drawing, editing, simulation, and formal verification [9].
- CPN models are XML based and therefore can easily be imported exported, and edited using third-party applications.
- The structure of a CPN model is defined using a document-type definition [17]. Consequently, the models could easily be checked for the validity of their structure.
- CPN models offer various programmable elements that significantly reduce the size of formal models.

REFERENCES

1. *CPN Documentation*, January 2012.
2. J. A. Bondy and U. S. R Murty. *Graph Theory*. Springer-Verlag, Berlin, 2008.
3. E. Clarke, O. Grumberg, and D. Peled.*Model Checking*. MIT Press, Cambridge, MA, 2000.
4. S. Evangelista. High level petri net analysis with Helena. In *Proceedings of the 26th International Conference on Applications and Theory of the Petri Nets, ICATPN 2005*, Volume 3536, *of Lecture notes in computer science*, pages 445–464. Springer-Verlag, Berlin, 2005.
5. R. Fehling. A concept of hierarchical petri nets with building blocks. In *Proceedings of the 12th International Conference on Applications and Theory of Petri Nets ICAPTN '93*, pages 148–168. Springer-Verlag, Berlin, 1993.
6. G. J. Holzmann. *The SPIN Model Checker: Primer and Reference Manual*. Addison-Wesley, Reading, MA, 2003.
7. K. Jensen. *Colored Petri Nets: Basic Concepts, Analysis Methods and Practical Use*, volumes 1–3. Springer-Verlag, Berlin, 1996.

8. K. Jensen and L. M. Kristensen. *Colored Petri Nets: Modelling and Validation of Concurrent Systems*. Springer-Verlag, Berlin, 2009.
9. K. Jensen, L. M. Kristensen, and L. Wells. Colored petri nets and CPN tools for modelling and validation of concurrent systems. *International Journal of Software Tools for Technology, Transfer* 9(3):213–254, 2007.
10. C. Lakos. The object orientation of object petri nets. In *Proceedings of the Workshop on Object Oriented Programming and Models of Concurrency*, pages 2–7, 1995.
11. R. Milner, M. Tofte, and D. Macqueen. *The Definition of Standard ML*. MIT Press, Cambridge, MA, 1997.
12. T. Murata. Petri nets: properties, analysis and applications. In *Proceedings of the IEEE*, 77, 541–580, 1989.
13. A. V. Ratzer, L. Wells, H. M. Lassen, M. Laursen, J. F. Qvortrup, M. S. Stissing, M. Westergaard, S. Christensen, and K. Jensen. CPN tools for editing, simulating, and analysing colored petri nets. In *Proceedings of the 24th International Conference on Applications and Theory of Petri Nets, ICATPN 2003* volume 2679 of *Lecture Notes in Computer Science*, pages 450–462. Springer-Verlag, Berlin, June 2003.
14. Karsten Schmidt. LoLA: a low level analyser. In M. Nielsen, and D. Simpson, Eds., In *Proceedings of the 21st International Conference on Applications and Theory of Petri Nets, ICATPN 2000*, volume 1825, *of Lecture Notes in Computer Science*, pages 465–474. Springer-Verlag, Berlin, 2000.
15. A. Tanenbaum. *Computer Networks*. Prentice Hall, Upper Saddle River, NJ, 2002.
16. W. M. P. van der Aalst. The application of petri nets to workflow management. *Journal of Circuits, Systems, and Computers*, 8(1):21–66, 1998.
17. M. Westergaard, K. Jensen, S. Christensen, and L. Kristensen. *CPN Tools DTD*, December 2005.

CHAPTER 4

WEB SERVICES

In recent years, companies have been actively exposing their software as a service to be used by other applications over the network. These services have uncovered various business opportunities by exploiting the ubiquitous nature of the web. They adhere to the associated service description, irrespective of the underlying implementation. However, as shown in Figure 4.1, these services, by themselves, might not be very useful. In the scenario illustrated, a customer needs to make several individual web-service calls to complete a shopping event. Furthermore, the calls need to be made in a specific order wherein the reference from the preceding call is used in the succeeding invocation. Apart from being a cumbersome and error-prone process, this scenario unnecessarily exposes the underlying business logic of the application.

Figure 4.2 illustrates an alternative scenario wherein the business logic is encapsulated within the application. The customer only needs to provide the payment and address details to finish shopping. However, this necessitates composing the involved web services based on the business logic of the application. Such a state of affairs has resulted in the emergence of different service composition languages. In recent years, the Business Process Execution Language (BPEL) has emerged as the de facto standard language for composing web services.

Verification of Communication Protocols in Web Services: Model-Checking Service Compositions, First Edition. Zahir Tari, Peter Bertok, Anshuman Mukherjee.

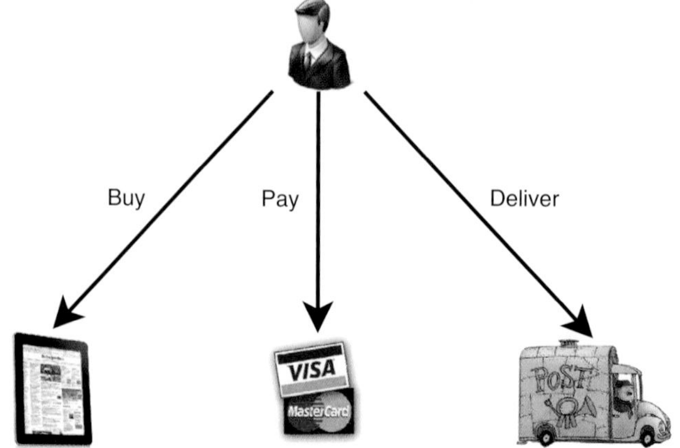

FIGURE 4.1 Using individual exposed services for online shopping.

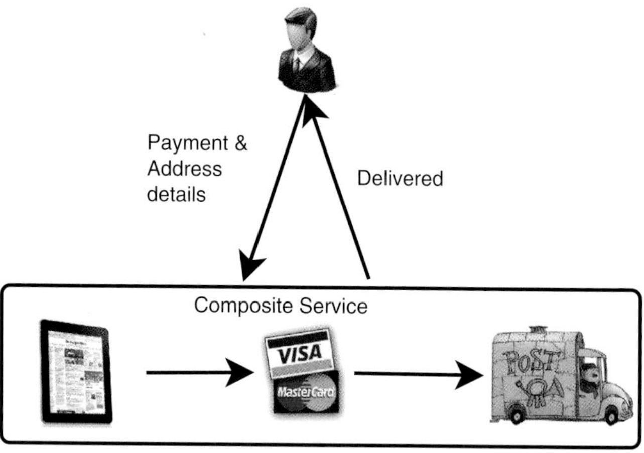

FIGURE 4.2 Using service composition for online shopping.

Service-oriented architecture (SOA) is an emerging paradigm for harmonizing and consuming the services offered by disparate vendors. These services can span across several organizational and national boundaries and have any underlying implementations. Such a state of affairs has made it possible to alleviate software interoperability issues and has catapulted SOA into the forefront of software development architectures. SOA-based applications are built as an assembly of existing web services that are invoked in a sequence based on the business logic and the workflow of the application. The rapid inroads made by such applications can be attributed to their agility maintainability, and modularity.

Service discovery and composition form the basis of SOA. The former involves finding an appropriate service provider for a service requester. Usually, a provider registers its service with a middle agent (e.g., Universal Description Discovery and

Integration) to allow search and discovery. However, such centralized registries can be avoided by using Web Services Dynamic Discovery (WS-Discovery), wherein the services are searched over a local network using multicast.

The services discovered are composed to render an SOA-based application wherein each service constitutes a component of the application. These services are composed based on the requirements and workflow of the application. Considering that the services were discovered at design time, such compositions are static.

Static compositions require the services involved to be perpetual and consistent throughout the lifetime of an application. However, existing web services can break and newer (probably better) services can surface. Furthermore, a change in the business logic of an application during its lifetime might necessitate additional web services to be composed dynamically. Such states of events have culminated in dynamic composition. Compared to its static counterparts, an application based on dynamic composition is open for modification, extension, and adaptation at runtime.

The aforementioned composition approaches are centralized by means of a central controller that collaborates on a set of suitable services to constitute an application. The controller orchestrates individual services and integrates their functionalities based on the requirements of the application envisioned. However, considering the large number of individual web services that might be involved in creating an enterprise application, any centralized composition technique suffers from a performance bottleneck and a single point of failure. Furthermore, as observed previously, web services are distributed across several physical and geographical domains, where they are constantly modified, removed, and updated. Therefore, to ensure that the location of services is transparent to the application, the composition technique must support an equivalent extent of distribution. Dynamic and distributed composition of a set of services ensures that the resulting application (1) is open for modification, extension, and adaptation at runtime, (2) does not have a single point of failure, (3) scales well on integrating additional services to extend its functionalities, and (4) is more robust than individual services. However, an enterprise application is expected to be void of deadlocks, live-locks, and conflicts. Furthermore, the integrity of an application could be jeopardized by a rough application that does not confirm to its advertised functionality. Therefore, an application ought to be checked for correctness throughout its lifetime.

4.1 BUSINESS PROCESS EXECUTION LANGUAGE

A BPEL process specifies the exact order in which the constituent web services should be invoked. When calling a service, the information sent (or the result returned) could be read from (or stored into) a variable. Consequently, the result from services called hitherto could be used for any forthcoming calls. It also supports conditional and iterative invocation of services and offers handlers that execute when an event occurs.

Although it is possible to compose services using a programming language (e.g., Java or C++), there are specific advantages to using BPEL:

- Contrary to popular programming languages (e.g., C++), BPEL is platform independent. Therefore, it can be used to compose services regardless of the platform used to create them (e.g., Java, PHP, C++, C, Ruby).
- Business processes often require asynchronous interactions with high turnaround time. The BPEL activities have been created to handle such scenarios better than can any programming language.
- It is easier to introduce concurrency into a BPEL process than with most other programming languages.
- BPEL activities are XML based and consequently can be imported, exported, and edited easily using third-party tools.

A BPEL specification consists of steps known as *activities*, classified further as *basic activities*, *structured activities*, or other activities. Some important BPEL activities are discussed below.

Process Activity. The *process* activity represents a BPEL process and is the root tag for any BPEL specification. It has the set of attributes listed in Table 4.1.

Partner Links. A BPEL process needs to interact with other web services to conform to a specific workflow. These services are specified in a BPEL process using *partner links*. If a partner link is used to specify the link to another web service, it is called an *invoked partner link*. The partner links that specify links to the client invoking a BPEL process are called *client partner links* [5]. Usually, a BPEL process contains at least one each of client and invoked partner links. This is essentially because (1) a client needs to invoke the BPEL process, and (2) the process needs to invoke other services.

A partner link activity has the following attributes:

- *name:* the name of the link that is used as a reference for interactions.
- *partnerLinkType:* used to describe the partner web service and is part of the corresponding document written in Web Services Description Language (WSDL).

TABLE 4.1 Attributes of the *Process* Activity

Attribute	Description	Optional?
name	Name of the BPEL process	No
targetNamespace	Target namespace of the BPEL specification	No
xmlns	BPEL namespace	No
queryLanguage	Query language used for node selection	Yes
expressionLanguage	Expression language used	Yes
suppressJoinFailure	Used in handling join failures	Yes
enableInstanceCompensation	Used to enable compensation for the BPEL process	Yes
abstractProcess	Specifies if the process is abstract	Yes

```
<portType name="ComputeInsurancePremiumPT">
  <operation name="...">
    <input message="..." />
  </operation>
</portType>

<portType name="ComputeInsurancePremiumCallbackPT">
  <operation name="...">
    <input message="..." />
  </operation>
</portType>
...
<plnk:partnerLinkType name="insuranceLT">
  <plnk:role name="insuranceService">
    <plnk:portType name="ins:ComputeInsurancePremiumPT"/>
  </plnk:role>
  <plnk:role name="insuranceRequester">
    <plnk:portType name="ins:ComputeInsurancePremiumCallbackPT"/>
  </plnk:role>
</plnk:partnerLinkType>
```

FIGURE 4.3 *partnerLinkType* declared in WSDL [5].

```
<partnerLinks>
   <partnerLink name="insurance"
                partnerLinkType="tns:insuranceLT"
                myRole="insuranceRequester"
                partnerRole="insuranceService"/>
</partnerLinks>
```

FIGURE 4.4 Declared *partnerLinkType* used in a partner link declaration for BPEL specification [5].

- *myRole:* indicates the role that the BPEL process plays in an interaction with a partner.
- *partnerRole:* indicates the role of the partner in the interaction.

The roles are specified in the *partner link type* that is defined in the WSDL document.

Figure 4.3 illustrates declaring a partner link type, which is used in Figure 4.4 to declare a partner link. Since this is an asynchronous service, the BPEL role involves invoking the service, and the partner role involves invoking the callback.

Variable Activity. A BPEL process interacts with several services wherein the result received from one needs to be supplied to another. Variables are used to store the results temporarily, before being used later in the process. In addition, they are used to store the state of a BPEL process. A variable needs to be declared before it is used, by specifying its name and type. The possible variable types are listed in Table 4.2.

Assign Activity. As mentioned previously, variables are used in a BPEL specification to store some intermediate results. Consequently, it is often necessary to copy data into a variable, from a variable, or between variables. This is done using

TABLE 4.2 **Possible Types for the *Variable* Activity**

Type	Description
messageType	WSDL message can be stored
element	XML schema element can be stored
type	XML schema simple type

TABLE 4.3 **Attributes of the *Invoke* Activity**

Attribute	Description
partnerLink	Link to the web service
portType	Port type to be used
operation	Operation name
inputVariable	Store input message
outputVariable	Store result

the *assign* activity. It copies the data using the *copy* activity and requires a source (specified using the *from* activity) and a destination (specified using the *to* activity).

```
<assign>
<copy>
<from variable="fromVar"/>
<to variable="toVar"/>
</copy>
</assign>
```

Invoke Activity. The BPEL activity *invoke* is used to trigger a web service. Its attributes are listed in Table 4.3.

It has five attributes: *partnerLink*, *operation*, *outputVariable*, *inputVariable*, and *portType*. The attribute *partnerLink* gives information about the role of a partner web service. In the case of a synchronous invocation, the role of a partner web service is to provide an *operation* that takes *inputVariable* as input and returns the result in *outputVariable*. In the case of an asynchronous invocation, the *operation* takes *inputVariable* as input, but the result is returned using *callback*. We need a *receive* activity to fetch the result. Hence, for asynchronous *invoke*, the role of partner is to provide *operation*, and the role of BPEL is to receive the result.

Receive Activity. The BPEL activity *receive* waits for an incoming message, either from a client to start the BPEL process, or from a partner in the case of *callback*. The attributes of *receive* are shown in Table 4.4.

It has an attribute *createInstance*. When this attribute is set to "yes," a new instance of the BPEL process is created. The incoming message is stored in the *variable* attribute.

TABLE 4.4 **Attributes of the *receive* Activity**

Attribute	Description
partnerLink	Link to the web service
portType	Port type to be used
operation	Operation name
createInstance	Create new instance of process
variable	Store request or result

Reply Activity. In the case of a synchronous *receive*, the result is returned to the client using the *reply* activity. All attributes of the *reply* activity must be the same as the corresponding *receive*, except that the variable now has a result to be returned. The activities *invoke*, *receive*, and *reply* allow a BPEL process to interact with its constituent web services. The advantages that these activities provide over conventional programming languages are as follows:

- An operation specified in WSDL can easily be invoked using the *operation* attribute of the invoke activity.
- The schema for input and output messages of an operation can be used to define the aforementioned variables.
- Both synchronous and asynchronous interactions are natively supported.

Flow and Sequence Activities. The BPEL *flow* activity defines a set of subtasks or sub activities that must execute concurrently. It is also used to define guarded links. It terminates when the final subactivity in it is completed. The BPEL activity *sequence* defines a set of subtasks or subactivities that are to be executed in a specific order. This order is usually the same as the order of occurrence of subactivities within the sequence. As with *flow*, a *sequence* activity terminates when the final subactivity in it is completed.

The *flow* and *sequence* activities offer an easy mechanism to control the flow of business processes. Examples are given in Figures 4.5 and 4.6.

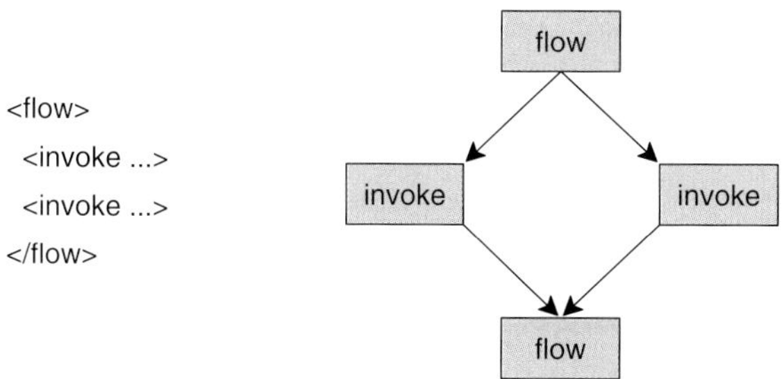

FIGURE 4.5 Structure of the *flow* activity.

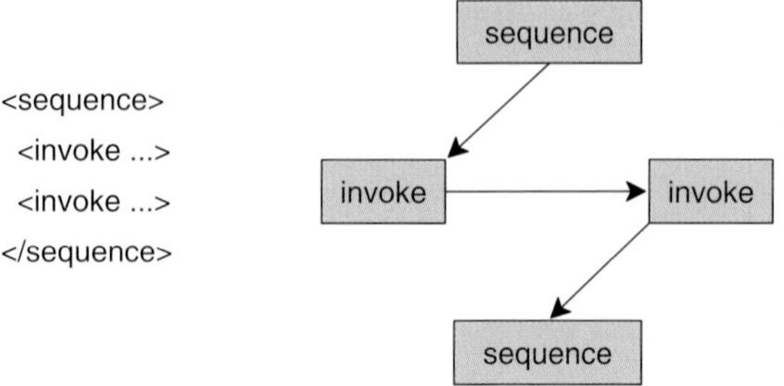

FIGURE 4.6 Structure of the *sequence* activity.

While Activity. The BPEL activity *while* is used to repeat the enclosed activities until the boolean condition specified is no longer true. The condition is specified using the *condition* attribute. The condition is evaluated before each iteration. Therefore, if the condition fails at first iteration, the enclosed activities are skipped altogether.

```
<while condition="boolean-exp">
  <!– List the activities that need to be repeated until
     the condition specified is false –>
</while>
```

Switch Activity. The BPEL activity *switch* is a multi way conditional branching control. When there are multiple possible paths of execution for a BPEL process, the decision to select a path is taken by the *switch* activity (Figure 4.7). Each of these paths is wrapped in a *case* activity and listed inside *switch*. Just like *while*, each `case` has a condition. The condition for each case is evaluated in the order in which they are listed under *switch*. If a condition evaluates to *true*, the corresponding activities specified for that case are executed and the *switch* activity terminates; otherwise, the

```
<switch>

  <case condition="boolean-expression">
    <!-- some activity -->
  </case>

  <case condition="boolean-expression">
    <!-- some activity -->
  </case>
  ...
  <otherwise>    <!-- optional -->
    <!-- some activity -->
  </otherwise>

</switch>
```

FIGURE 4.7 Structure of the *switch* activity [5].

TABLE 4.5 Attributes for the *Wait* Activity

Attribute	Description
for	Used to specify delay for a period of time
until	Used to delay untill a certain date and time

TABLE 4.6 Characters for Specifying *Duration*

Character	Description
P	Duration expression begins with a P
Y	Is preceded by the number of years
M	Is preceded by the number of months (or minutes)
D	Is preceded by the number of days
T	Indicates the beginning of time representation
H	Is preceded by the number of hours
S	Is preceded by the number of seconds

TABLE 4.7 Characters for Specifying *Deadline*

Character	Description
C	Expresses the century
Y	Expresses the number of years
M	Expresses the number of months
D	Expresses the number of days
H	Expresses the number of hours
m	Expresses the number of minutes
s	Expresses the number of seconds
Z	Follows the time element and represents coordinated universal time

next case condition is evaluated. If all case conditions evaluate to *false*, the activities specified under the optional *otherwise* are executed.

Delays. The BPEL activities are processed in the order in which they are specified inside a structured activity (e.g., flow or sequence). However, it might sometimes be necessary to introduce a delay between two activities. This delay could be for a specific amount of time or until a particular deadline. Delays are specified using the *wait* activity and support the two attributes shown in Table 4.5.

The characters used for duration expression are shown in Table 4.6.

An example of a duration expression is

```
<wait for="P2Y3M10DT2H35M10S"/>
```

The characters used for deadline expression are shown in Table 4.7.

Empty Activity. BPEL offers the *empty* activity, which does not perform any operation. It is used in cases where an activity needs to be added only to conform to the BPEL schema. For example, the BPEL schema does not allow an empty *case* for a *switch* activity. Consequently, adding an *empty* activity helps in conforming the specification to the BPEL schema.

```
<empty/>
```

Terminate Activity. The *terminate* activity is used to terminate a BPEL process. Normally, it is used when the BPEL process has entered an erroneous state and cannot continue any further. The executing process is terminated immediately.

```
<terminate/>
```

Fault Handling. The loosely coupled nature of SOA-based applications make them vulnerable to faults and failures. This is essentially because web-service interactions take place over Internet connections that can be unreliable [5]. Faults can also occur in the execution of a BPEL process, due to an error in the specification. In addition, faults can be thrown explicitly using the *throw* activity.

```
<throw faultName="fn" faultVariable="fv"/>
```

The *faultName* is used to handle the fault using a fault handler. In addition, the information associated with the fault is stored in the *faultVariable* specified. When faults occur in a BPEL process, the invoking client needs to be notified of it. This is done using the *reply* activity discussed earlier.

```
<reply partnerLink = "pl"
  portType = "pt"
  operation = "op"
  variable = "var"
  faultName = "fn" >
</reply>
```

The name of the fault is stored in *faultName*, and the information associated with it is stored in *faultVariable*.

When a fault occurs, the BPEL process terminates by default. However, certain faults might be minor and should not necessarily require the process to terminate. In such scenarios, the fault should be handled using a fault handler. The fault handlers are specified at the beginning of the BPEL specification, after declaring the partner links and variables. They are structured as follows:

```
<faultHandlers>
<catch faultName="f1" faultVariable="fv1">
```

TABLE 4.8 **Attributes for the *Catch* Activity**

Attribute	Description
faultName	Name of the fault handled by the catch
faultVariable	Type of variable that stores the fault information

```
   <!- The activities to handle the fault->
</catch>
<catch faultName="f2" faultVariable="fv2">
   <!- The activities to handle the fault->
</catch>
<catchAll>
   <!- The activities to handle other faults->
</catchAll> </faultHandlers>
```

A fault handler consists of one or more *catch* activities and a *catchAll* activity. While the *catch* activities handle specific faults, *catchAll* handles faults that are not handled by any of the preceding *catch* activities. Consequently, it is important to order the *catch* and *catchAll* activities correctly for a fault handler.

The *catch* activity has two attributes, at least one of which should be specified. These attributes are shown in Table 4.8.

The faults associated with an *invoke* activity can also be handled efficiently using an inline fault handler [5].

```
<invoke partnerLink = "pl"
   portType = "pt"
   operation = "op"
   inputVariable = "invar"
   outputVariable = "outVar">
   <catch faultName="f1" faultVariable="fv1">
   <!- The activities to handle the fault->
</catch>
<catch faultName="f2" faultVariable="fv2">
   <!- The activities to handle the fault->
</catch>
<catchAll>
   <!- The activities to handle other faults->
</catchAll>
</invoke>
```

Event Handling. BPEL provides event handlers to specify a set of activities that need to be executed when an event occurs. The activities are executed parallel to the business process. As with fault handlers, they are specified at the top of a BPEL specification.

TABLE 4.9 Attributes for the *onMessage* Activity

Attribute	Description
partnerLink	Specifies the link from which the message will be received
portType	Specifies the port type of the incoming message
operation	Specifies the operation to wait for the message
variable	Variable to store the message

An event handler can respond on receiving a message or on expiration of a timeout. The former is handled using, the *onMessage* activity; the latter is handled using the *onAlarm* activity. The *onMessage* activity has the four attributes shown in Table 4.9.

```
<onMessage partnerLink = "pl"
  portType = "pt"
  operation = "op"
  variable = "var" >
  <!- The activities to be executed after receiving the messages ->
</onMessage>
```

The *onAlarm* activity has the same attributes as *wait*, as listed in Table 4.5. A typical event handler is

```
<eventHandlers>
<onMessage partnerLink = "pl"
  portType = "pt"
  operation = "op"
  variable = "var" >
  <!- The activities to be executed after receiving the messages ->
</onMessage>
<onAlarm for="PT5H">
  <!- The activities to be executed after 5 hours ->
</onAlarm>
<onAlarm until="10:00:00Z">
<!- The activities to be executed at a specified time ->
</onAlarm>
</eventHandlers>
```

Synchronization of Concurrent Activities. As discussed earlier, the *flow* activity ensures concurrent execution of its subactivities. However, the subactivities might have certain interdependencies that need to be observed during execution. Although most simple dependencies could be handled using nested flow and sequence activities, *flow* offers *links* for complex scenarios.

The BPEL activity *link* is used to synchronize concurrent subtasks of *flow* activity. These links make it possible to specify if and when a subtask can execute based on the execution of other subtasks. Each link is identified by a unique `name`, and all the links are grouped under the *links* activity.

```
<links>
  <link name="link1"/>
  <link name="link2"/>
</links>
```

The subtasks of a *flow* activity can be either the *source* or *target* of one of the links defined. A subtask is defined as a source by declaring the source element nested within it.

```
<invoke ... >
  <source linkName = "name" transitionCondition = "boolean-exp"/>
</invoke>
```

Similarly, a subtask is defined as the target for a link by declaring a nested target element within it.

```
<invoke ...>
  <target linkName = "name" />
</invoke>
```

The *target* activity for a link can execute only when its source activity has finished execution. This allows synchronizing the subtasks of a *flow* activity. The *source* for a link might have a *transitionCondition* attribute specified, which evaluates a boolean expression. The result of this expression is sent to *target* activities for this link. If no *transitionCondition* is specified, *true* is sent by default. The result from the *transitionCondition* expression determines the status of the outgoing link.

Each subtask with a nested target element has a *joinCondition* attribute that evaluates the status of incoming links. By default it is calculated as the logical OR of the status values for all incoming links. However, this can be overridden by specifying any boolean expression for the join condition. Before the target activity starts, the join condition expression is evaluated. If it is true, the activity executes; otherwise, a *joinFailure* fault is thrown. Unless this fault is handled, this action would terminate the BPEL process. However, if an attribute *suppressJoinFailure* for target activity is set to "yes", the target activity is simply ignored and no fault is thrown. The default value for this attribute is "no".

```
<flow>
<links>
  <link name="link1"/>
  <link name="link2"/>
</links>
<invoke partnerLink = "pl1"
  portType = "pt1"
  operation = "op1"
  inputVariable = "invar1"
  outputVariable = "outVar1">
  <source linkName = "link1" transitionCondition = "boolean-exp"/>
</invoke>
<invoke partnerLink = "pl2"
  portType = "pt2"
  operation = "p2"
  inputVariable = "invar2"
  outputVariable = "outVar2">
  <source linkName = "link2" transitionCondition = "boolean-exp"/>
</invoke>
<invoke partnerLink = "pl3"
  portType = "pt3"
  operation = "op3"
  inputVariable = "invar3"
  outputVariable = "outVar3"
  joinCondition ="bool-exp"
  suppressJoinFailure = "yes">
  <target linkName = "link1" />
  <target linkName = "link2" />
</invoke>
```

4.2 SPRING FRAMEWORK

Spring is an open-source, lightweight, and loosely coupled Java application framework. It was created by Rod Johnson and described in his book *Expert One-on-One: J2EE Design and Development* [4]. Although it was created to address the complexity of server-side development, it has made its way into a multitude of other Java applications (e.g., Spring Mobile [2] and Spring Android [1]). Furthermore, vast community support has allowed the framework to be extended even for non-Java applications (e.g., Spring.NET [3]).

The Spring framework consists of several modules that offer most of the services required to develop enterprise-ready applications. As shown in Figure 4.8, these modules are stacked over the core module that forms the basis of the Spring framework. It is possible to use a subset of these modules, in combination with the core

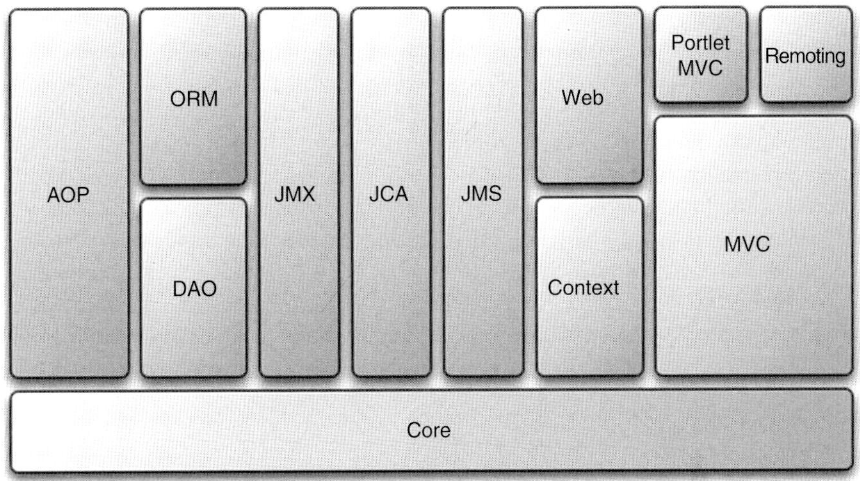

FIGURE 4.8 Modules of the Spring framework [6].

module, to build an enterprise application. Furthermore, Spring offers interfaces to plug into other frameworks that might be required by an application. Consequently, Spring can work in harmony with other frameworks, if necessary.

The core module acts as a container for application objects. It is responsible for creating, configuring, and managing these objects. The aspect-oriented-programming (AOP) module addresses the system-wide concerns of an application (e.g., security). The data-access-object (DAO) and object-relational-mapping (ORM) modules help in interacting with a data source. The model-view-controller (MVC) module helps in developing web applications in which the business logic is segregated from the user interface. In this book we use only the core module of the framework.

Any nontrivial application (based on an object-oriented paradigm) constitutes of a set of objects, each corresponding to an instance of a real-world object, concept, or data. These objects interact and collaborate to meet the business objectives of the underlying application. Traditionally, this interplay required an object to create instances for all objects that it would need. As shown below, this is done using *new* in the Java programming language.

```
class A {
    B b = new B( );
    public int add(int a,int b) {
        return b.sum(a,b);
    }
}
```

```
class B {
    public int sum(int x,int y) {
        return x+y;
    }
}
```

Such strong coupling among objects makes them difficult to test and reuse. This is exacerbated further for enterprise applications that comprise thousands of objects. The crux of the problem is the necessity for an object to manage its dependencies.

The Spring framework resolves this problem by managing the dependencies among application objects. Instead of objects having to create and maintain their own dependencies, they are injected by the framework. Considering that Spring creates each object in the system, it has all the objects required to resolve any dependency. The process of configuring dependencies among application objects is known as *wiring*. Although Spring supports multiple ways of wiring components, it is more often done using XML documents. As shown below, each application object is instantiated by the framework as a bean. In doing so, it assigns all dependencies of a bean as its properties. The appropriate *setter* methods are used for wiring.

```
class A {
    B bobj;
    public void setBobj(B bobj) {
        this.bobj=bobj; }
    public int add(int a,int b) {
        return bobj.sum(a,b); }
}

class B {
    public int sum(int x,int y) {
        return x+y;
    }
}

<bean id="a" class="A">
    <property name="bobj" ref="b">
</bean>

<bean id="b" class="B">
</bean>
```

The core module of the Spring framework acts as the *container* for application objects. It contains an interface *BeanFactory*, which creates, configures, and manages beans. This interface has several implementations (e.g., *XmlBeanFactory*, *Simple-JndiBeanFactory*), each of which acts as a simple container.

Other modules of the framework that are stacked over the core module in Figure 4.8 have the following functionalities:

- *AOP*. Aspect-oriented programming increases the modularity of code by separating cross-cutting concerns such as logging, and transaction management. Although AspectJ extends Java for aspect-oriented programming, Spring provides extensive AOP support wherein the application objects are loosely coupled in using dependency injection.
- *DAO*. Accessing a database using JDBC creates a lot of boilerplate code. This is essentially because each access requires (1) opening a connection,

(2) creating an SQL query, (3) executing the query to get a result, and (4) closing the connection. Spring not only reduces code redundancy but it also supports transaction management services for application objects. Furthermore, it translates any vendor-specific exceptions into meaningful error messages.

- *ORM*. Spring provides an ORM package on top of DAO to provide object-relational mapping APIs. Instead of building its own ORM framework, it supports several popular frameworks, including Java Persistent APIs, Java Data Objects, Hibernate, and iBatis.
- *JMX*. Using Java management extensions, technology is a standard way of monitoring applications, systems, and networks. The Spring framework automatically registers each bean as a JMX MBean (managed bean) that can be monitored.
- *JCA*. Spring provides a standard way to connect to legacy enterprise applications using Java connector architecture. This makes it possible to connect disparate applications that are running on heterogeneous servers and platforms.
- *Context*. The context package builds on the core package and adds support for internationalization, event propagation, resource loading, and the creation of contexts.
- *MVC*. The MVC package provides a web application framework that has a clear separation between the user interface and application logic. However, unlike other MVC frameworks, such as Apache Struts, JSF, Tapestry, and so on, MVC has all the advantages of the Spring framework (e.g., loose coupling).
- *Portlet MVC*. The Spring portlet MVC builds on Spring MVC to support JSR-168 Java portlet specification. The portlet workflow differs from the servlet workflow in having two distinct phases. The first phase is known as an *action phase*, wherein any backend changes are accomplished. The *render phase* sets in when the content is displayed to the user.
- *Web*. The web module contains support classes for Spring MVC and Spring portlet MVC. Additionally, it supports multipart file uploads and binding of request parameters.
- *Remoting*. The remoting module allows exposing the functionality of an application as remote objects. Remoting also helps another application to access and use these objects as if they were local Java beans. Remote Method Invocation (RMI), Hessian, Burlap, JAX-RPC, and Spring's HTTP Invoker can be used for remoting.
- *JMS*. The Java message service package complements remoting in communication over the network. While remoting is driven by the network reliability and the availability of communicating applications, JMS guarantees the delivery of messages irrespective of the status of network and endpoints. Spring simplifies the JMS APIs and shields the user from the differences across multiple versions.

The Spring framework is used in this book to formalize a BPEL specification because:

- The technique for automatic formalization of a BPEL specification required instantiating and initializing the DTOs corresponding to BPEL activities (as discussed in Chapter). The convenience offered by the Spring framework in this transformation led to its adoption.
- The Spring framework uses XML-based files to specify beans. This made it possible to extend the Spring framework to parse the activities in a BPEL specification (which is also XML based) to create their beans.
- Spring helps in developing lightweight and loosely coupled applications.

4.3 JAXB 2 APIs

Java Architecture for XML Binding (JAXB) 2 APIs offer a practical, efficient, and standard way of mapping between XML and Java code. Transforming a Java object hierarchy into an XML document is known as *marshaling*, and the reverse is known as *unmarshaling*. JAXB 2 APIs, which support both marshaling and unmarshaling, consist of two basic components:

1. The binding compiler (i.e., *xbj*) transforms an XML schema into a set of Java classes. In doing so, the compiler embeds in these classes the structure specified in the XML schema. This is done using special JAXB annotations that are used by the runtime framework.
2. The runtime framework provides marshaling and unmarshaling features. The annotated classes generated by the compiler are used for this transformation.

An XML schema describes the precise structure of an XML document. This includes the set of elements and the attributes allowed in it. In addition, a schema might contain details about the order and number of child elements allowed for a parent element. When the binding compiler processes a schema, it includes all available information in the classes produced. The compiler creates a corresponding class for each element defined in the schema.

```
>xjc test.xsd -p package.test -d src/generated
```

The options *p* and *d* are used to specify the package and directory for the classes generated.

4.3.1 Unmarshaling XML Documents

Unmarshaling requires creating a *javax.xml.bind.JAXBContext* object using the package name for classes that were produced by the binding compiler.

```
JAXBContext context
        = JAXBContext.newInstance("package.test");
```

Unmarshaling a document requires creating a *javax.xml.bind.Unmarshaler* object from the context.

```
Unmarshaler unmarshaler = context.createUnmarshaler();
```

Finally, the unmarshaler object processes an XML document to return an object. This object is an instance of the class corresponding to the root element of the XML that was generated by the binding compiler. It is worth mentioning that the XML document used herein must adhere to the schema compiled earlier.

```
File f = new File("test.xml");
RootElementClass obj
        = (RootElementClass) unmarshaler.unmarshal(f);
```

4.3.2 Marshaling Java Objects

The process for marshaling is almost the reverse of that for unmarshaling. As with unmarshaling, initially a *javax.xml.bind.JAXBContext* object is created using the package name for the classes generated.

```
JAXBContext context
        = JAXBContext.newInstance("package.test");
```

Then the class corresponding to the root element of the XML document envisioned is instantiated and initialized. The initialization involves assigning the attributes and subelements.

```
RootElementClass obj = new RootElementClass();
obj.setAttribute1 = "att1";
...
```

Finally, a marshaler object is created and the object is marshaled.

```
context.createMarshaler().marshal(obj, System.out);
```

The XML rendered is written to standard output. JAXB 2 APIs are used in this book because:

- The intermediate DTOs rendered by the Spring framework need to be marshaled into an XML-based formal model.

- JAXB 2 provides a compiler that can be used to compile a schema into a hierarchy of classes. These classes help in creating XML documents that conform to the schema definition.
- The APIs are convenient and powerful.

REFERENCES

1. *Spring Android*, January 2011.
2. *Spring Mobile*, January 2011.
3. *Spring.Net Application Framework*, January 2011.
   E. Clarke, O. Grumberg, and D. Peled. *Model Checking*. MIT Press, Cambridge, MA, 2000.
4. R. Johnson. *Expert One-on-One J2EE Design and Development*. Wrox Press, Birmingham, UK, 2002.
5. M. Juric. *Business Process Execution Language for Web Services*. Packt Publishing, Birmingham, UK, 2006.
6. C. Walls and R. Breidenbach. *Spring in Action, 2nd ed.* Manning Publications, Greenwich, CT, 2007.

CHAPTER 5

MEMORY-EFFICIENT STATE-SPACE ANALYSIS IN SOFTWARE MODEL CHECKING

Formal methods have an unprecedented ability to endorse the correctness of a system. Despite that, they have been limited to safety- and mission-critical systems, owing to the significant time and memory costs involved. Our ever-increasing dependency on software in many aspects of life has necessitated the use of formal methods for a wider range of software. In this chapter we present two techniques to reduce the memory requirement of *model checking*, a widely used formal method. To ensure termination a model checker stores in memory all states explored. The techniques presented slash memory costs by storing a state according to how different it is from one of its neighboring states. Our experiments report a memory reduction of 95% while only doubling the computation delay. This reduction allows model checking in a machine with only a fraction of the memory required otherwise. Consequently, the advantage is twofold: (1) the savings substantial are, as a smaller physical memory suffices; and (2) as more states can now be stored in a memory of the same size, the chances of accomplishing complete state-space analysis are considerably higher.

Verification of Communication Protocols in Web Services: Model-Checking Service Compositions, First Edition. Zahir Tari, Peter Bertok, Anshuman Mukherjee.

5.1 MOTIVATION

Traditionally, software is considered "fail-safe" if it has passed a rigorous testing phase [1]. However, the crash of the *Ariane 5* launcher [5] and the deaths due to malfunctioning of the Therac-25 radiation therapy machine [18], despite rigorous software testing, suggest otherwise. The team investigating these accidents recommended using formal methods (FMs) to complement testing, as the former assures exhaustive verification of a system [5,18].

The problem is exacerbated further by SOA-based applications that are loosely coupled and dynamically composed. Despite the advances in sophisticated techniques to allow automatic matching and composition of web services [10,17], such applications rely overwhelmingly on automated verification methods to attest to their credibility and reliability. As model checking is an automated verification technique that scrutinizes exhaustively all possible behavior of a system, it is an obvious choice for use with SOA-based applications.

However, most nontrivial systems have a gigantic number of states (known as the *state-space explosion* problem [4]), so FMs are associated with a high price tag. This is essentially due to (1) the time taken to generate such a large number of states, and (2) the enormous space requirements for storing these states. Consequently, developers are often compelled to skip FMs completely to meet the software budget. In this chapter we present two techniques for reducing the FM cost so that they can be used more widely.

Model checking [5] is a formal verification method that involves scrutinizing the reachable states of a system for a set of predefined undesirable properties. However, during state-space exploration, states might be generated more than once. To prevent analyzing the same states repeatedly for the properties desired, it is necessary to remember the states already explored by storing them in memory. This also ensures termination, a condition where no new states are generated. Nevertheless, model checking is plagued with the state-space explosion problem, wherein a gigantic number of states need to be scrutinized to find a counterexample. This causes a manyfold increase in memory costs, as each new state has to be stored. Such bottlenecks in available memory hinder model checking.

Some solutions based on *partial storage* address the problem by storing only a subset of the states explored [4,9,16]. Although this reduces the memory requirement, it is difficult to decide the set of states to be deleted (i.e., not stored). If a deleted state is reached again in the future, it would be treated as a new state and explored further. The solution presented here has no such issues, as it uses an *exhaustive storage* technique, in which all states explored are compressed and stored in a suitable data structure (e.g., a hash table). The states need to be decompressed before comparison, as it is possible for more than one state to have a similar compressed state.

In this chapter we describe two techniques to reduce the memory costs of model checking. These techniques require storing the states as the difference from one of the neighboring states. Based on the neighboring state used to calculate the difference, the model generated can be classified as either a *sequential model*, which stores a state in terms of how different it is from its immediately preceding state, or as a *tree model*, which stores a state in terms of how different it is from its nearest state in explicit form. As observed previously, each state produced during state-space exploration is remembered by storing it in memory. When the state is stored in any of these alternative forms, there is a significant reduction in memory costs. The reduction is attributed to the assertion that a change in state is smaller than the state itself.

As mentioned previously, the first step in model checking requires creating a formal representation of the system. This representation depends on the model-checking tool to be used for verification. Some common languages for system representation are Promela for SPIN [12], the C programming language for BLAST [2], and colored petri nets (CPNs) for CPN Tools [15]. Due to subtle differences between the representation languages, it is difficult to present a generic memory-reduction technique. The models discussed in this chapter specifically target CPN models but do not gain any advantage from using CPN models. The relative storage technique will work for all representation languages, as systems usually change in many small steps rather than in a single large step. Hence, the assertion that "change in a state is smaller than the state itself" is valid. Indeed, experiments report a 95% reduction in memory, which further endorses the assertion.

The solutions presented in this chapter can be summarized as follows:

1. Relative storage techniques to reduce the memory requirement for model checking by storing states in difference form. The results indicate up to a 95% reduction in the memory requirement.
2. A backtracking method to transform a difference state to its explicit form. Considering the possibility of multiple explicit states having the same difference state, this backtracking mechanism allows us to decompress the states before comparison and thereby prevents false duplicates. The decompression technique only doubles the time needed to generate the state space. This is 33% lower than the time reported by Evangelist and Pradat-Peyre [8].

The remainder of the chapter is organized as follows. In Section 5.2 we introduce the problem being deliberated and provide an insight into the solution. Prior to describing the sequential and tree models in Section 5.4, related work is reviewed in Section 5.3. We tabulate and plot the experimental results in Section 5.5 and discuss the outcome in Section 5.6. Finally, we summarize the solution in Section 5.7.

5.2 OVERVIEW OF THE PROBLEM AND SOLUTION

In this section we discuss the problem in detail and outline the solution presented. State-space analysis of a model is done by generating a *reachability graph* [14].

Definition 5.1 *The reachability graph of a model C is a directed graph $G(C) = (V,E,v_0)$ wherein:*

(a) *The vertices in V correspond to the set of reachable states in C.*
(b) *The edges in E correspond to the binding elements in C.*
(c) *The root vertex v_0 corresponds to the initial state of C.*

Each model has a unique initial state, and this is represented by the root node of a reachability graph. At its initial state, the system might have a set of enabled events which can cause a change in state. Each of these events is represented by a separate edge from the root node of the reachability graph and leads to a new node representing the new state. These new states are then analyzed for the set of events enabled. For each such event, an outgoing edge is added to the corresponding node. This, in turn, generates another set of new states to be analyzed identically. This analysis continues until the set of new states has no enabled event.

However, it might be possible to reach a state from the initial state by executing different sequences of events. Suppose that S_0 is the initial state of a model M, and let S' be a state reached by the following two sequences of events:

$$S_0[e_1\rangle S_1[e_2\rangle S_2[e_3\rangle \cdots [e_m\rangle S'$$
$$S_0[e'_1\rangle S'_1[e'_2\rangle S'_2[e'_3\rangle \cdots [e'_n\rangle S'$$

where $\forall i \in [1,m]$: e_i and $\forall j \in [1,n]$: e'_j are events and $S_{i-1}[e_i\rangle S_i$ denotes the fact that event e_i in state S_{i-1} leads to state S_i. This is shown in Figure 5.1.

If $\exists i \in [1,n]$: $(i < m) \wedge (e_i \not\equiv e'_i)$, the state S' can be reached using two different sequences of events and therefore is a *duplicate state*. The reachability graph for M will have two nodes representing the same state, S'. However, analyzing both the nodes and their children (each of which will also have a duplicate node) is a waste of resources. The larger the number of duplicate nodes for a state, the greater the wast of resources. Furthermore, if there exists a nonempty sequence of events $[e_1e_2\cdots e_r\rangle : r > 0$ that causes no net change in state of a model M, the model checker might never terminate. This is shown in Figure 5.2. Let S be some state of model M and $\forall i \in [1,r]$: e_i be events such that

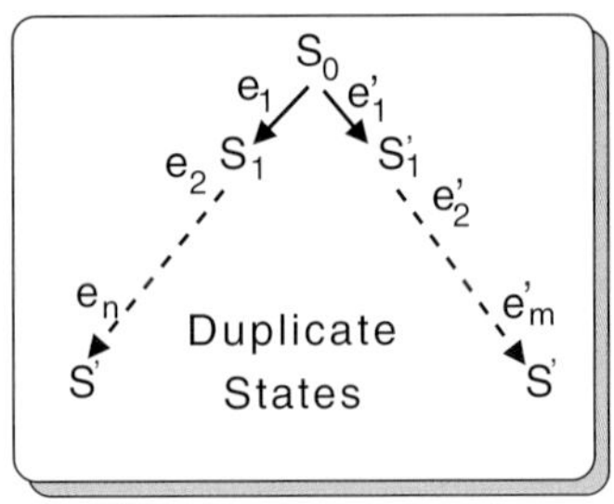

FIGURE 5.1 S' reached using two different sequences of events from S_0.

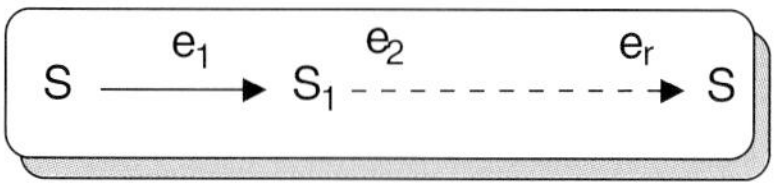

$$S \xrightarrow{e_1} S_1 \xrightarrow{e_2} \cdots \xrightarrow{e_r} S$$

FIGURE 5.2 The sequence of events $[e_1 e_2 \cdots e_r\rangle$ causes no net change in state.

$$S[e_1\rangle S_1[e_2\rangle S_2[e_3\rangle \cdots [e_r\rangle S \text{ or } S[e_1e_2e_3 \cdots e_r\rangle S$$

Such a state of affairs would lead to analysis of the set of states $\{S, S_1, S_2, \ldots, S_{r-1}\}$ forever, and state-space analysis might never finish.

Consequently, it is necessary to remember the states already explored and ignore any duplicate states encountered. A model checker remembers the states explored by storing them in memory. When a state is generated during state-space exploration, it is compared with the stored states to determine if it is new or a duplicate of a state generated previously. If it is a duplicate state, the corresponding node in the reachability graph becomes a terminal node and it is not analyzed further. Otherwise, the new state is stored in memory and is analyzed for enabled events. However, due to state-space explosion, a large amount of memory is needed to store all unique states. In this chapter we present two relative storage techniques to reduce the memory requirement by storing a state in terms of how different it is from the preceding state.

At any time, there might be thousands of explored states stored in memory. Comparing each state generated with all stored states might take a long time. Hence, the states are stored in a hash table to ensure constant time lookup.

We illustrate the problem using an example. Figures 5.3 and 5.4 show a colored petri net model and a part of its reachability graph. All duplicate nodes in Figure 5.4 are shaded. Initially, the CPN model has two tokens in place A and three in place C. This is represented by state 1 in Figure 5.4, and being the root node of the reachability graph, it is stored in memory. The events enabled at this state are (T1,x=5) and (T1,x=7), where T1 is the transition enabled and x=5 or 7 is the binding for which it is enabled. Corresponding to these two enabled events, the root node in Figure 5.4 has two outgoing edges, one for each event. When T1 fires with x=5, there is no change in state, as all tokens remain in their previous places and the edge corresponding to this event leads to a duplicate state in Figure 5.4. To save time and to ensure termination duplicate states are not analyzed further. The other event (T1,x=7) results in moving a token from A to B, leading to state 2. Being a new state, it is represented using a bright node in Figure 5.4. Furthermore, it is stored and analyzed further for enabled transitions. State 2 has three enabled events: (T2,y=0), (T2,y=1), and (T2,y=2). The first event causes no change in state and is represented by a shaded node in Figure 5.4. The other two events change the value of the token in B, leading to States 3 and 4, which are represented by bright nodes in Figure 5.4. Being new states, they are stored in memory and analyzed further for enabled events. The remaining states are explored analogously to generate the complete reachability graph.

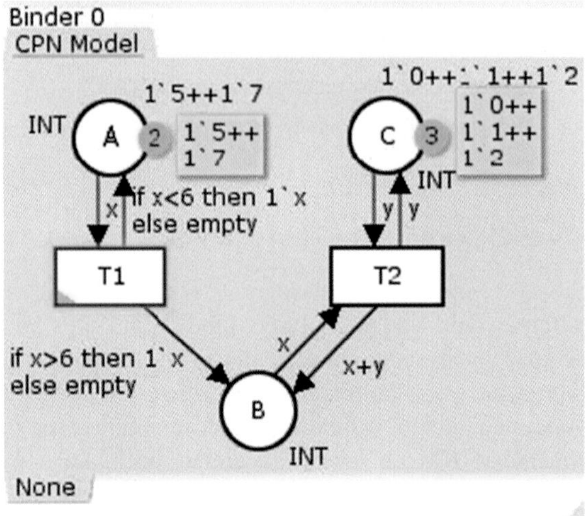

FIGURE 5.3 Colored petri net model. Variables x and y are of type INT.

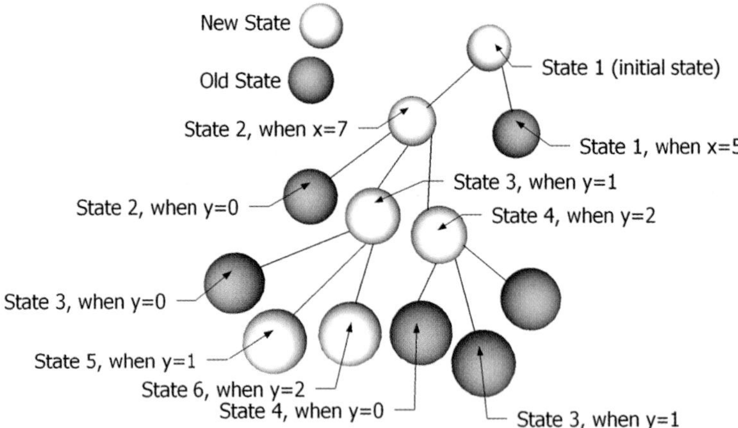

FIGURE 5.4 Part of a reachability graph for the CPN model in Figure 5.3.

The reachability graph in this example has an infinite number of states. Other models might have a finite number of states. However, the number of states is almost always huge, leading to state-space explosion [6]. Complete state-space analysis is possible only when the available memory (α_A) in a machine is sufficient to store all unique states in the reachability graph (α_M) of model M. Otherwise, if $\alpha_A < \alpha_M$, only a partial state-space analysis can be performed, and the analysis will stop when the memory is full. In this chapter we describe models for compact representation and storage of a state so as to dramatically reduce the memory requirements for model checking. Using the models presented, the memory needed to store all unique states in the reachability graph of model M is reduced to α'_M. This allows (1) complete reachability analysis in a machine with a smaller memory α'_A if $\alpha'_A \geq \alpha'_M$, where $\alpha'_A < \alpha_A$ and $\alpha'_M < \alpha_M$, and (2) even when $\alpha_A < \alpha'_M$, the partial state-space analysis can have at least a few more steps. That is, with the available memory remaining the same, we are able to create a reachability graph with more states, due to the fact that less memory is needed to store a state.

5.3 RELATED WORK

All solutions proposed to store state space can be classified as either (1) partial storage, (2) lossy storage, or (3) exhaustive storage. The solution described in this chapter is based on exhaustive storage.

As the name indicates, only a subset of the states explored is stored, using *partial storage* techniques. The sweep-line method [4] is such an approach, wherein a state is deleted if it cannot be reached again in future. However, it is difficult to decide the states to be deleted. Furthermore, it is not a generic solution, as for different systems we might need to delete a different set of states. *Lossy storage* techniques produce the entire state space in which each explored state is compressed and stored in a suitable data structure (e.g., a hash table) to ensure constant time lookup. However, the compression algorithm used is not reversible. To determine if a state is new, it is also compressed and compared with stored states. As pointed out previously, multiple states can have the same compressed form. This often results in falsely identifying a state as a duplicate. There are several interesting solutions based on lossy storage:

- *An ordered binary decision diagram* (OBDD) *with compression* uses a decision tree to store a state visited [20]. Figure 5.5 shows an acyclic graph that can store eight possible states. These states are represented using 3 bits, from 000 to 111.

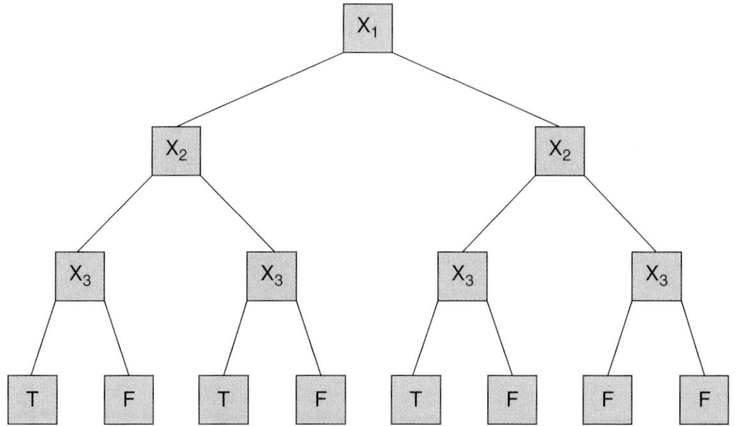

FIGURE 5.5 Decision tree for boolean function $f(x_1, x_2, x_3) = \overline{x_1} \cdot \overline{x_2} \cdot \overline{x_3} + \overline{x_1} \cdot x_2 \cdot \overline{x_3} + x_1 \cdot \overline{x_2} \cdot \overline{x_3}$.

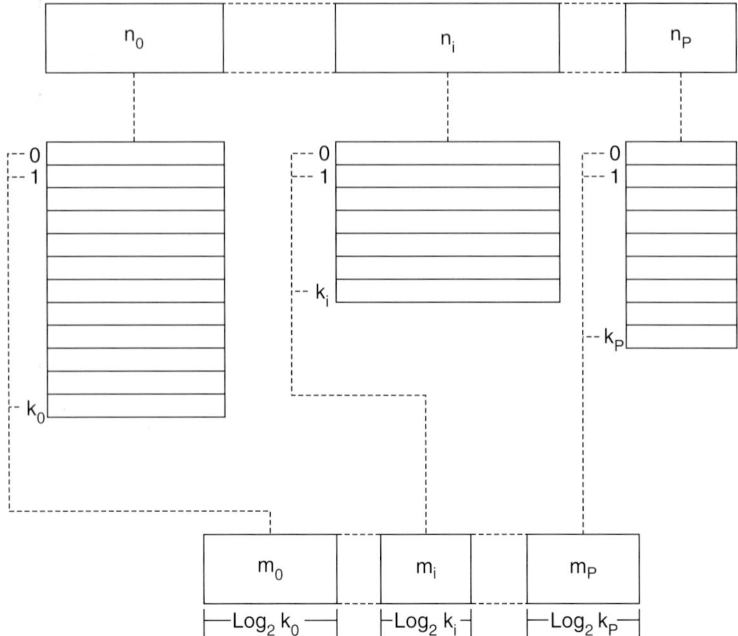

FIGURE 5.6 Compression of states represented by bits.

Each left arm of the acyclic graph represents a 0, and each right arm represents a 1. For example, starting at the root, a state 100 would use the right arm at the first level and the left arm at the remaining two levels. Finally, after traversing all the arms based on bit values, a terminal node is encountered that stores either *true* or *false*. A terminal node with *true* denotes that the marking that leads to it has been visited. Consequently, the terminal nodes for an acyclic graph need to be updated whenever a new state is generated. The compression algorithm divides the bits representing a state into $p + 1$ parts such that part d has n_d bits. Each of these bit pieces has a table, and the table for the dth bit piece has k_d entries such that $m_d = \log_2 k_d << n_d$. This reduces the size of the graph by ensuring that a state is represented by using fewer bits. Figure 5.6 illustrates the compression technique.

- *An automaton representation of reachable states* stores each state as a sequence of bits [13]. This is similar to an OBDD, where x bits are used to represent 2^x states. However, instead of an acyclic graph, an automaton is used to store the states. Its edges are inscribed with bit values *0* and *1*. Starting from the root node, the edges are followed based on the bits representing a state. If the terminal node has a *1*, the state is established as a duplicate. Figure 5.7 shows an automaton that leads to a *1* node for the set of states represented by {000, 001, 101}. The automaton is modified whenever a new marking is generated, to ensure that its corresponding bit sequence leads to a *1* node.

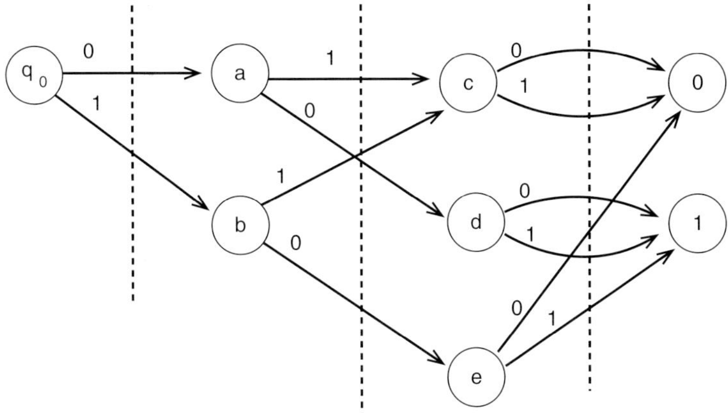

FIGURE 5.7 Storing states visited using an automaton.

- *A graph-encoded tuple set* (GETS) makes possible compact representation of states which the common prefix and suffix for a set of states are used to reduce the size of graphs. A reduction is obtained only when the state space is large. Otherwise, there might be an expansion of the storage required instead of the reduction envisioned. Results indicate that a GETS can decrease the memory requirements up to sevenfold with a tripling of processing time.

Exhaustive storage techniques also produce the entire state space in which each state explored is compressed and stored in a suitable data structure (e.g., a hash table) to ensure constant time lookup. However, unlike lossy storage, the compression algorithm needs to be reversible; otherwise, the states cannot be regenerated for comparison. Both the tree and sequential models incorporate compression techniques that are reversible. Other compression techniques include Δ-markings, shown in Figure 5.8, wherein a state is stored as the transition instance that leads to it from the preceding state. Such solutions are specific to petri nets and related formalisms where the transitions are deterministic. Nevertheless, the compression rendered has an inevitable associated delay. The existing models offer a generic solution within an acceptable time frame.

Table 5.1 compares the sequential model with other solutions based on this approach and the state-space compression they provide. The table also gives the additional delay incurred when using a solution. The sequential model provides reduction equivalent to that of Evangelists and Pradat-Peyre [8] with only two-thirds of its delay.

Table 5.2 illustrates the advantage of exhaustive storage over related techniques. In the table, *false positive* means that two different states are identified erroneously as being the same; *false negative* refers to missing duplicate states. The models are based on exhaustive storage techniques that are not subject to the aforementioned shortcomings.

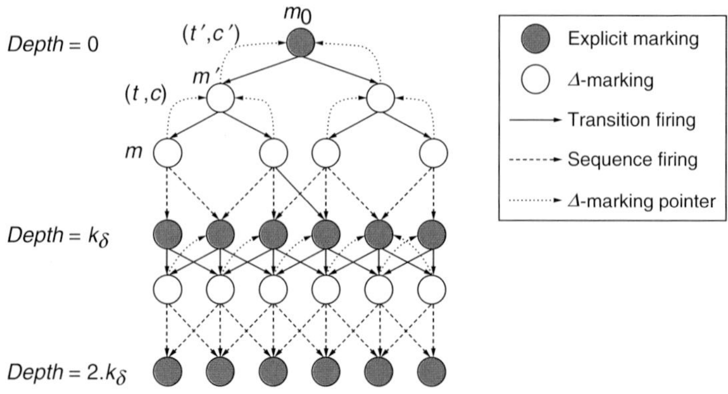

FIGURE 5.8 Generating state space with Δ-mappings [8].

TABLE 5.1 Comparison of Solutions Based on Exhaustive Storage

Method	Run Time	Memory Use
No algorithm	100%	100%
[19]	130%	60%
[8]	300%	5%
[11]	280%	18.3%
Sequential model	200%	5%

TABLE 5.2 Comparison of Storage Techniques for Memory Reduction[a]

	Storage Technique		
Feature	Partial Storage	Lossy Storage	Exhaustive Storage
States stored	◐	●	●
Compression algorithm	⊗	$\not\rightleftarrows$	$\rightleftarrows$
False positive	×	✓	×
False negative	✓	×	×
Generic	×	✓	✓

[a] ◐, satisfies Partially; ●, satisfies; ⊗, does not satisfy; $\not\rightleftarrows$, non-reversible technique; $\rightleftarrows$, reversible technique

5.4 MODELS FOR MEMORY-EFFICIENT STATE-SPACE ANALYSIS

In this section we provide details of the sequential and tree models with memory-efficient state-space analysis. Although these models specifically target CPN models, the solutions do not rely on any CPN-specific characteristic; they are valid for all modeling languages that satisfy the condition that "a change in a state is smaller than the state itself." For CPN, a change in state occurs if one or more tokens (1) move to another place, (2) change their value, (3) are created in the model, (4) are deleted from the model, or (5) combine these such that the color of each token matches the color set of a containing place. In a CPN model, these changes are brought in by a transition. However, a transition usually modifies the place and value information of only a small number of tokens. Furthermore, a very small number of tokens are usually created or deleted by a transition. Therefore it is substantially cheaper to store how different a state S is from the preceding state than to store the full state S. Based on this, in the next section we describe the sequential model used to generate a memory-efficient reachability graph.

5.4.1 Sequential Model

The model aims at reducing the memory requirements for model checking. Such a reduction will increase the affordability and consequent use of model checking in software development. The focus of this model is storing states in difference form, which is defined as follows:

Definition 5.2 *The difference form of a state S_{st}, denoted as D_{st}, is defined as the changes in its preceding state S_{pv} necessary to generate it.*

Corollary 5.1 *If D_{st} is the difference form of a state S_{st}, and S_{pv} is its preceding state, S_{st} can be regenerated in explicit form as $S_{st} = S_{pv} + D_{st}$.*

An explicit state has information for all tokens, and in this chapter it is often referred to simply as a *state*. Below we illustrate how to find the difference form of a state using a simple example.

Figure 5.9 presents a portion of the reachability graph for the CPN model (shown in Figure 5.3) using a sequential model. Initially, the model is in state 1, and since it does not have a preceding state, it is stored in explicit form (see Figure 5.9). The tokens in the model are arbitrarily termed a to e (see Figure 5.9). Furthermore, their

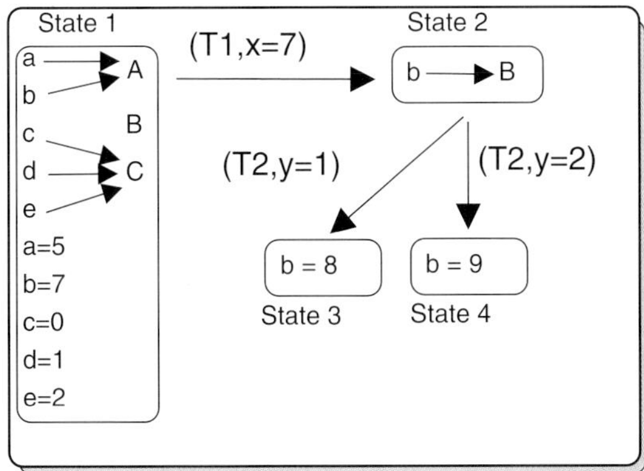

FIGURE 5.9 Part of the reachability graph in Figure 5.4 using a sequential model. The corresponding model is shown in Figure 5.3.

places are assigned by an arrow (→) and values are assigned by an equals (=) sign. For example, the token 1`5 in place $A$ of Figure 5.3 is named $a$. Its place is assigned as $a \rightarrow A$ while the value is assigned as $a = 5$. Similarly, the token 1`7 in A is termed b and assigned the place and value $b \rightarrow A$ and $b = 7$.

When the event (T1,x=5) occurs, the model persists in state 1. As a result, the difference form is empty (or null) and not drawn (see Figure 5.9). However, (T1,x=7) takes it to state 2. To store the new state in difference form, we need to find the changes in state 1 brought on by this event. We find that the event moved token 1`7 to place B. This information is sufficient to construct state 2 from state 1. We therefore store state 2 in difference form as $b \rightarrow B$.

The event (T2,y=1) in state 2 leads to state 3. Similarly, the event (T2,y=2) leads to state 4. To store these new states in difference form, the changes in state 2 brought by these events need to be found. On inspecting these events, both are found to change the value of the token in place B. While (T2,y=1) changes the value to 8, (T2,y=9) changes it to 9. Given state 2 in explicit form, this information is sufficient to construct states 3 and 4. Accordingly, state 3 is stored as $b = 8$ and state 4 is stored as $b = 9$. The difference forms for other states are calculated identically. Additionally, each state stores a pointer to its preceding state. This is necessary to regenerate the states, as explained later. As is evident from this example, it takes less space to store states in difference form.

A state change also occurs when an event creates or deletes one or more tokens. If an event deletes a token a, the new state can be represented in difference form by assigning the place for a as null ($a \rightarrow$ null). Similarly, when an event creates a new token, it is given an arbitrary name and assigned the corresponding place and value information. This is illustrated by the example in Figure 5.10. The CPN model in

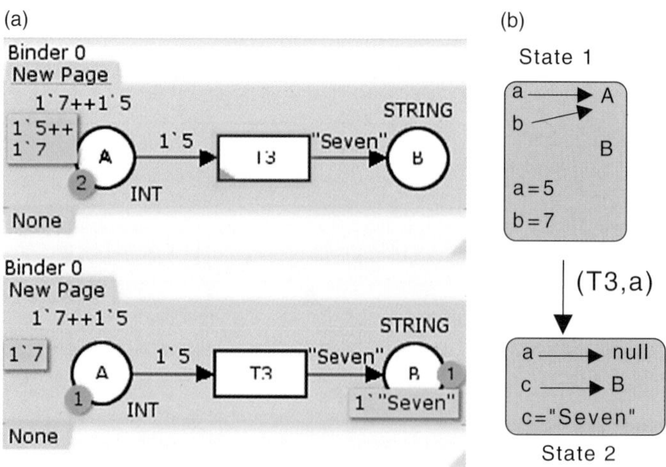

FIGURE 5.10 State change when tokens are created and/or deleted. (a) A CPN model where $T3$ fires to delete token 1`5 and create token 1'"Seven". (b) Reachability graph using a sequential model.

Figure 5.10(a) has a transition T3, which removes token 1`5 from place A and adds 1"Seven" to place B. Considering the value in the latter token, place B is assigned the color set STRING. The reachability graph of the model using a sequential model is presented in Figure 5.10(b).

The tokens in place A are assigned the terms a and b. The initial state of the model is stored explicitly in Figure 5.10(b), as there is no previous state to calculate a difference. When event (T3,1`5) occurs, it deletes the token $a$ and creates a new token, which we term $c$. The new state can be stored in difference form by assigning the place of $a$ to `null` and assigning the place and value information for the newly created token. Given state 1 in explicit form, the aforesaid information is sufficient to regenerate State 2. This example further endorses a reduction in the memory requirement when states are stored in difference form.

In this section we explained how to obtain the difference form of a state and demonstrated the memory reduction when states are stored in difference form. However, more than one explicit state can produce the same difference state. This necessitates converting states into explicit forms before comparison. This is explained in the next section by means of an example.

Expanding a State in Difference Form. Here we demonstrate backtracking to cause a difference state to revert. This is necessary for comparison, as more than one explicit state can produce the same difference state.

When a state is generated during state-space exploration, it has to be compared with stored states to determine if it is new. However, compressing and comparing it with states stored in difference form might lead to an error, owing to multiple states having the same difference form. Suppose that three states S_a, S_b, and S_c produce the same difference form D_{abc}. When either of the three states is encountered for the first time, D_{abc} is stored in memory. When the other two states are encountered and compared with stored states in compressed form, they are interpreted incorrectly as duplicate states. Therefore, before comparing it is essential to revert a stored state. Such a conversion, called *expanding*, is done by *backtracking*.

Definition 5.3 *Backtracking is the process of regenerating a state by recursively adding the most recent changes for each token to its preceding state until a state stored in explicit form is reached.*

Corollary 5.2 *If S_n and D_n are the explicit and difference states at depth n of a reachability graph, the former can be obtained from the latter using a backtracking function BK, where $S_n = BK(D_n) = D_n + S_{n-1}$.*

Corollary 5.3 *Since S_0 is always in explicit form, the equation in Corollary 5.2 can be solved for all $n \leq h$, where h is the height of the reachability graph.*

We illustrate backtracking with an example. State 4 is stored in difference form in Figure 5.9, and to expand it we need to backtrack until an explicit state is encountered, as shown in Figure 5.11. Initially, state 4 contains a new value for

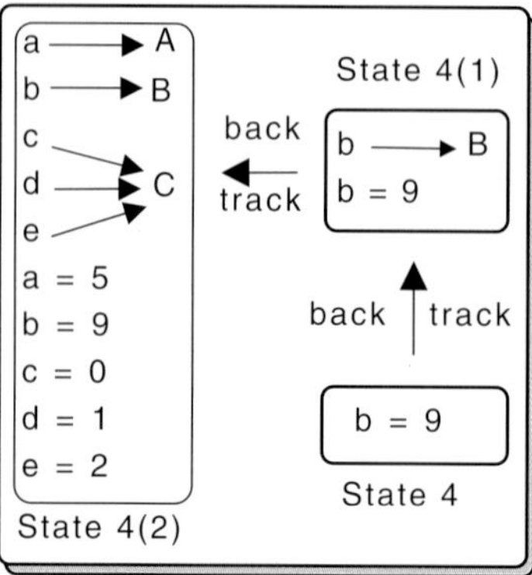

FIGURE 5.11 Backtracking to expand state 4 in Figure 5.9.

token b and a link to its preceding state. Using Definition 5.2, we should get state 4 in explicit form by updating its preceding state (which we hope is in explicit form) with this value. However, on backtracking one step in Figure 5.9, we reach state 2, which is also stored in difference form. But it gives additional information about the place of token b and a link to its preceding state. We add the place information from state 2 with the value information from state 4 and get metastate 4(1), shown in Figure 5.11. We call 4(1) a metastate as it was obtained by combining two different states. Using Definition 5.3, state 4 can now be obtained by updating the preceding state of state 2 with information in metastate 4(1). On further backtracking, state 1 is encountered, which is actually in expanded form. We update it with the information in 4(1) and get another metastate, 4(2). By Definition 5.3, metastate 4(2) is state 4 in expanded form.

As backtracking is an additional overhead when states are stored in difference form, they increase the time needed for state-space analysis. Definition 5.3 requires backtracking to initial state S_0 for expanding each state. However, this leads to a large delay with an increase in height of the reachability graph. In the next section we discuss ways to reduce this overhead.

Decreasing the Cost of Expanding. Here we discuss various ways of reducing the additional delay incurred while backtracking. Reducing this delay will reduce the overall time required for model checking.

So far we have stored only the initial state in explicit form, while all other states are to be stored in difference form. Although this should ensure maximum reduction in memory requirements, Definition 5.3 will require backtracking to the initial state for expanding. As a result, the states far from the initial state take a long time to expand.

To reduce the delay, the number of backtracking steps need to be minimized. If every state at depth $i\delta: i \in N$ steps from the initial state is stored in expanded form, expanding a state will never require backtracking more than $\delta - 1$ steps. (N is the set of natural numbers starting from zero.) Therefore, starting from the initial state, the

δth, 2δth, 3δth, ... states are stored in expanded form. The model can be tuned by accepting different values of δ.

Algorithm for the Sequential Model. As specified previously, the sequential model achieves memory reduction by storing states in difference form. Starting from the initial state, it explores the remaining reachable states of the model using a depth-first search (DFS) algorithm [7]. Each state explored is stored in a hash table.

When a state is generated, a hash-function is used to find its index in a hash table. If this index is empty, the state is new. Its difference form is calculated and inserted at this index. Furthermore, the transitions enabled are identified, and one of them is fired. Otherwise, if there are states already stored at this index, they are all expanded and compared with the state generated. If there is no match, the state is new and it is inserted at the head of the list at this index. Additionally, one of its enabled transitions is executed. In case of a match, the state is a duplicate of a state analyzed previously. It is neither stored nor analyzed for enabled transitions.

The algorithm presented calculates the difference form of a state by comparing it with its preceding state. However, to reduce delay in backtracking, all states at depth $i\delta$: $i \in N$ from the initial state are stored in explicit form, where δ is the shortest distance between two explicit states. To expand a state, the algorithm implements backtracking until an explicit state is encountered.

The algorithm presented also implements two-level hashing at an index if the number of states stored at that index exceeds a threshold. In our algorithm we set the threshold as $M/10$, where M is an estimation of the total number of reachable states. When two-level hashing is used, the index of the primary hash table contains a hash function for a secondary hash table.

The algorithm presented for the sequential model has three parts:

1. SEARCH. The steps are listed in Algorithm 5.1. This algorithm accepts a state (S_{st}), its preceding state (S_{pv}), and the distance of S_{st} from the last expanded state (depth) as input. A hash function H is used to find the index for state S_{st}, as shown in step 1. The algorithm then checks the content of the hash table at this index. There can be three possibilities.
   (a) *The hash table contains NULL at this index.* In this case it is the first time that this state is generated. Hence, Algorithm 5.2 is called to store the state at this index. Any enabled event at this state is fired. Steps 2 to 4 in Algorithm 5.1 check and handle this case.
   (b) *The hash table contains a linked list at this index.* In this case each state in the linked list has hashed to this index. S_{st} is compared with each state in this list. If a state is stored in difference form, it is expanded before comparison using Algorithm 5.3. In case of a match, the state is neither stored nor analyzed for an enabled event. Otherwise, the state is stored at the head of the linked list using Algorithm 5.2 and an enabled event is fired. Steps 5 to 11 in Algorithm 5.1 check and handle this case.

Algorithm 5.1 SEARCH (State S_{st}, int depth, State S_{pv})

Data: Current state S_{st} steps away from the last explicit state (depth), preceding state S_{pv}

Result: Decide if a state generated is new

```
1  i←H[S_st] ;
2  if HASH[i]=NULL then
3  |   INSERT(S_st,depth,S_pv);
4  |   foreach S' such that S_st[(t,c)⟩S' do SEARCH(S',(depth+1)mod δ,S_st);
5  else if HASH[i] points to a linked list then
6  |   foreach state D in linked list do
7  |   |   if D is in difference form then D←RECONSTRUCT(D);
8  |   |   if D=S_st then return;
9  |   end
10 |   INSERT(S_st,depth,S_pv);
11 |   foreach S' such that S_st[(t,c)⟩S' do SEARCH(S',(depth+1)mod δ,S_st);
12 else if HASH[i] contains a hash function then
13 |   H' ← HASH[i];
14 |   j←H'[S_st] ;
15 |   if HASHi [j] is empty then
16 |   |   INSERT(S_st,depth,S_pv);
17 |   |   foreach S' such that S_st[(t,c)⟩S' do SEARCH(S',(depth+1)mod δ,S_st);
18 |   else
19 |   |   if HASHi[j] is in difference form then
20 |   |   |   HASHi[j]←RECONSTRUCT(HASHi[j]);
21 |   |   end
22 |   |   if HASHi[j]=S_st then return;
23 |   |   INSERT(S_st,depth,S_pv);
24 |   |   foreach S' such that S_st[(t,c)⟩S' do SEARCH(S',(depth+1)mod δ,S_st);
25 |   end
26 end
```

(c) *The hash table contains a hash function at this index.* In this case all states that hashed to this index are stored in a separate hash table, HASHi, indexed by the function H' stored at this index. In step 14, the index in the second hash table is calculated using this hash function. Step 15 checks if this index is empty or has a state stored. In case this index is empty or does not contain this state, it is inserted at this index using Algorithm 5.2, and its enabled events are fired. Otherwise, the algorithm returns. Steps 15 to 24 in Algorithm 5.1 handle these cases.

2. INSERT. This algorithm is responsible for inserting a state into the hash table and is listed in Algorithm 5.2. It accepts a state (S_{st}), its preceding state (S_{pv}), and the distance of S_{st} from the last expanded state (depth) as input. The fields of a pointer *new* are assigned the required values before storing

Algorithm 5.2 INSERT(State S_{st}, int depth, State S_{pv})

```
   Data: current state S_st steps away from the last explicit state (depth),
         preceding state S_pv
   Result: Insert state S_st into the hash table
1  if depth=0 then // when depth is 0
2  |  new.type←explicit;                /* store in explicit form */
3  |  new.state←S_st;
4  else
5  |  new.type←difference;              /* else difference form */
6  |  new.state←S_st-S_pv;
7  |  new.prev←S_pv;
8  end
9  i← H[S_st] ;
10 if HASH[i]=NULL then
11 |  HASH[i]=new;                                /* no conflict */
12 else if HASH[i] points to a linked list then
13 |  insert new at the head of linked list;   /* multiple states hash
   |  to same index */
14 |  if length(linked list)≥ |M|/10 then
15 |  |  foreach state d in linked list do
16 |  |  |  if d is in difference form then
17 |  |  |  |  d←RECONSTRUCT(d); /* get explicit state */
18 |  |  |  end
19 |  |  |  add d to HASHi[H′[d]];   /* store in secondary hash
   |  |  |  table */
20 |  |  end
21 |  |  HASH[i]←H′;  /* store secondary hash function */
22 |  end
23 else if HASH[i] points to a hash function then
24 |  H′ ← HASH[i];           /* get secondary hash function */
25 |  j←H′[S_st] ;
26 |  HASHi[j]←new;
27 end
```

it in an appropriate index. Based on the value of delta, the state is stored in either explicit or difference form, and this is assigned to the *type* field of the pointer *new*. In the case of the former, the explicit state S_{st} is assigned to the *state* field of *new*. Otherwise, the difference, given by $S_{st} - S_{pv}$ is assigned to the *state* field. Additionally, in the latter case, a pointer to the preceding state, is stored in the *prev* field of *new*. This is shown in steps 1 to 8 of Algorithm 5.2.

The index of the hash table at which this state is to be stored is calculated in step 9. Three cases are possible:

Algorithm 5.3 RECONSTRUCT(State D_{st})

Data: State D_{st} in difference form
Result: Expanded form of D is returned

```
1 while d.type=difference do
2     sum=sum+d.state ;
3     d=d.prev;
4 end
5 return d+sum;
```

(a) *The hash table contains NULL at this index.* This is the case when S_{pv} is generated for the first time. The contents of the pointer *new* is simply copied to this index of the hash table. This is shown in steps 10 and 11 of Algorithm 5.2.

(b) *The hash table contains a linked list at this index.* In this case, the contents of 'new' is copied to the head of the linked list. Furthermore, the list is checked to see if it contains more than 10% of an estimated total number of states. In that case, the states in this linked list are stored in another hash table, and the hash function is stored at this index. This is done in steps 12 to 22 of Algorithm 5.2.

(c) *The hash table contains a hash function at this index.* In this case the hash function stored at this index is used to find the index in the secondary hash table, and the contents of the pointer *new* are copied to that index. Steps 23 to 26 in Algorithm 5.2 handle this case.

3. RECONSTRUCT. This algorithm accepts a difference state and expands it by backtracking. The steps are listed in Algorithm 5.3. In steps 1 to 4, the algorithm backtracks and adds each state encountered until an explicit state is reached. Finally, state D_{st} in explicit form can be calculated by adding the sum to the explicit state encountered. This is shown in step 5.

Complexity Analysis. The algorithm presented for the sequential model reduces the amount of space necessary to store the states by using difference states. However, this reduction process induces an increase in the delay, due to backtracking. In this section we show an estimation of the reduction and derive the time needed for extra processing.

Let δ be the distance between two expanded states. We pointed out earlier that the initial state is stored in expanded form. Other states in expanded form are those at depths δ, 2δ, and so on. If a reachability graph has height n, the depth of the last node expanded is $\lfloor n/\delta \rfloor \delta$.

Assuming that the average number of new states generated by a transition is $k(> 1)$, the number of states at depth d is given by k^d. This is illustrated in Figure 5.12, where dark circles represent explicit states and shaded circles represent difference states. The number of expanded states in a reachability graph of height n

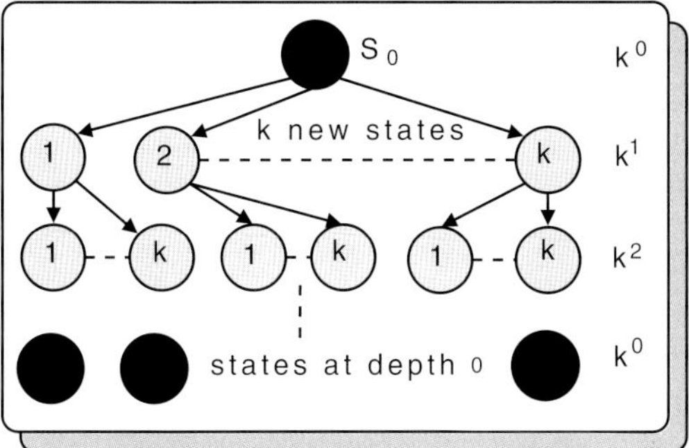

FIGURE 5.12 At depth d the number of states is k^d. All states at depth δ are explicit.

is the sum of the number of expanded states at depth 0, δ, 2δ, ..., $\lfloor n/\delta \rfloor \delta$. This is given by

$$\beta_{\text{expanded}} = k^0 + k^{\delta} + k^{2\delta} + \cdots + k^{\lfloor n/\delta \rfloor \delta}$$

This is a geometric progression [3] with initial term $a = 1$ and ratio $r = k^{\delta}$. Hence, the sum is given by

$$\beta_{\text{expanded}} = \frac{a(r^{n+1} - 1)}{r - 1} = \frac{k^{(\lfloor n/\delta \rfloor + 1)\delta} - 1}{k^{\delta} - 1} \tag{5.1}$$

Similarly, the total number of states is another geometric progression with initial term $a = 1$ and ratio $r = k$.

$$\beta_{\text{total}} = k^0 + k^1 + k^2 + \cdots + k^n = \frac{a(r^{n+1} - 1)}{r - 1} = \frac{k^{n+1} - 1}{k - 1} \tag{5.2}$$

Therefore, the number of states in difference form is given by

$$\beta_{\text{difference}} = \beta_{\text{total}} - \beta_{\text{expanded}}$$

Assigning β_{expanded} from equation (5.1) and β_{total} from equation (5.2), we get

$$\beta_{\text{difference}} = \frac{k^{n+1} - 1}{k - 1} - \frac{k^{(\lfloor n/\delta \rfloor + 1)\delta} - 1}{k^{\delta} - 1} \tag{5.3}$$

Percentage Reduction in Memory. The number of states in difference and explicit forms are given by equations (5.3) and (5.1). Suppose that the memory occupied by an explicit state is λ, while a state stored in difference form occupies $x\lambda$ memory, where $0 < x < 1$. Therefore, the memory needed to generate a reachability graph of depth n without using our algorithm is

$$\Lambda_{\text{without algo.}} = \beta_{\text{total}}\lambda \tag{5.4}$$

When using the algorithm presented, the memory needed to generate the same reachability graph is

$$\Lambda_{\text{with algo.}} = \beta_{\text{difference}}\lambda x + \beta_{\text{expanded}}\lambda \tag{5.5}$$

The percentage reduction in memory denoted by Δ is

$$\Delta = \frac{\Lambda_{\text{without algo.}} - \Lambda_{\text{with algo.}}}{\Lambda_{\text{without algo.}}} \tag{5.6}$$

Using equations (5.4) and (5.5) in (5.6), we get

$$\Delta = \frac{\beta_{\text{total}}\lambda - \beta_{\text{difference}}\lambda x - \beta_{\text{expanded}}\lambda}{\beta_{\text{total}}\lambda}$$

Substituting $\beta_{\text{difference}}$ as $\beta_{\text{total}} - \beta_{\text{expanded}}$, we will have

$$\Delta = (1 - x)\left(1 - \frac{\beta_{\text{expanded}}}{\beta_{\text{total}}}\right)$$

$$\Delta = (1 - x)\left(1 - \frac{(k^{(\lfloor n/\delta \rfloor + 1)\delta} - 1)(k - 1)}{(k^{\delta} - 1)(k^{n+1} - 1)}\right)$$

Time Needed for Extra Processing. The extra time required when states are stored in difference form is now calculated. We consider only the delays due to backtracking as any other delay is common for both explicit and difference states.

Let i be an integer between 1 and n. If the height of reachability graph is i, the number of states in explicit and difference forms are given by

$$\beta'_{\text{total}} = \frac{k^{i+1} - 1}{k - 1}, \quad \beta'_{\text{expanded}} = \frac{k^{(\lfloor i/\delta \rfloor + 1)\delta} - 1}{k^{\delta} - 1}$$

and

$$\beta'_{\text{difference}} = \frac{k^{i+1} - 1}{k - 1} - \frac{k^{(\lfloor i/\delta \rfloor + 1)\delta} - 1}{k^{\delta} - 1}$$

When a state S_{st} is generated, this is compared with the state stored at an index given by the hash function. The probability that this state is stored in expanded or difference form can be calculated as

$$P_{\text{expanded}} = \frac{\beta'_{\text{expanded}}}{\beta'_{\text{total}}} \quad \text{and} \quad P_{\text{difference}} = \frac{\beta'_{\text{difference}}}{\beta'_{\text{total}}}$$

If the state is stored in difference form, it first has to be expanded by backtracking and then compared with S_{st}. Hence, the time taken for comparing S_{st} with the stored states is given by

$$T_{\text{comparison}} = T_{\text{expanded}} + T_{\text{difference}}$$

Suppose that the time for comparing two expanded states is ϵ, while it takes $y\epsilon$ time for backtracking a single step. In the worst case, a backtracking of $\delta - 1$ steps is necessary to expand the state. Therefore, the time can be calculated as

$$\begin{aligned}
T_{\text{comparison}} &= P_{\text{expanded}}\epsilon + P_{\text{difference}}\epsilon(\delta - 1)y \\
&= \frac{\epsilon(1 - y(\delta - 1))\beta'_{\text{expand}}}{\beta'_{\text{total}}} + \epsilon(\delta - 1)y \\
&= \frac{\epsilon(k^{(\lfloor i/\delta \rfloor + 1)\delta} - 1)(k - 1)(1 - y(\delta - 1))}{(k^{\delta} - 1)(k^{i+1} - 1)} + \epsilon(\delta - 1)y
\end{aligned}$$

This is the time taken for comparing a state generated with a state stored in difference form. All comparison at a particular depth takes place concurrently. Hence, the total time taken to generate a reachability graph of height n is the sum of time taken for one comparison at each level. This is denoted by π, where

$$\pi = \sum_{i=0}^{n} \frac{\epsilon(k^{(\lfloor i/\delta \rfloor + 1)\delta} - 1)(k - 1)(1 - y(\delta - 1))}{(k^{\delta} - 1)(k^{i+1} - 1)} + \epsilon(\delta - 1)y$$

Since $\lfloor n/\delta \rfloor = 0$ for $0 \le i < \delta$, $\lfloor n/\delta \rfloor = 1$ for $\delta \le i < 2\delta$, and so on,

$$\begin{aligned}
\pi &= \sum_{i=0}^{\delta} \frac{\epsilon(k^{\delta} - 1)(k - 1)(1 - y(\delta - 1))}{(k^{\delta} - 1)(k^{i+1} - 1)} \\
&\quad + \sum_{i=\delta}^{2\delta} \frac{\epsilon(k^{2\delta} - 1)(k - 1)(1 - y(\delta - 1))}{(k^{\delta} - 1)(k^{i+1} - 1)} \\
&\quad + \cdots \\
&\quad + \sum_{i=z\delta}^{n} \frac{\epsilon(k^{(z+1)\delta} - 1)(k - 1)(1 - y(\delta - 1))}{(k^{\delta} - 1)(k^{i+1} - 1)} + \epsilon(\delta - 1)y
\end{aligned}$$

where $z = \lfloor n/\delta \rfloor$. This is the time taken to generate a reachability graph of height n when the algorithm presented is used.

5.4.2 Tree Model

This model is an enhancement of the sequential model. In this section we provide details of this model, including the basic concepts (related to the algorithm) as well as the corresponding algorithm.

Overview A difference state in Definition 5.2 is expressed as the variation from its immediately preceding state. Although this reduced the memory requirement, regenerating a difference state required backtracking all the way to a state stored in explicit form. Consequently, this involves significant costs for regenerating states that were far from an explicit state. To prevent such scenarios, we alter the definition of a difference state.

Definition 5.4 *Let S_{st} be a state with state S_{ex} as its nearest state in explicit form. The difference form of S_{st}, denoted as D^t_{st}, is defined as the changes necessary in S_{ex} to generate S_{st}.*

Corollary 5.4 *Let D^t_{st} be the difference form of a state S_{st} with state S_{ex} as its nearest state in explicit form. The state S_{st} can be regenerated in explicit form as $S_{st} = S_{ex} + D_{st}$.*

Instead of defining a difference state as the changes required in the immediately preceding state, it is now defined as the changes required in the nearest explicit state. This ensures that a state can always be regenerated by backtracking once the required changes recorded in D^t are applied in the nearest explicit state. However, the nearest explicit state could also be a successor state. Considering that the successor states are not known in advance, states from $[\lceil \delta - 1/2 \rceil + 1]$ to $\delta - 1$ are stored initially in explicit form and later transformed when the successor is known.

The difference between sequential and tree models is illustrated using Figures 5.13 and 5.14. Figure 5.13 presents a portion of the reachability graph for the CPN model in Figure 5.3 using a tree model. Initially, the model is in State 1,

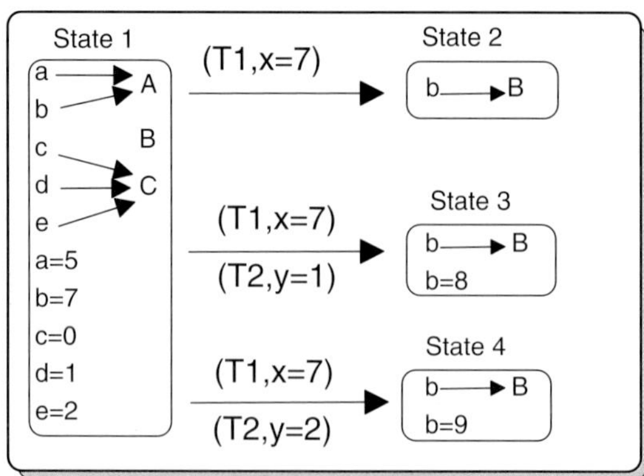

FIGURE 5.13 Part of the reachability graph in Figure 5.4 using the tree algorithm.

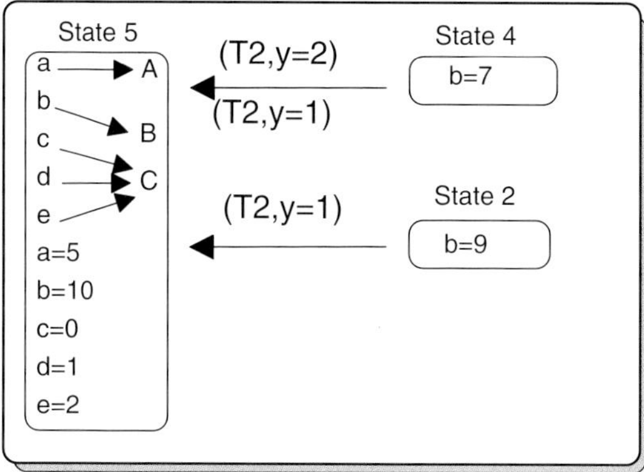

FIGURE 5.14 The difference form is determined using the nearest explicit state, even if latter is a child (or descendent) of the former.

and since it does not have a preceding state, it is stored in explicit form. As with the sequential model, the tokens in the model are arbitrarily termed a to e, and their place and values are assigned using "→" and "=". However, compared to the sequential model, states 2 to 4 are stored as their difference from state 1 (supposing that state 1 is the nearest explicit state for states 2 to 4). Furthermore, contrary to the sequential model, the difference is not always calculated using the a preceding state. As shown in Figure 5.14, states 4 and 2 might also be stored as the difference from a child state (state 5 in Figure 5.4) if it is deemed to be the nearest explicit state.

On comparing Figure 5.13 with Figure 5.9, certain difference states for the tree model are found to contain more information than their counterparts in the sequence model. This is essentially because the difference between two consecutive states (stored in the sequential model) is often less than the states separated by intermediate markings. Consequently, the memory reduction offered by the tree model is sometimes less that offered by the sequential model. However, as emphasized previously, the tree model allows single-step reconstruction of a difference state. Consequently, the tree model is more time-efficient than the sequential model, and the choice depends on priorities when exploring the state space.

Figure 5.14 shows that the nearest explicit state need not always be a preceding state. Considering that there are $\delta - 1$ difference states between any two explicit states S_{before} and S_{after}, the first $\lceil \delta - 1/2 \rceil$ states have the former as their nearest explicit state, while the remaining have the latter. However, considering that the successor states are not known in advance, the states from $[\lceil \delta - 1/2 \rceil + 1]$ to $\delta - 1$ are stored initially in explicit form and later transformed when S_{after} is known.

The tree model uses the nearest explicit states to ensure a minimal size for difference states. This is based on the assertion that systems usually change in many small steps, wherein each event inches it away from its preceding state toward a terminating state. Consequently, a small δ reduces the memory requirement of the tree the model. In case this assertion is invalid, either S_{before} and S_{after} can be used to transform all the $\delta - 1$ states.

The Algorithm. As with the sequential model, this algorithm reduces the memory requirement by storing states in difference form. However, it differs in the mechanism used to determine the difference form of a state.

The state-space exploration begins at the initial state of a system and traverses all states that are reachable from it. Each unique state encountered is stored in a hash table after determining the index using a hash function. Furthermore, starting with the initial state, each state at depth δ is stored in explicit form. The form in which the remaining states are stored depends on their proximity to explicit states:

- The difference form for states at depth $(i\delta + 1)$ to $(i\delta + \lfloor \delta - 1/2 \rfloor)$ can be determined immediately using the explicit state at $i\delta$. Consequently, they are stored in difference form.
- The difference form for remaining states at depth $i\delta + \lfloor \delta - 1/2 \rfloor + 1$ to $(i + 1)$ δ-1 cannot be determined, immediately, as the explicit state at $(i+1)\delta$ is unknown. Consequently, they are stored in explicit form until $(i + 1)\delta$ is determined. To save time, a buffer of size $\lfloor \delta - 1/2 \rfloor$ is used to store these explicit states temporarily.

As compared to the sequential model, the algorithm for the tree model has four parts:

1. SEARCH. The steps are listed in Algorithm 5.4. It accepts a state (S_{st}), its previous state (S_{pv}), and the distance of S_{st} from the last expanded state (depth) as input. A hash function H is used to find the index for S_{st}, as shown in step 1. The algorithm then checks the content of the hash table at this index. Again, there can be three possibilities.
   (a) *The hash table contains NULL at this index.* In this case it is the first time that this state is generated. Consequently, Algorithm 5.5 is invoked to store the state at this index. Thereafter any enabled event at this state is fired. Steps 2 to 4 in Algorithm 5.4 check and handle this case.
   (b) *The hash table contains a linked list at this index.* In this case, each state in the linked list has hashed to this index. Consequently, S_{st} is compared with each state in this list. For explicit states in the list, this comparison is direct. However, difference states need to be expanded before making a comparison using Algorithm 5.6. In case of a match, S_{st} is neither stored nor analyzed for any enabled events. Otherwise, Algorithm 5.5 stores the marking at the head of the linked list, and any enabled event is executed. Steps 5 to 11 in Algorithm 5.4 check and handle this case.
   (c) *The hash table contains a hash function at this index.* If this case, all states that hashed to this index are stored in a separate hash table HASHi, indexed by the function H' stored at this index. The index in the second hash-table is calculated in step 14. In step 15 this index is checked to determine if it is empty or stores a state. It it is empty, the state is inserted

Algorithm 5.4 SEARCH (State S_{st}, int depth State S_{pv})

Data: State S_{st}, int depth, state S_{pv}
Result: Decide if a marking generated is new
1 i←H[S_{st}] ;
2 **if** *HASH[i]=NULL* **then**
3   INSERT(S_{st},depth,S_{pv});
4   **foreach** S_{nx} *such that* $S_{st}[(t,c)\rangle S_{nx}$ **do** SEARCH(S_{nx},(depth+1)mod δ,S_{st});
5 **else if** *HASH[i] points to a linked list* **then**
6   **foreach** *state d in linked list* **do**
7   **if** *d is compact* **then** d←RECONSTRUCT(d);
8   **if** $d=S_{st}$ **then** return;
9   **end**
10   INSERT(S_{st},depth,S_{pv});
11   **foreach** S_{nx} *such that* $S_{st}[(t,c)\rangle S_{nx}$ **do** SEARCH(S_{nx},(depth+1)mod δ,S_{st});
12 **else if** *HASH[i] contains a hash function* **then**
13   H′ ← HASH[i];
14   j←H′[S_{st}] ;
15   **if** *HASHi [j] is empty* **then**
16   INSERT(S_{st},depth,S_{pv});
17   **foreach** S_{nx} *such that* $S_{st}[(t,c)\rangle S_{nx}$ **do** SEARCH(S_{nx},(depth+1)mod δ,S_{st});
18   **else**
19   **if** *HASHi[j] is in compact form* **then**
20   HASHi[j]←RECONSTRUCT(HASHi[j]);
21   **end**
22   **if** *HASHi[j]=*S_{st} **then** return;
23   INSERT(S_{st},depth,S_{pv});
24   **foreach** S_{nx} *such that* $S_{st}[(t,c)\rangle S_{nx}$ **do** SEARCH(S_{nx},(depth+1)mod δ,S_{st});
25   **end**
26 **end**

using Algorithm 5.5 and any enabled event is executed. Steps 15 to 24 in Algorithm 5.4 handle this case.

2. INSERT. The second algorithm is responsible for inserting a state into a hash table and its steps are listed in Algorithm 5.5. It accepts a state (S_{st}), its preceding state (S_{pv}), and the distance of S_{st} from the last expanded state (depth) as input. The first step determines the index of state S_{st} using a hash function. Thereafter, the offset from the last expanded state (stored in *depth*) is checked. If the depth is 0, the state is stored in expanded form. Furthermore, this instigates calculating the difference form for each of last $\delta/2$ states. As discussed earlier, initially these states are stored in explicit form until their nearest explicit state is determined. Otherwise, the difference form for S_{st} is

Algorithm 5.5 INSERT(State S_{st}, int depth, State S_{pv})

```
Data: State S_st,int depth, state S_pv
Result: Insert state S_st into hash table
i← H[S_st] ;                    // H is used to calculate the index
if depth=0 then       // when depth is 0, store in explicit form
    new.type←explicit;
    new.state←S_st;
    for i=1; i≤ δ/2;i++,S_pv=S_pv.prev do
        S_pv.state←S_st-S_pv.state; // difference form for δ/2 previous
        states
        S_pv.near←S_st;          // that were temporarily stored in
        explicit form
    end
    nearest←S_st;
else if depth≥ δ/2 then
    new.type←explicit;       // store temporarily in explicit form
    new.state←S_st;
    new.prev←S_pv;
else
    new.type←difference;                  // store in difference form
    new.state← S_st-nearest;
    new.near←nearest;
    new.prev←S_pv;
end
if HASH[i]=NULL then
    HASH[i]=new;                                          // no conflict
else if HASH[i] points to a linked list then
    insert new at the head of linked list; // multiple states hash to same
    index
    if length(linked list)≥ |M|/10 then   // if length is longer than 10
    percent
        foreach state d in linked list do        // create a new hash table
            if d is in compact form then
                d1←d;
                d←RECONSTRUCT(d);            // get explicit state
            end
            j←H[d] ;
            add d1 to HASHi[j];     // store in secondary hash table
        end
    end
else if HASH[i] points to a hash function then
    H′ ← HASH[i];                    // get secondary hash function
    j←H′[S_st] ;
    HASHi[j]←new;
end
```

Algorithm 5.6 RECONSTRUCT(State d)

```
Data: State d in difference form
Result: Explicit form of d is returned
return d.state+d.near;
```

determined. In any case, the state is stored in the pointer *new* which has a field *type* to identify it if it is stored in difference or explicit form. It also has a field to store the state itself (either explicit or difference) and a couple of pointers to record the nearest explicit state and the immediately preceding state. Thereafter, the content of the hash table at the index calculated in step 1 is checked. There could be three possibilities.

(a) *The hash table contains NULL at this index.* In this case it is the first time that this marking is generated. The contents of the *new* is simply copied to this index of the hash table. It is worth mentioning that this element is hereafter treated as a linked list with a single node. This allows generalizing the handler for hash collisions. The logic for this case is handled in steps 20 and 21 of Algorithm 5.5.

(b) *The hash table contains a linked list at this index.* In this case the contents of *new* is copied to the head of linked list to handle hash collision. Then the list is checked to ensure that it contains no more than 10% of all possible states. Otherwise, the states in it are moved into another hash table, and the hash function used is stored at this index. The logic for this case is shown in steps 22 to 33 of Algorithm 5.5.

(c) *The hash table contains a hash function at this index.* In this case the hash function stored at this index is used to find the position of the state in the secondary hash table and *new* is copied into it. Note that having discrete hash functions for each index of the primary hash table makes it possible to minimize collisions in the secondary hash table. Steps 35 to 37 of Algorithm 5.5 handle this case.

3. RECONSTRUCT. The third algorithm accepts a state in difference form and returns its explicit form. The transformation basically involves applying the differences in the nearest explicit state. The steps are listed in Algorithm 5.6.

Comparison with the Sequential Model. The algorithm presented for the tree model promises to reduce the amount of space necessary to store states by using difference states. Furthermore, it eliminates any associated delay due to backtracking. In this section we evaluate the tree model by comparing its time and memory requirements with those of the sequential model.

Comparing Percentage Increase in Memory for the Tree Model. Suppose that the memory occupied by an explicit state is λ and the average difference between consecutive states is $x\lambda$, where $0 < x < 1$. In the sequential model case, each explicit state would occupy a space λ, and each difference state would occupy $x\lambda$. While the former remains the same for the tree model, the latter changes because the difference states contain the difference from the nearest explicit state instead of the immediately preceding state. In the worst case, the difference of a state from the nearest explicit state would be the sum of the differences stored in the intermediate states. Therefore, the memory needed to store the difference states between any two explicit states would be

$$
\begin{cases}
2\left(x\lambda + 2x\lambda + 3x\lambda + \cdots + \dfrac{\delta}{2}x\lambda\right) & \text{if } \delta \text{ is even} \\[2ex]
2\left(x\lambda + 2x\lambda + 3x\lambda + \cdots + \dfrac{\delta - 1}{2}x\lambda\right) + \dfrac{\delta + 1}{2}x\lambda & \text{otherwise}
\end{cases}
$$

These equations can be simplified to

$$
\begin{cases}
x\lambda\dfrac{\delta(\delta + 2)}{4} & \text{if } \delta \text{ is even} \\[2ex]
x\lambda\dfrac{(\delta + 1)^2}{4} & \text{otherwise}
\end{cases}
$$

As with the sequential model, we assume that the average number of new states generated by a transition is $k(k > 1)$. The number of states at depth d is given by k^d, as illustrated in Figure 5.12. All dark circle represent explicit states and shaded circles represent difference states. The number of expanded states in a reachability of height n is the sum of the number of expanded states at depth $0, \delta, 2\delta, \ldots, \lfloor n/\delta \rfloor \delta$. This is given by

$$\beta_{\text{expanded}} = k^0 + k^\delta + k^{2\delta} + \cdots + k^{\lfloor n/\delta \rfloor \delta}$$

This is a geometric progression [3] with initial term $a = 1$ and ratio $r = k^\delta$. Hence, the sum is given by

$$\beta_{\text{expanded}} = \frac{a(r^{n+1} - 1)}{r - 1} = \frac{k^{(\lfloor n/\delta \rfloor + 1) * \delta} - 1}{k^\delta - 1}$$

The number of explicit states for the tree model is the same as that for the sequential model, and therefore no extra memory is required to store them. From our earlier discussion, the difference states at depth $i(\delta - 1)$ and $i(\delta + 1)$ require space $x\lambda$, which is again the same as for the sequential model. However, the difference states at other depths account for the additional memory requirement.

Between any two explicit states at depth $i\delta$ and $(i+1)\delta$, the difference in memory requirements for the tree and sequential models are

$$\begin{aligned}
\partial_{i\delta+2} &= 2x\lambda k^{i(\delta+2)} - x\lambda k^{i(\delta+2)} = x\lambda k^{i(\delta+2)} \\
\partial_{i\delta+3} &= 3x\lambda k^{i\delta+3} - x\lambda k^{i\delta+3} = 2x\lambda k^{i\delta+3} \\
&\vdots \\
\partial_{i\delta+\frac{\delta}{2}} &= \frac{\delta}{2}x\lambda k^{i(\delta+\delta/2)} - x\lambda k^{i\delta+\delta/2} = \left(\frac{\delta}{2}-1\right)x\lambda k^{i(\delta+\delta/2)} \qquad \text{if } \delta \text{ is even}
\end{aligned}$$

We take advantage of the symmetry of difference around $\delta/2$ and evaluate the difference only for the first half of difference states. The remaining states are accounted for by doubling the sum of the differences above, which is evaluated as

$$\begin{aligned}
\partial &= x\lambda k^{i\delta+2} + 2x\lambda k^{i\delta+3} + \cdots + \left(\frac{\delta}{2}-1\right)x\lambda k^{i\delta+\delta/2} \quad \text{if } \delta \text{ is even} \\
\partial &= x\lambda k^{i\delta+1}\left[k + 2k^2 + \cdots + \left(\frac{\delta}{2}-1\right)k^{\delta/2-1}\right] \quad \text{otherwise}
\end{aligned} \tag{5.7}$$

To simplify the equation, we assign the part in square brackets to E.

$$E = k + 2k^2 + \cdots + \left(\frac{\delta}{2}-1\right)k^{\delta/2-1}$$

or

$$kE = k^2 + 2k^3 + \cdots + \left(\frac{\delta}{2}-2\right)k^{\delta/2-1} + \left(\frac{\delta}{2}-1\right)k^{\delta/2}$$

Therefore,

$$E - kE = k + k^2 + k^3 + \cdots + k^{\delta/2-1} - \left(\frac{\delta}{2}-1\right)k^{\delta/2}$$

or

$$E(1-k) = \frac{k\left(k^{\delta/2}-1\right)}{k-1} - \left(\frac{\delta}{2}-1\right)k^{\delta/2}$$

or

$$E = \frac{1}{k-1}\left[\left(\frac{\delta}{2}-1\right)k^{\delta/2} - \frac{k(k^{\delta/2}-1)}{k-1}\right]$$

Assigning E in equation (5.7), we get

$$\partial = x\lambda k^{i\delta+1}\frac{1}{k-1}\left[\left(\frac{\delta}{2}-1\right)k^{\delta/2}-\frac{k(k^{\delta/2}-1)}{k-1}\right]$$

The value in ∂ gives the additional memory needed to store difference states between $i(\delta+2)$ and $i(\delta+\delta/2)$. Due to symmetry around $\delta/2$, the additional memory needed to store difference states between $i(\delta+2)$ and $(i+1)(\delta-2)$ is 2∂. The memory required by the sequential model to store these difference states is

$$x\lambda(\delta-3)$$

Therefore the percentage increase in memory requirement for the tree model is given as

$$\frac{2\partial}{x\lambda(\delta-3)}\%$$

or

$$\frac{2x\lambda k^{i\delta+1}\frac{1}{k-1}\left[\left(\frac{\delta}{2}-1\right)k^{\delta/2}-\frac{k(k^{\delta/2}-1)}{k-1}\right]}{x\lambda(\delta-3)}\%$$

or

$$\frac{2\left[\left(\frac{\delta}{2}-1\right)k^{\delta/2}-\frac{k(k^{\delta/2}-1)}{k-1}\right]}{2(\delta-3)(k-1)}\%$$

Comparing Percentage Reduction in Time. As discussed earlier, the tree model eliminates any delay due to backtracking. Consequently, this comparison considers only the backtracking delays, as any other delay is common for both the sequential and tree models.

Let i be an integer between 1 and n. If the height of the reachability graph is i, the number of states in the explicit and difference forms is given by

$$\beta'_{\text{total}} = \frac{k^{i+1}-1}{k-1}$$

$$\beta'_{\text{expanded}} = \frac{k^{(\lfloor i/\delta\rfloor+1)\delta}-1}{k^{\delta}-1}$$

$$\beta'_{\text{difference}} = \frac{k^{i+1}-1}{k-1}-\frac{k^{(\lfloor i/\delta\rfloor+1)\delta}-1}{k^{\delta}-1}$$

When a state S_{st} is generated, it is compared with the state stored at an index given by the hash-function. The probability that this state is stored in expanded or difference form can be calculated as

$$\begin{aligned} P_{\text{expanded}} &= \frac{\beta'_{\text{expanded}}}{\beta'_{\text{total}}} \\ P_{\text{difference}} &= \frac{\beta'_{\text{difference}}}{\beta'_{\text{total}}} \end{aligned} \tag{5.8}$$

If the state is stored in difference form, it first has to be expanded by backtracking and then compared with S_{st}. Hence, the time taken for comparing S_{st} with the stored states is given by

$$T_{\text{comparison}} = T_{\text{expanded}} + T_{\text{difference}}$$

Suppose that the time for comparing two expanded states is ϵ and that it takes $y\epsilon$ time for backtracking a single step. While the tree model always requires backtracking a single step, the sequential model would need a backtracking of $\delta - 1$ steps in the worst case for expanding the state. Therefore, the time taken for the two models to be calculated is

$$\begin{aligned} T^{\text{seq}}_{\text{comparison}} &= P_{\text{expanded}}\epsilon + P_{\text{difference}}\epsilon(\delta - 1)y \\ T^{\text{tree}}_{\text{comparison}} &= P_{\text{expanded}}\epsilon + P_{\text{difference}}\epsilon y \end{aligned}$$

Consequently, the difference in time taken for each comparison would be

$$\begin{aligned} T^{\text{seq}}_{\text{comparison}} - T^{\text{tree}}_{\text{comparison}} &= [P_{\text{expanded}}\epsilon + P_{\text{difference}}\epsilon(\delta - 1)y] \\ &\quad - (P_{\text{expanded}}\epsilon + P_{\text{difference}}\epsilon y) \\ &= P_{\text{difference}}\epsilon(\delta - 2)y \\ &= \frac{\beta'_{\text{difference}}}{\beta'_{\text{total}}}\epsilon(\delta - 2)y \\ &= \left(1 - \frac{\beta'_{\text{expanded}}}{\beta'_{\text{total}}}\right)\epsilon(\delta - 2)y \\ &= \epsilon(\delta - 2)y - \frac{\beta'_{\text{expanded}}}{\beta'_{\text{total}}}\epsilon(\delta - 2)y \\ &= \epsilon(\delta - 2)y - \frac{(k^{(\lfloor \frac{i}{\delta} \rfloor + 1)\delta} - 1)(k - 1)}{(k^{i+1} - 1)(k^{\delta} - 1)}\epsilon(\delta - 2)y \end{aligned}$$

This is the additional time taken by the sequential model for comparing a state generated with a stored state in difference form. All comparison at a particular depth takes place concurrently. Hence, the additional time taken to generate a reachability graph of height n is the sum of extra time taken for one comparison at each level. This is denoted by ∂', where

$$\partial' = \epsilon(\delta - 2)y - \epsilon(\delta - 2)y \sum_{i=0}^{n} \frac{\left(k^{(\lfloor i/\delta \rfloor + 1)\delta} - 1\right)(k - 1)}{(k^{\delta} - 1)(k^{i+1} - 1)}$$

Since $\lfloor n/\delta \rfloor = 0$ for $0 \leq i < \delta$, $\lfloor n/\delta \rfloor = 1$ for $\delta \leq i < 2\delta$, and so on.

$$\begin{aligned}
\partial' &= \epsilon\,(\delta - 2)y - \epsilon(\delta - 2)y \sum_{i=0}^{\delta} \frac{(k^{\delta} - 1)(k - 1)}{(k^{\delta} - 1)(k^{i+1} - 1)} \\
&\quad + \epsilon(\delta - 2)y \sum_{i=\delta}^{2\delta} \frac{(k^{2\delta} - 1)(k - 1)}{(k^{\delta} - 1)(k^{i+1} - 1)} \\
&\quad + \cdots \\
&\quad + \epsilon(\delta - 2)y \sum_{i=z\delta}^{n} \frac{(k^{(z+1)\delta} - 1)(k - 1)}{(k^{\delta} - 1)(k^{i+1} - 1)}
\end{aligned}$$

where $z = \lfloor n/\delta \rfloor$. This is the additional time taken by the sequential model to generate a reachability graph of height n.

5.5 EXPERIMENTAL RESULTS

In Section 5.4 we provided a theoretical evaluation of the tree model by comparing it with the sequential model. In this section we provide san experimental evaluation (of the sequential model). Six different colored petri net models are used to run the experiments. The number of places and tokens in each CPN model is listed in Tables 5.3 and 5.4. If a model had m tokens and n places, each token was assigned an integer name $i : i \in [0, m - 1]$ and each place was assigned an integer name $j : j \in [0, n - 1]$. Initially, all tokens were in place 0. At each state the set of enabled transitions was selected randomly, and one of these transitions was fired. This makes possible having a large number of transitions in a model without specifying the bindings for which they are enabled.

For each CPN model, the time and space needed to generate the first 500 unique states were calculated using the sequential model and without using it. Furthermore, the sequential model requires a nonnegative integer value of δ, and the set of values $\{1,2,3,7,20\}$ were assigned. When the sequential algorithm is not used, 0 to δ is assigned. The results are listed in Tables 5.3 and 5.4. δ is the shortest distance between two explicit states. Table 5.3 shows the memory needed (given by Λ) to store the first 500 states of the CPN models used and the percentage reduction in

TABLE 5.3 **Space Occupied (in bytes) by the First 500 States of CPN Models (Λ) and the Percentage Decrease in Space (Δ)**

		$\delta = 0$	$\delta = 1$		$\delta = 2$		$\delta = 3$		$\delta = 7$		$\delta = 20$	
n^a	m^a	Λ	Λ	Δ	Λ	Δ	Λ	Δ	Λ	Δ	Λ	Δ
4	5	9980	9980	0%	5996	40%	4668	53%	3148	68%	2396	76%
60	90	179640	179640	0%	90996	49%	61448	66%	27628	85%	10896	94%
200	400	798400	798400	0%	400996	50%	268528	66%	116908	85%	41896	95%
400	700	1397200	1397200	0%	700996	50%	468928	66%	203308	85%	71896	95%
800	1000	1996000	1996000	0%	1000996	50%	669328	66%	289708	85%	101896	95%
1500	2000	3992000	3992000	0%	2000996	50%	1337328	67%	577708	86%	201896	95%

[a] n and m are the number of places and tokens in these models.

TABLE 5.4 Time (in msec) to Generate the First 500 States of CPN Models (π) and Percentage Increase in Time (η).

		δ=0	δ=1		δ=2		δ=3		δ=7		δ=20	
n^a	m^a	π	π	η	π	η	π	η	π	η	π	η
4	5	≈0	20	∞	90	∞	160	∞	430	∞	1490	∞
60	90	20	40	100%	80	300%	100	400%	210	950%	570	2750%
200	400	80	130	62%	170	112%	200	150%	320	300%	680	750%
400	700	140	220	57%	260	85%	290	107%	410	193%	770	450%
800	1000	200	310	55%	350	75%	380	90%	500	150%	850	325%
1500	2000	400	620	55%	660	65%	680	70%	820	105%	1200	200%

[a] n and m are the number of places and tokens in these models.

the memory requirement (given by Δ) for different values of δ. For each model, the memory requirement is highest either when not using the sequential algorithm ($\delta = 0$) or when using it with $\delta = 1$. In Figure 5.15, the memory required is plotted against the value of δ. On increasing the value of δ, the memory requirement decreases for all models. Furthermore, the decrease is significantly higher for large models, with a significantly greater number of places and tokens than those for small models. For examples, a CPN model with 1500 places and 2000 tokens used 95% less space when the sequential algorithm was used with $\delta = 20$. Compared to this, the reduction was 76% for a CPN model with four places and five tokens. Nevertheless, the reduction is massive for models of all sizes and for all values of δ, as is evident from Table 5.3 and Figure 5.15.

Table 5.4 shows the time needed (given by π) to generate the first 500 states of the CPN models used and the percentage increase in delay (given by η) for different values of δ. For each model the delay is minimal when the sequential algorithm is not used ($\delta = 0$). In Figure 5.16, delay is plotted against the value of δ. When the sequential algorithm is used the delay increases with an increase in the value of δ. A model with four states and five tokens generates 500 states almost instantly ($\pi = 0$) without using the sequential algorithm. The same model needs 1.5 seconds when the sequential algorithm is used with $\delta = 20$. The percentage increase in delay (η) decreases with increased model size. The model with 1500 places and 2000 tokens has twice the delay when the sequential algorithm is used with $\delta = 20$ as compared to $\delta = 0$ (algorithm not used). A comparison of the results in Tables 5.3 and 5.4 show clearly that the reduction in memory requirements comes at the cost of an extra delay in processing. This is further evident in Figure 5.17, where the memory required decreases and the delay increases with an increase in the value of δ. However, the memory reduction envisioned is massive compared to the increase in delay, especially for moderate to large models. A model with 1500 places and 2000 tokens had a 95% reduction in memory with double the delay. Due to the inherent complexity of most modern systems, their models are almost always large. The sequential and tree models address a niche for such systems.

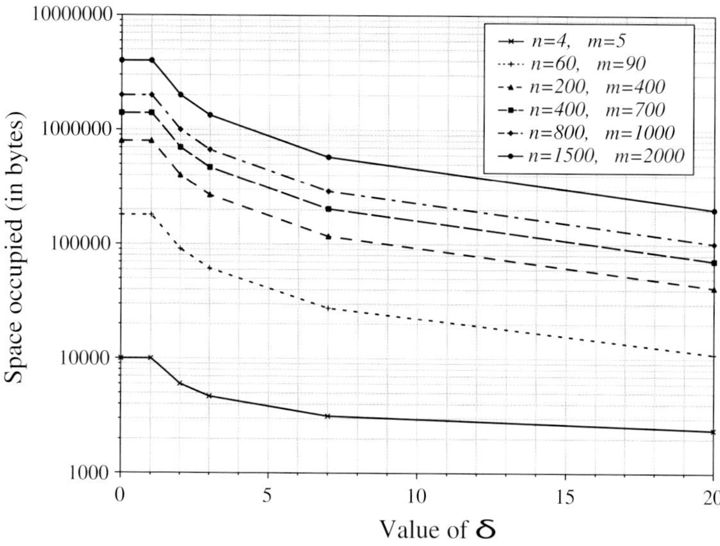

FIGURE 5.15 Memory requirement decrease with increase in the value of δ, the distance between two explicit markings. $\delta = 0$ means that the algorithm was not used. The y-axis uses the log scale.

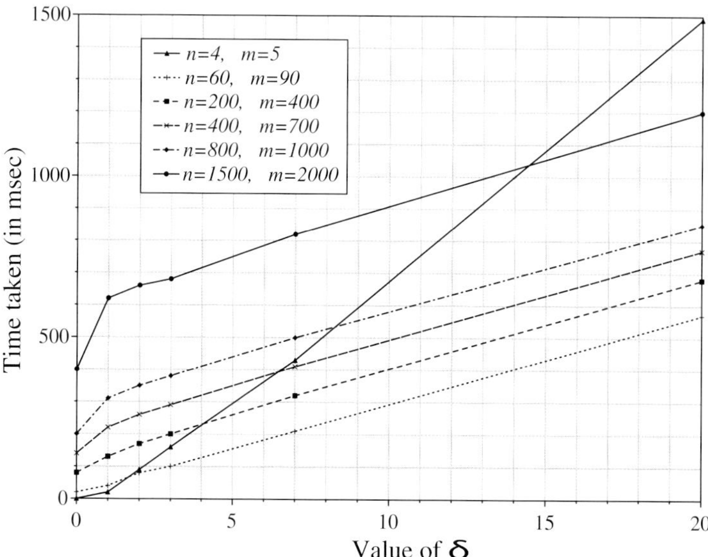

FIGURE 5.16 Delay increases with an increase in the value of δ. $\delta = 0$ when the algorithm is not used.

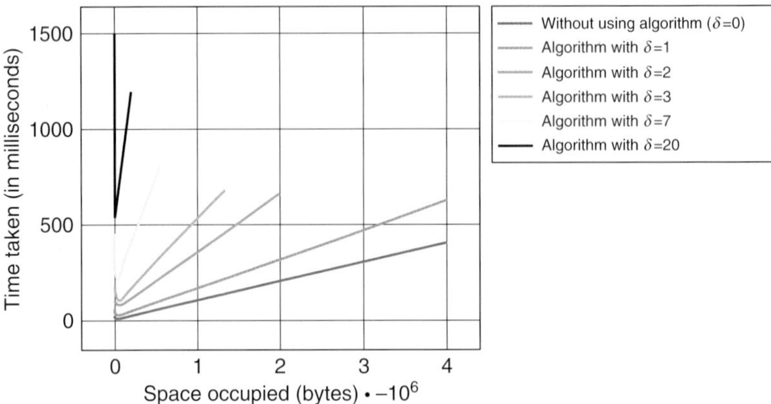

FIGURE 5.17 Delay and the memory requirement decrease with an increase in the value of δ. Each curve is for a different value of δ, as indicated by the legend. The six points on a curve correspond to the six CPN models used.

5.6 DISCUSSION

The sequential model reduces the memory requirements for model checking by storing states in difference form, making it possible to model-check in a machine with a fraction of the memory required otherwise. This might lead to a wider use of model checking in software verification and subsequent production of reliable software systems. Although there is an increase in delay due to backtracking, the results illustrate that the delay is small compared to the massive reduction in memory obtained.

***Reduction in Memory Requirement* Λ.** The sequential model is found to reduce the memory requirement increasingly with an increase in the value of δ. State-space analysis without using the sequential algorithm will store all states in explicit form, leading to maximum memory requirement. This holds for the results shown in Figure 5.15. Furthermore, using the sequential algorithm with $\delta = 1$ also stores all states in explicit form, keeping Λ unchanged. However, when $\delta = 2$, every alternative state is stored in explicit form. This leads to almost a 50% reduction in Λ, as only half the total number of states are in explicit form. Similarly, when $\delta = 3$, one in every three states is stored in explicit form, leading to a 66% reduction in Λ. When $\delta = 7$, one in seven states is stored in explicit form, leading to an 85% reduction in Λ. Finally, when $\delta = 20$, one in 20 states is stored in explicit form, resulting in a 95% reduction in the value of Λ.

The reduction for a CPN model with four places and five tokens is low compared to that of other models because the size of an explicit state is almost the same as that of a difference state for a small model. Therefore, replacing an explicit state with a difference state does not make a big difference.

Increase in Delay π. The sequential model is found to increase the delay with an increase in the value of δ and a corresponding decrease in the memory requirement. Two factors contribute to overall delay: (1) backtracking to expand a difference state; and (2) when state space is being explored using the DFS algorithm and a duplicate state is encountered, the stack is popped until a state with an enabled event (transition) is encountered. Popping a stack is a time-intensive operation.

A small model has fewer possible states, and therefore the chances of encountering a duplicate state is high. A CPN model with four places and five tokens encountered 469 duplicate states before generating the 500th unique state. As compared to this, a model with 60 places and 90 tokens encountered only one duplicate state before generating the 500th state. The delay in popping the stack, together with the backtracking delay, leads to a large π value for small models.

When model checking, we need not backtrack if all states are in explicit form. This leads to a low π value when there is no difference state ($\delta = 0$ or $\delta = 1$). However, due to extra the processing delay of the sequential algorithm, the delay for $\delta = 1$ is higher than that for $\delta = 0$. On further increasing δ, the delay increases due to backtracking. The higher the value of δ, the more backtracking is needed to expand a state and the greater the delay.

Reducing the cost of model checking would encourage its wider use in the software development life cycle. This, in turn, would enhance the reliability and usability of software systems. Considering our widespread dependency on such systems (e.g., traffic signals, elevators), this would also ensure our safety and well-being.

5.7 SUMMARY

In this chapter we showed how the memory requirement for model checking could be reduced by storing states in difference form. Consequently, model checking would acquire a bigger role in the verification of a wide range of software. This ensures the safety and reliability of software systems and enhances their usability. Experimental results indicate that the models presented require significantly less memory to verify a software system. Furthermore, the solutions presented are found to perform better with larger models. Contemporary systems have a high level of complexity, often leading to large models. Therefore, the solutions presented are addressing a niche for such systems.

REFERENCES

1. B. Beizer. *Software Testing Techniques*. Van Nostrand Reinhold, New York, 1990.
2. D. Beyer, T. A. Henzinger, R. Jhala, and R. Majumdar. The software model checker blast: applications to software engineering. *International Journal on Software Tools for Technology Transfer*, 9:505–525, October 2007.
3. I. N. Bronshtein, K. A. Semendyayev, and K. A. Kirsch. *Handbook of Mathematics*, 3rd ed. Springer-Verlag, Berlin, 1997.

4. S. Christensen, L. M. Kristensen, and T. Mailund. A sweep-line method for state space exploration. In *Proceedings of the 7th International Conference on Tools and Algorithms for the Construction and Analysis of Systems, TACAS 2001*, pages 450–464, 2001.
5. E. Clarke, O. Grumberg, and D. Peled. *Model Checking*. MIT Press, Cambridge, MA, 2000.
6. E. M. Clarke and S. Berezin. Model checking: historical perspective and example (extended abstract). In *Proceedings of the International Conference on Automated Reasoning with Analytic Tableaux and Related Methods*, TABLEAUX '98, pages 18–24. Springer-Verlag, Berlin, 1998.
7. T. H. Cormen, C. E. Leiserson, R. L. Rivest, and C. Stein. *Introduction to Algorithms, 2nd ed.* MIT Press, Cambridge, MA, 2001.
8. S. Evangelista and J.-F. Pradat-Peyre. Memory efficient state space storage in explicit software model checking. In *Proceedings of the 12th International SPIN Workshop on Model Checking of Software*, volume 3639 of *Lecture Notes in Computer Science*, pages 43–57. Springer-Verlag, Berlin, 2005.
9. P. Godefroid, G. J. Holzmann, and D. Pirottin. State-space caching revisited. In *Proceedings of the 4th International Workshop on Computer Aided Verification*, pages 178–191. Springer-Verlag Berlin, 1993.
10. Y. Hao and Y. Zhang. Web services discovery based on schema matching. In *Proceedings of the 30th Australasian Conference on Computer Science, ACSC '07,* volume 62, pages 107–113, Australian, Computer Society, Darlinghurst, Australia, 2007.
11. G. J. Holzmann. State compression in spin: recursive indexing and compression training runs. In *Proceedings of the 3rd International SPIN Workshop*, 1997.
12. G. J. Holzmann. *The SPIN Model Checker: Primer and Reference Manual.* Addison-Wesley, Reading, MA, 2003.
13. G. J. Holzmann and A. Puri. A minimized automaton representation of reachable states. *Software Tools for Technology Transfer*, 2:270–278, 1999.
14. K. Jensen. *Colored Petri Nets: Basic Concepts, Analysis Methods and Practical Use*, volumes 1–3. Springer-Verlag, Berlin, 1996.
15. K. Jensen, L. M. Kristensen, and L. Wells. Colored petri nets and CPN tools for modelling and validation of concurrent systems. *International journal of Software Tools, for Technology, Transfer*, 9(3):213–254, 2007.
16. T. Mailund and M. Westergaard. Obtaining memory-efficient reachability graph representations using the sweep-line method. In *Proceedings of the 10th International Conference, on Tools and Algorithms for the Construction and Analysis of Systems, TACAS 2007*, pages 177–191, Springer-Verlag, Berlin, 2004.
17. M. Paolucci, T. Kawamura, T. R. Payne, and K. P. Sycara. Semantic matching of web services capabilities. In *Proceedings of the First International Semantic Web Conference on the Semantic Web*, ISWC '02, pages 333–347. Springer-Verlag, Berlin, 2002.
18. J. Rushby. Formal methods and critical systems in the real world. In *Formal Methods for Trustworthy Computer Systems, FM '89*, pages 121–125, 1989.
19. K. Schmidt. Using petri net invariants in state space construction. In *Proceedings of the 9th International Conference on Tools and Algorithms for the Construction and Analysis of Systems, TACAS 2003*, pages 473–488, Springer-Verlag, Berlin, 2003.
20. W. Visser. Memory efficient state storage in spin. In *Proceedings of the 2nd SPIN Workshop*, pages 21–35. American Mathematical society, Providence, RI, 1996.

CHAPTER 6

TIME-EFFICIENT STATE-SPACE ANALYSIS IN SOFTWARE MODEL CHECKING

In Chapter 5 we identified the significance of formal methods for service compositions as well as their associated massive time and memory costs. Considering the ubiquity of software systems in our daily life, Chapter 5 vouched for the wider use of formal methods to warrant their correctness and usability. The sequential and tree models were described to pursue this inducement by reducing the memory costs involved in model checking, a widely used formal method. However, as with any memory-reduction technique, the models were found to have an associated time overhead.

In this chapter we seek to reduce the aforementioned delay by introducing concurrency into the paradigm of model checking. Contemporary model-checking languages offer different levels of abstraction by defining a notion of hierarchy wherein a system is modeled as a set of interdependent modules. The reduction in time offered is attributed to the concurrent exploration of all such modules in a hierarchical model and exposing the outcome using special data structures. This allows the modules to interact with each other and resolve their dependencies when generating

Verification of Communication Protocols in Web Services: Model-Checking Service Compositions, First Edition. Zahir Tari, Peter Bertok, Anshuman Mukherjee.

the state space. Experiments report a time reduction of 86% in generating the first 25,000 markings. Furthermore, the reduction offered increases as more markings are generated. Compared to recent solutions, which depend on the existence of *stubborn sets* and/or *symmetry* in the state space, the technique only necessitates a hierarchical model. Considering that most modern modeling languages have incorporated the notion of hierarchy, this is a fairly lenient prerequisite.

6.1 MOTIVATION

In Chapter 5 we identified the significance of formal methods for service compositions. Thereupon the sequential and tree models presented enable the reduction in memory costs for model checking. In this chapter we describe a novel method for reducing the time requirements for model checking so that they could be used more widely.

The delay in model checking could be attributed to a range of factors. A significant delay could be accredited to the primary job of model checking, wherein each state of a system is checked for a set of undesirable properties. This delay is formidable for systems that exhibit a state-space explosion problem. This is exacerbated further by the delay in storing states of a system explored hitherto by the model checker and comparing them with the states to be produced hereafter. As observed in Chapter 5, certain states of the system might be generated repeatedly and prevent the model checker from terminating. Consequently, it is necessary to store and compare states in order to identify duplicate states and ensure termination of the model checking process. Regardless of the data structure used for storage and the efficiency of comparison, there is an associated time overhead. This is in addition to the delay considered earlier in generating and processing a state. As observed earlier, the state-space explosion problem could further aggravate the delay. Furthermore, considering the cost and stringent upper bounds (based on the architecture, operating system, processor, motherboard, etc.) of memory in a system, there has been extensive research in reduce the memory requirements for storing states. Unfortunately, as explained in Chapter 5, all attempts to reduce the memory requirements for model checking are accompanied by a doubling or tripling of the time requirements [13]. This provides further inducement in proposing a technique to reduce the delay that could be used either independently or with a memory-reduction algorithm.

Some solutions based on partial order reduction [14] address this problem by exploiting the independence of events that execute concurrently. However, detecting such independent events might sometimes be as difficult as the underlying verification problem [15]. A few other solutions are based on detecting symmetry in the state space [11], wherein the state space is partitioned into equivalent classes corresponding to isomorphic graphs, and one state is used to represent each class. However, this requires determining the representative state (known as the orbit problem [7,11]), which is at least as difficult as the graph isomorphism problem [7,19].

In this chapter we provide details of a novel method to reduce the time requirements for model checking a hierarchical model. A hierarchical model consists of a set of interdependent modules. We explore each of these modules in parallel to generate its *parameterized reachability graph* (PRG) and *access tables*, which act as a repository of corresponding module behavior. Thereafter a module can use these data structures to determine the behavior of any other module without actually executing it. In addition to concurrency, exposing such a module behavior repository for each module helps in reducing the delay. For each module, the dependency on it of other modules is injected into its repository using parameters. Later, these parameters are assigned specific values to obtain the corresponding *reachability graph* for the hierarchical model.

As discussed previously, the first step in model checking involves modeling the target system. This can be accomplished using an array of available modeling languages that offer varying convenience in modeling a system. These languages exhibit different levels of elegance and expressiveness. Among all offerings, the notion of hierarchy in a modeling language sets it apart. Other than stepwise refinement and different levels of granularity, a hierarchical modeling language allows sharing and reuse of modules [2]. Some common hierarchical languages, along with the model-checking tool they support are SMV [23] for CMU SMV, v-Promela [22] for SPIN, a hierarchical timed automata [9] for UPPAAL, and CPN ML for CPN Tools [18]. The subtle differences between each of these languages forbid us from proposing an all-inclusive algorithm; the technique presented in this chapter specifically targets CPN models. However, we do not claim any advantage in using CPN ML over other modeling languages. The method can be adapted for languages that have an underlying notion of hierarchy.

The innovative ideas described in this chapter could be summarized as:

- A technique to explore concurrently the modules in a hierarchical model and produce a repository of their behavior. Any dependency of other modules on it is epitomized as a set of parameters. Such concurrent exploration helps to reduce the time requirement. Furthermore, the repository makes it possible to determine module behavior without actually executing it.
- A related technique to assign specific values to the parameters in each PRG and to generate a reachability graph for the hierarchical model. Assigning values to the parameters helps in resolving dependency between modules.

The rest of the chapter is organized as follows. In Section 6.2 we introduce a problem and provide insight into the solution proposed. In Section 6.3 we present an overview of the hierarchical colored petri net model, which is used later in discussing the solution. Prior to proposing a technique for time-efficient state-space analysis in Section 6.5, the related work is given in Section 6.4. The experimental results are discussed in Section 6.6, and the outcomes are given in Section 6.7. In Section 6.8 we conclude the chapter.

6.2 OVERVIEW OF THE PROBLEM AND SOLUTION

State-space analysis of a model is performed by generating a reachability graph in which each node (or state) is scrutinized to determine if a set of undesirable and/or desirable properties holds. Depending on the number of properties to be analyzed at each state, there is an associated time overhead. Furthermore, an additional delay is incurred in determining the set of events enabled at each state and in taking turns to execute them.

The ever-increasing intricacies in a contemporary software system dramatically increases the number of states in the reachability graph. This phenomenon, better known as the *state-space explosion* problem [5], leads to exorbitant delays in producing and analyzing the state space. This is undermined further by the necessity of storing states that were generated hitherto and comparing them to any state produced henceforth (as discussed in Section 5.2). Regardless of the numerous ingenious algorithms proposed for efficient storage and comparison of states, there is always an associated time overhead. Even worse, all attempts at memory-efficient storage are accompanied by an increased delay [13,24]. Unfortunately, the sheer volume of research on memory efficiency suggests that reducing the memory costs has always been a priority, even when this has an associated time delay. We recognize the necessity of reducing both the memory and time requirements. In Chapter 5 we addressed the issue of memory costs in model checking (using the sequential and tree models). In this chapter we describe a technique to reduce the time requirement that could be used either independently or with a memory-reduction algorithm.

As pointed out previously, a system needs to be modeled using one of several available modeling languages prior to generating its state space. These languages offer different levels of abstraction, elegance, and expressiveness. Among all offerings, the notion of hierarchy in a modeling language sets it apart. A hierarchical model consists of a set of interdependent modules, and the reduction in delay envisioned is attributed to the exploration of these modules in parallel.

Most existing hierarchical formalisms are limited to modeling a system (e.g., hierarchical colored petri nets [16], hierarchical state machines [3]). Prior to generating the state space, a hierarchical model is usually flattened for convenience. Despite being a legitimate solution, there is no parallelism and concurrency in the process of generating the state space. The technique presented here preserves the hierarchical structure and the individual modules of the model when generating the state space. Furthermore, to reduce the delay associated with generating the reachability graph, these modules are explored in parallel. As a result of this exploration, an access table and a parameterized reachability graph are obtained for each module, which act as a repository of module behavior. The parameterized reachability graph for a module contains a set of parameters that epitomizes the dependency on it of other modules. Considering that the behavior of all modules in a hierarchical model is available in these repositories, the reachability graph can be produced by assigning appropriate values to these parameters and resolving the intermodule dependencies.

6.3 OVERVIEW OF HIERARCHICAL COLORED PETRI NETS

A *hierarchical colored petri net* (HCPN) [16] model consists of a finite set of nonhierarchical CPN models, also known as *modules*. Figures 6.1 and 6.2 represent a collection of modules that together constitute a HCPN model. The modules depict a simple stop-and-wait *Protocol* [25] for transferring a number of data packets from *Sender* to *Receiver* over an unreliable *Network* (module names in italic). For multiple receivers, as is the case here, a copy of the packet is delivered to each receiver independently. The three receivers here are identified as *Recv*(1), *Recv*(2), and *Recv*(3). The technique for time-efficient state-space analysis, described later, is discussed in reference to this example net.

Definition 6.1 *A module [17] $s \in S$ is a four-tuple $s = (CPN^s, T^s_{sub}, P^s_{port}, PT^s)$, where*

(a) $CPN^s = (P^s, T^s, A^s, \sum^s, V^s, C^s, G^s, E^s, I^s)$ *is a nonhierarchical colored petri-net.*
(b) $T^s_{sub} \subseteq T^s$ *is a set of substitution transitions.*
(c) $P^s_{port} \subseteq P^s$ *is a set of port places.*
(d) $PT: P^s_{port} \rightarrow \{IN, OUT, I/O\}$ *is a port-type function that specifies the port type for each port place.*

For all $s_1, s_2 \in S$: $s_1 \neq s_2$, we have $(P^{s_1} \bigcup T^{s_1}) \bigcap (P^{s_2} \bigcup T^{s_2}) = \phi$. This implies that no two modules should share their places and/or transitions.

Corollary 6.1 *A module containing a substitution transition is known as a super-module; the module it substitutes is known as a submodule.*

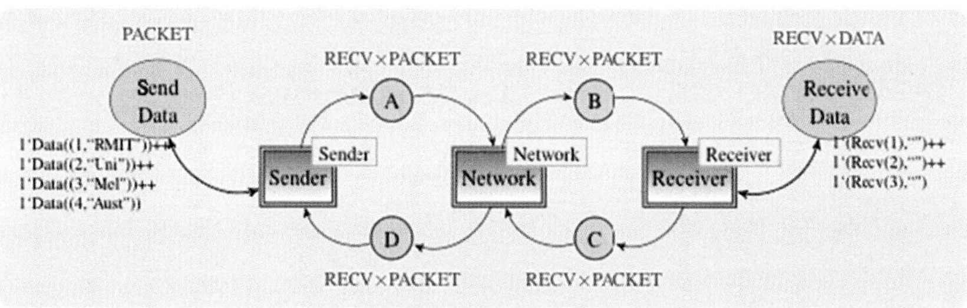

FIGURE 6.1 Module for *Protocol*.

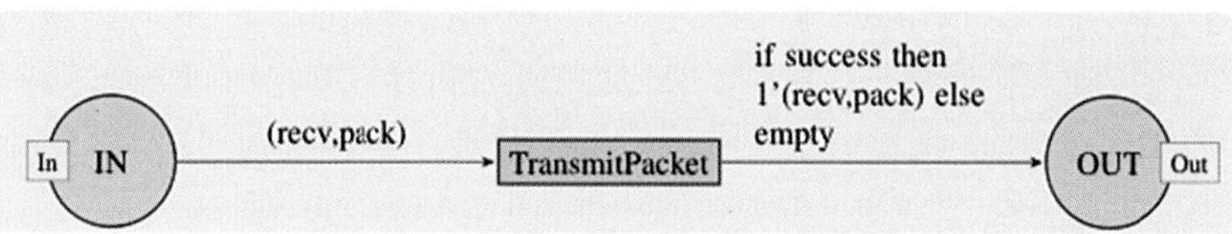

FIGURE 6.2 Module for *Transmit* in Figure 6.4.

Figure 6.1 illustrates the module *Protocol*, containing six places (the ellipses), and three substitution transitions (bordered rectangles), connected by arcs (arrows). As the name emphasizes, a *substitution transition* acts as a substitute for another module that executes whenever it fires. The module substituted is indicated by an associated tag. For example, the substitution transition *Sender* replaces a module by the same name that is shown in Figure 6.3. Similarly, the module *Network* in Figure 6.4 has two substitution transitions, each with an associated tag *Transmit*. However, it is important to point out that they replace different copies (or instances) of the module *Transmit*. The real power of HCPN lies in the fact that a module can have multiple instances, one for each substitution transition.

Definition 6.2 *A substitution transition* $t \in T^s_{sub}$ *is defined as the 3-tuple* $t = \{SM^s, P^t_{sock}, PS^s\}$, *where*

(*a*) $SM^s : T^s_{sub} \rightarrow S\text{-}s$ *is the submodule function for module s and associates a module (other than s) with each substitution transition* $t \in T^s_{sub}$. *If* $s' = SM^s(t)$, *then* $s, s' \in S : s \neq s'$ *and there exists a nontrivial path* $s \xrightarrow{t} s'$. *The module* s' *is denoted as the submodule of s.*

(*b*) $P^t_{sock} \subseteq P^s$ *is the set of adjoining places of t, referred to as its socket.*

(*c*) $PS^s(t) \subseteq P^t_{sock} \times P^{SM^s(t)}_{port}$ *is a port–socket function that is used to "glue" a module and its submodule. This is accomplished by mapping each port in a submodule with a socket in a corresponding module.*

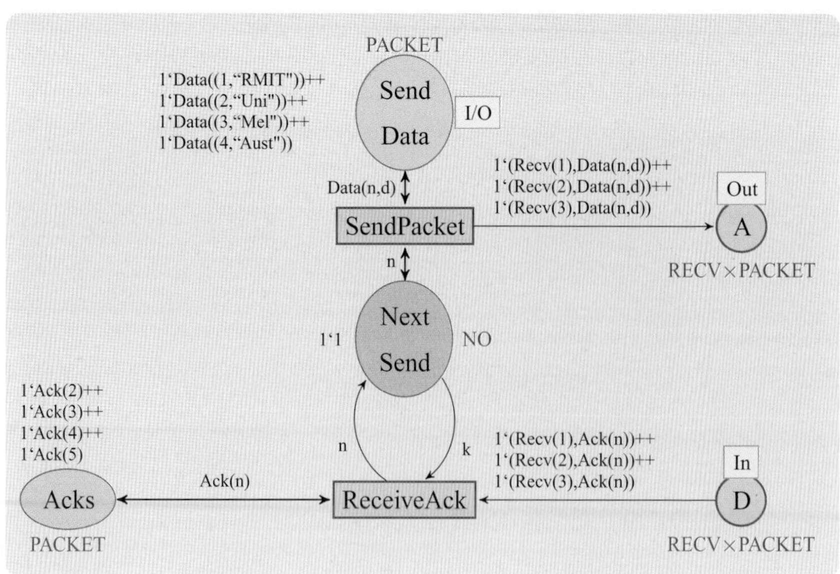

FIGURE 6.3 Module for *Sender* in Figure 6.1.

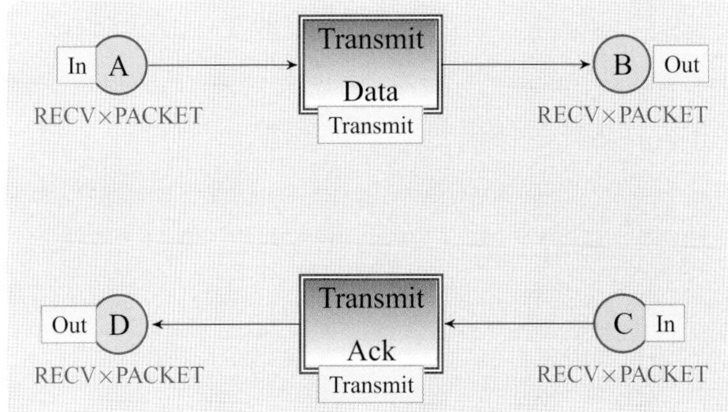

FIGURE 6.4 Module for *Network* in Figure 6.1.

A supermodule and its submodules are glued by defining a one-to-one relationship between a subset of their places. Each place adjacent to a substitution transition is known as a *socket* and has a counterpart in the associated submodule known as a *port*. Although not necessary, the port–socket pairs in our example net have the same name. Furthermore, considering that a socket could be either an input, an output, or an I/O place of substitution transition, an equivalent tag is attached to the corresponding port to indicate its permitted type.

If each module is linked to its submodules using directed arcs, the resulting graph is known as *module hierarchy*. Figure 6.5 illustrates the module hierarchy of our example HCPN model. Each directed arc in this figure is labeled with the name of a substitution transition that represents its target module. Considering that a module cannot be its own submodule, the module hierarchy is essentially an acyclic directed graph [4]. Roots of the module hierarchy with no incoming arcs are known as *prime modules* [17] and are denoted by S_{PM}. A module hierarchy can have multiple prime modules.

Each place in a module has an affiliated data type (known as its color), and all data values (known as *tokens*) in it must confirm to this type. For example, the token 1 *'Data((*1, *"RMIT"))* in the place *Send Data* is of type *PACKET*. The preceding number followed by a backquote (e.g., 1') indicates the count of a token, and a "++" separates two tokens.

A module might also have nonhierarchical transitions (rectangles with no border) that can manipulate these data values when *enabled* and move them between places through an arc. To enable a transition, an appropriate value needs to be assigned to each variable associated with it, a process known as *binding*. A binding enables a transition iff (1) each arc expression on an input arc evaluates to a subset of markings of the corresponding input place, and (2) the guard condition (if one exists) is satisfied. Accordingly, a binding b enables a transition t if the following holds:

$$\forall p \in P_{\text{In}}(t) : (E(p,t)\langle b\rangle \subseteq M(p)) \wedge G(t)\langle b\rangle \tag{6.1}$$

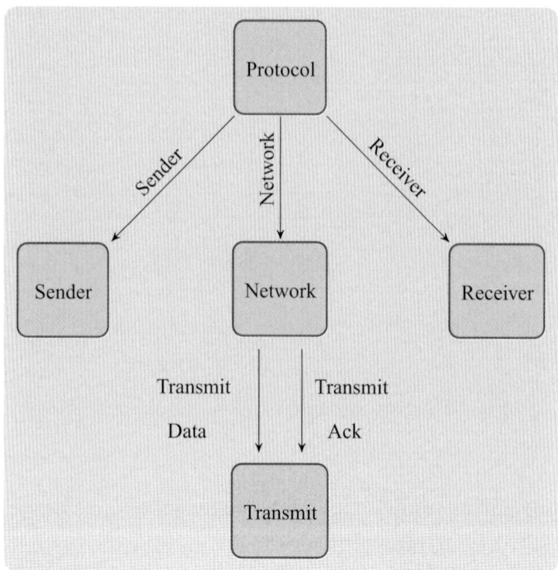

FIGURE 6.5 Module hierarchy for the example HCPN model.

where $P_{\text{In}}(t)$ is a set of input places of t, $E(p, t)$ is the expression on an arc connecting p to t, $M(p)$ denotes the set of tokens in p (known as its *marking*), and $G(t)$ denotes the guard, which is nothing but a boolean expression attached to t. For example, the transition *ReceiveAck* (in Figure 6.3) has two variables, n and k, and a binding $\langle n = 3, k = 2\rangle$ would enable it only when $2 \in M(\textit{Next Send})$ and $Ack(3) \in M(D)$. None of the transitions in the example net have an associated guard condition.

It is worth mentioning that a substitution transition has no associated variables. Consequently, it cannot be bound and cannot get enabled. For a particular substitution transition, the tokens in its adjoining places (i.e., sockets) are concurrently available to their associated ports in the submodule, and vice versa. For example, the socket *Send Data* (in Figure 6.1) and its port (see Figure 6.3) have the same marking. This allows one or more nonhierarchical transitions in the submodule to become enabled and consume these tokens. After the submodule finishes execution, the leftover tokens at its ports can be claimed back by the sockets.

Reachability Graph for HCPN. Prior to generating the reachability graph for a HCPN model, all its modules are joined to constitute a single large module. This is accomplished by overlapping each port–socket pair, rendering the substitution transitions useless. Each place in the newly constituted module is known as a *compound place*. However, only a subset of compound places is an outcome of the aforementioned port–socket fusion.

Table 6.1 lists the initial marking for each compound place that is constituted from the example HCPN model. Each port–socket pair in the HCPN model would join to constitute a compound place for the new module. Furthermore, a place in an HCPN model that is neither a port nor a socket (e.g., *Next Send*) would be a compound place by itself. The compound place corresponding to a place p in an HCPN model

TABLE 6.1 Compound Places in the HCPN Model and Their Initial Marking

Compound Place	Initial Marking M_0
$[SendData^*_{Protocol}] \sim_{cp} [SendData^*_{Sender}]$	$1`Data((1, ``RMIT''))$ ++ $1`Data((2, ``Uni''))$ ++ $1`Data((3, ``Mel''))$ ++ $1`Data((4, ``Aust''))$
$[A^*_{Protocol}] \sim_{cp} [A^*_{Sender}] \sim_{cp} [A^*_{Network}] \sim_{cp} [IN^*]$	ϕ
$[D^*_{Protocol}] \sim_{cp} [D^*_{Sender}] \sim_{cp} [D^*_{Network}] \sim_{cp} [OUT^*]$	ϕ
$[B^*_{Protocol}] \sim_{cp} [B^*_{Network}] \sim_{cp} [B^*_{Receiver}] \sim_{cp} [OUT^*]$	ϕ
$[C^*_{Protocol}] \sim_{cp} [C^*_{Network}] \sim_{cp} [C^*_{Receiver}] \sim_{cp} [IN^*]$	ϕ
$[ReceiveData^*_{Protocol}] \sim_{cp} [ReceiveData^*_{Receiver}]$	$1`(Recv(1), ``'')$ ++ $1`(Recv(2), ``'')$ ++$1`(Recv(3), ``'')$
$[NextSend^*]$	$1`1$
$[Acks^*]$	$1`Ack(2)$ ++ $1`Ack(3)$++$1`Ack(4)$ ++ $1`Ack(5)$
$[NextRec^*]$	$1`(Recv(1), 1)$ ++ $1`(Recv(2), 1)$ ++ $1`(Recv(3), 1)$

is denoted as $[p^*]$. Furthermore, $[p^*] \sim_{cp} [q^*]$ denotes that p and q belong to the same compound place. Any conflict in place names is resolved by including the module name as a subscript. The new module has eight compound places, corresponding to the eight rows (see Table 6.1). The multiple entries of the compound places $[IN^*]$ and $[OUT^*]$ in Table 6.1 correspond to separate instances of the module *Transmit*. whereas the place *IN* from the first instance forms a compound place with *A*, the same place from another instance forms a compound place with *C*. Similarly, the two instances of *OUT* form compound places with *B* and *D*.

The initial marking constitutes the root node of the reachability graph. The events enabled at this marking can bring about a change in state. The root node has an outgoing edge for each enabled marking, leading to a new node. The markings that correspond to these new nodes are then analyzed to find the next set of enabled events that would lead to another set of new nodes. The analysis continues until there are no enabled events.

However, if there exists a nonempty sequence of events that causes no net change in a marking M (i.e., $M[e_1\rangle M_1[e_2\rangle M_2 \cdots M_{r-1}[e_r\rangle M$: $r > 0$), the states $\{M, M_1, \ldots, M_{r-1}\}$ would be analyzed forever. To ensure termination, all the unique markings encountered hitherto are stored and compared with the markings generated hereafter.

6.4 RELATED WORK

All existing solutions to reducing the time requirements for model checking can be categorized as either partial order reduction, symmetry-based reduction, or modular

TABLE 6.2 Comparison of Existing Solutions

Method	Runtime	Number of Markings
No Algorithm	100%	Any
[12]	49.18%	45,780
[21]	89.3%	25
Technique presented here	14%	25,000

state-space generation. The solutions related to each of these categories are discussed and compared to the technique presented.

Partial order techniques for HCPN involve determining *stubborn sets* and executing only the enabled transitions in each set. A stubborn set consists of a set of transitions such that a transition outside the set cannot affect their behavior. Consequently, such a set requires the presence of *concurrent independent transitions*, which would lead the system to the same marking, irrespective of their order of execution. However, the problem of deciding if a set of transitions is stubborn at a state is at least as difficult as the reachability problem [8]. Partial order techniques for colored petri nets have been proposed [12,21], and the worst efficiencies observed are illustrated in Table 6.2.

The symmetry method exploits the presence of any underlying symmetry or symmetrical components in the target system. The symmetric components in such systems exhibit identical behavior and have identical state graphs. The subgraphs of these components in the reachability graph of the entire system are usually interchangeable, with some permutation of states. Therefore, the system reachability graph could be broken into symmetrical graph quotients. One of these graph quotients, when annotated with corresponding permutations, could be enough to verify the properties of the entire system. However, it is difficult to determine a graph quotient whose permutations would produce other graph quotients (known as the *orbit problem* [7,11]). Solving the orbit problem is at least as difficult as solving the *graph isomorphism problem* [7,19], which requires determining if two finite graphs are isomorphic. A symmetry method for colored petri nets has been proposed [10]. The performance of symmetry-based algorithms depends on the extent of symmetry in the target system.

Modular state-space generation involves generating the reachability graph of each module independently and then composing them to generate the reachability graph for the entire system. The algorithm presented is based on this technique. Although one algorithm proposed [6] is also based on this technique, the semantics of "transition fusion" used in this algorithm is no longer defined in CPN tools and is best avoided. Solutions based on this technique only necessitate a hierarchical modeling language to be used for system representation. Consequently, it is not necessary to linger in identifying stubborn sets or symmetrical markings. Furthermore, it is possible to reduce the overhead time by generating a reachability graph for each module in parallel.

TABLE 6.3 Comparison of Categories of Existing Solutions

	Category of Existing Solutions		
Criterion	Partial Order	Symmetry	Modular
Requires	Stubborn sets	Symmetry	Modules
Mechanism	Determine concurrent independent transitions	Determine representative states	Determine and merge the reachability graphs of different modules
Complexity	NP	NP	P
Estimation	Heuristic	Heuristic	

Table 6.2 compares the technique presented in this chapter with several others [12,21] based on partial order techniques. Whereas the former offers a reduction of 50.82% in a worst-case scenario, the latter offers a meager 10.7% reduction. These are significantly less than the 86% reduction offered by the technique presented here. Furthermore, the prerequisite of the solution described here (i.e., a hierarchical model) is less stringent than that of these techniques, for which a stubborn set is mandatory. The reduction offered by symmetrical reduction techniques depends largely on the extent of symmetry in the model under deliberation.

Table 6.3 compares broad categories of existing solutions. The solution described here is based on a modular technique that has a polynomial solution.

6.5 TECHNIQUE FOR TIME-EFFICIENT STATE-SPACE ANALYSIS

As noted previously, the modules of a HCPN model are joined prior to generating the reachability graph. This in effect amounts to flattening the model and analyzing its equivalent nonhierarchical counterpart. Despite this being a legitimate solution, it lacks concurrency and parallelism. The technique (described here) installs these features by exploring the HCPN modules in parallel instead of joining them together. The existing dependencies on a module are represented using parameters. Such a setup provides the reduction envisioned under the time requirement.

Figure 6.6 illustrates the concurrent exploration of HCPN modules. However, as depicted in Figure 6.5, the *Protocol* module is dependent on three of its submodules. Consequently, it needs to access the reachability graph (RG) for each *Sender*, *Network*, and *Receiver* when generating its own reachability graph. Similarly, the *Network* module requires the reachability graph for the *Transmit* module. The vertical lines in Figure 6.6 denote the execution of a module, and the horizontal lines denote a module trying to access the reachability graph for one of its submodules. In case the reachability graph for a submodule is available, it is returned at once. Otherwise, the module needs to wait until it becomes available. For example, when *Protocol* tries to fetch the reachability graph for *Sender* at time T_p2, the latter has not yet finished generating it. Consequently, it waits until time

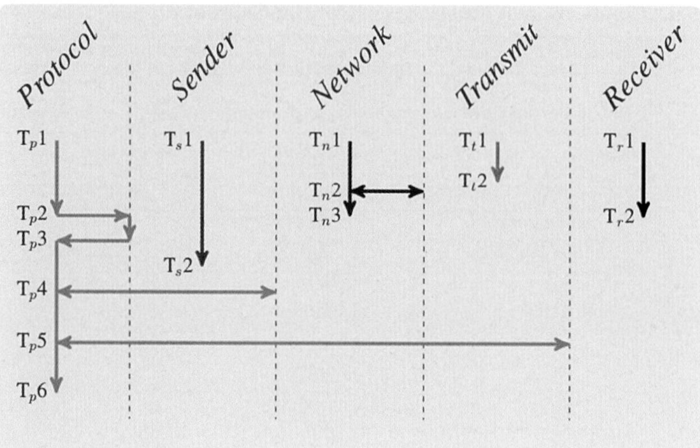

FIGURE 6.6 Order of access for modules in the example HCPN model.

T_p3, when the required reachability graph is available. However, it is not necessary to wait when it tries to fetch the reachability graph for *Network* or *Receiver*, as these modules have finished execution by then and the reachability graph is available immediately.

Algorithm 6.1 lists the steps for executing all modules concurrently. A new thread is created for each module in S and all the threads explore the corresponding module concurrently. The steps for exploring a module are illustrated in Algorithm 6.3. In the next section we deliberate using parameters to represent dependency between modules.

6.5.1 Access Tables and Parameterized Reachability Graph

Access tables and parameters are used to manage the dependencies on a module. Figure 6.5 depicts existing dependencies: for example, HCPN.

A substitution transition executes by furnishing the associated submodule with tokens at each of its input places. The submodule receives these tokens at ports

Algorithm 6.1 ConcurrentRG(S)

Data: The set of modules S
Result: Each module is explored concurrently

```
foreach module m ∈S do
    Thread t=new Thread(new Explore(m));
    t.start();
end
```

termed "In" and executes all the transitions enabled. Thereafter, the tokens at ports termed "Out" are made available to a substitution transition at its output places. On furnishing different sets of tokens to the submodule, the substitution transition might expect different sets of tokens returned to their output places. From the perspective of substitution transition, the submodule is a black box which when supplied with a particular set of tokens always returns another set of tokens. If a table contains all the possible inputs that this submodule can accept and the result is produced in each case, we can replace the submodule with this table. Considering the deterministic nature of a submodule, the substitution transition would never know that the results are being fetched from a table. Since the result of executing a module is available without actually executing it, the scheme would render a massive reduction in delay. This table is known as an *access table*, and the steps in generating it for a module are given later as an algorithm.

An access table has one column for each port and a set of additional columns to check the validity of conditions. Each entry in the access table consists of (1) a minimum set of tokens required in input ports, (2) possible values of listed conditions (if applicable), and (3) a set of tokens at the output ports under each condition. Table 6.4 shows the access table for the *Sender* module. The first entry requires that the port *Send Data* contain at least a token *Data(n,d)*, where n and d are parameters. The use of parameters helps in reducing the number of rows in the access table by allowing a range of token values. The column for conditions lists all possible results when evaluating the specified condition $n = v$?. The variable v stores the value of the token at the place *Next Send*. Finally, the marking of output ports for each of these conditions is listed. It is worth mentioning that we treat I/O ports as a combination of input and output ports. Consequently, they have one column under each of these

TABLE 6.4 Access Table for *Sender*

Input Ports			Output Ports	
Send Data	*D*	Conditions: $n = v$?	*A*	Send Data
Data(n,d)$^-$	Empty	Yes	1'*(Recv*(1),*Data(n,d))*$^+$ ++ 1'*(Recv*(2),*Data(n,d))*$^+$ ++ 1'*(Recv*(3),*Data(n,d))*$^+$	*Data(n,d)*$^+$
		No	Empty	*Data(n,d)*$^+$
Empty	1'*(Recv*(1),*Ack(m))*$^-$ ++ 1'*(Recv*(2),*Ack(m))*$^-$ ++ 1'*(Recv*(3),*Ack(m))*$^-$	—	Empty	Empty

categories. The superscript of a token indicates if it is being added or removed (+ = add, − = remove).

If a substitution transition uses an access table instead of actually executing its submodule, any changes required in marking nonport places would be omitted. This is because the access table accounts only for the port places of a submodule. For example, an access table does not account for a change in marking the place *Next Send* when the module *Sender* executes with a token *Ack(m)* in place *D* (second row of Table 6.4). Nevertheless, this could steer the model into incorrect marking to produce an incorrect reachability graph. Consequently, each row of the access table is associated with a *parameterized reachability graph* (PRG). A PRG is generated by initializing the input port places of a submodule with tokens in the corresponding row of an access table and exploring it. Figures 6.7 and 6.8 illustrate the parameterized reachability graphs corresponding to the two rows of its access table. The parameterized reachability graphs corresponding to the second row now account for the change in marking of the nonport place *Next Send.*

When generating the reachability graphs for *Protocol*, the substitution transition *Sender* is encountered. Supposing that the access table and parameterized reachability graphs for *Sender* have already been generated, all that is required is to determine the most appropriate entry in the access table. Considering that the place *Send Data*

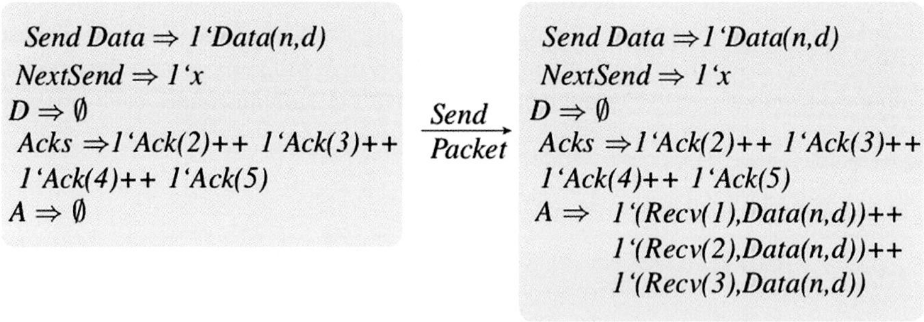

Send Data ⇒ *1'Data(n,d)*
NextSend ⇒ *1'x*
D ⇒ ∅
Acks ⇒ *1'Ack(2)++ 1'Ack(3)++ 1'Ack(4)++ 1'Ack(5)*
A ⇒ ∅

—*Send Packet*→

Send Data ⇒ *1'Data(n,d)*
NextSend ⇒ *1'x*
D ⇒ ∅
Acks ⇒ *1'Ack(2)++ 1'Ack(3)++ 1'Ack(4)++ 1'Ack(5)*
A ⇒ *1'(Recv(1),Data(n,d))++ 1'(Recv(2),Data(n,d))++ 1'(Recv(3),Data(n,d))*

FIGURE 6.7 Reachability graph for the the first row of Table 6.4.

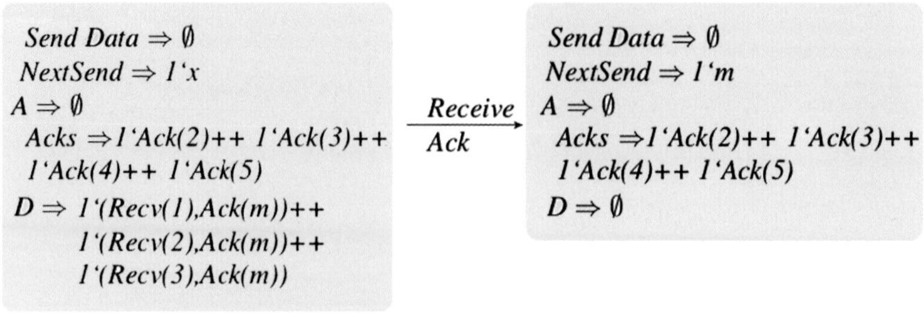

Send Data ⇒ ∅
NextSend ⇒ *1'x*
A ⇒ ∅
Acks ⇒ *1'Ack(2)++ 1'Ack(3)++ 1'Ack(4)++ 1'Ack(5)*
D ⇒ *1'(Recv(1),Ack(m))++ 1'(Recv(2),Ack(m))++ 1'(Recv(3),Ack(m))*

—*Receive Ack*→

Send Data ⇒ ∅
NextSend ⇒ *1'm*
A ⇒ ∅
Acks ⇒ *1'Ack(2)++ 1'Ack(3)++ 1'Ack(4)++ 1'Ack(5)*
D ⇒ ∅

FIGURE 6.8 Reachability graph for the second row of Table 6.4.

TABLE 6.5 Values Assigned to Parameters by Tokens

Token	n	d
Data(1, *"RMIT"*)	1	*"RMIT"*
Data(2, *"Uni*)	2	*"Uni"*
Data(3, *"Mel"*)	3	*"Mel"*
Data(4, *"Aust"*)	4	*"Aust"*

has three tokens whereas D has none, the first row in Table 6.4 turns out to be the obvious choice. The values assigned to parameters n and d by each of these three tokens are shown in Table 6.5.

The value of the variable v is 1, owing to the token *1‘1* in the place *Next Send*. Consequently, only the token 1 *‘Data*(1, *"RMIT")* satisfies the condition $n = v?$, and the only token added to place A is 1 *‘Data*(1, *"RMIT")*. This being an output port, the token also appears in an output place of the substitution transition *Sender*, where it is available for the module *Network*. Finally, the parameterized reachability graph is checked to update the markings of any nonport places of the module *Sender*.

The discussion above emphasizes the role played by access tables and parameterized reachability graphs in concurrent state-space analysis. Each submodule generates its own access table and associated parameterized reachability graphs in parallel, as shown in Figure 6.6. As observed previously, a supermodule needs to wait if its submodule is still in the process of generating them. In the next section we illustrate further the importance of access tables and explain the steps involved in constructing them.

6.5.2 Exploring a Module

When generating the access table or parameterized reachability graph of a module, the most challenging aspect is to determine the set of initial marking for the input port places that enable the module. Each distinct initial marking that enables the module would add a new row to the access table and create an associated parameterized reachability graph. If a substitution transition queries an access table with the tokens at its input places and does not find a match, it concludes that the associated submodule is not enabled for the particular marking. Therefore, omitting a marking that enables the module would lead to potential error.

The algorithm determines the initial markings by identifying the set of bindings that enable the output transitions of input port places. This follows from the fact that enabling any of these transitions enables the module. For each of these bindings, the marking of input port places could be established by evaluating the corresponding arc expressions. Considering that each of these markings would enable at least one transition of the module, all possible combinations of these markings would return the exhaustive set of initial markings required. We now discuss the underlying strategy before proposing the algorithm.

Each arc connecting a transition t to its adjoining places has an associated arc expression. In addition, t might also have an associated expression as a guard condition. The variables constituting these expressions are known as *free variables* (FVs) [20]. Accordingly, the set of free variables for transition t is given by

$$\mathrm{FV}(t) = \bigcup_{p \in P_{\mathrm{in}}(t)} \mathrm{FV}(E(p,t)) \cup \bigcup_{p \in P_{\mathrm{out}}(t)} \mathrm{FV}(E(t,p)) \cup \mathrm{FV}(G(t)) \tag{6.2}$$

where $E(p,t)$ denotes the arc expressions on input arcs of t $E(t,p)$ denotes the arc expressions on output arcs of t and $G(t)$ denotes the guards condition for t. The set of FV for the transition *ReceivePacket* appearing in Figure 6.9 is expressed as

$$\mathrm{FV}(\mathit{ReceivePacket}) = \{n, recv, k, data, d\} \tag{6.3}$$

It should be noted that the scope of a CPN FV is limited by a transition; that is, an FV appearing in multiple arc expressions or as a guard for a transition t is the same variable. For example, the variable *recv* appearing in each input arc expression of *ReceivePacket* is the same.

When generating the reachability graph for a module, it is necessary to determine the set of enabled transitions at every step. To determine if a transition is enabled, all the FVs associated with it need to be bound to values and the corresponding arc expression evaluated. This was observed in Section 6.3.

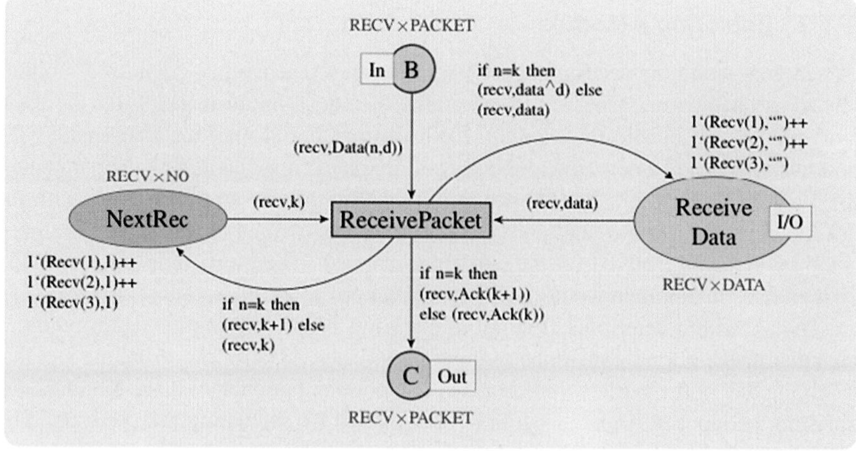

FIGURE 6.9 Module for *Receiver* in Figure 6.1.

Definition 6.3 *Binding is the process of assigning values to each FV associated with a transition. It is written in the form* $b = <v_1 = c_1, v_2 = c_2, \ldots, v_n = c_n>$, *where* $FV(t) = \{v_i | i \in 1 \cdots n\}$ *and* c_i *is the value bound to* v_i.

The result on evaluating an arc expression e for binding $b = < v_1 = c_1, v_2 = c_2, \ldots v_n = c_n >$ is defined as

$$e < b > = (fn(v_1, \ldots, v_n) \Rightarrow e)(c_1, \ldots, c_n) \tag{6.4}$$

The place *NextRec* in Figure 6.9 contains three tokens. To ensure that *ReceivePacket* is enabled, the expression on arc connecting *NextRec* to *ReceivePacket* must evaluate to one of these three tokens. Consequently, the possible bindings should be

$$b_1 = < recv = Recv(1), k = 1 > \tag{6.5}$$

$$b_2 = < recv = Recv(2), k = 1 > \tag{6.6}$$

$$b_3 = < recv = Recv(3), k = 1 > \tag{6.7}$$

On evaluating the expression *(recv,k)* with b_1, b_2, and b_3, the resulting arc expressions obtained should culminate in removal of either of the three tokens in *NextRec*.

However, out of the five FVs of *ReceivePacket* shown in equation (6.3), only two have been bound in either of b_1, b_2, or b_3. Other variables will be bound similarly by matching the tokens at input places with the expressions appearing on input arcs. This requirement is captured by the *pattern binding basis* [20].

Definition 6.4 *A pattern binding basis PBB(t) for a transition t is a set of input arc expressions of t satisfying:*

(a) $FV(t) = \bigcup_{E(p,t) \in PBB(t)} FV(E(p,t))$.
(b) $\forall E(p,t) \in PBB(t)$: *PATTERN(E(p,t)).*

Definition 6.5 *A pattern is an expression comprising constructors, identifiers, and constants.*

The first item ensures that the FVs of a transition t appear in at least one of the expressions in PBB(t). The second item ensures that each expression in PBB(t) is a pattern (Definition 6.5). The PBB for the transition *ReceivePacket* in *Receiver* is

$$\text{PBB}(ReceivePacket) = \{(recv, k), (recv, Data(n, d)), (recv, data)\} \tag{6.8}$$

The bindings b_1, b_2, and b_3 are only *partial bindings*, as they assign values to a subset of variables in FV*(ReceivePacket)*. In general, matching the tokens at an input place to the expression on the arc connecting it to a transition t would normally bind only a subset of free variables fv $\subseteq$ FV (t) of t. The partial bindings that are obtained for the transition *ReceivePacket* from bindings in equations (6.5), (6.6), and (6.7) are

$$pb^1_{ReceivePacket} = < recv = Recv(1), k = 1, n = \bot, d = \bot, data = \bot > \quad (6.9)$$

$$pb^2_{ReceivePacket} = < recv = Recv(2), k = 1, n = \bot, d = \bot, data = \bot > \quad (6.10)$$

$$pb^3_{ReceivePacket} = < recv = Recv(3), k = 1, n = \bot, d = \bot, data = \bot > \quad (6.11)$$

where $\bot$ denotes that a variable is not bound to a value.

Since the remaining two input places of *ReceivePacket* are port places, they do not have a fixed marking. Their binding is determined by the input places of the corresponding substitution transition; consequently, they cannot be used to bind free variables. To enable the transition *ReceivePacket*, we add tokens to each of these input ports based on the following rules:

- The tokens added to a port place are determined by evaluating the expression on the arc connecting it to the transition. The partial bindings of the transition are used in evaluating these arc expressions.
- When evaluating the arc expression in the preceding step, each FV that is unbound in partial binding is assigned a unique parameter.
- The color of the token added must be same as that of the containing port place.

Using these rules, the tokens added to the input port places of *ReceivePacket* are

$$B = 1`(Recv(1), Data(n_p, d_p)) ++ 1`(Recv(2), Data(n_p, d_p)) ++ 1`(Recv(3), Data(n_p, d_p)) \quad (6.12)$$

$$Receive\ \ Data = 1`(Recv(1), data_p) ++ 1`(Recv(2), data_p) ++ 1`(Recv(3), data_p) \quad (6.13)$$

The expression on the arc connecting place B to *ReceivePacket* is *(recv,Data(n,d))*. Because neither n nor d was assigned a value in the partial binding $pb^1_{ReceivePacket}$, $pb^2_{ReceivePacket}$, or $pb^3_{ReceivePacket}$[equations (6.9) to (6.11)], they are now assigned parameters n_p and d_p. For the same reason, FV *data* is assigned parameter $data_p$. The bindings after adding these tokens are as follows:

$$b^1_{ReceivePacket} = < recv = Recv(1), k = 2, n = n_p, d = d_p, data = data_p > \quad (6.14)$$

$$b^2_{ReceivePacket} = < recv = Recv(2), k = 1, n = n_p, d = d_p, data = data_p > \quad (6.15)$$

$$b^3_{ReceivePacket} = < recv = Recv(3), k = 2, n = n_p, d = d_p, data = data_p > \quad (6.16)$$

When the transition *ReceivePacket* fires, it removes the token from input places and moves tokens to output places. The tokens removed and added depend on the binding for which the transition fires. The tokens removed for each binding are shown in Table 6.6.

TABLE 6.6 Tokens Removed by *ReceivePacket* from Its Input Places for Each Binding

	Input Places		
Binding	*B*	NextRec	Receive Data
$b^1_{ReceivePacket}$	1'(*Recv*(1),*Data*(n_p, d_p))	1'(*Recv*(1), *k*)	1'(*Recv*(1), $data_p$)
$b^2_{ReceivePacket}$	1'(*Recv*(2),*Data*(n_p, d_p))	1'(*Recv*(2), *k*)	1'(*Recv*(2), $data_p$)
$b^3_{ReceivePacket}$	1'(*Recv*(3),*Data*(n_p, d_p))	1'(*Recv*(3), *k*)	1'(*Recv*(3), $data_p$)

The entry for each binding in Table 6.6 maps to a row in the corresponding access table. However, only information for port places *B* and *Receive Data* is used, as access tables do not have columns for other places. The value of *k* in each entry is fetched from the corresponding binding.

The output arcs of *ReceivePacket* have a conditional expression *if* $n = k$ and the tokens added to output places depend on the boolean result obtained on evaluating this expression. Accordingly, there is an additional column in the access table to check this condition, which contains all possible results of evaluating the expression. The tokens added to each output place for each possible outcome of conditional expression are shown in Table 6.7.

Each entry in Table 6.7 corresponds to a row in the corresponding access table. However, only the information for port places *B* and *Receive Data* are used, as access tables do not have columns for other places. The value of *k* in each entry is fetched from the corresponding binding. The access table for *Receiver* can be constituted from Tables 6.6 and 6.7 by joining the entries for identical bindings and removing the excess columns. The access table obtained is shown in Table 6.8.

TABLE 6.7 Tokens Added by *ReceivePacket* to Its Output Places for Each Binding

		Output Places		
Binding	Conditions: $n = k$?	*C*	NextRec	Receive Data
$b^1_{\text{ReceivePacket}}$	Yes	1'(*Recv*(1), *Ack*(*k*+1))	1'(*Recv*(1), *k*+1)	1'(*Recv*(1), $data_p \wedge$d))
	No	1'(*Recv*(1), *Ack*(*k*)	1'(*Recv*(1), *k*)	1'(*Recv*(1), $data_p$)
$b^2_{\text{ReceivePacket}}$	Yes	1'(*Recv*(2), *Ack*(*k*+1))	1'(*Recv*(2), *k*+1)	1'(*Recv*(2), $data_p \wedge$d))
	No	1'(*Recv*(2), *Ack*(*k*)	1'(*Recv*(2), *k*)	1'(*Recv*(2), $data_p$)
$b^3_{\text{ReceivePacket}}$	Yes	1'(*Recv*(3), *Ack*(*k*+1))	1'(*Recv*(3), *k*+1)	1'(*Recv*(3), $data_p \wedge$d))
	No	1'(*Recv*(3), *Ack*(*k*)	1'(*Recv*(3), *k*)	1'(*Recv*(3), $data_p$)

TABLE 6.8 Access Table of *Receive* from Tables 6.6 and 6.7

Input Ports			Output Ports	
B	Receive Data	Conditions: $n=k$?	*C*	Receive Data
1‘(*Recv*(1), *Data*(n_p, d_p))$^-$	1‘(*Recv*(1), $data_p$)$^-$	Yes	1‘(*Recv*(1), *Ack*(*k*+1))$^+$	1‘(*Recv*(1), $data_p \wedge d$))$^+$
		No	1‘(*Recv*(1), *Ack*(*k*))$^+$	1‘(*Recv*(1), $data_p$)$^+$
1‘(*Recv*(2), *Data*(n_p, d_p))$^-$	1‘(*Recv*(2), $data_p$)$^-$	Yes	1‘(*Recv*(2), *Ack*(*k*+1))$^+$	1‘(*Recv*(2), $data_p \wedge d$))$^+$
		No	1‘(*Recv*(2), *Ack*(*k*))	1‘(*Recv*(2), $data_p$))
1‘(*Recv*(3), *Data*(n_p, d_p))$^-$	1‘(*Recv*(3), $data_p$)$^-$	Yes	1‘(*Recv*(3), *Ack*(*k*+1))$^+$	1‘(*Recv*(3), $data_p \wedge$d))$^+$
		No	1‘(*Recv*(3), *Ack*(*k*))$^+$	1‘(*Recv*(3), $data_p$))$^+$

Since the module *Receiver* contains a single transition, its access tables could be constructed using tables that contain information about the tokens it adds and removes. However, if the module had additional transitions, we would have required similar tables for all those transitions in order to generate the access table.

Often, it is only the output arc expressions that contain conditional expressions. The expressions on input arcs are almost always very simple. Hence, the column “Condition” is missing from the table, which illustrates the tokens removed from input places.

6.5.3 Access Table and Parameterized Reachability Graph for a Super-module

In section 6.5.2 we discussed the role played by access tables and parameterized reachability graphs in concurrent state-space analysis. However, the discussion was limited to modules that do not have any other submodules. In this section we discuss producing the parameterized reachability graph and access tables for such super modules.

For example, as illustrated in Figure 6.5, the module *Network* has a submodule *Transmit*. Accordingly, as shown in Figure 6.6, it would need the access table for *Transmit* to produce its own access table. Considering that *Transmit* does not have a submodule, its access table can be created based on the aforementioned discussion and is shown in Table 6.9. Note that the parameters used in this table are of simple types (e.g., INT, STRING) instead of user-defined types (i.e., RECV, PACKET, or their product) that appear in an arc expression. This requires modifying the arc

TABLE 6.9 Access Table for *Transmit*

Input Port, IN	Conditions: Success?	Output Port, OUT
1‘(*Recv(k),Data(n,d)*)$^-$	Yes	1‘(*Recv(k),Data(n,d)*)$^+$
	No	Empty
1‘(*Recv(k),Ack(n)*)$^-$	Yes	1‘(*Recv(k),Ack(n)*)$^+$
	No	Empty

expression before applying the three rules described in Section 6.5.2 for adding tokens to input ports. Using parameters of simple types throughout a model prevents any ambiguities in assigning them values. This is illustrated further toward the end of this section.

Network has two input ports, *A* and *C*. Considering that these are input places of substitution transitions *Transmit Data* and *Transmit Ack*, there are no free variables or arc expressions to evaluate and determine the minimum number of tokens to be added to these ports to enable the module *Network*. Consequently, the access-table for the *Transmit* module (corresponding to these substitution transitions) is used to ascertain the enabling tokens to be inserted into these ports.

From Table 6.9 it can be inferred that the presence of either *(Recv(k),Data(n,d))* or *(Recv(k),Ack(n))* in place *IN* enables the *Transmit* module. Considering that (1) enabling of the *Transmit* module enables the substitution transitions, which in turn enable the module *Network*, and (2) the port *IN* of *Transmit* maps to socket places *A* and *C* of *Network*, it can be deduced that adding either of these tokens to place *A* or *C* would enable the *Network* module. Accordingly, the access table for *Network* contains an entry for adding each of these tokens into a socket place and is shown in Table 6.10.

In general, prior to generating the access table for a supermodule, the tokens that enable each of its submodules need to be determined from their access tables. The columns of an access table convey the tokens that need to be added into each input port place to enable the submodule. The supermodule has one or more substitution transitions corresponding to each of these submodules, and based on the port–socket mapping, its sockets are populated with the enabling tokens from their ports. A socket could be either of the following:

- An input port place of the supermodule. In that case, the tokens in it add entries to the access table of the supermodule.
- A noninput port place of the supermodule. In that case, the set of tokens in input port places needs to be determined that would produce the enabling tokens in the socket. This is done by backtracking. Furthermore, the set of tokens in input port places that produce the enabling tokens add entries to the access table for the supermodule.

TABLE 6.10 Access Table for *Network*

Input Port			Output Port	
A	*C*	Conditions: Success?	*B*	*D*
1'(*Recv*(*k*), *Data*(*n*, *d*))$^-$	Empty	Yes	1'(*Recv*(*k*), *Data*(*n*, *d*))$^+$	Empty
		No	Empty	Empty
1'(*Recv*(*k*), *Ack*(*n*))$^-$	Empty	Yes	1'(*Recv*(*k*), *Ack*(*n*))$^+$	Empty
		No	Empty	Empty
Empty	1'(*Recv*(*k*), *Data*(*n*, *d*))$^-$	Yes	Empty	1'(*Recv*(*k*), *Data*(*n*, *d*))$^+$
		No	Empty	Empty
Empty	1'(*Recv*(*k*), *Ack*(*n*))$^-$	Yes	Empty	1'(*Recv*(*k*), *Ack*(*n*))$^+$
		No	Empty	Empty

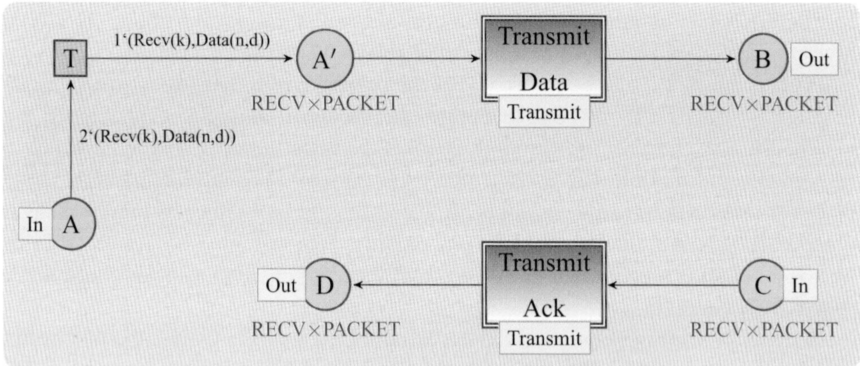

FIGURE 6.10 Module for the network in Figure 6.1.

The first case was observed for the *Network* module, where socket places *A* and *C* were also the input port places. To demonstrate the second case, the *Network* module is modified as shown in Figure 6.10.

Socket *A*′ is not an input port place of *Network*. Therefore, the tokens in the input port places need to be determined to generate the access table. The enabling tokens that could be added to *A*′ are 1 *'(Recv(k), Data(n,d))* and 1'(*Recv(k), Ack(n)*). The corresponding tokens on input port places *A* and *C* are shown in Table 6.11.

While two instances of *(Recv(k), Data(n,d))* in *A* produce the first enabling token in *A*′, the other enabling token cannot be produced for any combination of tokens in input port places. Accordingly, the access table for a modified *Network* module does not have a entry for the second enabling token, as shown in Table 6.12.

TABLE 6.11 Tokens in Input Port Places that Produce Enabling Tokens in the Socket

A'	A	C
1‘$(Recv(k), Data(n,d))$	2‘$(Recv(k), Data(n,d))$	None
1‘$(Recv(k), Ack(n))$	None	None

TABLE 6.12 Access Table for Modified *Network* Module

Input Port			Output Port	
A	C	Conditions: Success?	B	D
2‘$(Recv(k), Data(n,d))^-$	Empty	Yes	1‘$(Recv(k), Data(n,d))^+$	Empty
		No	Empty	Empty
Empty	1‘$(Recv(k), Data(n,d))^-$	Yes	Empty	1‘$(Recv(k), Data(n,d))^+$
		No	Empty	Empty
Empty	1‘$(Recv(k), Ack(n))^-$	Yes	Empty	1‘$(Recv(k), Ack(n))^+$
		No	Empty	Empty

Furthermore, the entry for the first enabling token now requires two instances of *(Recv(k), Data(n,d))* in *A*.

Comparison of Table 6.10 with Tables 6.4 and 6.8 exemplifyies the advantages in using simple parameters. Columns *A*, *B*, *C*, and *D* in all these tables contain tokens that are compatible (i.e., of the same data type) and similar. Consequently, when the tokens move between modules, a simple assignment of enabling tokens would determine the result required.

6.5.4 Algorithms for Generating Access Tables and Parameterized Reachability Graphs

We now show the algorithms for generating the access table and parameterized reachability graphs of a module. First, few terms are defined.

Definition 6.6 *Partial bindings pb_1 and pb_2 for a transition t are said to be compatible, which is denoted as Compatible(pb_1,pb_2), if they have consistent values bound to their variables* [*i.e.,* $\forall v \in \mathrm{FV}(t)$: $pb_1(v) \neq \perp \wedge pb_2(v) \neq \perp \Rightarrow pb_1(v) = pb_2(v)$].

Definition 6.7 *If pb_1 and pb_2 are two partial bindings, such that Compatible (pb_1,pb_2), they can be combined, denoted as Combine(pb_1,pb_2), to obtain another* *partial binding pb, where*

$$pb(v) = \left\{ \begin{array}{ll} pb_1(v): & pb_1(v) \neq \perp \\ pb_2(v): & pb_2(v) \neq \perp \\ \perp: & \text{otherwise} \end{array} \right\} \tag{6.17}$$

Definition 6.8 *Merging is the process of combining two sets of partial bindings such that for any two sets B_1 and B_2,*

$$\begin{aligned} \text{Merge}(B_1, B_2) = \{&\text{Combine}(pb_1, pb_2) \mid \exists (pb_1, pb_2) \in B_1 \times B_2: \\ &\text{Compatible}(pb_1, pb_2)\} \end{aligned} \tag{6.18}$$

Definition 6.9 *$PB(exp, tok_{val})$ is the partial binding obtained by matching an expression exp with a token value tok_{val}. If they do not match, then $PB(exp, tok_{val}) = \perp$.*

Algorithm 6.2 lists the steps for determining the enabled bindings for a particular transition. It is a modified version of the algorithm proposed by kristensen and

Algorithm 6.2 GetBindings(PBB(t))

```
Data: PBB(t)
Result: The set of bindings enabled
C ← φ
foreach E(p, t) ∈ PBB(t) do
    if p ∈ P_port then continue
    C′ ← φ
    foreach c ∈ M(p) do
        b′ ← PB(E(p, t), c)
        if b′ ≠ ⊥ then
            C′ ← C′ ⋃ {b′}
        end
    end
    C ← Merge(C, C′)
end
foreach b ∈ C do
    foreach v ∈ FV(t) do
        if b(v) = ⊥ then
            b(v) ← c_param;
        end
    end
end
C ← {b ∈ C | G(t)⟨b⟩}
C ← {b ∈ C | ∀p ∈ P_in(t) : p ∉ P_port ∧ E(p, t)⟨b⟩ ⊆ M(p)}
return C
```

christensen [20] and can now handle port places. The loop in steps 2 to 12 fetches each pattern $E(p,t)$ from PBB(t) and computes the associated partial binding C' by comparing the pattern with the tokens in the corresponding input place p. However, as shown in step 3, the pattern is not compared if p is a port place. This follows from the fact that a port can have disparate markings obtained from its associated sockets. Before considering the next pattern, this partial binding is then merged with the current partial binding C.

The set of partial bindings obtained is then processed in a loop (steps 13 to 19) wherein each unassigned free variable in a binding is attached to a unique parameter. As described later, this allows ports to have generic tokens that can be assigned values from any token supplied by a socket. The value of an FVv in a binding b is contained in $b(v)$ (steps 15 and 16).

Finally, the bindings in C are subjected to the guard condition in step 20 in order to filter out any bindings in conflict. Furthermore, if the pattern in PBB(t) does not include an input arc expression $E(p,t)\,:\; p \notin P_{\text{port}}$, the corresponding input place p is checked (step 21) to ensure that it contains the minimum number of tokens required.

Algorithm 6.3 shows the various steps for generating all possible initial markings that enable a module. The single most important thing to do before exploring a model is to populate its input ports with generic tokens. In this pursuit, the set of output transitions for all port places are determined (in step 2), and their enabled bindings are ascertained (steps 4 to 7) using Algorithm 6.2. Thereafter the marking for each port place p is modified to contain additional tokens (steps 8 to 10). Each additional token added to a port corresponds to the result of evaluating its arc expression with an enabled binding.

To generate all possible parameterized reachability graphs for a module, all legitimate combinations of initial markings are produced (steps 12 to 33) and sent to Algorithm 6.4 for processing (step 19). Prior to generating these combinations, the loop in steps 13 to 17 store each input port $p \in P^{m}_{\text{inport}}$ in an array *ports*[] (step 14), while the number of tokens in it is stored in *tokenCount*[] (step 15). Furthermore, the number of possible initial markings for a port is stored in *activeTokens*[]. A port with x tokens can accept either of $0, 1, 2, \ldots, x$ tokens from a socket initially. The number of ways in which it can accept these tokens is

$$ {}^{x}C_0 + {}^{x}C_1 + {}^{x}C_2 + \cdots + {}^{x}C_x = 2^{x} \tag{6.19} $$

Consequently, *activeTokens*[] is defined as $2^{tokenCount[]}$ in step 16.

Thereafter the algorithm executes a loop (steps 18 to 33), wherein M_0 is assigned with all possible combinations of tokens at each of its port places. Considering that the port places in M_0 were initialized with all possible tokens that enable one or more bindings (steps 8 to 10), the required combinations are obtained by successive removal of tokens from these places, starting with the lowest index of array *ports*[]. A port place with x tokens is assumed to have them numbered $1, 2, \ldots, x$. At each step, the value of *activeTokens*[] for the lowest index of *ports* is decreased (step 22) and the tokens in it are selected using the function *onlyTokens*( ) (step 23).

Algorithm 6.3 Explore(*m*)

```
Data: Module m
Result: A module is explored to generate its reachability graph
Tran ← φ
foreach p∈P^m_port do Tran ← Tran ⋃ T_out(p)
foreach t ∈ Tran do
    foreach p∈P_in(t) do
        if PATTERN(E(p,t)) then PBB(t) ← PBB(t) ⋃ E(p,t)
    end
    C ← GetBindings(PBB(t))
    foreach b∈C do
        foreach p∈P^m_port∧p∈P_in(t) do M_0(p) ← M_0(p) ⋃ E(p,t)⟨b⟩
    end
end
i ←0
foreach p∈P_port do
    ports[i] ← p
    tokenCount[i] ← M_0(p).numOfTokens()
    activeTokens[i++] ← 2^tokenCount[i]
end
while activeTokens[i-1]!=0 do
    Process(M_0)
    j ← 0
    if activeTokens[j]!=0 then
        activeTokens[j] = activeTokens[j] − 1
        M_0(ports[j]).onlyTokens(activeTokens[j])
    else
        while activeTokens[j]!=0 & j<i do j++
        if j≥i then break
        activeTokens[j] = activeTokens[j] − 1
        M_0(ports[j]).onlyTokens(activeTokens[j])
        foreach k∈ [0···j − 1] do
            activeTokens[k] = 2^tokenCount[k]
            M_0(ports[k]).onlyTokens(activeTokens[k])
        end
    end
end
```

This function selects the set of tokens numbered $\{n_1, n_2, \ldots, n_k\}$ out of all tokens in *ports*[*j*] such that

$$2^{n_1} + 2^{n_2} + \cdots + 2^{n_k} = activeTokens[j] \tag{6.20}$$

Algorithm 6.4 Process(M_0)

```
Data: Initial state
Result: Generate reachability graph and access table
foreach p∈P^m_inport do accessTable.insertInPort(M0(p))
Unprocessed ← {(M0, "")}
Nodes ← {M0}
while !Unprocessed.empty() do
    (M, conditions) ← Unprocessed.getNextMarking()
    foreach ((t,b),M') such that M[(t,b)⟩M' do
        if !Nodes.contains(M') then
            Nodes.add(M')
            Unprocessed.add((M',conditions))
            if p∈P_outport∧p∈P_out(t) then
                accessTable.insertOutPort(M'(p),conditions)
            end
        end
    end
    b_param=conditions
    foreach ((t,b)^ParaCond,?) such that M[(t,b)^ParaCond⟩? do
        foreach E(p,t)∈ParaCond do
            if E(p,t)⟨b_p⟩=true then b_param=Combine(b_param,b_p)
        end
        if G(t)∈ParaCond & G(t)⟨b_p⟩=true then b_param=Combine(b_param,b_p)
        foreach E(t,p)∈ParaCond do
            if E(t,p)⟨b_p⟩=true & M[(t,b_p)⟩M' then
                Unprocessed.add((M',Combine(b_param,b_p)))
                Node.add(M')
                if p∈P_outport then
                accessTable.insertOutPort(M'(p),Combine(b_param,b_p))
            end
        end
    end
end
```

The function *onlyTokens* is computationally linear because it simply involves checking the value of the nth bit in *activeTokens*[j]. If it is 1, the token numbered n is included in the marking. The function is listed in Algorithm 6.5. The function $x >> i$ returns the ith bit of x. Step 3 always checks the first bit of *activeTokens*[j], which is eliminated in step 6 using an integer division. This operation recursively reduces the value of *activeTokens*[j] and thereby ensures that the algorithm eventually terminates.

Returning to Algorithm 6.3, when the value of *activeTokens*[] for the lowest index of *ports*[] becomes 0, its values for higher indices are polled until a nonzero value

Algorithm 6.5 *onlyTokens(activeTokens)*

```
Data: The value in activeTokens (NOT the reference)
Result: Select the tokens corresponding to this value
i ←1;
while activeTokens!=0 do
    if activeTokens>>1 == 1 then
        include token numbered i in M0;
    end
    activeTokens←activeTokens / 2;
    i++;
end
```

is found (step 25). The value of *activeTokens*[] at this index is decreased (steps 27 and 28) and its value is restored at all lower indices (steps 29 to 32) to establish the next possible combination. This is continued until the value of *activeTokens* for the highest index becomes 0, indicating that none of the port places have any tokens (step 18). Each initial marking obtained is sent to Algorithm 6.4 for processing (step 19).

Algorithm 6.4 shows the steps for generating the parameterized reachability graph corresponding to an initial marking. It also adds new entries into the access table corresponding to the module.

When an initial marking is passed into the algorithm, the tokens at each input port place are written into the access table as a new entry (step 1). Thereafter the sets *Unprocessed* and *Nodes* are initialized as shown in steps 2 and 3. In addition to the initial marking, each entry in *Unprocessed* contains a field to store the conditions that must be satisfied to reach the marking. This condition is the specific value that needs to be assigned to a subset of parameters to reach a marking. Since there is no condition to reach the initial marking, it is left empty in step 2.

The algorithm executes a loop (steps 4 to 30) to process the markings in *Unprocessed* until it is empty. At any marking, there could be two possible cases:

- A transition does not require a parameter to have a specific value in order to get enabled. Furthermore, the result of execution of the transition does not depend on any of the parameters. This case is illustrated using transition *case1* in Figure 6.11 and is handled by the algorithm in steps 6 to 14.
- The transition requires one or more parameters to be bound to specific values either to get enabled or to determine the result of its execution. This case is illustrated using transition *case2* in Figure 6.11 and is handled by the algorithm in steps 15 to 26.

In the first case, binding b for transition t is found, which leads to a new marking M'. The set *Nodes* is scanned for M' and its absence ensures that the state was not explored previously. To process a new marking, it is added to *Unprocessed* along

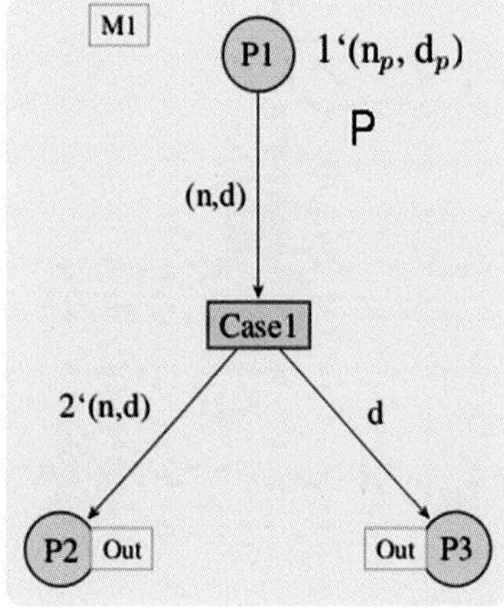

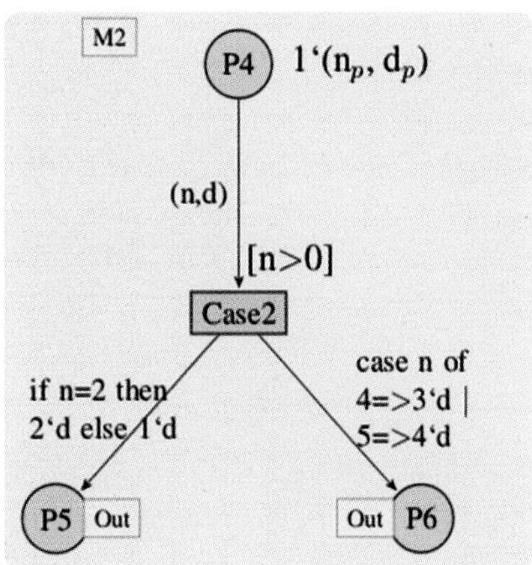

FIGURE 6.11 Two possible cases when generating a parameterized reachability graph.

with the conditions that needs to be satisfied to reach that marking. Furthermore, if the new marking adds any tokens to an output port, it is reflected in the access table.

The processing is similar in the second case, with the exception that the new marking M' cannot be determined unless the conditions are resolved. Consequently, it is represented using a "?" symbol in step 16. Furthermore, *ParaCond* is assigned with the set of conditions associated with t that requires assigning specific values to at least one parameter. The subset of parameters that have already been assigned values are fetched from conditions in step 15. A condition in *ParaCond* could be either an input arc expression, an output arc expression, or a guard condition. For input arc expressions, specific values are assigned to parameters until they all evaluate to true (steps 17 to 19). If necessary, required values are assigned to additional parameters until the guard condition evaluates to *true* (step 20). The condition on output arcs is checked thereafter. Since the output arc expressions can contain one or more nested if/switch or case conditions, a different value of bindings leads to a different new marking M'. Each of these markings is stored in *Unprocessed* along with the condition (step 23). The latter is updated to contain the values that were assigned to the parameters. Furthermore, if any of the output places is a port, the contents are written into the access table (step 25). The entry added to the access table when both $P5$ and $P6$ in Figure 6.11 are output port places is shown in Table 6.13.

6.5.5 Additional Memory Cost for Storing Access Tables and Parameterized Reachability Graphs

As observed earlier, each module has an access table that is used by a substitution transition to determine the result of its execution. The rows in this table comprise a combination of bindings that enable the output transitions of the input port places. Consider a module M with the output transitions of input port places in TS^M_{out}, where

$$TS^M_{\text{out}} = \{t_1, t_2, t_3, \ldots, t_{x-1}, t_x\} \tag{6.21}$$

TABLE 6.13 Entry in Access Table for Module $M2$

Conditions			Output Port	
if $n > 0$?	if $n = 2$?	Case n of	$P5$	$P6$
Yes	Yes	2 =≥	2‘d	Empty
No	No	4 =≥	1‘d	3‘d
		5 =≥	1‘d	4‘d
		—	Empty	Empty

For simplicity, we consider these transitions to be independent. This allows a transition in TS^M_{out} to be enabled for a binding irrespective of other transitions. Suppose that a transition t_i in TS^M_{out} is enabled by nb^{t_i} bindings. Therefore, the number of possible combinations in which these bindings can enable t_i is

$$^{nb^{t_i}}C_1 + {}^{nb^{t_i}}C_2 + \cdots + {}^{nb^{t_i}}C_{nb^{t_i}} \tag{6.22}$$

Equation (6.22) follows from the fact that any one or more of these bindings can enable the transition. However, the only way of not enabling the transition would be to use none of these bindings, as shown in the equation.

$$^{nb^{t_i}}C_0 \tag{6.23}$$

The total number of combinations in which a transition can be either enabled or disabled is the sum of equations (6.22) and (6.23):

$$^{nb^{t_i}}C_0 + {}^{nb^{t_i}}C_1 + {}^{nb^{t_i}}C_2 + \cdots + {}^{nb^{t_i}}C_{nb^{t_i}} \tag{6.24}$$

or

$$2^{nb^{t_i}} \tag{6.25}$$

Enabling a module requires enabling any one of the transitions in TS^M_{out}. This in turn requires at least one transition in TS^M_{out} to use an enabling binding. Therefore, the total combination of bindings that would enable a module would be all possible combinations except the one that disables all transitions in TS^M_{out}.

$$\text{TOT}_M = \left\{ 2^{nb^{t_1}} 2^{nb^{t_2}} \cdots 2^{nb^{t_x}} - 1 \right. \tag{6.26}$$

$$\left\{ 2^{nb^{t_1} + nb^{t_2} + \cdots + nb^{t_x}} - 1 \right. \tag{6.27}$$

This is nothing but the number of entries in an access table. If each entry occupies α space, the total memory needed to store the access table would be $\text{TOT}_M \cdot \alpha$.

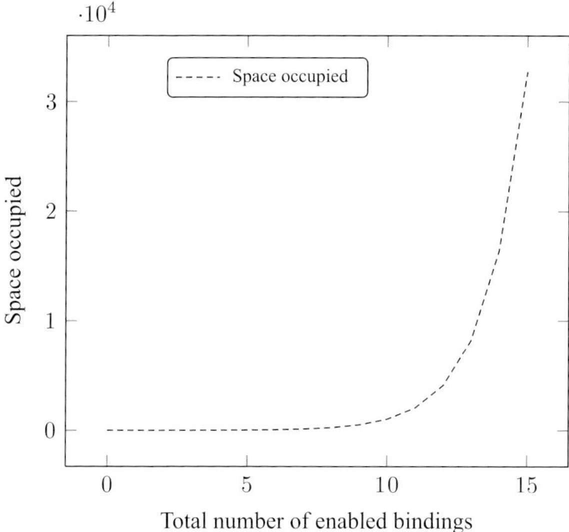

FIGURE 6.12 Space occupied by an access table increases with the number of enabling bindings.

Figure 6.12 shows the increase in the space requirement with an increase in the number of bindings enabled. Considering the sharp rise in the curve, our technique might not be suitable for modules that have a large number of output transitions for input port places. Each row of the access table is associated with a parameterized reachability graph that also requires additional memory. When the substitution transition uses a particular row of an access table, the corresponding parameterized reachability graph is also fetched. This is done to account for the states that could be reached when actually executing the module.

When a substitution transition fetches a parameterized reachability graph, it assigns the parameters to determine the new states. These states are then stored in memory for detecting duplicate states (as explained in Chapter 5). If a particular row of the access table is used only once by the substitution transition, each state in the parameterized reachability graph has a counterpart in memory (after assigning values). Therefore, the memory required is twice what it would be otherwise. However, if the row is accessed twice, each state in the parameterized reachability graph would have two other counterparts in memory. Therefore, an additional 1.5 times memory is required in this case. In general, the percentage of additional memory required would decrease with an increase in the average use of parameterized reachability graphs. This is shown in Figure 6.13.

6.5.6 Theoretical Evaluation of the Reduction in Delay

The technique presented here reduces the delay in model checking by exploring modules in parallel. However, the degree of reduction depends on a range of factors.

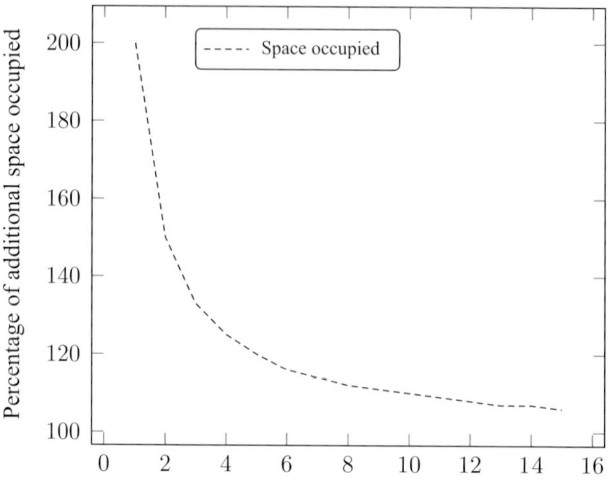

FIGURE 6.13 Percentage of additional space occupied decreases with an increase in the use of parameterized reachability graphs.

For example, if (1) the root module does not have any enabled transitions and (2) the tokens in its socket places do not enable any submodule, the delay in model checking might increase. This is essentially because the access tables and parameterized reachability graph for each submodule would be created anyway. In this section we evaluate the reduction in delay offered by the technique presented.

Consider a row i in the access table for module M whose parameterized reachability graph was derived in time x. When a substitution transition uses this row, it also fetches the associated parameterized reachability graph to assign the parameters and determine new states. Considering that this does not require executing any transitions, the time required should be a fraction of x $(= \beta x : 0 < \beta < 1)$. Without using our technique, the substitution transition could have executed the transitions in the submodule and determined the new states in time x. Therefore, the difference in time delay is

$$x - (x + \beta x + \alpha) = -(\beta x + \alpha) \tag{6.28}$$

where α is the time to access a row in the access table. The negative result indicates that the delay has increased when using our technique. However, if the row i is accessed twice, the difference in the time delay is

$$2x - (x + 2\beta x + 2\alpha) = x - 2(\beta x + \alpha) \tag{6.29}$$

Considering that β and α are substantially smaller than x, equation (6.29) should yield a positive difference in delay. The value of β that ensures a positive difference in delay is derived using equations (6.30) to (6.33). From equation (6.29), a positive difference in delay requires that

$$x - 2(\beta x + \alpha) > 0 \tag{6.30}$$

or

$$x(2\beta - 1) < -2\alpha \tag{6.31}$$

Since β and α are positive constants and x is a positive variable, equation (6.31) holds iff

$$2\beta - 1 < 0 \tag{6.32}$$

or

$$\beta < \frac{1}{2} \tag{6.33}$$

In general, as shown in equations (6.34) and (6.35), the difference in delay follows an identical pattern, as more substitution transitions use row i.

$$3x - (x + 3\beta x + 3\alpha) = 2x - 3(\beta x + \alpha) \tag{6.34}$$

$$cx - (x + c\beta x + c\alpha) = (c - 1)x - c(\beta x + \alpha) \tag{6.35}$$

The general equation (6.35) returns a positive difference in delay when

$$x(c - 1) - c(\beta x + \alpha) > 0 \tag{6.36}$$

or

$$x(c\beta - c + 1) < -c\alpha \tag{6.37}$$

Since β, α, and c are positive constants and x is a positive variable, equation (6.37) holds iff

$$c\beta - c + 1 < 0 \tag{6.38}$$

or

$$\beta < \frac{c - 1}{c} : c > 0 \tag{6.39}$$

Equation (6.39) justifies the negative difference of delay in equation (6.28) when $c = 1$. Furthermore, equation (6.42) renders the value of β for which equation (6.35) is strictly increasing:

$$\frac{d}{dx}((c-1)x - c\beta x - c\alpha) > 0 \tag{6.40}$$

or

$$c - 1 - c\beta > 0 \tag{6.41}$$

or

$$\beta < \frac{c-1}{c} : c > 0 \tag{6.42}$$

The conditions for a positive difference in delay and its strict increase in value are found to be the same.

To determine the *O( )* function, we consider a model with m modules which are used M times (in some combination) during the state-space analysis. If the average probability of using module K_i during state-space analysis is $p(i)$, it is used $Mp(i)$ times in total. Using equation (6.35), the total time taken by module K_i can be calculated as

$$T_i = x_i + Mp(i)\beta_i x_i + Mp(i)\alpha_i \tag{6.43}$$

where the symbols have their usual meaning and the subscripts denote the module number. Consequently, the total time taken for state-space exploration is

$$T = T_1 + T_2 + \cdots + T_m \tag{6.44}$$

$$= \sum_{i=1}^{m} x_i + M \sum_{i=1}^{m} p(i)\beta_i x_i + M \sum_{i=1}^{m} p(i)\alpha_i \tag{6.45}$$

Since in most cases the modules of a model would be heavily used,

$$M \sum_{i=1}^{m} p(i)\beta_i x_i >>> \sum_{i=1}^{m} x_i \tag{6.46}$$

where $>>>$ denotes *far exceeds*. Furthermore, since the time for executing a module (x_i) far exceeds the time to read the access table (α_i),

$$M \sum_{i=1}^{m} p(i)\beta_i x_i >>> M \sum_{i=1}^{m} p(i)\alpha_i \tag{6.47}$$

Therefore, the expression in equation (6.45) that determines the delay is

$$M \sum_{i=1}^{m} p(i)\beta_i x_i \tag{6.48}$$

Considering that M and β are constant for a model, the total time depends essentially on the product of probability and the time of execution for each module. Consequently,

$$T = O(px) \tag{6.49}$$

6.6 EXPERIMENTAL RESULTS

An implementation of the model checker is described in this section for evaluating the technique for time-efficient state-space analysis. Instead of a full-fledged model checker, a cut-down version of the full implementation is described, and this will handle only integer color sets. Furthermore, the model checker assumes that the value in each token will be 1. Such a setup simplifies the experiment without capitulating any advantages offered by a model checker. The results obtained from CPN Tools [18] have been used as a benchmark for comparison. To ensure a fair comparison, both model checkers explore the same HCPN model (which is shown in Figure 6.14).

Experimental Setup. The model checker is implemented using Java (Standard Edition, Runtime Environment Version 6) programming language. The object model is created using the Eclipse Modeling Framework (EMF) [1], which generates Java classes for the model, in addition to representing it structurally. It also generates a set of adapter classes that enable viewing and command-based editing of the model.

Figure 6.15 illustrates the object model that contains the classes corresponding to the various elements in a CPN model. These classes need to be instantiated and their properties initialized before the CPN model can be model-checked. In this pursuit, we created an importer that accepts a CPN model as an XML document and parses it to instantiate these classes. However, it is also possible to instantiate these classes

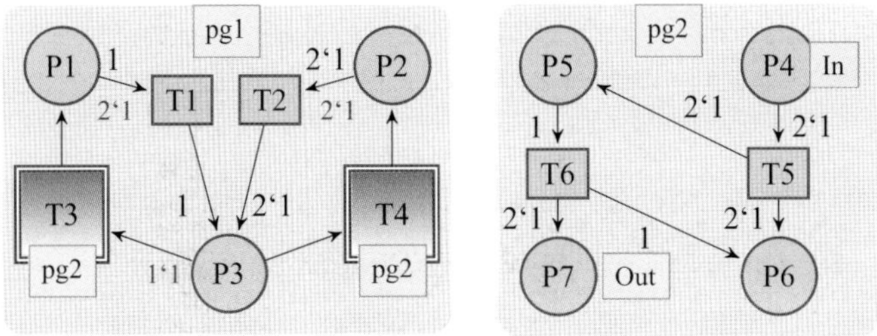

FIGURE 6.14 HCPN model used for evaluation.

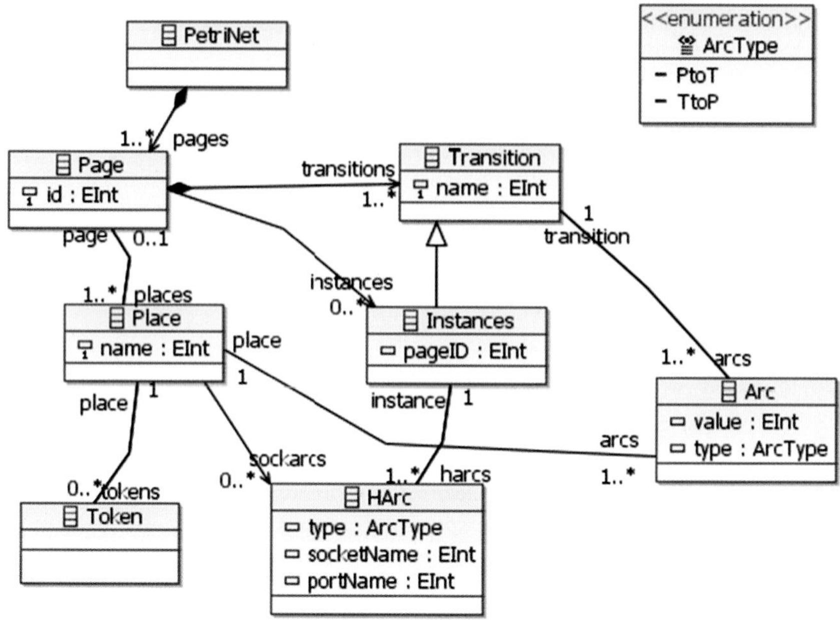

FIGURE 6.15 Object model implementation using EMF.

programmatically and assign their properties. All attempts have been made to ensure that the object model is similar to that of Access/CPN [26]. Such a similarity ensures the portability of a CPN model from our implementation into CPN Tools [18].

The class corresponding to a petri net is known as *PetriNet* and sits at the top of the hierarchy. It can have one or more *Pages*, each corresponding to a module. A *Page*, in turn, has one or more *Places* and *Transitions*. Additionally, it can have any number of *Instances*, the CPN Tools' equivalent of substitution transition and a subclass of *Transition*.

Each arc has a corresponding class that stores its arc expression and arc type. Since we consider only integer tokens, the arc expression is always an integer. An arc type could be either *PtoT* or *TtoP*, defined by the enumeration *ArcType*. The class *HArc* corresponds to arcs connecting a place and an instance. In addition to arc type, it has the name of its adjoining socket place and the port place associated with it. The arc value is not stored, as it holds no significance in this context. Furthermore, the class *Token* corresponds to a token in a CPN model. For simplicity, the value of each token is assumed to be 1.

Results. The HCPN model shown in Figure 6.14 is explored by the aforesaid model checkers to produce the results. As required by the simplifications in our implementation, all the places in this model have an integer color set and all tokens in them have the value 1.

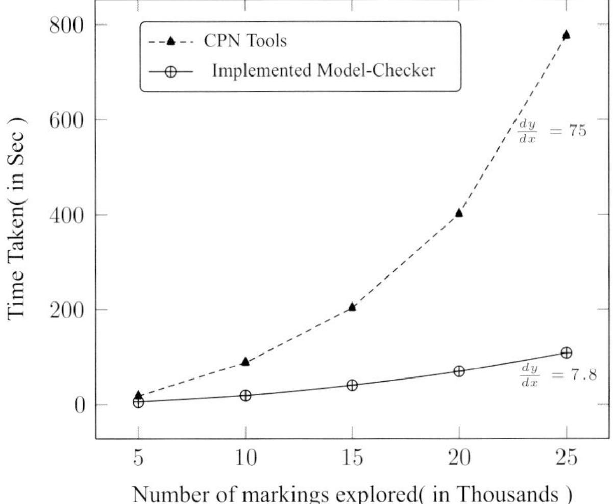

FIGURE 6.16 Time taken for model checking the HCPN model shown in Figure 6.14.

Figure 6.16 compares the time taken in model-checking the HCPN model, both with and without using our time-efficient state-space analysis technique. The latter is obtained using CPN Tools, currently the default model-checking tool for HCPN models. While the x-axis records the number of markings generated (in thousands), the time taken to generate them is accounted for along the y-axis. Considering that the model has an infinite state space, the plots are restricted to the time taken in generating the first 25,000 unique markings.

Figure 6.16 clearly exhibits the time reduction offered by our time-efficient technique. Compared to CPN Tools, the model checker implemented offers a massive 86% reduction for generating the first 25,000 markings. Considering that the slope for its plot (= 7.8) is one-tenth that for CPN Tools (= 75), the reduction offered would only increase as more markings are generated.

The technique presented requires some additional memory to store access tables and parameterized reachability graphs. This memory is insignificant compared with the memory occupied by the state space of a HCPN model. Consequently, the cost of this additional memory is not accounted for.

6.7 DISCUSSION

The experimental results indicate a massive reduction in time requirements when using the implemented model checker. Considering that these algorithms do not make any assumptions about the value in tokens or the data type(or color) of places, a full-fledged model checker incorporating our algorithm is also expected to deliver an identical reduction.

TABLE 6.14 Access Table for *pg2*

Input Port, *P4*	Conditions	Output Port, *P7*
2‘1	—	4‘1

The example HCPN in Figure 6.14 has two modules, *pg1* and *pg2*. When using the algorithms, an access table and a parameterized reachability graph are created for *pg2*. No such tables or graphs are created for *pg1* because the model does not have a module that is dependent on it.

The substitution transitions *T3* and *T4* execute by probing the access table for *pg2*, shown in Table 6.14. This in turn prevents *T5* and *T6* from firing and accounts for the reduction in time the requirement. As discussed previously, there is an additional memory requirement to store the access table and parameterized reachability graphs. However, this being a very small model, the additional space requirement was negligibly small and could not be measured and taken into account. Furthermore, the additional space need not necessarily be measured even for larger models. This is because the memory occupied by the access table and parameterized reachability graph is static and does not change as the state space is explored.

As observed previously, state-space exploration involves determining the reachable states of the system and investigating them for a set of undesirable properties. To ensure efficiency, the model checker maintains a list of states explored and rejects any duplicate state. The *x*-axis in Figure 6.16 accounts only for unique states of the system that were reached by the model checker. However, its *y*-axis accounts for the time in producing both unique and duplicate markings. This is because a model checker needs to generate a marking and compare it with the states stored before determining if it is new. Regardless of the technique used for this comparison, the model checker spends time in processing duplicate states. Therefore, a surge in duplicate markings would lead to a rapid increase in the *y*-coordinate, propelling a steep increase in the slope of the associated curve. For large models, the algorithm presented offers a massive reduction, owing to its ability to reduce the time requirement for producing duplicate and unique markings alike.

6.8 SUMMARY

In this chapter we described a technique to reduce the time requirement for model-checking a hierarchical model. The reduction obtained is attributed to generating the reachability graph for each module in parallel. Compared to CPN Tools experimental results indicate a time reduction of 86% when generating the first 25,000 states. The technique is found to have a very small time overhead, negligible for practical situations, at the expense of a small increase in the memory requirement. Considering the inherent complexities of modern software systems, more and more model checkers ought to embrace a hierarchical representation to ensure multiple levels of abstraction. The algorithm presented addresses a niche for such systems.

REFERENCES

1. *Eclipse Modeling Framework (EMF)*, July 2010.
2. R. Alur. Formal analysis of hierarchical state machines. In *Verification: Theory and Practice*, volume 2772 of *Lecture Notes in Computer Science*, pages 434–435. Springer-Verlag, Berlin, 2004.
3. R. Alur and M. Yannakakis. Model checking of hierarchical state machines. *ACM Transactions on Programming Languages and Systems*, 23(3):273–303, 2001.
4. J. A. Bondy and U. S. R Murty. *Graph Theory*. Springer-Verlag, Berlin, 2008.
5. S. Christensen, L. M. Kristensen, and T. Mailund. A sweep-line method for state space exploration. In *Proceedings of the 7th International Conference on Tools and Algorithms for the Construction and Analysis of Systems*, TACAS 2001, pages 450–464, 2001.
6. S. Christensen and L. Petrucci. Modular state space analysis of colored petri nets. In *Proceedings of the 16th International Conference on Application and Theory of Petri Nets*, ICATPN 1995, pages 201–217. Springer-Verlag, Berlin, 1995.
7. E. M. Clarke, E. A. Emerson, S. Jha, and A. P. Sistla. Symmetry reductions in model checking. In *Computer Aided Verification*, volume 1427 of *Lecture Notes in Computer Science*, pages 147–158. Springer-Verlag, Berlin, 1998.
8. E. Clarke, O. Grumberg, and D. Peled. *Model Checking*. MIT Press, Cambridge, MA, 2000.
9. A. David and M. O. Möller. From HUPPAAL to UPPAAL: a translation from hierarchical timed automata to flat timed automata. *Research Series RS-01-11*, BRICS, Department of Computer Science, University of Aarhus, Denmark, March 2001.
10. L. Elgaard. *The Symmetry Method for Colored Petri Nets: Theory, Tools and Practical Use*. Ph.D. dissertation, University of Aarhus, Denmark, 2002.
11. E. A. Emerson and A. P. Sistla. Symmetry and model checking. *Formal Methods in System Design*, 9(1–2):105–131, 1996.
12. S. Evangelista and J.- F. Pradat-Peyre. On the computation of stubborn sets of colored petri nets. In *Proceedings of the 27th International Conference on Application and Theory of Petri Nets*, ICATPN '06, pages 146–165. Springer-Verlag, Berlin, 2006.
13. S. Evangelista and J.- F. Pradat-Peyre. Memory efficient state space storage in explicit software model checking. In *Proceedings of the 12th International SPIN Workshop on Model Checking of Software*, volume 3639 of *Lecture Notes in Computer Science*, pages 43–57. Springer-Verlag, Berlin, 2005.
14. P. Godefroid. *Partial-Order Methods for the Verification of Concurrent Systems: An Approach to the State-Explosion Problem*. Springer-Verlag, New York, 1996.
15. G. Gueta, C. Flanagan, E. Yahav, and M. Sagiv. Cartesian partial-order reduction. In *Proceedings of the 14th International SPIN Conference on Model Checking Software*, pages 95–112, 2007.
16. K. Jensen. *Colored Petri Nets: Basic Concepts, Analysis Methods and Practical Use*, volumes 1–3. Springer-Verlag, Berlin, 1996.

17. K. Jensen and L. M. Kristensen. *Colored Petri Nets: Modelling and Validation of Concurrent Systems*. Springer-Verlag, Berlin, 2009.

18. K. Jensen, L. M. Kristensen, and L. Wells. Colored petri nets and CPN tools for modelling and validation of concurrent systems. *International Journal of Software Tools for Technology Transfer*, 9(3):213–254, 2007.

19. J. Köbler, U. Schöning, and J. Torán. *The Graph Isomorphism Problem: Its Structural Complexity*. Birkhauser Verlag, Basel, Switzerland, 1993.

20. L. M. Kristensen and S. Christensen. Implementing colored petri nets using a functional programming language. *Higher-Order and Symbolic Computation*, 17(3):207–243, 2004.

21. L. M. Kristensen and A. Valmari. Finding stubborn sets of colored petri nets without unfolding. In *Proceedings of the 19th International Conference on Application and Theory of Petri Nets*, ICATPN '98, pages 104–123. Springer-Verlag, Berlin, 1998.

22. S. Leue and G. Holzmann. v-promela: a visual, object-oriented language for spin. In *Proceedings of the 2nd IEEE International Symposium on Object-Oriented Real-Time Distributed Computing*, ISORC '99, page 14. IEEE Computer Society, Washington, DC, 1999.

23. K. McMillan. *SMV Manual*, November 2000.

24. A. Mukherjee, Z. Tari, and P. Bertok. Memory efficient state-space analysis in software model-checking. In *33-rd Australasian Computer Science Conference, ACSC*. Australian Computer Society, Darlinghurst, Autralia, 2010.

25. A. Tanenbaum. *Computer Networks*. Prentice Hall, Upper Saddle River, NJ, 2002.

26. M. Westergaard and L. Kristensen. Two interfaces to the CPN tools simulator. *In Proceedings of the 9th Workshop and Tutorial on Practical Use of Colored Petri Nets and the CPN Tools, CPN'08*, October 2008.

CHAPTER 7

GENERATING HIERARCHICAL MODELS BY IDENTIFYING STRUCTURAL SIMILARITIES

Model checking requires formulating a formal representation of a system prior to verifying it. Considering the parallel components in a service composition, this translation often leads to an enormous increase in the size of the representation obtained, which eventually becomes a computational bottleneck in model-checking algorithms. Such a massive model is difficult to draw and impractical to analyze and maintain [9]. Consequently, it is prone to errors and omissions that impair the benefits of model checking. Furthermore, the lack of abstraction and classification in such voluminous formal models prevents a human modeler from developing a thorough understanding.

To obtain a more succinct representation with multiple levels of abstraction, any system needs to embrace the notion of hierarchy [2]. In a hierarchical setup, each system component is represented by a module wherein the module for a high-level component refers to its underlying components using their module name or reference. Apart from rendering an elegant, abstract, and expressive model, such a setup also makes it possible to avoid a state-space explosion by applying *compositional model checking* [8].

In this chapter we describe a *decrease-and-conquer*-based method for installing hierarchy into an otherwise "flat" model. This method involves determining

Verification of Communication Protocols in Web Services: Model-Checking Service Compositions, First Edition. Zahir Tari, Peter Bertok, Anshuman Mukherjee.

structurally similar components in a flat model and creating a module for each of them. A decrease-and-conquer-based strategy breaks the bigger problem into a set of smaller problems, and the solutions to smaller problems are combined to solve the original problem. Apart from the aforementioned benefits, such a method also helps to extend the time-efficient state-space analysis technique presented in Chapter 6 for nonhierarchical models. The experimental results indicate a linear time complexity, $O(n)$, where n is the number of nodes in the flat model. Furthermore, as opposed to the related techniques [3,10,12], the decrease-and-conquer method ensures that the transformed model is equivalent to the original model.

7.1 MOTIVATION

Model checking is an automatic verification technique that is rapidly being embraced for quality assurance of software systems. However, for verification, a model checker requires formal representation of a system. Considering that the components in a *component-based system* [16] could be nested arbitrarily, such a representation would be much too large for human comprehension. A large model would be difficult to draw and impractical to analyze and maintain [14]. *Model* is used synonymously with *formal representation*. The crux of the problem is the set of nested components that require representation of a low-level component to be added once for each overlaid component that is using it.

Alternatively, a model could be constituted out of a set of modules wherein each module represents a system component. In such a hierarchical setup, the module for a high-level component refers to its underlying components using their module name or reference. This avoids an acute increase in model size, owing to the inclusion underlying components in actual representation. Furthermore, the benefits increase with each additional high-level component sharing an underlying component. Consequently, the model obtained would be significantly more succinct, owing to the notion of hierarchy introduced. In addition, modifying a component would only require altering the corresponding module.

Recently there have been a number of attempts in autogenerating the formal representation of software systems [5,11]. The primary objective in autogenerating a model is to produce the input for a model checker. Regardless of the structure of input (flat or hierarchical), the model checker verifies the system under deliberation. Consequently, these tools often render flat models, as there is limited incentive in introducing hierarchy. However, the model rendered might assist in accomplishing additional objectives, such as identifying the overall architecture of the system, understanding its dependencies, visualizing the flow of information through it, identifying its capabilities and limitations, and calculating its complexity [7]. Nevertheless, it might be impossible to scrutinize the flat model because of its massive size. In this chapter we present methods for accomplishing these additional objectives by introducing hierarchy into a flat model and rendering it exponentially more succinct.

Some solutions based on *pre-* [12] and *post-agglomeration* [10,12] reduce the size of a model by merging some sequential events. However, these reduction techniques address primarily the problem of state-space explosion [6] by reducing the number of execution traces to be analyzed. Consequently, the technique itself, as well as the reduction it offers, depend on the property to be analyzed when exploring the state space. Furthermore, the reduced model obtained using these solutions differs from the original model. In Chapters 5 and 6 we described techniques to alleviate the state-space explosion problem. Subsequently, the solution presented here installs hierarchy into a given model to obtain an equivalent concise model.

The method described has two distinct parts: (1) a *lookup method*, which identifies the set of structurally similar components in a model, and (2) *a clustering method*, which establishes a hierarchy thereupon. The former is based on the decrease-and-conquer [20] strategy, in which the bigger problem is broken into smaller problems, and the solutions to smaller problems are combined to solve the original problem. Consequently, it starts by identifying the smallest components in a model that are identical. Thereafter it progressively determines the larger components by recursively attaching the adjoining elements of the identical components determined in the preceding step and comparing them for similarity. This translates, in effect, to identifying the fine-grained components in the system followed by the determination of their overlaying components bottom-up. Later, to establish a hierarchy, these components are mapped into modules by the clustering method.

A decrease-and-conquer algorithm requires the solution of at least one subproblem in order to use it and determine the solution of larger problems. This is different from the divide-and-conquer technique, in which a the solution of several subproblems is required. Considering the ease in determining and solving the smallest subproblem of the original problem, decrease-and-conquer has been selected as the appropriate design technique. The technique for solving the smallest problem is included in the lookup method.

The innovative ideas of this chapter can be summarized as follows:

- The *lookup method* identifies the structurally similar components of a model. Essentially it identifies the identical components in a model that would be used for creating individual modules of an equivalent hierarchical model. The algorithm for this method has a linear time complexity for sufficiently large CPN models (up to 141 places and 132 transitions).
- The *clustering method* establishes hierarchy over a flat model by forking a module out of each identical component identified by the lookup method. This is elaborated only in the context of establishing hierarchy in colored petri net models.

Although a wide array of languages are available to model a software system, each model-checking tool essentially supports only a specific modeling language. Some common modeling languages, along with the model-checking tool supported, are Promela for SPIN [1], the C programming language for BLAST [4], and colored petri nets for CPN Tools [15]. Considering the subtle differences between these modeling languages, it is difficult to come up with a generic method for installing hierarchy. Consequently, the lookup and clustering methods described in this chapter specifically target CPN models. These methods offer no additional advantage in using CPN models, and they can be adapted independently for any other language that defines a notion of hierarchy and structural similarity.

Throughout this chapter, a CPN or petri net model is sometimes referred to as a *net*, while their subparts are referred to as *subnets* or *components*. In Section 7.2 we introduce the problem and provides an insight into the solution. In Section 7.3 we introduce the basics of substitution transitions. Prior to proposing the lookup and clustering methods in Section 7.5, related work is compiled in Section 7.4. The various experimental results are plotted in Section 7.6 and discussed in Section 7.7. Finally, a summary of the chapter is given in Section 7.8.

7.2 OVERVIEW OF THE PROBLEM AND SOLUTION

As pointed out previously, a system needs to be modeled (using available modeling languages) prior to generating and analyzing its state space. This is a tedious and error-prone activity, but several methods enable autogeneration of formal representations of software systems [5,11]. However, the complex and concurrent components in contemporary systems lead to an enormous increase in model size. Many modeling languages support hierarchical constructs and offer multiple levels of abstraction. However, there are limited incentives in using a hierarchical modeling language and enhancing the human understandability and modularity of the model rendered. The primary objective in formalizing a system is to produce the input for a model-checking tool that is indifferent to the orientation and structure of the formal model. Nevertheless, we identify the advantages of introducing hierarchy and modularity in a formal model. A formal model might assist a human modeler in identifying the overall architecture of the system, understanding its dependencies, visualizing the flow of information through it, identifying its capabilities and limitations, and calculating its complexity [7]. However, the flat model produced by autogenerating techniques poses a serious challenge in accomplishing these objectives. In this chapter we describe a novel method for realizing these objectives by introducing hierarchy into a flat model and rendering it more succinct.

A software system is usually composed of a set of components, and on formalizing it using an autogenerating tool, the model rendered has footprints of the individual components [21]. Consequently, any effort to identify structurally similar subparts of the model should yield models corresponding to individual components. These models can thereupon be used to create the modules of a hierarchical model. This follows from an earlier discussion in Section 7.1, in which hierarchical models were shown to consist of modules corresponding to the components of a system.

Some of the steps in the method described are illustrated in Figure 7.1. Initially, the flat model is scrutinized to determine the set of identical subparts. These correspond to the components of the overlying system. Nevertheless, modeling this system directly using a hierarchical formalism will render a representation consisting of modules corresponding to each of the components. Consequently, the flat model could be transformed into its equivalent hierarchical model by creating modules

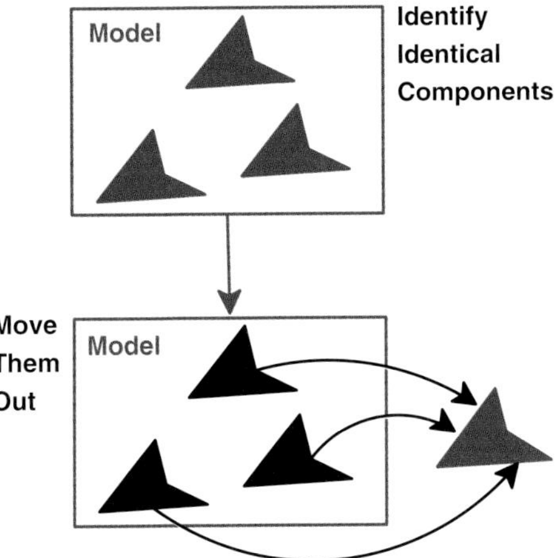

FIGURE 7.1 Identical components are identified and moved out.

from the subparts identified. As shown in Figure 7.1, this is done by replacing these subparts in the model with a stub to the actual module.

The aforementioned transformation involves two discrete steps: (1) to identify the structurally similar subparts of the model, and (2) to use the subparts in creating the modules of a hierarchical model. The first step is accomplished by using the lookup method; subsequently, the clustering method is used.

The lookup method, which is based on the decrease-and-conquer paradigm, determines the identical components bottom-up starting from the elementary subparts of the model. It is worth mentioning that these elementary subparts depend on the modeling language being used. For graph (or bipartite graph, e.g., CPN)-based models, these are essentially the vertices of the graph. Consequently, the smallest problem boils down to finding the identical vertices in a graph, as defined in Definition 7.1. The smallest problem is solved by classifying each disjoint set of vertices based on their indegree and outdegree. This yields the set of smallest identical components that consists of single vertices. The solutions to the smaller problems are used in solving the bigger problem. In this context, the bigger problem is to determine even larger components. In each step henceforth, the adjoining nodes of these similar vertices are attached before comparing the components rendered. Considering that the existing components were compared in an earlier step, the lookup method can determine the similarity of new components by comparing the last nodes attached.

Finally, the clustering method produces a module for each component identified to generate the corresponding hierarchical model. Again, this depends on the semantics of the hierarchical modeling language being used. Since CPN is used in this chapter, the hierarchy is established using the semantics of *substitution transition* for colored petri nets.

Compared to other transformation techniques [3,10,12], the lookup and clustering methods render an equivalent hierarchical model. In addition, they address a niche for contemporary software systems that consists of parallel components. Identifying and modeling individual components help the human modeler to understand a system. Furthermore, the transformation renders a valid hierarchical CPN model that could be both simulated and verified using CPN Tools.

7.3 BASICS OF SUBSTITUTION TRANSITION

In this section we explain briefly the semantics of substitution transitions for CPN that are used by the clustering method. As discussed previously, a hierarchical model consists of a set of modules. However, unless these modules are correlated, they cannot constitute a formal model. The substitution transitions act as stubs to associate and connect these modules.

Each module of a hierarchical CPN model has a substitution transition as its proxy. A module using the services of another module has a proxy for the latter as a substitution transition. On executing this transition, the corresponding module executes and delivers the services required. Consequently, replacing each proxy with its underlying module does not alter the behavior of the formal model. However, this would destroy the hierarchy and render a flat model.

This is explained further using Figures 7.2 and 7.3. Figure 7.2 shows a CPN model with two identical components: *A-T1-F-T3-G-T2-B* and *C-T4-H-T6-I-T5-D*. These components are replaced using substitution transitions *Hier1_1* and *Hier1_2* in Figure 7.3. Furthermore, the components themselves have been moved out to constitute a separate module. A module that contains a substitution transition is called a *supermodule* and the module substituted is called a *submodule*. In Figure 7.3, *Page1* is a supermodule and *Subpage1* is a submodule. In addition, each proxy has its own instance of the submodule. For example, the two instances of submodule *Subpage1*

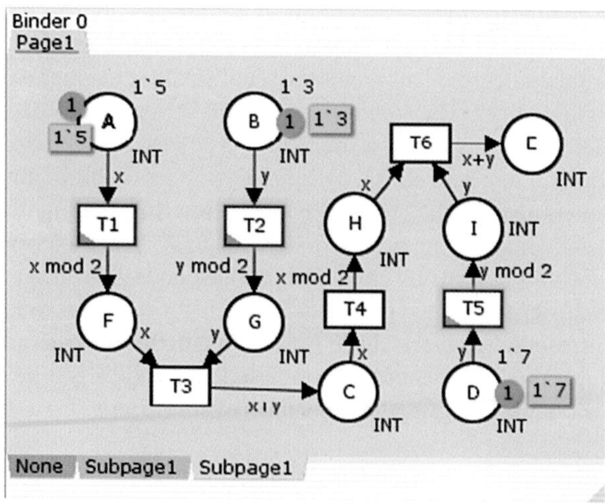

FIGURE 7.2 Colored petri net model with identical components.

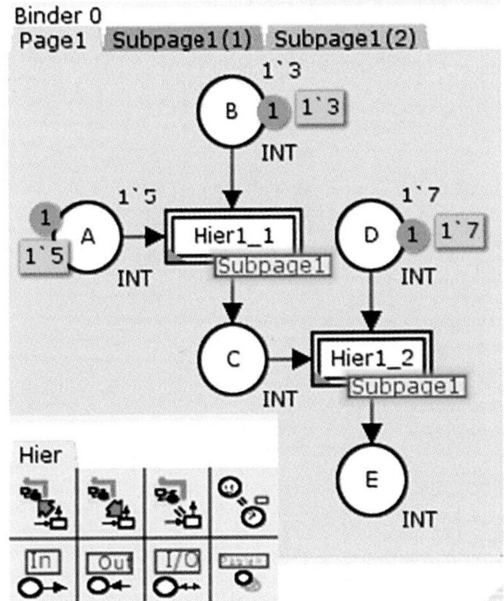

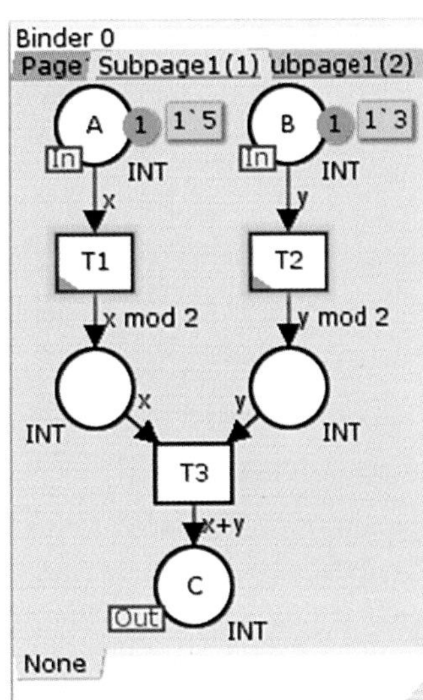

FIGURE 7.3 CPN model in Figure 7.2 with hierarchy installed using a *substitution transition*. *Page1* is the supermodule; *Subpage1(1)* and *Subpage1(2)* are two instances of submodules corresponding to the two substitution transitions.

[i.e., *Subpage1(1) and Subpage1(2)*] in Figure 7.3 correspond to the substitution transitions *Hier1_1* and *Hier1_2*.

A supermodule and its submodules are glued by defining a one-to-one relationship between subsets of their places. Each place adjacent to a substitution transition is known as a *socket* and has a counterpart in the associated submodule that is known as a *port*. Furthermore, considering that a socket could be either an input, an output, or an I/O place of the substitution transition, an equivalent tag is attached to the corresponding port to indicate its permitted type. A port assigned *In* can only be associated with an input place of the substitution transition. Similarly, a port assigned *Out* can only be paired with an output place of the substitution transition. A port assigned *I/O* can be associated with a socket that is both the input and output place of the substitution transition. For example, port A in Figure 7.3 is assigned port type *In* and consequently linked to socket A, which is an input place of the substitution transition.

The services of a submodule can be used by any number of supermodules by including them as a substitution transition. This makes it possible to reuse a defined submodule and forms the basis of the reduction method described in this chapter. However, as mentioned earlier, a separate instance of the submodule is created for each substitution transition.

7.4 RELATED WORK

A set of transformations proposed by Berthelot [3] aim to reduce the size of a PN model by merging two or more of its places or transitions based on certain specific

TABLE 7.1 Comparison of Related Reduction Methods[a]

Method	Resulting Net Same as Original Net	Model Size Reduced	State Space Reduced	Properties Preserved
[3]	⊗	●	●	◐
[12]	⊗	●	●	◐
[10]	⊗	●	●	◐
[19]	●	⊗	●	●
Lookup	●	●	⊗	●

[a] ⊗, does not satisfy; ●, satisfies; ◐, satisfies partially.

conditions. These transformations preserve several classical properties of nets (e.g., boundedness, safety, liveness) and also reduce the number of reachable states when performing state-space analysis. The implicit place simplification and pre- and post-agglomeration of transitions are the most frequently used transformations [3] and have been extended for CPN models [12]. In implicit place simplification, a place is removed if its marking is always sufficient to allow firing of any transition attached to it. In pre-agglomeration, two transitions, t_1 and t_2, are merged if a place p is the sole input place for t_2 and is also an output place for t_1. Similarly, in post-agglomeration, two transitions t_1 and t_2 are merged if a place p is the sole output place of t_1 and is also an input place for t_2. More recently, colored petri net reductions based-on post-agglomerations have been proposed [10].

Table 7.1 compares the features of these related algorithms with the method described in this chapter. Apart from reducing the size of the model, the transformations [3,10,12] also diminish the state space by reducing the number of execution traces to be analyzed. However, the net obtained after transformation is not equivalent to the original net, nor does it preserve the properties of the original net other than those specifically targeted. Consequently, we address the problem in two separate steps. The lookup and clustering methods reduce the size by transforming a net into an equivalent hierarchical model.

7.5 METHOD FOR INSTALLING HIERARCHY

In this section we describe a method for identifying the structurally similar components in a CPN model and installing hierarchy in it. Considering that a CPN model is a folding [13] of an equivalent petri net, the method is immediately applicable for the latter. Although the method is discussed only in the context of CPN language, it could be extended for other modeling languages that have the notion and semantics of hierarchy and structural similarity.

The method presented here is applicable to modern software systems that embrace a component-based model as opposed to a monolithic model. Whereas the former allows separating discrete functionalities and features of a system as separate components that could be reused, the latter focuses on building an indivisible monolithic system that is difficult to use and maintain, despite being functionally equivalent to the component-based counterparts. After autogenerating a model, the lookup method helps in determining the structurally similar subparts in it that would correspond to the components in a system. The hierarchy can be installed thereafter by formulating a module out of these individual identical components.

7.5.1 Lookup Method

The lookup method determines the identical components in a model. To provide good understanding of the principles of such a method, it is also enacted on the example shown in Figure 7.6. Additionally, the various steps of the lookup method are listed as an agglomeration of three related short algorithms instead of a single lengthy algorithm. This allows the reader to deal with fewer details simultaneously. As illustrated in Figures 7.4 and 7.5, the three algorithms constitute the two phases of the method. These phases are introduced here briefly before analyzing them in subsequent sections.

Lookup is based on the decrease-and-conquer strategy [20], wherein the bigger problem is broken into smaller problems, and the solutions to the smaller problems are combined to solve the original problem. The first phase, in effect, solves the smallest problem of finding structurally similar vertices in a graph-based model.

Definition 7.1 *A set of vertices* $\{v_1, v_2, \ldots, v_k\}$ *in a directed graph* $G = (V_1, V_2, \ldots, V_n, E)$, *with n disjoint sets of vertices* $\{V_1, V_2, \ldots, V_n\}$, *are said to be identical iff*

(a) $\forall i \in (1, k), \exists j \in (1, n)$: $v_i \in V_j$.

(b) $\exists i \in (1, k), \forall j \in (1, k)$: *Indegree*$(v_i)$ = *Indegree*(v_j) *and Outdegree*(v_i) = *Outdegree*(v_j).

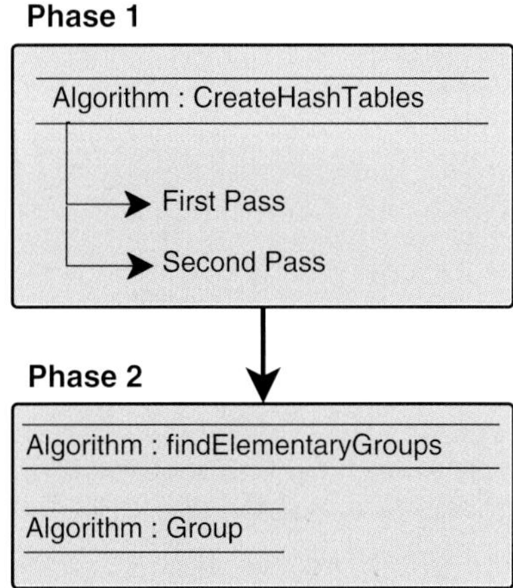

FIGURE 7.4 Three algorithms constituting the two phases of the lookup method.

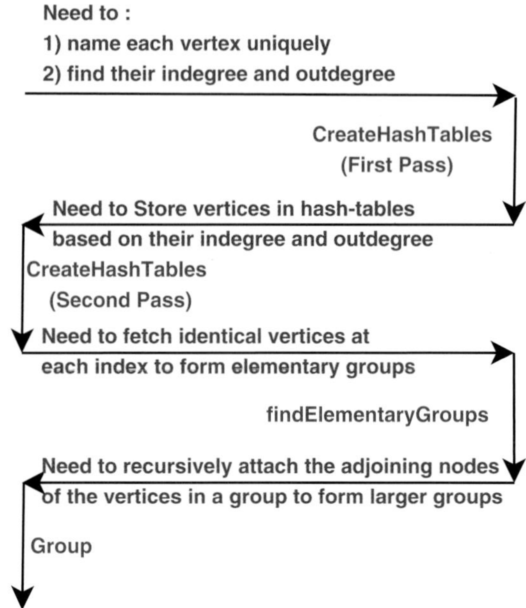

FIGURE 7.5 Road map of the method presented. Blue indicates a requirement that is addressed by the immediately following algorithm (in red).

Corollary 7.1 *If the edges* $\{e_1, e_2, \ldots, e_m\} \subseteq E$ *lead to vertex* $v \in V$ *in a graph* $G = (V, E)$, *then Indegree*$(v) = |\{e_1, e_2, \ldots, e_m\}|$.

Corollary 7.1 is used in Algorithm 7.1 to determine the indegree of vertices.

Corollary 7.2 *If the edges* $\{e_1, e_2, \ldots, e_m\} \subseteq E$ *lead away from vertex* $v \in V$ *in a graph* $G = (V, E)$, *then Outdegree*$(v) = |\{e_1, e_2, \ldots, e_m\}|$.

Corollary 7.2 is used in Algorithm 7.1 to determine the outdegree of vertices.

Using Definition 7.1, the smallest problem can be solved by classifying the vertices in each disjoint set based on their indegrees and outdegrees. Nevertheless, the indegree and outdegree for each vertex need to be determined before making such a classification. As illustrated in Figure 7.5, the first pass of Algorithm 7.1 scrutinizes the vertices to determine these values.

However, classifying these vertices solves only half of the problem. These vertices must be stored in an appropriate data structure to allow constant time lookup. This would allow the next phase to fetch the results efficiently from this phase and solve the larger problem. Considering that hash tables have constant time lookup, they are used to store the vertices wherein each possible combination of indegrees and outdegrees map into a distinct index. Furthermore, for simplicity, each disjoint set of vertices is stored in a separate hash table. As illustrated in Figure 7.5, the second pass of Algorithm 7.1 populates the hash tables. It should be noted that the hash tables store a list of vertices at each index, and the hash function ensures that these vertices are all structurally similar.

The identical vertices determined in the first phase form the smallest components. The second phase then steps in and recursively attaches the adjoining nodes of these vertices to create larger components. As shown in Figure 7.5, Algorithm 7.2 fetches the identical vertices from each index of the aforementioned hash tables and delivers them to Algorithm 7.3 for attaching their adjoining vertices recursively. Then at each stage the adjoining vertices of the components in a group are attached, and these new components are compared to determine their similarity. Given that the existing components had been compared in an earlier step, the lookup method compares these new components by comparing the last attached nodes. This continues until a component has no identical counterparts. Identifying components with multiple counterparts is beneficial because they will all be replaced by substitution transitions when a new module is constituted for the component. This forms the basis of the reduction method.

Phase 1: Creating and Populating Hash Tables. Finding identical vertices of a CPN model by storing them into the appropriate index of a hash table constitutes the very first phase of the lookup method. The index at which a vertex is stored depends on its indegree (number of input-adjoining vertices) and outdegree (number of output-adjoining vertices). Considering that the vertices at any particular index of a hash table have the same values for indegree and outdegree, they are all structurally similar. The two disjoint sets of vertices in a CPN model (*places* and *transitions*) are stored in two separate hash tables.

However, this phase has two basic prerequisites that need to be addressed. Primarily, all places and transitions in the net must have unique names. This is essential in order to identify them in a hash table. Additionally, each vertex must store its indegree and outdegree. This is necessary to determine the index in the hash table at which it would be stored. Therefore, a "two-pass" method is appropriate for creating the hash tables, with the two basic prerequisites fulfilled in the first pass and the hash tables created in the second pass.

Steps for Creating and Populating Hash Tables. Algorithm 7.1 lists the steps involved in creating and populating the two hash tables. The loop in steps 2 to 14 constitutes the first pass; the other loop (in steps 23 to 26) constitutes the second pass. In the first pass the algorithm needs to provide a new name for each vertex and to scrutinize them to determine their indegree and outdegree. In pursuit of fulfilling the first requirement, the algorithm uses two global identifiers, *placeId* and *transitionId*. As the names indicate, the former is used for naming places and the latter is used for naming transitions. When a place is encountered during the first pass, the value stored in *placeId* is assigned as the name of the place, as shown in step 4. This is followed by an increment of the value in *placeId* to ensure that the next place encountered is assigned a different name. Similarly, when a transition is encountered, its name is assigned using *transitionId*, as shown in step 9. As the identifiers are initialized

Algorithm 7.1 CreateHashTables(CPN N)

```
   Data: CPN N
   Result: Hash tables are generated
1  placeId←transitionId←1;
2  foreach Vertex V in N do // first pass
3  |  if V is a Place then
4  |  |  V.name←placeId++;                               // assign unique name
5  |  |  V.numInTran←V.numOutTran←0;                     // initialize
6  |  |  foreach input transition T_in of V do V.numInTran++;    // find
   |  |  indegree
7  |  |  foreach output transition T_out of V do V.numOutTran++; // find
   |  |  outdegree
8  |  else if V is a Transition then
9  |  |  V.name←transitionId++;                          // assign unique name
10 |  |  V.numInPlace←V.numOutPlace←0;                   // initialize
11 |  |  foreach input place P_in of V do V.numInPlace++;        // find
   |  |  indegree
12 |  |  foreach output Place P_out of V do V.numOutPlace++;     // find
   |  |  outdegree
13 |  end
14 end
15 numPlace=placeId-1;      // total number of places in net N
16 numTran=transitionId-1;  // total number of transitions in
   net N
17 fun hashFun(v)=switch v do // define hash function
18 |  case v is a Place
19 |    return v.numInTran∗(numTran+1)+v.numOutTran;
20 |  otherwise
21 |    return v.numInPlace∗(numPlace+1)+v.numOutPlace;
22 endsw
23 foreach Vertex V in N do // second pass
24 |  if V is a Place then hashPlace[hashFun(V)]=V; // hash table for
   |  place
25 |  if V is a Transition then hashTran[hashFun(V)]=V;  // hash table
   |  for tran
26 end
```

to 1 in step 1, the assigned names are integer values starting from 1. This is one possible scheme for assigning unique names and can be replaced by other possible schemes. To fulfill the other requirement, the *numInTran* and *numOutTran* properties of a vertex are incremented once for each of its input and output nodes (steps 6 and 7 and 11 and 12). Considering that these properties were initialized to zero in steps 5 and 10, they record the indegree and outdegree of the corresponding places and transitions. The indegree and outdegree of a vertex can be either a positive integer or zero.

Once the prerequisites are fulfilled, the second pass can start creating the hash tables using the hash function defined in steps 17 to 22. It accepts a vertex and returns the index of the hash table where it should be inserted. It calculates the index using the indegree and outdegree of the vertex that were determined during the first pass. Additionally, it also requires the total number of places and transitions in the net. These are determined in steps 15 and 16 and stored in the identifiers *numPlace* and *numTran*. The hash function for a vertex v is defined as

$$hashFun(v) = v.numInTran(numTran + 1) + numOutTran \quad \text{for a place} \tag{7.1}$$

$$= v.numInPlace(numPlace + 1) + v.numOutPlace \quad \text{otherwise} \tag{7.2}$$

where

- $v.numInTran, v.numOutTran \in [0, numTran]$: $v.numInTran + v.numOutTran \neq 0$
- $v.numInPlace, v.numOutPlace \in [0, numPlace]$: $v.numInPlace{+}v.numOutPlace \neq 0$.
- $v.numInXxxx$ and $v.numOutXxxx$ store the indegree and outdegree for a vertex v.

These conditions ensure that isolated places or transitions are not processed. It is necessary to filter out isolated vertices, as they have no adjoining nodes.

As discussed earlier, the hash tables are used to classify the vertices of a graph based on their indegree and outdegree. The legitimacy of the hash function in Algorithm 7.1 depends on its ability to ensure that no two dissimilar vertices hash to the same index. This can be proved by demonstrating that any two arbitrary vertices v_1 and v_2 hashing to the same index must be structurally similar. Consider any two places p_1 and p_2 in a net with

$$\text{indegree of } p_1 = p_1.numInTran = x_1$$

$$\text{outdegree of } p_1 = p_1.numOutTran = y_1$$

$$\text{indegree of } p_2 = p_2.numInTran = x_2$$

$$\text{outdegree of } p_2 = p_2.numOutTran = y_2$$

$$\text{total number of transitions} = numTran = z - 1 (z \geq 2)$$

Since both v_1 and v_2 are places, their indices are determined using the hash function *hashFun(v)* as defined in equation (7.2). Supposing that both of these places hash to index I, we get

$$x_1 z + y_1 = x_2 z + y_2 = I \tag{7.3}$$

or

$$z(x_1 - x_2) + (y_1 - y_2) = 0 \tag{7.4}$$

We know that the difference between two positive integers cannot be greater than the bigger integer. That is, if $m \geq 0, n \geq 0$ are two integers such that $m > n$ and $m + n \neq 0$, then

$$|m - n| \leq m \tag{7.5}$$

Since $0 \leq y_1, y_2 < z$ and $0 \leq x_1, x_2 < z$, it can be deduced from equation (7.5) that

$$0 \leq |y_1 - y_2| < z \quad \text{and} \quad 0 \leq |x_1 - x_2| < z \tag{7.6}$$

where |y| is the modulus function that returns the absolute value of an enclosed variable or expression. Although $|x_1 - x_2| \in [0,z)$, we find it particularly interesting when $|x_1 - x_2| \geq 1$. Multiplying the positive integer z on both sides, we get

$$z|x_1 - x_2| \geq z \tag{7.7}$$

when $|x_1 - x_2| \geq 1$. However, since we deduced $|y_1 - y_2| < z$ in equation (7.6), the first term in equation (7.4) is greater than the second term and cannot cancel it to produce zero. Consequently, $|x_1 - x_2| < 1$ and equation (7.4) only holds for $|x_1 - x_2| = 0$ (as $|x_1 - x_2|$ cannot be a fraction). This imparts $x_1 = x_2$, and using this result in equation (7.4), we get $y_1 = y_2$. The two places p_1 and p_2 are therefore structurally similar, demonstrating that any two vertices hashing to the same index must be identical. The proof also applies when p_1 and p_2 are transitions. The potency of the hash function is thereby established.

Figure 7.7 shows the model in Figure 7.6 after the first pass, wherein each vertex is assigned a unique name and its degree determined. The vertices are represented using color codes wherein all vertices marked with the same color have the same values for indegree and outdegree and are therefore structurally similar. For example, all red spots correspond to an indegree of 1 and an outdegree of zero. Similarly, a black spot in a transition corresponds to an indegree of 1 and an outdegree of 2. Furthermore, to avoid confusion we have appended a "*P*" or a "*T*" to place and transition names. For example, a place named "1" in the first pass is called "*P*1" in Figure 7.7, and a transition named "1" is called "*T*1".

The second pass populates the hash tables for places and transitions based on their indegrees and outdegrees. The places and transitions are hashed into separate hash tables known as *hashPlace* and *hashTran*, as shown in steps 24 and 25. The hash tables created for this model in the second pass are shown in Tables 7.2 and 7.3. The first column in these tables indicates the index of the hash table where the vertices were inserted.

At the conclusion of the second pass, the smallest problem, finding all structurally similar vertices in a CPN (i.e., the graph-based model), is solved. As the lookup

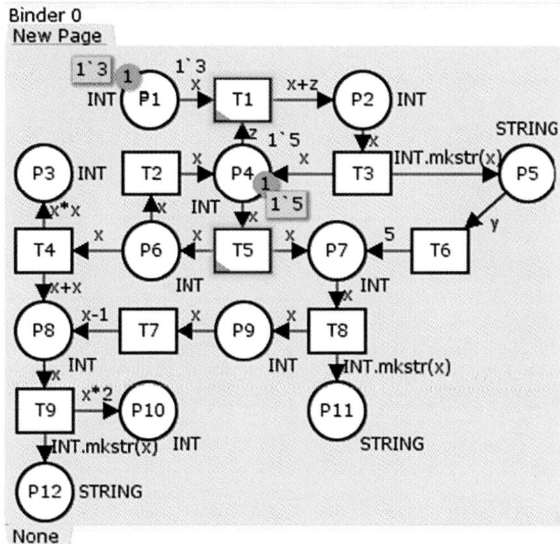

FIGURE 7.6 Example net for demonstrating the lookup method.

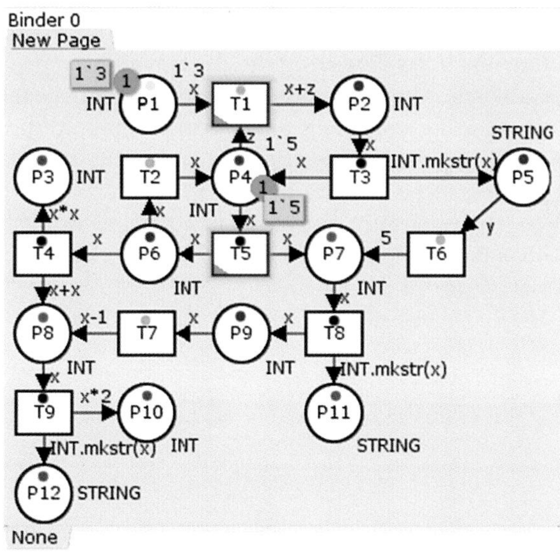

FIGURE 7.7 Example net after phase 1.

method is a decrease-and-conquer algorithm, the results obtained in this phase are used in the next phase to solve a larger problem. Consequently, the hash tables are sent to Algorithm 7.2 for further processing.

TABLE 7.2 Hash Table for Places Created on the Second Pass

Index	H(in,out)	Color	List of Places(in:out Transition)
1	$H(0,1)$	Yellow	$P1(T1)$
10	$H(1,0)$	Red	$P11(T8),P12(T9),P10(T9),P3(T4)$
11	$H(1,1)$	Blue	$P2(T1{:}T3),P5(T3{:}T6),P9(T8{:}T7)$
12	$H(1,2)$	Purple	$P6(T5{:}T4,T2)$
21	$H(2,1)$	Green	$P7(T5,T6{:}T8),P8(T4,T7{:}T9)$
22	$H(2,2)$	Brown	$P4(T2,T3{:}T1,T5)$

TABLE 7.3 Hash Table for Transitions Created on the Second Pass

Index	H(in,out)	Color	List of Transitions(in:out Places)
14	$H(1,1)$	Cyan	$T2(P5{:}P3),T6(P4{:}P6),$ $T7(P8{:}P7)$
15	$H(1,2)$	Black	$T3(P1{:}P3,P4),T4(P5{:}P2,P7),$ $T5(P3{:}P5,P6),$ $T8(P6{:}P8,P10),$ $T9(P7{:}P9,P11)$
27	$H(2,1)$	Orange	$T1(P3,P12{:}P1)$

Phase 2: Adding Vertices Recursively. As demonstrated previously, the hash function *hashFun(v)* defined in equations (7.2) and (7.3) ensures that all vertices at an index of a hash table are structurally similar. Such similar vertices form a group known as an *elementary group*.

Definition 7.2 *A group is defined as a maximal set of nonoverlapping components in a graph (or graph-based model) that are all structurally similar.*

Corollary 7.3 *Two components of a graph are nonoverlapping if they do not share vertices.*

Corollary 7.4 *For a graph N,* $\alpha_N = \{G_1, G_2, \ldots, G_g\}$ *denotes the set of groups in it.*

Corollary 7.5 *A group* $G_i \in \alpha_N$ *is a maximal set if* $\forall j \in [1, g] : (i \neq j) \wedge (G_i \not\subseteq G_j)$.

Corollary 7.6 *A group consisting only of a single vertex is called an elementary group.*

Corollary 7.7 *The set of groups* α_N *for a graph N is not unique for a graph.*

Figure 7.8 demonstrates a possible set of groups in our example CPN. The groups in this set are listed in equation (7.8). The blue and red vertices in this figure form elementary groups, and the set of brown vertices connected with brown

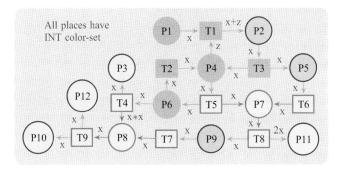

FIGURE 7.8 Possible set of groups in α_{example} for our example CPN.

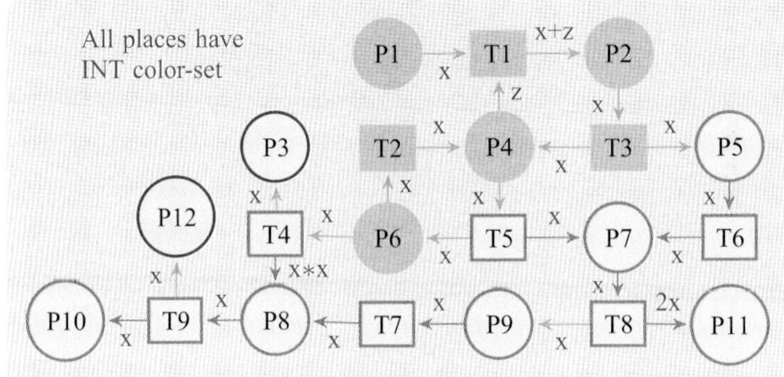

FIGURE 7.9 α is not unique: another possible set of groups in α_{example} for the same CPN.

arcs constitute identical components. The notation *node(list of input vertices: list of output vertices)* is used to illustrate the input and output vertices of a node.

$$\begin{aligned}\alpha_{\text{example}} = \{ & \{P3, P10, P11, P12\}, \{P2, P5, P9\}, \\ & \{P8(T4, T7 : T9), P7(T5, T6 : T8)\}\}\end{aligned} \tag{7.8}$$

However, from Corollary 7.7, α is not unique for a graph-based model. Figure 7.9 demonstrates another possible set of groups in the example CPN, and these are listed in the equation.

$$\begin{aligned}\alpha_{\text{example}} = \{ & \{P3, P12\}, \{P8(T4, T7(P9) : \\ & T9(: P10)), P7(T5, T6(P5) : T8(P11))\}\}\end{aligned} \tag{7.9}$$

Since at this point the smallest problem has been solved, the results are available for the aforementioned bottom-up resolution of larger problems. This is handled by the second phase of the lookup method, which rolls in after the first phase populates the hash tables. This phase has two related subphases. The first subphase, the steps for which are listed as Algorithm 7.2, renders all elementary groups of places from the hash tables. Considering that any particular index of a hash table contains all identical vertices, this subphase in effect fetches the vertices at each index to constitute elementary groups. Each of these elementary groups is then forwarded to the other subphase (listed in Algorithm 7.3) to attach the adjoining vertices recursively and compare them to determine similarity. Attaching adjoining vertices makes it possible to determine larger components.

Why Use Additional Hash Tables? Before passing the elementary groups to the second subphase, some additional information is stored into them in the first subphase. For efficiency and convenience, this information is stored in two levels of hash tables. In this section, the information that is stored and the reason for storing it is discussed using Figure 7.10. An insight into this would ensure better understanding of the two subphases and the related algorithms introduced later.

Consider an elementary group G, shown in Figure 7.10, that consists of five places:

$$G = \{P1, P2, P3, P4, P5\}$$

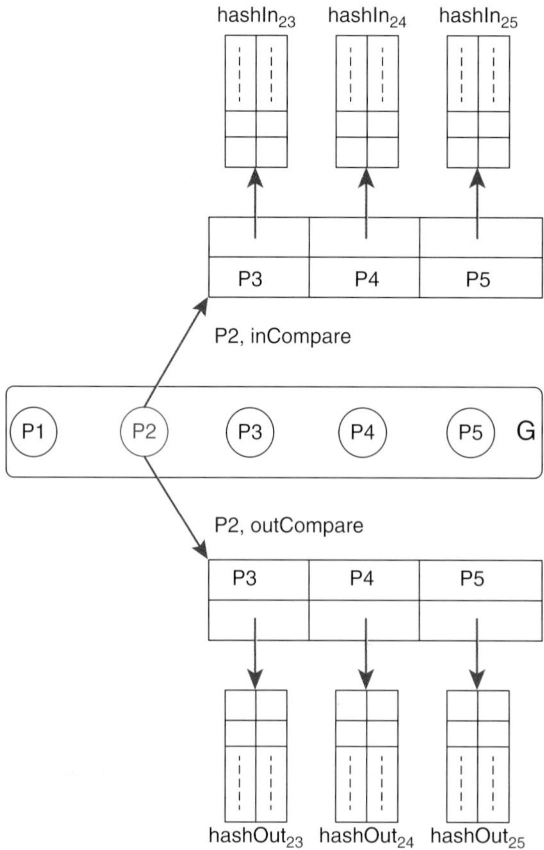

FIGURE 7.10 Hash tables corresponding to a place.

The ordering of these places is crucial and cannot be changed at a later stage because of the underlying data structures used. Each place in a group contains the two hash tables known as *inCompare* and *outCompare*. For a place P, these hash tables are referred to as *P.inCompare* and *P.outCompare* in Figure 7.10. The keys in these hash tables consist of places that are on the right-hand side of P in its group. For example, in Figure 7.10, the hash tables for $P2$ have $\{P3, P4,$ and $P5\}$ as its keys because these places happen to be at $P2$'s right in group G. Hereafter the position of these places needs to be maintained in the group to ensure the validity of entries in these hash tables. The value corresponding to a key consists of a pointer to another hash table, as shown using the blue arrows in Figure 7.10. The significance of these hash tables ($hashIn_{ij}$ and $hashOut_{ij}$) is explained using Figure 7.11, which consists of two identical components (shown in brown) obtained by adding the adjoining transitions of $P7$ and $P8$. Because these components are identical, each transition in a component has an identical counterpart in the other component ($T4 \leftrightarrow T5, T6 \leftrightarrow T7$, and $T8 \leftrightarrow T9$ from Table 7.3). The next step involves attaching the adjoining places of these transitions to obtain even larger components. However, to ensure that the components are similar even after adding these place, we need to compare the adjoining places of each transition with that of its counterpart prior to attaching them. These hash tables map similar vertices between two components to help us in making this comparison. For example, $P7.inCompare[P8]$ will have two entries $\{(T6, T7), (T5, T4)\}$ whose input places need to be compared i.e. $\forall(v_1, v_2) \in P_x.inCompare[P_y]$ compares the input vertices of v_1 and v_2, while $P7.outCompare[P8]$ will also have two entries $\{(T8, T9), (T5, T4)\}$ whose output places need to be compared i.e. $\forall(v_1, v_2) \in P_x.outCompare[P_y]$ compares the output vertices of v_1 and v_2. Note that $(T5, T4)$ appears in both tables because both its input and output places need to be compared. Moreover, $P7$ and $P8$ do not appear in any of these tables despite being similar because they do not have adjoining vertices that need to be compared.

To further elaborate on the necessity of these hash tables, consider the components formed after adding the adjoining transitions of any two places $P2$ and $P4$, as shown in Figure 7.12. For determining the structural similarity of these components, we first need to find the hash tables *hashIn* and *hashOut*.

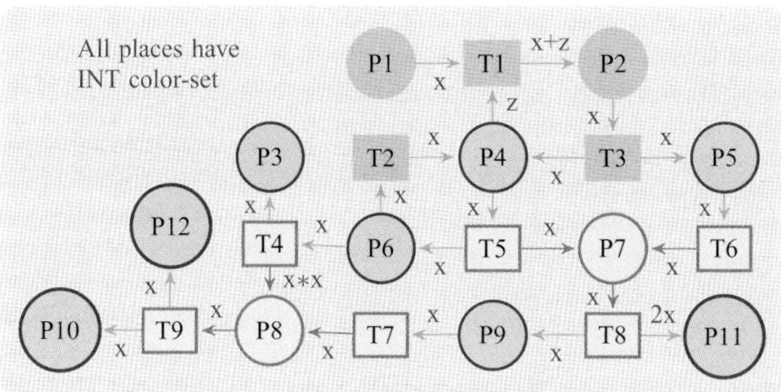

FIGURE 7.11 Adjoining places of identical components to be added next.

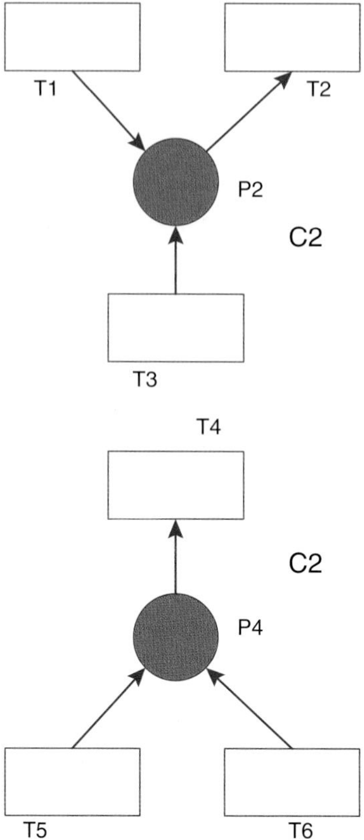

FIGURE 7.12 After adding the adjoining transitions to $P2$ and $P4$.

$$\texttt{hashIn}_{24} = P2.\texttt{inCompare}[P4] \text{ and } \texttt{hashOut}_{24} = P2.\texttt{outCompare}[P4]$$

Considering that the similarity of these two components can only be determined by comparing the input and output transitions of places $P2$ and $P4$ (and not any other vertices), both hash tables should contain a single entry $(P2, P4)$ as a key-value pair and are shown in Tables 7.4 and 7.5.

This being a trivial case, the hash-tables were initialized with these entries when they were created. Hereafter, the entries in these hash tables would be updated after each successful comparison. For example, if the components in Figure 7.12 are found to be similar, the previous entries in the hash table would be deleted and new entries would be added. The new entries will depend on how the transitions in a component

TABLE 7.4 Initial $\textit{hashIn}_{24}$

Key	Value
P2	*P4*

TABLE 7.5 **Initial *hashOut*$_{24}$**

Key	Value
$P2$	$P4$

TABLE 7.6 ***hashIn*$_{24}$ After Adding the Adjoining Transitions**

Key	Value
$T1$	$T5$
$T3$	$T6$

TABLE 7.7 ***hashOut*$_{24}$ After Adding the Adjoining Transitions**

Key	Value
$T2$	$T4$

could be mapped to their structurally similar counterparts in other components. If this mapping corresponds to the shades as shown in Figure 7.13, the new entries would be as shown in Tables 7.6 and 7.7.

The usefulness of these hash tables could be further illustrated by comparing larger components. This is accomplished by comparing the components $C1'$ and $C2'$ in Figure 7.13 that are formed after appending the adjoining places to components $C1$ and $C2$. The similar components $C1$ and $C2$ are bordered in red in Figure 7.13, and their adjoining places are bordered in blue. To decide on the usefulness of the hash tables, we first try to compare $C1'$ and $C2'$ without using them. Considering that $C1$ and $C2$ were already found to be similar, only their adjoining places need to be compared to determine the similarity of $C1'$ and $C2'$. However, there is no way to decide on a place in the first component that should be compared with a place in the second component. For example, we do not know the place in the second component to which $R1$ should be compared. Similarly, the place in the first component to which $R8$ should be compared is unknown. The hash tables returned by *inCompare* and *outCompare* provide the additional information required for undertaking these decisions. The entry $(T1, T5)$ in *hashIn* prompts us to compare the input places of $T1$ with those of $T5$. Similarly an entry $(T2, T4)$ in *hashOut* prompt us to compare the output places for $T2$ and $T4$. The benefits that justify using these additional hash tables are:

- For any two components $C1$ and $C2$, the hash tables *inCompare* and *outCompare* are needed to fetch the secondary hash tables $hashIn_{ij}$ and $hashOut_{ij}$.
- The secondary hash tables are needed to fetch the vertices whose input and output nodes need to be compared to determine the similarity of $C1$ and $C2$.

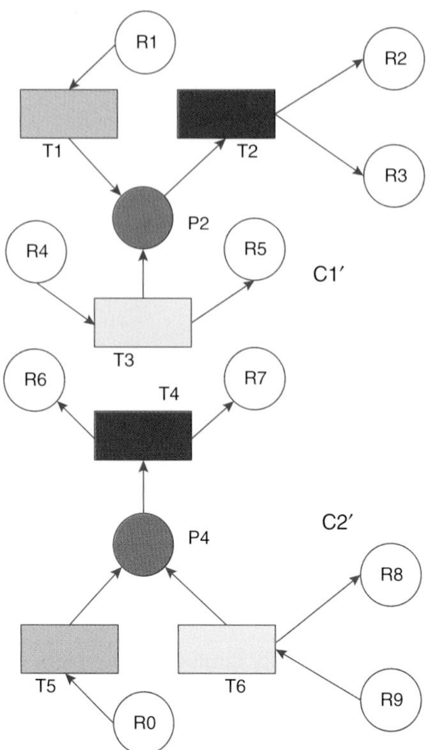

FIGURE 7.13 After adding the adjoining places to the component in Figure 7.12.

Subphase 2.1: Finding All Elementary Groups of Places. In a decrease-and-conquer strategy, the solution for a smaller problem is used to solve a larger problem. After addressing the smallest problem, finding identical vertices in a model, we use the results to determine identical components of larger size. This phase, in effect, fetches the vertices from each index of the hash tables populated in the first phase and forwards them to the second subphase. However, as discussed in earlier, additional hash tables are initialized for each vertex before forwarding.

Algorithm 7.2 lists the steps in finding all elementary groups of places. All places at an index of *hashPlace* are retrieved and stored in the list *P*, as illustrated in step 2. The places in *P* constitute an elementary group, wherein the name of a component is the same as that of its sole constituent place. Each place *pl* in *P* is added to *pl.iList* and *pl.oList* (step 5) and later used by Algorithm 7.3 to create a hash table for indices. Then the algorithm initializes the hash tables $hashIn_{ij}$ and $hashOut_{ij}$ with (P_i, P_j) in steps 8 and 9, as their adjoining transitions need to be compared next, to ascertain the equality of components. These hash tables are stored in *Pi. inCompare*[*Pj*] and *Pi.outCompare*[*Pj*] in steps 10 and 11.

Algorithm 7.2 findElementaryGroups(hashPlace)

```
Data: Hash table for places
Result: Elementary group of places
foreach index i in hashPlace do
    list P←hashPlace[i] ;     // places at index i are copied to P
    for i←1 to P.count() do //P.count gives the number of places in P
        place pl=P.at(i); // get place at position i of list P
        pl.iList=pl.oList=pl;
        for j←i+1 to P.count() do
            place pl2←P.at(j);
            hashIn_ij[pl]←pl2;
            hashOut_ij[pl]←pl2;
            pl.inCompare[pl2]=hashIn_ij;
            pl.outCompare[pl2]=hashOut_ij;
        end
    end
    Group(P);                 // add transitions and regroup
end
```

This being a decrease-and-conquer algorithm, the results obtained in this step are used in the next step to solve a larger problem, which in this case is finding larger identical components. In this pursuit, the list of places P, along with all additional information, is passed to Algorithm 7.3 for adding adjoining vertices and forming new groups.

Subphase 2.2: Determining Larger Groups Recursively. Algorithm 7.3 lists the steps for creating a metagroup from a group by augmenting each component with vertices from its immediate vicinity. As contrasted to a group, a metagroup consists of components that are not essentially similar. After creating a metagroup, the algorithm compares the components in it to forge new groups.

Definition 7.3 *A metagroup is defined as a maximal set of non-overlapping components of a graph which are not necessarily similar.*

Corollary 7.8 *A metagroup should always be reducible to a group by removing the most recently added adjoining vertices.*

Corollary 7.9 *An elementary metagroup does not exist because it cannot be reduced to a group.*

After determining the elementary group of places, Algorithm 7.2 delivers them to Algorithm 7.3 one after the other. The latter stores each group into list V before

Algorithm 7.3 Group(list V)

```
Data: List of vertices V
Result: β_N, the superset groups of N
if numberOfElements(V)=1 then return // list has one item
foreach Vertex E in V do
    for i←1 to E.iList.count( ) do
        Vertex D←E.iList.at(i);                          // get the vertex at position i
        foreach Vertex C in D.inVertices( ) do hashInIndex[D]←hashFun(C);
        newInList.append(D.inVertices( ));                // copy input vertices
        E.iList.remove(D);                                // remove this vertex from E.iList
    end
    for i←1 to E.oList.count( ) do
        Vertex D←E.oList.at(i);                          // get the vertex at position i
        foreach Vertex C in D.outVertices( ) do hashOutIndex[D]←hashFun(C);
        newOutList.append(D.outVertices());               // copy output vertices
        E.oList.remove(D);                                // remove the vertex from E.oList
    end
    E.iList←newInList; E.oList←newOutList;                // copy vertices
end
foreach i←1 to V.count() do //form groups out of metagroup V
    E←V.at(i);                                            // get the vertex at i
    list newV.append(E);                                  // add it to new list
    V.remove(E);                                          // remove it from V
    flag=0;                                               // a flag to find equality
    foreach j←i+1 to V.count() do // E appears prior to F in V
        F←V.at(j);                                        // get vertex at j
        hashIn←E.inCompare[F];                            // get the hash-tables containing
        hashOut←E.outCompare[F];                          // i/o vertices to be compared
        foreach V_in1,V_in2,V_out1,V_out2:hashIn[V_in1]=V_in2 & hashOut[V_out1]=V_out2 do
            list inIndex1←hashInIndex[V_in1];
            list inIndex2←hashInIndex[V_in2];
            list outIndex1←hashOutIndex[V_out1];
            list outIndex2←hashOutIndex[V_out2];
            hashIn.remove(V_in1); hashOut.remove(V_out1);
            if (inIndex1≠inIndex2) or (outIndex1≠outIndex2) then
                flag←1; break;
            else
                foreach I_1 ∈V_in1.inVertices & O_1 ∈V_out1.outVertices do
                    if I_2 ∈ V_in2.inVertices & hashFun(I_1)=hashFun(I_2) then hashIn[I_1]←I_2;
                    if O_2 ∈V_out2.outVertices & hashFun(O_1)=hashFun(O_2) then hashOut[O_1]←O_2;
                end
            end
        end
        if flag=0 then {newV.append(F); V.remove(F);}
    end
    Group(newV);                                          // add vertices and regroup
end
```

processing it. If a group has only a single component, the algorithm terminates at the very first step without processing. This is consistent with the objective of the lookup method to determine groups with multiple identical components.

Why Use Additional Lists and Hash Tables? Earlier we introduced the hash tables *inCompare*, *outCompare*, *hashIn*, and *hashOut*. These hash tables specifically contain the vertices that need to be compared to determine the similarity of two components. In this section we introduce lists that are used to store the vertices whose adjoining nodes are to be added to the components in the next recursion of Algorithm 7.3. For a component C, these lists are stored in *C.iList* and *C.oList*. As the names indicate, the input vertices for all $v_i \in C.iList$ and output vertices for all $v_o \in C.oList$ are added to C in the next recursion. In addition, the hash tables *hashInIndex* and *hashOutIndex* are used to store the indices of the vertices to be added in the next step. As explained later, these indices are calculated using the hash function in Algorithm 7.1, and they help to compare the components for similarity.

Algorithm 7.3 stores each elementary group of places into V before processing it. As mentioned earlier, each place $E \in V$ has a pair of lists (i.e., $E.iList$ and $E.oList$) that were assigned to E by Algorithm 7.2. Consequently, this ensures that the adjoining vertices of E are attached to it in the next recursion. For a place $P2 \in V$, these lists are illustrated using Figure 7.14. Then the vertices in these lists are fetched by Algorithm 7.3 to determine the indices of their input and output nodes. The nested *for* loop in steps 3 to 8 is responsible for determining the indices of input vertices for each node in *iList* and subsequently for storing them in the hash table *hashInIndex*. Similarly, the nested loop in steps 9 to 14 determines the indices of output vertices for each node in *oList* before storing them in the hash table *hashOutIndex*. For simplicity, the algorithm does not process the output vertices for the nodes in *iList* and the input vertices for the nodes in *oList*. The place $P2$ in Figure 7.14 has two input transitions,

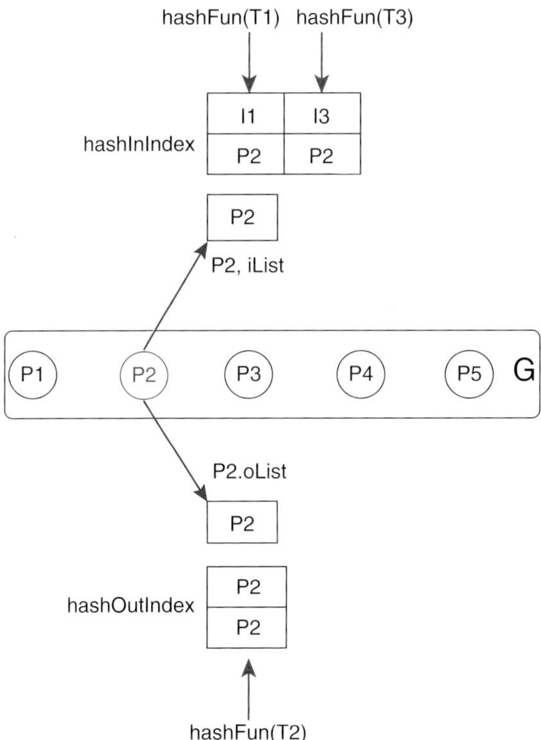

FIGURE 7.14 Key-value pairs inserted into the hash tables *hashInIndex* and *hashOutIndex* in the first execution of Algorithm 7.3.

$T1$ and $T3$, and an output transition, $T2$. Assuming that these transitions occupy the following indices in the hash tables that were populated in the first phase,

$$hashFun(T1) = I1$$

$$hashFun(T2) = I2$$

$$hashFun(T3) = I3$$

the entries $(P2, I1)$ and $(P2, I3)$ would be added to hashInIndex while a single entry $(P2, I2)$ would go into *hashOutIndex*, as shown in Figure 7.14. As a result, `hashInIndex`[$P2$] would return the list of indices corresponding to all input vertices of $P2$ (i.e., $[I1, I2]$). It should be noted that the hash tables *hashInIndex* and *hashOutIndex* can contain multiple entries for the same key value. Furthermore, these hash tables have a single instance each to store the indices for all the vertices. After the loop terminates in step 16, each input node for the vertices in *E.iList* and each output node for the vertices in *E.oList* are considered "added" to the subnet, wherein all the subnets together form a metagroup. The vertices in these lists are thereupon replaced by their input and output nodes. This ensures that the next set of adjoining vertices is attached in the following recursion of Algorithm 7.3. For example, place $P2$ is deleted from $P2.iList$ and replaced by its input transitions $T1$ and $T3$. Similarly, $P2$ is deleted from $P2.oList$ and replaced with its sole output, transition $T2$, as illustrated in Figure 7.15.

As evident from Figures 7.14 and 7.15, hash tables *hashInIndex* and *hashOutIndex* are updated on every recursion of Algorithm 7.3. In the next recursion of Algorithm 7.3, the entries added to *hashInIndex* depend on the indices of input places for transitions in $P2.iList$. Similarly, the entries added to *hashOutIndex* would depend on the indices of output places for transitions in $P2.oList$. Supposing that the component formed after attaching $T1$, $T2$, and $T3$ to $P2$ is similar to $C1'$ in Figure 7.13 and that the adjoining places $R1$, $R2$, $R3$, and $R4$ to be added occupy the following indices in the hash table for places determined in the first phase. These hash tables would store entries as shown in Figure 7.15.

$$hashFun(R1) = I4$$

$$hashFun(R2) = I6$$

$$hashFun(R3) = I7$$

$$hashFun(R4) = I5$$

It is worth mentioning that for any component E in the list V, vertex E is not the same as component E. If E is at position i in V, vertex E refers to place P_i in the corresponding elementary group. On the contrary, component E refers to place P_i along with all adjoining nodes attached to it by Algorithm 7.3. For example, in Figure 7.13, vertex $C1'$ refers to place $P2$ and vertex $C2'$ refers to place $P4$. Furthermore, even if E is a component, it is implicitly vertex E when referring to $E.iList$ or $E.inCompare$.

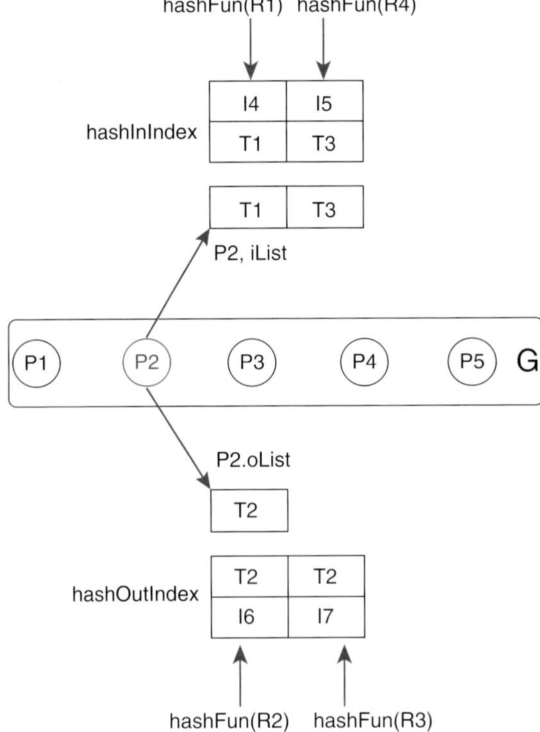

FIGURE 7.15 Key-value pairs inserted into the hash tables *hashInIndex* and *hashOutIndex* in the second execution of Algorithm 7.3.

The *foreach* loop in steps 17 to 44 compares the subnets in this metagroup to formulate the new groups. For any two components E and F in V, the hash tables *hashIn* and *hashOut* are fetched from $E.inCompare[F]$ and $E.outCompare[F]$ in steps 24 and 25. This is illustrated in Figure 7.16 for two components formed out of places $P2$ and $P4$. As manifested previously, $E.inCompare[F]$ and $E.outCompare[F]$ are defined only if E appears prior to F in V. If Algorithm 7.3 is processing an elementary group sent by Algorithm 7.3, both of these hash tables contain a single key-value pair, (pl_i, pl_j). Otherwise, as shown in Figure 7.16, these hash tables will contain vertices whose input and output nodes need to be compared to determine the similarity of the components. The metagroup MGr in Figure 7.16 and the group G to which it could be reduced are as follows:

$$MGr = \{P2(T1(R1), T3(R4){:}T2({:}R2, R3)), P4(T5(R0), T6(R9){:}T4(R6, R7))\}$$
$$= \{K1', K2'\}$$
$$Gr = \{P2(T1, T3{:}T2), P4(T5, T6{:}T4)\} = \{K1, K2\}$$

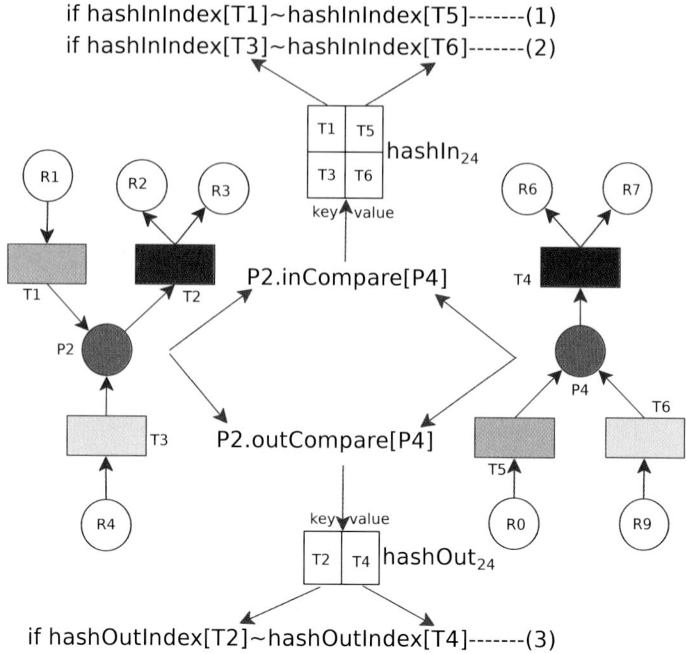

FIGURE 7.16 Comparing two components using Algorithm 7.3.

The structural similarity of components in metagroup *MGr* can be determined by comparing the places added to $K1$ and $K2$ to form $K1'$ and $K2'$. In other words, the similarity of $K1'$ and $K2'$ could simply be determined by comparing the input vertices for each key-value pair in *hashIn* and output vertices for each key-value pair in *hashOut*. For example, in Figure 7.16 the two components can be compared by comparing:

1. The input places of $T1$ with those of $T5$
2. The input places of $T3$ with those of $T6$
3. The output places of $T2$ with those of $T4$

If these places are found to be structurally similar, these components are also determined to be similar and together form a group.

However, instead of comparing two vertices for structural similarity, we compare their indices in the corresponding hash table. If two places occupy the same indices in the hash table for places, they are deemed to be identical. This follows from an earlier demonstration that if $hashFun(v_1) = hashFun(v_2)$, the vertices v_1 and v_2 must be structurally identical [equations (7.4) to (7.7)]. We have mentioned that *hashInIndex* stores the indices for all input vertices for a node while *hashOutIndex* stores the indices for all output vertices for a node. Therefore, *hashInIndex*[$T1$] would give the set corresponding to indices of its input places. If this set is found to be similar to the set returned by $hashInIndex[T5]$, we can conclude that each input place in $T1$ has a structurally similar counterpart that is an input place of $T5$.

Additionally, if we determine the following:

$$hashInIndex[T1] \sim hashInIndex[T5]$$

$$hashInIndex[T3] \sim hashInIndex[T6]$$

$$hashOutIndex[T2] \sim hashOutIndex[T4]$$

we can conclude that $K1'$ and $K2'$ are structurally similar. A new group can be constituted using $K1'$ and $K2'$ into which other identical subnets are added after a similar comparison.

Later this new group is handed over to Algorithm 7.3 for further processing in step 43. The symbol $\sim$ is used to represent the similarity of two sets. Two lists are considered similar if they contain the same number of elements and one is a permutation of other.

Determining Similarity in an Example Net. We now consider applying Algorithms 7.2 and 7.3 to the example net in Figure 7.6. The elementary groups are fetched by Algorithm 7.2, and their additional hash tables are initialized before passing them to Algorithm 7.3. The set of places $\{P11, P12, P10, P3\}$ are all at $index2$ of Table 7.2 and consequently form an elementary group V_1. For any two places, $pl_i, pl_j \in V_1$: pl_i appears before pl_j in V_1, $pl_i.inCompare[pl_j]$ is assigned a hash table that is initialized with a single entry (pl_i, pl_j). This is illustrated in Figure 7.17 for each pair of places in V_1. Additionally, for each place $pl \in V_1$, the lists $pl.iList$ and $pl.oList$ are initialized with a single entry pl. Subsequently, Algorithm 7.2 passes V_1 to Algorithm 7.3 for further processing.

As shown in Figure 7.17, Algorithm 7.3 attaches each place $pl \in V_1$ to its sole input transitions and produces a metagroup:

$$M_1 = \{P11 \leftarrow T8, P12 \leftarrow T9, P10 \leftarrow T9, P3 \leftarrow T4\}$$

The transitions attached are shown in blue. The index for each input transition in *iList* is found and stored in *hashInIndex*. As explained earlier, this is done using Figures 7.14 and 7.15. The other list *oList* is empty, owing to zero output transitions. The values added to *hashInIndex* and the corresponding changes to *inList* are listed in Table 7.8.

Subsequently, the metagroup members need to be compared to establish new groups consisting of identical subnets. For any two places $pl_i, pl_j \in V_1$: pl_i appears before pl_j in V_1, the components formed out of pl_i and pl_j can be compared by obtaining the hash table $hashIn_{ij} (= pl_i.inCompare[pl_j])$ and checking if $hashInIndex[v1] \sim hashInIndex[v2]$ for each entry $(v1, v2)$ in $hashIn$. These hash tables are shown in Figure 7.17. Considering that $hashInIndex$ returns similar sets for each pair of vertices in the hash table $hashIn$,

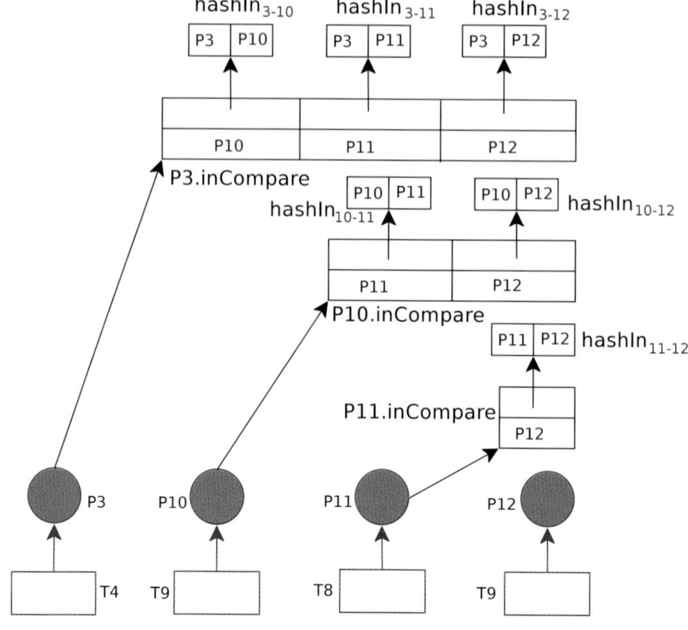

FIGURE 7.17 Hash tables in metagroup M_1.

TABLE 7.8 Initialization of *hashInIndex* Is Followed by a Change in *iList* for Each Subnet in M_1

Initial *inList*	*hashInIndex* Initialization	Updated *inList*
$P11.inList = \{P11\}$	$hashInIndex[P11] = \{hashFun(T8)\} = \{2\}$	$P11.inList = \{T8\}$
$P12.inList = \{P12\}$	$hashInIndex[P12] = \{hashFun(T9)\} = \{2\}$	$P12.inList = \{T9\}$
$P10.inList = \{P10\}$	$hashInIndex[P10] = \{hashFun(T9)\} = \{2\}$	$P10.inList = \{T9\}$
$P3.inList = \{P3\}$	$hashInIndex[P3] = \{hashFun(T4)\} = \{2\}$	$P3.inList = \{T4\}$

$$hashInIndex[P3] \sim hashInIndex[P10] \sim \{2\}$$
$$hashInIndex[P3] \sim hashInIndex[P11] \sim \{2\}$$
$$hashInIndex[P3] \sim hashInIndex[P12] \sim \{2\}$$
$$hashInIndex[P10] \sim hashInIndex[P11] \sim \{2\}$$
$$hashInIndex[P10] \sim hashInIndex[P12] \sim \{2\}$$
$$hashInIndex[P11] \sim hashInIndex[P12] \sim \{2\}$$

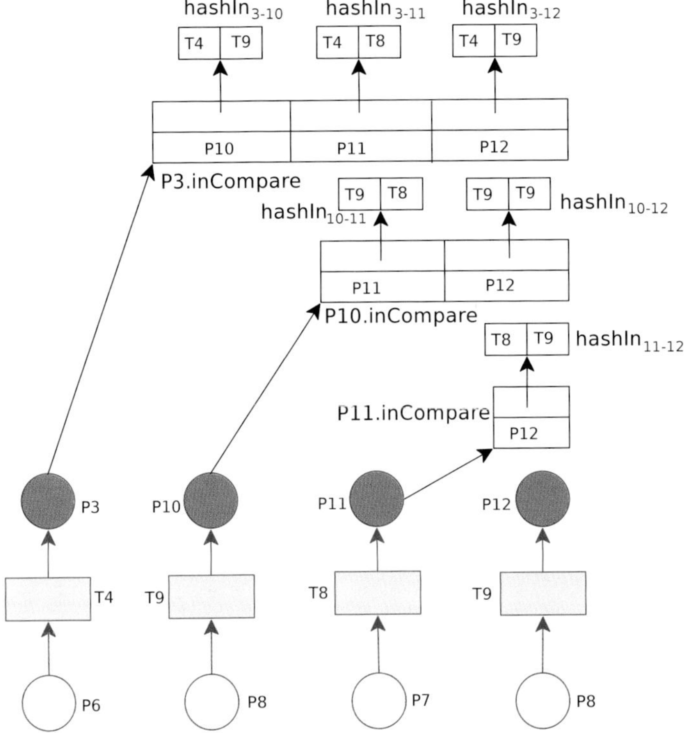

FIGURE 7.18 Hash tables in metagroup M_2.

the metagroup has all identical subnets and the new group V_2 is equivalent to metagroup M_1, or

$$V_2 = M_1 = \{P11 \leftarrow T8, P12 \leftarrow T9, P10 \leftarrow T9, P3 \leftarrow T4\}$$

This group is shown in Figure 7.18, where it is circled in red for easy identification. The corresponding shades indicate identical places and transitions. Each hash table *hashIn* is modified to contain an entry for the corresponding pair of transitions found similarly. These modified hash tables are also illustrated in Figure 7.18. V_2 is then sent back to Algorithm 7.3 for further processing.

The process described above is then repeated when Algorithm 7.3 attaches input places to each subnet $S \in V_2$. Consequently, a new metagroup,

$$M_2 = \{P11 \leftarrow T8 \leftarrow P7, P12 \leftarrow T9 \leftarrow P8, P10 \leftarrow T9 \leftarrow P8, P3 \leftarrow T4 \leftarrow P6\}$$

is obtained, as shown in Figure 7.18. For each transition $T \in S.iList$, indices of its input places are found and inserted into *hashInIndex*$[T]$, as shown in Table 7.9.

TABLE 7.9 Initialization of *hashInIndex* Is Followed by a Change in *iList* for Each Subnet in M_2

Initial *inList*	*hashInIndex* Initialization	Updated *inList*
$P11.inList = \{T8\}$	$hashInIndex[T8] = \{hashFun(P7)\} = \{5\}$	$P11.inList = \{P7\}$
$P12.inList = \{T9\}$	$hashInIndex[T9] = \{hashFun(P8)\} = \{5\}$	$P12.inList = \{P8\}$
$P10.inList = \{T9\}$	$hashInIndex[T9] = \{hashFun(P8)\} = \{5\}$	$P10.inList = \{P8\}$
$P3.inList = \{T4\}$	$hashInIndex[T4] = \{hashFun(P6)\} = \{4\}$	$P3.inList = \{P6\}$

The subnets in the metagroup are compared to establish groups. For any two components $E, F \in V_2$ formed out of places pl_i, $pl_j \in V_1$:pl_i that appears before $pl_j inV_1$, the similarity of E and F can be determined by obtaining the hash table $hashIn_{ij}$ ($= pl_i.inCompare[pl_j]$) and checking if $hashInIndex[v1] = hashInIndex[v2]$ for each entry $(v1, v2)$ in *hashIn*. These hash tables are shown in Figure 7.18, comparing the sets returned by *hashInIndex* for each pair of vertices in the hash table *hashIn*,

$$hashInIndex[T4] \nsim hashInIndex[T9]$$

$$hashInIndex[T4] \nsim hashInIndex[T8]$$

$$hashInIndex[T4] \nsim hashInIndex[T9]$$

$$hashInIndex[T9] \sim hashInIndex[T8] \sim \{5\}$$

$$hashInIndex[T9] \sim hashInIndex[T9] \sim \{5\}$$

$$hashInIndex[T8] \sim hashInIndex[T9] \sim \{5\}$$

Only the first three subnets in M_2 are found to be similar. However, the second and third subnets are overlapping and cannot be together in the same group. Consequently, the new group is

$$V_3 = \{P11 \leftarrow T8 \leftarrow P7, P10 \leftarrow T9 \leftarrow P8\}$$

shown in Figure 7.19 by red borders. The figure also demonstrates the changes to each hashIn table to accommodate an entry for each pair of corresponding places found similarly.

If V_3 is processed further by Algorithm 7.3, a new meta group,

$$M_3 = \{P11 \leftarrow T8 \leftarrow P7^{\leftarrow T6}_{\leftarrow T5}, P10 \leftarrow T9 \leftarrow P8^{\leftarrow T7}_{\leftarrow T4}\}$$

is formed out of each subnet $S \in V_3$, as illustrated in Figure 7.19. For each place $P \in S.iList$, indices of its input transitions are found and inserted into $hashInIndex[T]$, as shown in Table 7.10.

Subsequently, the subnets in M_3 are compared to establish new groups. For any two components E, $F \in V_2$ that were formed out of places $pl_i, pl_j \in V_1$:

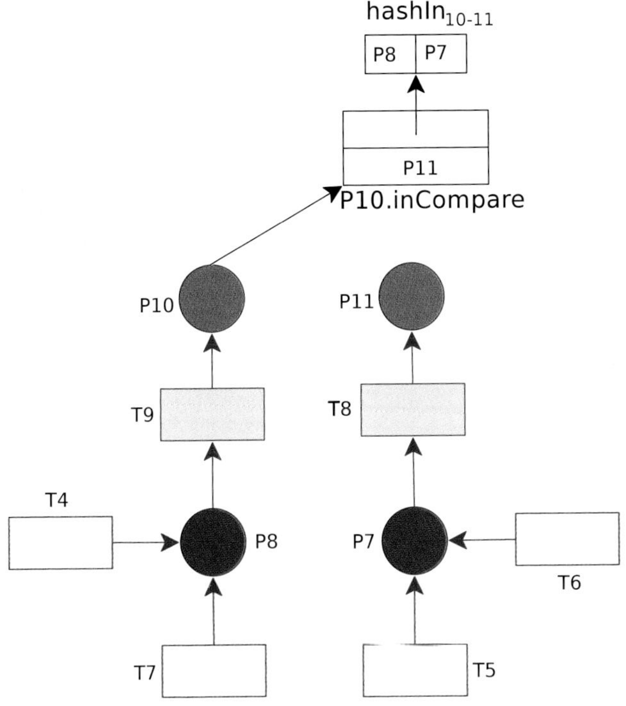

FIGURE 7.19 Hash tables in metagroup M_3.

TABLE 7.10 Initialization of *hashInIndex* Is Followed by a Change in *iList* for Each Subnet in M_3

Initial *inList*	$P10.inList = \{P8\}$
hashInIndex initialization	$hashInIndex[P8] = \{hashFun(T4), hashFun(T7)\} = \{2,1\}$
Updated *inList*	$P10.iList = \{T4,T7\}$
Initial *inList*	$P11.inList = \{P7\}$
hashInIndex initialization	$hashInIndex[P7] = \{hashFun(T5), hashFun(T6)\} = \{2,1\}$
Updated *inList*	$P11.iList = \{T5,T6\}$

(pl_i appears before pl_j in V_1), the similarity of E and F can be determined by obtaining the hash table $hashIn_{ij}(= pl_i.inCompare[pl_j])$ and checking if $hashInIndex[v1] = hashInIndex[v2]$ for each entry $(v1, v2)$ in *hashIn*. These hash tables are shown in Figure 7.19. Comparing the sets returned by *hashInIndex* for each pair of vertices in the hash table *hashIn*,

TABLE 7.11 Initialization of *hashInIndex* is Followed by a Change in *iList* for Each Subnet in M_4

Initial *inList*	$P10.inList = \{T4, T7\}$
hashInIndex initialization	$hashInIndex[T4] = \{hashFun(P6)\} = \{4\}$, $hashInIndex[T7] = \{hashFun(P9)\} = \{3\}$
Updated *inList*	$P10.iList = \{P6, P9\}$
Initial *inList*	$P11.inList = \{T5, T6\}$
hashInIndex initialization	$hashInIndex[T5] = \{hashFun(P4)\} = \{6\}$, $hashInIndex[T6] = \{hashFun(P5)\} = \{3\}$
Updated *inList*	$P11.iList = \{P4, P5\}$

$$hashInIndex[P8] \sim hashInIndex[P7] \sim \{2,1\}$$

the subnets in M_3 are found to be identical. Consequently, the new group, V_4, is same as M_3:

$$V_4 = M_3 = \{P11 \leftarrow T8 \leftarrow P7 \begin{smallmatrix} \leftarrow T6 \\ \leftarrow T5 \end{smallmatrix}, P10 \leftarrow T9 \leftarrow P8 \begin{smallmatrix} \leftarrow T7 \\ \leftarrow T4 \end{smallmatrix}\}$$

The new group is shown in Figure 7.20 by red borders. The figure also shows the hash table $hashIn_{10-11}$, containing two entries $(T7, T6)$ and $(T4, T5)$ that were found to be similar.

Finally, on applying Algorithm 14 to V_4, a metagroup M_4 is obtained as shown in Figure 7.20:

$$M_4 = \{P11 \leftarrow T8 \leftarrow P7 \begin{smallmatrix} \leftarrow T6 \leftarrow P5 \\ \leftarrow T5 \leftarrow P4 \end{smallmatrix}, P10 \leftarrow T9 \leftarrow P8 \begin{smallmatrix} \leftarrow T7 \leftarrow P9 \\ \leftarrow T4 \leftarrow P6 \end{smallmatrix}\}$$

The hash table *hashInIndex* is updated as shown in Table 7.11.

Subsequently, the subnets in M_4 are compared to establish new groups. On comparing the sets returned by *hashInIndex* for each pair of vertices in the hash table *hashIn*,

$$hashInIndex[T7] \sim hashInIndex[T6]$$

$$hashInIndex[T4] \nsim hashInIndex[T5]$$

the input places of $T7$ and $T6$ are found to be similar, whereas those of $T4$ and $T5$ are found to be distinct. Consequently, the input places of $T4$ and $T5$ are removed to obtain a new group V_5, as shown in Figure 7.21:

$$V_5 = \{P11 \leftarrow T8 \leftarrow P7 \begin{smallmatrix} \leftarrow T6 \leftarrow P5 \\ \leftarrow T5 \end{smallmatrix}, P10 \leftarrow T9 \leftarrow P8 \begin{smallmatrix} \leftarrow T7 \leftarrow P9 \\ \leftarrow T4 \end{smallmatrix}\}$$

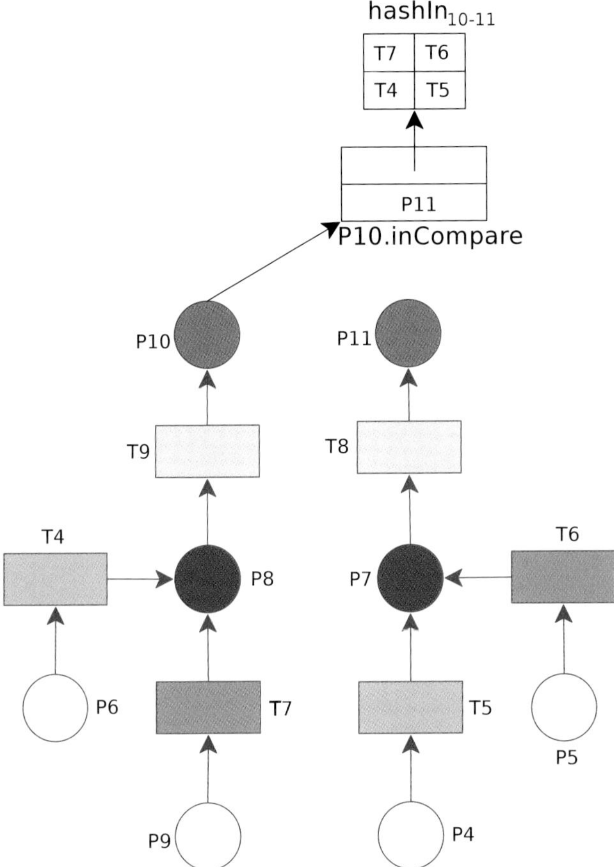

FIGURE 7.20 Hash tables in metagroup M_4.

Furthermore, the hash table now contains a single entry ($P9, P5$), as the other pair of places was found to be dissimilar.

The subnets identified in the example net are shown in Figure 7.22. Any further attempts to include more places or transitions in these subnets would result in overlapping, and thus these components would no longer constitute a group.

7.5.2 Clustering Method

The method presented here allows establishing hierarchy into a CPN model by creating a module out of each nonoverlapping group identified by the lookup method. Similar methods can be produced to install hierarchy into a non-CPN model by using the appropriate semantics for hierarchy as defined. The steps involved are explained herein with the example net in Figure 7.23 and its hierarchical counterpart in Figure 7.24.

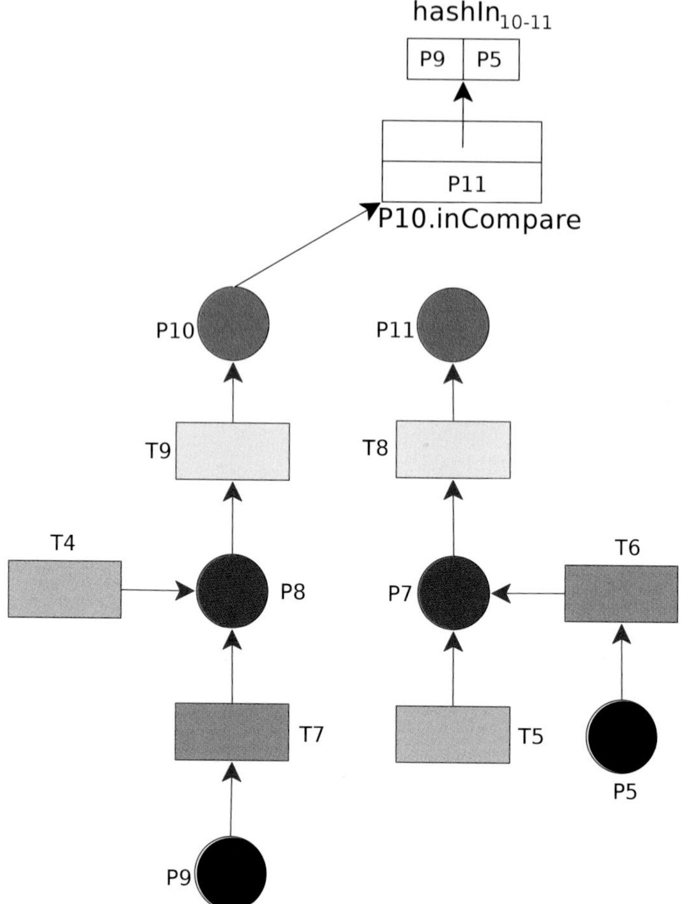

FIGURE 7.21 Subnets in group V_5.

- *Creating new modules.* A new module is created for each nonoverlapping group based on the structure of components in the group. If a transition in the new module has fewer adjoining places than it has in the original net, supplementary places are created and attached to it. This ensures that each socket in a supermodule has a port in a submodule. Figure 7.24 illustrates the new module $g2$ created from components identified in Figure 7.23. Additional ports are attached to $E1$ and $E2$ (dotted places), corresponding to the adjoining places for $T4/T5$ and $T9/T8$.
- *Declare union color sets if necessary.* On superimposing the components in a group, the places and transitions in each component would overlap with their counterpart in other components. However, if the color sets for any bunch of overlapping places are not the same, a new color set needs to be defined as the union of all these color sets and assigned to their counterpart in the new

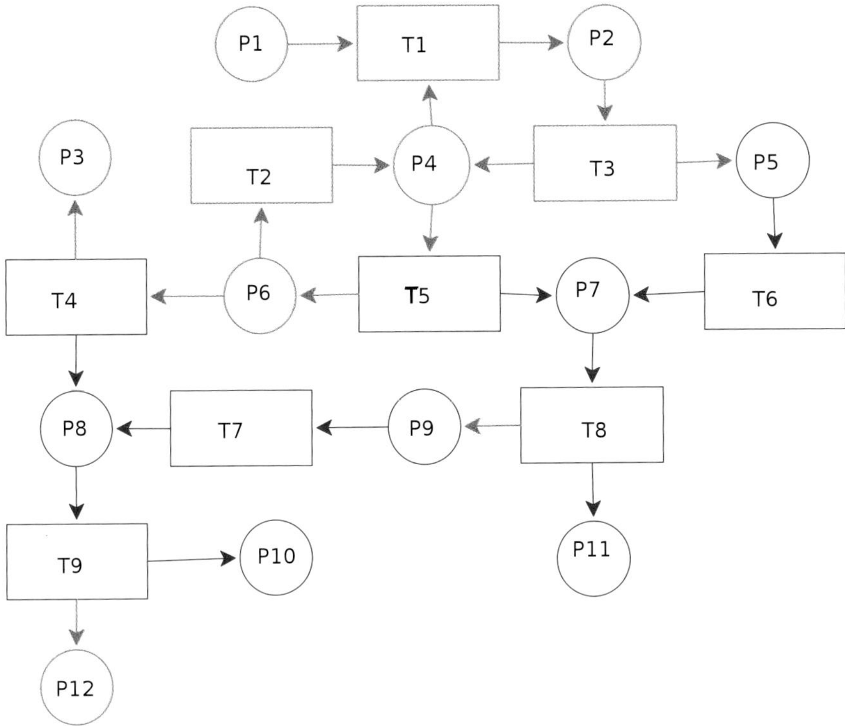

FIGURE 7.22 Subnets identified in the CPN model.

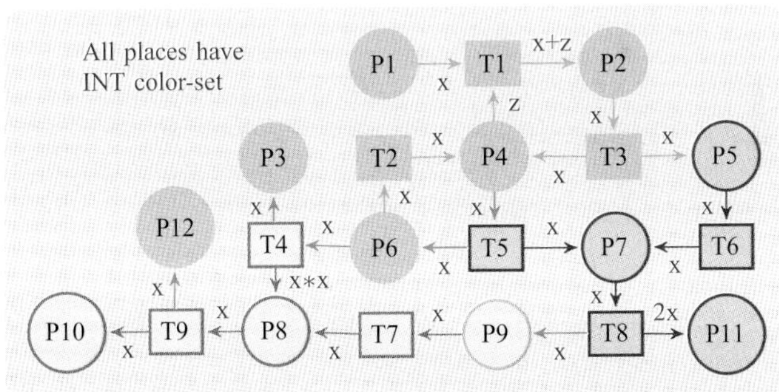

FIGURE 7.23 Two identical components (blue and brown) forming a group in an example net.

module. This ensures that their corresponding place in the new module can hold a token from any (or all) of them. For example, if *P7* had a STRING color set in Figure 7.23, it would be in conflict with the *INT* color set of *P8*. Accordingly, a union *INTnSTR* needed to be declared as

colset INTnSTR = union Int:INT + String:STRING;

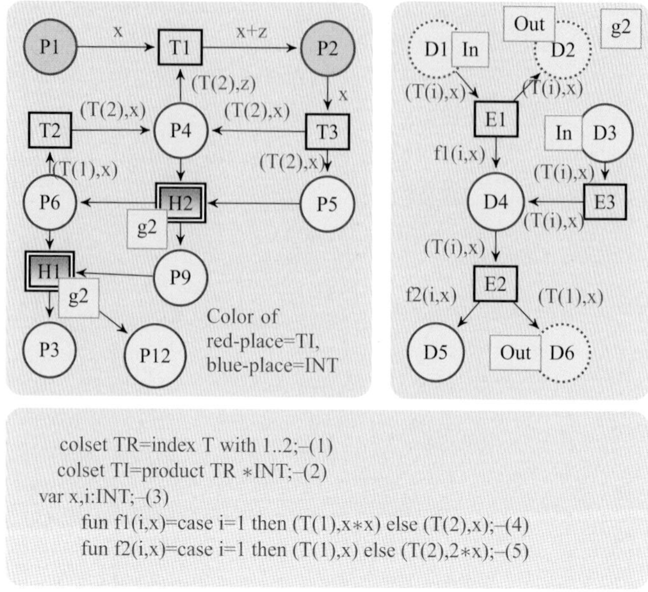

FIGURE 7.24 Equivalent hierarchical model obtained using the clustering algorithm.

and this would be assigned to corresponding place *D*4 in Figure 7.24 (after declaring a product color set, step 5). Furthermore, if any port–socket pair has disparate color sets, the union of their color set is assigned to the port and all its associated sockets. This ensures that port–socket pairs have consistent color sets.

- *Delete places and transitions from the original net.* For each component in a group, its constituent places and transitions are deleted from the original net, with the exception of peripheral places that constitute the sockets in a supermodule. The deleted nodes are subsequently replaced by substitution transitions with a tag containing the name of the new module. Any arc from socket places to a deleted node is now connected to a substitution transition. Figure 7.24 illustrates the nodes deleted from Figure 7.23.
- Assign ports. The ports are tagged (*In*, *Out*, or *I/O*) and mapped to their counterpart (sockets) in the original net.
- *Declare index color sets.* For each group, an index color set of the same size as the group is declared. The elements in this color set are used to identify the components that were replaced by substitution transition. This allows us to introduce component-specific behavior in the new module. For example, the two components of the example net differ in a few arc expressions. To account for this difference, an index color set has been defined as equation (1) of Figure 7.24. Furthermore, the expression on arcs with a socket at either end is modified to include the identity of components consuming the token (e.g., input arcs of *P*4 and *P*5). Accordingly, the color of socket places and the places

in the new module are also modified to contain component information (color TI for red places).

- *Declaring the functions.* The component-specific behavior of transitions in a component is obtained by declaring additional functions. For example, the function $f2$ doubles the value in the token $2x$ for the second component $(i = 2)$ while it keeps the value the same for the first component $(i = 1)$. Such component-specific behavior of transitions ensures that the behavior of the original net is not changed on installing hierarchy.
- *Tokens on output ports.* The place $P6$ in Figure 7.24 is the output socket for $H2$ and the input socket for $H1$. Consequently, before adding a token to $P6$, $H2$ updates the component information in the token (input arc expression of $D6$). Failing to do so will cause $H1$ to emulate the behavior of $H2$, and this might lead to potential errors.

The hierarchical model returned by the clustering method is shown in Figure 7.23.

7.5.3 Time Complexity of the Lookup Algorithm

Consider a net N with n_p places and n_t transitions such that

1. The maximum indegree of places$(\Delta_p^-) = m_p$.
2. The maximum outdegree of places$(\Delta_p^+) = l_p$.
3. The maximum indegree of transitions$(\Delta_t^-) = m_t$.
4. The maximum outdegree of transitions$(\Delta_t^+) = l_t$.

Hence, $\forall i \in [1,n_p]$, $deg^-(p_i) \in \{0, 1, 2, \ldots, m_p\}$ and $deg^+(p_i) \in \{0, 1, 2, \cdots, l_p\}$, where deg^- and deg^+ denote the *indegree* and *outdegree* of any node. Considering that a place in net N can have $(m_p + 1)$ possible values for deg^- and $(l_p + 1)$ possible values for deg^+, the number of rows in the hash table for places would be

$$x_p \leq (m_p + 1)(l_p + 1) - 1 \tag{7.10}$$

This value is 1 less than the product because both deg^- and deg^+ cannot be 0 for a place. Similarly, the number of rows in the hash table for transition would be

$$x_t \leq (m_t + 1)(l_t + 1) - 1 \tag{7.11}$$

If the probability that a place is at index k $(1 \leqslant k \leqslant x_p)$ is $\text{Prob}_p(k)$, the number of places at index k of the hash table would be $n_p\text{Prob}(k)$. Consider the functions In_p: $[1,x_p] \rightarrow [0,m_p]$ and Out_p: $[1,x_p] \rightarrow [0,l_p]$, which return the deg^- and deg^+ of places at some index $k(1 \leqslant k \leqslant {}_p)$. If z vertices could be compared in time $T(z)$, the time taken to compare input transition of a place at k would be $T(\text{In}(k))$. Similarly, the time for comparing output transitions of a place at k would be $T(\text{Out}(k))$. Consequently, the comparison time for all $n_p\text{Prob}(k)$ places at index k would be

$$n_p\text{Prob}(k)[T(\text{In}(k)) + T(\text{Out}(k))] \tag{7.12}$$

The overall delay in comparing places at each index of hash table would be

$$\sum_{k=1}^{x_p} n_p \text{Prob}(k)[T(\text{In}(k)) + T(\text{Out}(k))] \tag{7.13}$$

or

$$n_p \sum_{k=1}^{x_p} \text{Prob}(k)[T(\text{In}(k)) + T(\text{Out}(k))] \tag{7.14}$$

Equation (7.14) implies that the delay is linear on n_p. Similarly, it can be certified that the delay is linear on n_t. Creating the hash-tables is another linear process wherein the entire set of vertices is scanned once in each of the two passes. In the first pass, the number of times inner *foreach* loops execute for a vertex v_i is $deg^-(v_i) + deg^+(v_i)$. However, these values are independent of n_p and n_t. Evaluating the hash function in the second pass is also a constant time operation. Consequently, the time complexity of the lookup algorithm is $\theta(n_p + n_t)$.

7.6 EXPERIMENTAL RESULTS

The algorithm was implemented using Qt 4.5 SDK for 32-bit Linux and was tested on a PC with a 1.83-GHz Intel Core 2 Duo processor and 2 GB of RAM. The PC had Ubuntu 8.04 desktop version OS installed, and the C++ code was compiled using a GNU g++ compiler. The implementation can be downloaded [17].

A net consisting of all dissimilar places and transitions would have a single entry at each index of the hash tables generated by Algorithm 7.1. When these elementary groups are fetched by Algorithm 7.2 and sent to Algorithm 7.3, the latter quits at the very first step. This is because Algorithm 7.3 requires groups with multiple subnets for processing. Consequently, the time taken by the lookup algorithm would be minimal. On the contrary, if there are a large number of identical components in a net, a group passed to Algorithm 7.3 would have many subnets. Consequently, Algorithm 7.3 might need to execute several times recursively before the size of the group is reduced to 1 and causes the algorithm to stop. Therefore, given a net N, the best case occurs when it has no identical components and the performance of the algorithm degrades with the introduction of identical components.

To find the effect on the runtime of the lookup algorithm of incorporating identical components, the net in Figure 7.7 is used to create larger nets by joining multiple instances of the net in various patterns. Table 7.12 illustrates the patterns in which this net is joined to create new nets. Each bullet (•) in Figure 7.7 represents a net. The table assigns a number to each of these nets. The structure of net 17, which is the supergraph of all other nets, is easily available [18]. The structure of other nets could be interpreted from this structure. In Figures 7.25 to 7.28, the time taken by the lookup algorithm to process these nets is exhibited in red. However, modifying the structure of these nets to reduce the number of structurally similar components leads to a reduction in execution time of the lookup algorithm. The reduced execution

TABLE 7.12 Nets Used to Analyze Execution Time for the Lookup Method[a]

Net		Net		Net	
1	•	7	•• ••	13	•••• •••• ••••
2	• •	8	•• •• •	14	•••• •••• •••• ••••
3	••	9	•• •• ••	15	••••• ••••• ••••• •••••
4	•• •	10	•• • •• ••	16	••••• ••••• ••••• ••••• •••••
5	•• •	11	•• • • •• ••	17	•••• •• ••••• • ••••• • ••••• • ••••• •
6	• ••	12	•• • • •• • ••		

Source: [18].
[a] • represents the example net in Figure 7.7.

times are shown in blue. The possibility of being able to reduce the execution time by modifying the net structure indicates that the lookup algorithm depends on the number of structurally similar components in a net, apart from its size. This is demonstrated in further detail using Figures 7.29 to 7.32. The experiment is run 50 times for each net, and the average execution time is recorded as the time of execution for that particular net.

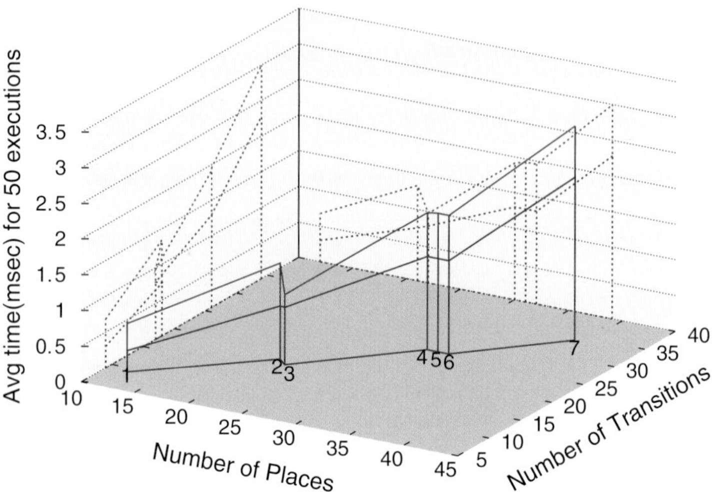

FIGURE 7.25 Average time (in ms) taken by the lookup algorithm for nets 1 to 7. The dotted lines indicate the projection of the curve on either axis.

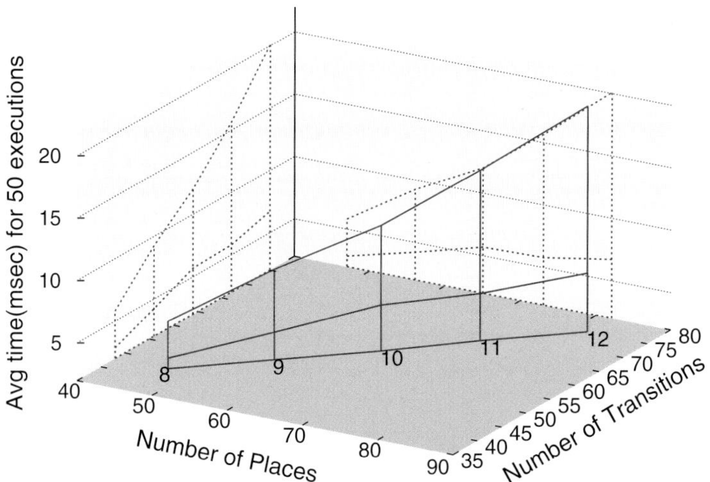

FIGURE 7.26 Average time (in ms) taken by the lookup algorithm for nets 8 to 12. The dotted lines indicate the projection of the curve on either axis.

Figure 7.25 illustrates the time taken by the lookup algorithm to find all groups in nets 1 to 7. The processing time increases as new instances of net 1 are attached. The time taken by the lookup algorithm to process nets 2 and 3 differ marginally, as they are composed of the same number of instances of an elementary net in Figure 7.7. This is also true for nets 4 to 6. However, a net with two instances of an elementary net joined vertically such as net 2 has a slightly larger processing time than that of net 3, where the instances are joined horizontally. This indicates the presence of

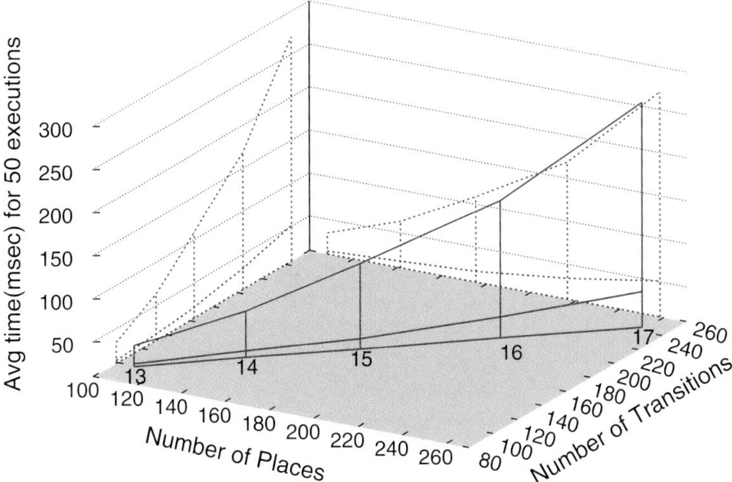

FIGURE 7.27 Average time (in ms) taken by the lookup algorithm for nets 13 to 17. The dotted lines indicate the projection of the curve on either axis.

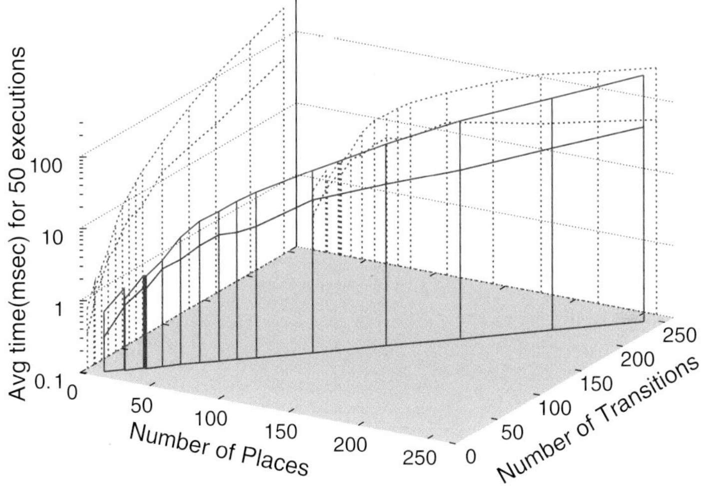

FIGURE 7.28 Average time (in ms) taken by the lookup algorithm for each net (1 to 17). The dotted lines indicate the projection of the curve on either axis.

additional identical components in net 3. For similar reasons, net 5 takes longer to process then does net 6 .

Figure 7.26 illustrates the time taken by the lookup algorithm to process nets 8 to 12. The increase in processing time is by and large linear as new instances of the elementary net are added. The processing time for nets 13 to 17, exhibited in Figure 7.27, increases more rapidly than does that of the smaller nets considered hitherto. However, deviation from the linear path for the curve is not large. Figure 7.28

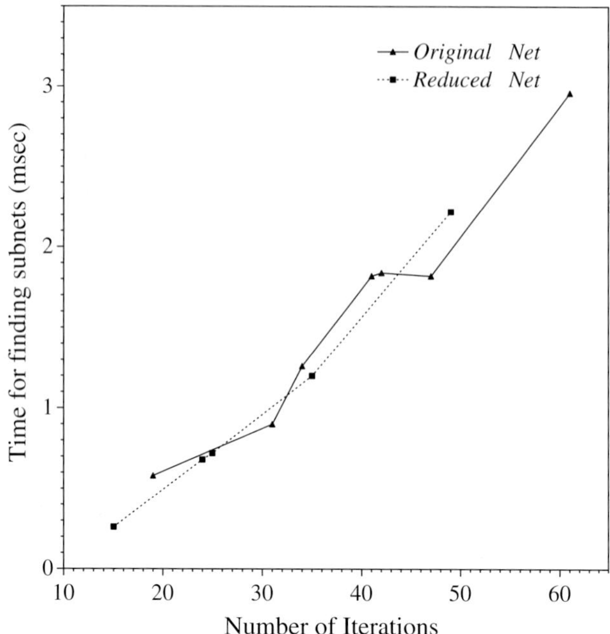

FIGURE 7.29 Average time (in ms) vs. the number of times that Algorithm 7.3 is invoked for nets 1 to 7.

compares the execution time for all 17 nets together. The increase in execution time is linear for the first 14 nets. Subsequently, the execution time increases more rapidly. However, considering that net 17 has 245 transitions and 258 places, an execution time of 270 ms can be considered fairly reasonable.

Furthermore, apart from the size of a net, the processing time also depends on the number of structurally similar components in the net. This is demonstrated in Figures 7.29 to 7.32, where the execution time for Algorithm 7.3 is plotted against its number of invocations. As discussed previously, the algorithm will be invoked more frequently for a net with many similar components. Comparing the curves corresponding to the original and modified nets, the processing time for an original net is found to be equal to that of a modified net of much smaller size provided that they invoke the algorithm the same number of times. The latter is an indication of their structural similarity. Considering the overlap between curves, it can be deduced that as the number of similar components in a net is reduced, its processing time will skid down the curve. This implies that the processing time for a net depends on the number of identical components in it.

Figures 7.33 and 7.34 demonstrate the time taken for each net by Algorithms 7.3 and 7.1. Considering that the latter takes a minuscule amount of time for processing, the execution time of the lookup algorithm is in effect the time taken by the former.

We have considered the worst-case scenario in Figures 7.29 to 7.32, wherein the number of identical components has been maximized by using multiple instances

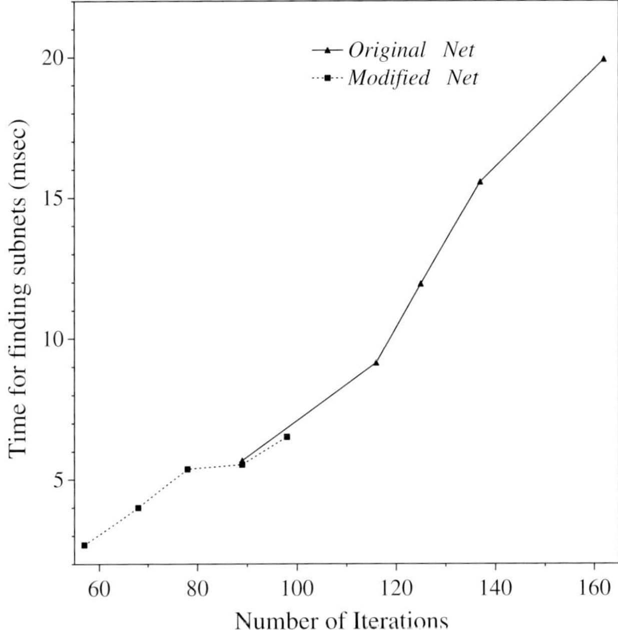

FIGURE 7.30 Average time (in ms) vs. the number of times that Algorithm 7.3 is invoked for nets 8 to 12.

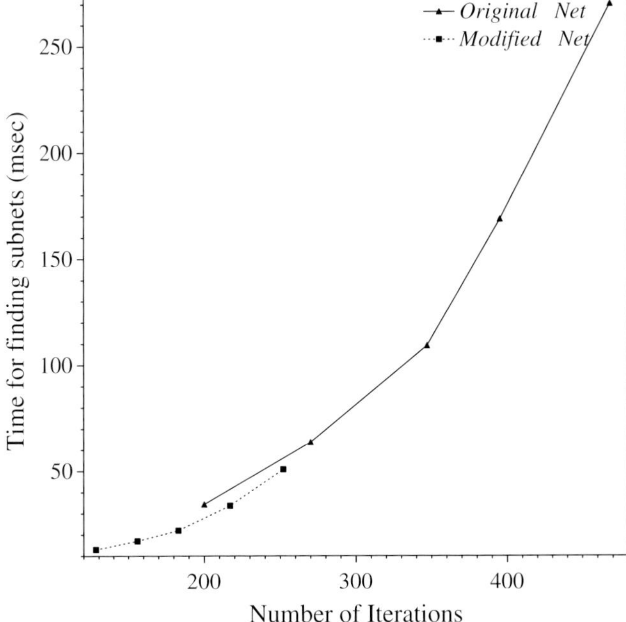

FIGURE 7.31 Average time (in ms) vs. the number of times that Algorithm 7.3 is invoked for nets 13 to 17.

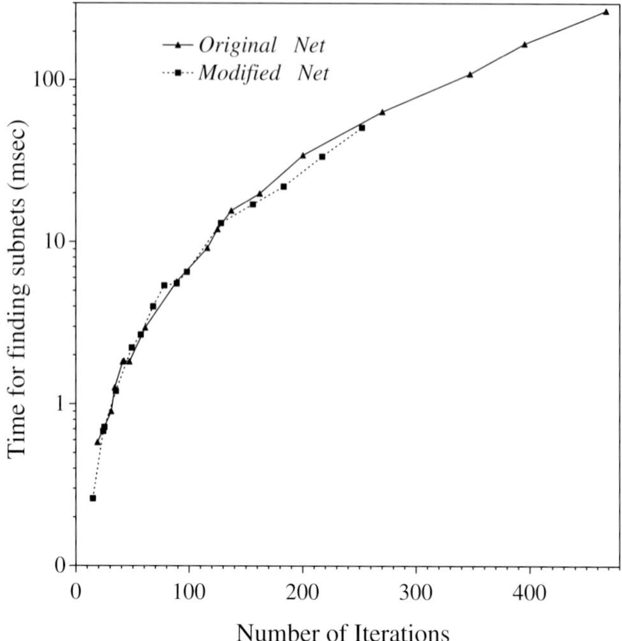

FIGURE 7.32 Average time (in ms) vs. the number of times that Algorithm 7.3 is invoked for all nets. Note that the curves overlap.

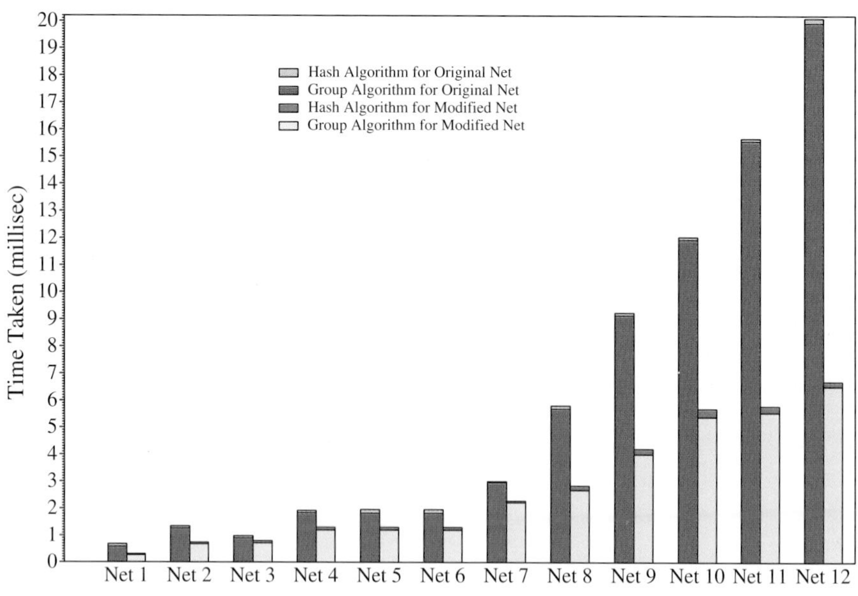

FIGURE 7.33 Processing time of Algorithms 7.3 and 7.1 for nets 1 to 12.

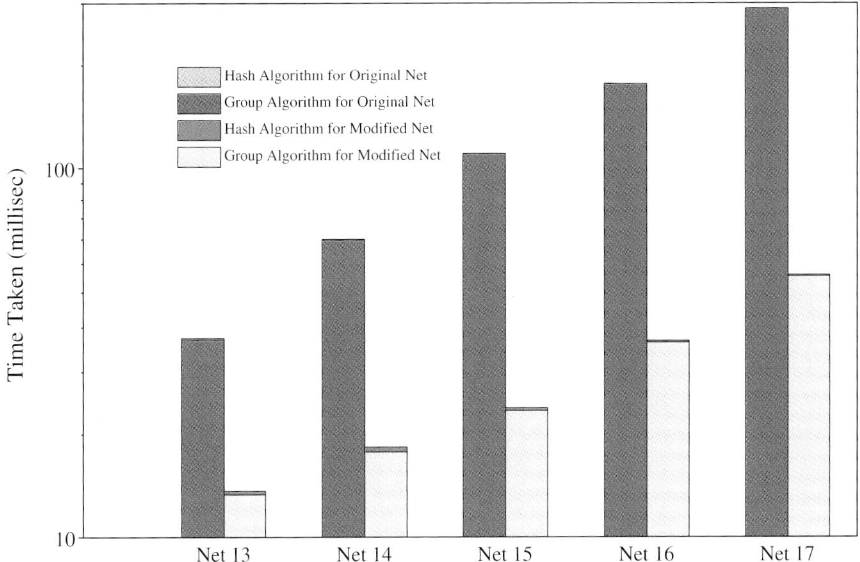

FIGURE 7.34 Processing time of Algorithms 7.3 and 7.1 for nets 13 to 17.

of the same elementary net in creating larger nets. As demonstrated previously, the execution time depends on the number of identical components in a net apart from the size of the net. Consequently, reducing the number of identical components in a net is followed by a reduction in execution time.

7.7 DISCUSSION

In this chapter we identify the problems in analyzing flat models and present a novel solution to address them. The complex and concurrent components in a contemporary software system often lead to a massive increase in the size of the corresponding formal representation. This is exacerbated further by the lack of abstraction and hierarchy in this representation. Consequently, a human modeler is required to deal with an overwhelming stockpile of information while analyzing a flat model. Such a state of affairs could lead to potential disasters, owing to any errors and omissions. To prevent such scenarios, we introduced hierarchy into an otherwise flat model. This allows a human modeler to analyze and acquire a better understanding of the system, owing to the modularity and abstraction introduced.

The solution is outlined in Figure 7.5. The hierarchy envisioned is installed by identifying the structurally similar components in a flat model and creating a module for each of them. The lookup method identifies the identical components bottom-up, starting from the elementary components of a model. It is based on the decrease-and-conquer strategy, in which the solutions to the smaller problems are used to solve a bigger problem. The results indicate that the lookup method takes linear time to find the groups in a sufficiently large net. Furthermore, the execution time of the lookup method is found to be dependent on the number of identical components in a model.

As discussed previously, the best case for the lookup method necessitates the absence of identical components. Such a scenario compels Algorithm 7.3 to quit without processing. However, as reflected in Figures 7.29 to 7.32, an increase in the number of identical components escalates the iterations of this algorithm and the associated delay.

To study the effect on delay of adding additional components, multiple instances of the example net are joined as shown in Table 7.12. From Figure 7.25, the time required to process the example net is 0.68 ms. When this net is attached to another instance of itself, the processing time is found to increase more than twofold. This is because in addition to the size, the number of identical components also doubles. Each component (places and transitions) in the first instance would have a counterpart in the other instance, leading to elementary groups of twice the size. Considering that (1) each iteration of Algorithm 7.3 attaches only a single layer of peripheral nodes to the components in a group, and (2) the size of identical components could be as large as the example net itself (because the model was formed by attaching two identical instances of the example net), the algorithm needs a large number of additional recursions to determine all identical components. The recursions required will increase further as additional instances of identical components are added. Consequently, the execution time in Figures 7.25 to 7.28 increase with an increase in the number of identical components.

The overlapping of curves for original and modified nets in Figures 7.29 to 7.32 further endorse the dependency of execution time on the number of identical components. When a net is modified to ensure that it has fewer identical components, its execution time is found to skid down along the curve. Consequently, the execution time of a larger net (e.g., modified net 17 in Figure 7.31) is found to be less than that of a much smaller net (original net 14 in Figure 7.31) when the former is modified to reduce the number of identical components. The consistency of this trend confirms the aforementioned dependency.

In Figure 7.28 we compare the average execution time for all 17 nets considered. Although the execution times are fairly linear for the first 14 nets, they increase more rapidly thereafter. This increase can be attributed to the comparison of indices in the second phase of the lookup method. Each entry in the hash tables *hashInIndex* and *hashOutIndex* consists of a list of indices corresponding to a vertex. As mentioned previously, these lists contain the indices for the input or output nodes corresponding to the key vertex. The delay is attributed to the comparison of these lists in step 32 of Algorithm 7.3. For big nets, these lists get significantly large, resulting in the delay observed.

7.8 SUMMARY

In this chapter we have described the lookup and clustering algorithms to install hierarchy into a CPN model. While the former identifies structurally similar components in a net, the latter uses these components to install hierarchy. The lookup algorithm is based on the decrease-and-conquer strategy, wherein the bigger problem is broken into smaller problems and the solutions to the smaller problems are combined to solve the original problem. It is a generic algorithm and can be used for a wide array of modeling languages that define a notion of hierarchy and structural similarity. On the contrary, the clustering algorithm uses the semantics of hierarchy defined for a particular modeling language and is consequently specific to the language. The results indicate that even in the worst-case scenario, the lookup algorithm has linear time complexity for sufficiently large nets.

The solutions presented address a niche for contemporary software systems that have a gigantic formal representation, owing to the high levels of concurrency and complexity. Our technique allows a human modeler to comprehend, analyze and maintain the representation by exploiting the abstraction and modularity. Considering that formal methods are applied at the early stage of application development, better understanding at this phase would significantly enhance the quality and reliability of the final product.

REFERENCES

1. *Basic Spin Manual*, June 2007.
2. R. Alur and M. Yannakakis. Model checking of hierarchical state machines. *ACM Transactions on Programming Languages and Systems*, 23(3):273–303, 2001.
3. G. Berthelot. Checking properties of nets using transformation. In *Advances in Petri Nets 1985, covers the 6th European Workshop on Applications and Theory in Petri Nets—Selected Papers*, pages 19–40. Springer-Verlag, Berlin, 1986.
4. D. Beyer, T. A. Henzinger, R. Jhala, and R. Majumdar. The software model checker blast: applications to software engineering. *International Journal on Software Tools for Technology Transfer*, 9:505–525, October 2007.
5. J. Chen and H. Cui. Translation from adapted UML to Promela for Corba-based applications. In *Proceeding of the 11th International SPIN Workshop*, pages 234–251, 2004.
6. S. Christensen, L. M. Kristensen, and T. Mailund. A sweep-line method for state space exploration. In *Proceedings of the 7th International Conference on Tools and Algorithms for the Construction and Analysis of Systems, TACAS 2001*, pages 450–464, 2001.
7. G. Christopher. Software modeling introduction. *Borland White Paper*. Borland Software Corporation, Austin, TX, March 2003.
8. E. Clarke, D. Long, and K. McMillan. Compositional model checking. In *Proceedings of the 4th Annual Symposium on Logic in Computer Science*, pages 353–362. IEEE Press, Piscataway, NJ, 1989.
9. E. Clarke, O. Grumberg, and D. Peled. *Model Checking*. MIT Press, Cambridge, MA, 2000.
10. S. Evangelista, S. Haddad, and J. F. Pradat-Peyre. Syntactical colored petri net reductions. In *Proceedings of the 3rd International Symposium on Automated Technology for Verification and Analysis, ATVA 2005*, volume 3707 of *Lecture Notes in Computer Science*, pages 202–216. Springer-Verleg, 2005.

11. X. Fu, T. Bultan, and J. Su. Analysis of interacting BPEL web services. In *Proceedings of the 13th World Wide Web Conference*, pages 621–630. ACM, New York, 2004.
12. S. Haddad. A reduction theory for colored nets. In *Advances in Petri Nets 1989, covers the 9th European Workshop on Applications and Theory in Petri Nets—Selected Papers*, pages 209–235. Springer-Verlag, Berlin, 1990.
13. K. Jensen. *Colored Petri Nets: Basic Concepts, Analysis Methods and Practical Use*, Vols. 1–3. Springer-Verlag, Berlin, 1996.
14. K. Jensen and L. M. Kristensen. *Colored Petri Nets: Modelling and Validation of Concurrent Systems*. Springer-Verlag, Berlin, 2009.
15. K. Jensen, L. M. Kristensen, and L. Wells. Colored petri nets and CPN tools for modelling and validation of concurrent systems. *International Journal of Software Tools for Technology Transfer*, 9(3):213–254, 2007.
16. G. T. Leavens and M. Sitaraman, Eds. *Foundations of Component-Based Systems*. Cambridge University Press, New York, 2000.
17. A. Mukherjee. Implementation of lookup algorithm. http://goanna.cs.rmit.edu.au/∼amukherj/project.tar.gz, December 2009.
18. A. Mukherjee. The structure of net 17. http://goanna.cs.rmit.edu.au/∼amukherj/net17.pdf, December 2009.
19. A. Mukherjee, Z. Tari, and P. Bertok. Memory efficient state-space analysis in software model-checking. In *33rd Australasian Computer Science Conference, ACSC*. Australian Computer Society, Darlinghurat, Australia, 2010.
20. A Puntambekar. *Analysis and Design of Algorithms*. Technical Publications, Pune, India, 2008.
21. P. Wohed, W. M. P. van der Aalst, M. Dumas, and A. H. M. ter Hofstede. Pattern-based analysis of BPEL4WS. *QUT Technical Report FIT-TR-2002-04*. Queensland University of Technology, Brisbane, Australia, 2002.

CHAPTER 8

FRAMEWORK FOR MODELING, SIMULATION, AND VERIFICATION OF A BPEL SPECIFICATION

In previous chapters we described methods for reducing the time and memory requirements for model checking. These methods offer incentives to use formal methods of verifying service-oriented architecture (SOA)–based applications. These chapters have also emphasized the ingenuity of formal methods in endorsing the safety and reliability of software systems. Following their widespread use in software engineering, they are increasingly being adopted for verification of SOA-based applications [14,19,32,33]. This is helping in identifying subtle errors in a *Business Process Execution Language* (BPEL) specification, the de facto industry standard for service composition. Such errors would often elude conventional simulation and testing techniques.

SOA-based applications have assumed widespread acceptance, owing to their agility, maintainability, and modularity. However, the safety and reliability of such loosely coupled systems depend entirely on the precision of service descriptions. Consequently, any implicit assumption or unforeseen usage scenarios can lead to catastrophic fiascos. This is exacerbated further by the overlapping constructs and inconsistencies in BPEL.

Verification of Communication Protocols in Web Services: Model-Checking Service Compositions, First Edition. Zahir Tari, Peter Bertok, Anshuman Mukherjee.

Conventional techniques cannot be used to verify an SOA-based application because (1) the fault, if any, is related primarily to the business logic for service composition rather than the source code or implementation of underlying services; (2) even if an issue is found with the implementation of a service, the source code is usually not available for rectification; and (3) even if the source code is available, it cannot be rectified immediately, as this would probably break thousands of other applications using this service. Consequently, an appropriate verification technique would investigate the service composition for all possible behaviors of the underlying services.

In recent years, several sophisticated techniques have been proposed to allow automatic matching and discovery of web services [16,23]. This empowers automatic and dynamic location of suitable web services and their composition to offer an envisioned complex service. Nevertheless, such techniques would overwhelmingly rely on automated verification methods to vouch for their credibility. Considering that model checking is an automated verification technique that scrutinizes all possible behaviors of a system exhaustively, it ought to be used for SOA-based applications. However, in the absence of a concrete framework, this verification process is essentially ad hoc.

In this chapter we extend the *Spring framework* to devise a verification framework for service composition wherein each BPEL activity is represented by a *Java bean*. This framework instantiates the beans corresponding to activities in a BPEL specification and injects the dependencies to yield a *bean factory*. Then *Java Architecture for XML Binding* (JAXB) 2 APIs are used to transform the bean factory into an XML-based formal model [e.g., colored petri nets (CPNs)] or an interchange format [e.g., Petri Net Markup Language (PNML)] for simulation and verification. In addition to automating the verification process, the framework helps to combat the ad hoc nature of existing solutions. Results indicate that the framework takes 0.7 s on average for formalization of a BPEL specification.

To evaluate the framework, a CPN template (which is XML based) is produced for each BPEL activity. The JAXB 2 APIs generate the formal model based on these templates. Each template is customized based on the attributes specified for the corresponding BPEL activity. A CPN model is essentially an XML document, and these templates confirm to the document type definition (DTD) supplied for CPN tools [30].

8.1 MOTIVATION

SOA-based applications are built as an assembly of existing web services that are invoked in some sequence based on the underlying business logic. Its component web services can span across several organizational boundaries and have any underlying implementation. Such a state of affairs has necessitated a tool for orchestrating the business workflow. Among all the domain-specific languages that were proposed, the BPEL for web services [3,5,10] stands out as the de facto industry standard for *web-service composition*.

SOA-based applications offer code mobility, cross-client support, code reuse, better scalability, and a distinct partition of application layers. However, the safety and reliability of such loosely coupled systems depend entirely on the precision of service descriptions. Consequently, any implicit assumption or unforeseen usage scenarios can lead to undesirable forms of interactions, such as a deadlock or race condition [25].

Considering the unprecedented ability of formal methods in ensuring the correctness of a system, they ought to be adopted for verifying SOA-based applications [8,20]. This would help to identify subtle errors in BPEL specifications that often elude conventional simulation and testing techniques.

Unfortunately, the overlapping constructs [31] and the lack of sound formal or mathematical semantics [24,28] in BPEL did not allow formal methods to be applied to its textual specification. These inconsistencies are the outcome of two conceptually contrasting languages, the Web Services Flow Language (WSFL) [17] of IBM and XLANG [27] of Microsoft, which were amalgamated to constitute BPEL [24].

Consequently, the textual specification of BPEL needs to be transformed into a formal specification prior to any formal verification. A BPEL specification is essentially a sequence of activities, and the aforesaid transformation involves formalization of each of these activities.

Most of the existing solutions incorporate an ad hoc mapping of BPEL activities into formal models [14,19,32,33]. Users are required to scan a BPEL specification and replace each activity with its corresponding formal model. Apart from being a cumbersome process, such an exercise is error-prone and time consuming. Although there exist some solutions that automate this translation, they are neither generic nor provide a pluggable interface to qualify as a framework [15]. Furthermore, they do not consider BPEL's most interesting and complicated activities, such as *eventHandler* and *links*, and overlook crucial scenarios such as *dead-path elimination* (DPE).

The crux of the problem lies in attempting to formalize a BPEL specification using a specific modeling language. Considering that many modeling languages are available (e.g., Promela, petri nets, automata, process algebras), targeting a specific language renders an ad hoc and temporary solution. Consequently, in this chapter we transform a BPEL specification into a generic intermediate specification formed before the actual formalization. In software engineering, data transfer objects (DTOs) are commonly used design patterns for storing and transferring data [9]. Therefore, we use DTOs to store the generic intermediate specification, wherein each BPEL activity is mapped to a separate DTO.

The aforementioned intermediate specification is obtained from a BPEL specification using the Spring framework. Despite the syntactical differences between a BPEL specification and a Spring configuration document, in this chapter we identify immense semantic similarity. Consequently, the Spring framework has been extended to recognize BPEL activities and populate corresponding DTOs. This helps to significantly automate the transformation envisioned.

As noted previously, the generic intermediate specification could be transformed into any modeling language. However, in this chapter we specifically target the modeling languages that are based on XML. This is done using the JAXB 2 APIs that transform the Spring bean factory into an XML-based formal model or an interchange format. The latter acts as an intermediate specification that can be transformed into a range of formal models. For example, PNML [6] can yield different versions of petri nets.

The innovative ideas provided in this chapter can be summarized as:

- A Spring-based verification framework to map individual BPEL activities into Java beans. This offers several advantages over existing techniques that map BPEL activities into formal models: (1) the transformation is automatic; (2) Java beans are generic intermediate specifications that can yield a range of formal models; and (3) the framework significantly reduces the time required for transformation.
- An object model to streamline the mapping of BPEL activities into Java beans. This model identifies the relationship among BPEL activities and forms the basis of (1) mapping from BPEL activities into DTOs and (2) CPN templates for BPEL activities.
- A JAXB 2-based component for the framework to transform the bean factory into an XML-based formal model. It forms a noncore component that could be replaced to transform the bean factory into non-XML formal models. The pluggability of formalizing a component into the framework forms the basis of its flexibility.
- A formalized BPEL activity as an XML templates that confirms to the DTD specified for CPN Tools. Templates are part of a complete formal model. Such templates are used by the JAXB 2 compiler to generate formal models. The templates exploit the hierarchical relationship among BPEL activities that is defined using the object model.

The rest of the chapter is organized as follows. In Section 8.2 we introduce a problem and provide an insight into the solution tendered. Prior to proposing the templates for formalizing a BPEL specification in Section 8.4, the existing work is compiled in Section 8.3. The experimental results are presented in Section 8.5, and the outcomes are discussed in Section 8.6. In Section 8.7 we summarize the major technical ideas of this chapter.

8.2 OVERVIEW OF THE PROBLEM AND SOLUTION

As pointed out previously, BPEL has emerged out of conflicting parent languages that differ vastly in the structure of control and message flows. Consequently, BPEL is infested with umpteen inherent inconsistencies and ambiguities that seriously undermine the reliability of a SOA-based application. This is aggravated further by the loosely coupled nature of a SOA-based application. The safety and reliability of loosely coupled systems depend entirely on the precision of service descriptions in which any implicit assumption or unforeseen usage scenarios can lead to undesirable forms of interactions, such as a deadlock or race condition [25]. Furthermore, as observed previously, dynamic service composition techniques rely overwhelmingly on automatic verification techniques to vouch for their reliability.

As emphasized in earlier chapters, *model checking* [8] is an automatic formal-verification technique that is being adopted increasingly as a standard procedure for quality assurance of software systems. Taking a cue from this tenacious trend, in this chapter we present a verification framework to enhance the reliability and usability of SOA-based applications. This has been done by mapping each BPEL activity into a Java bean that is instantiated and initialized by the Spring framework. This mapping is essentially between the properties of a class and the attributes of its corresponding BPEL activity. Furthermore, the classes corresponding to BPEL structured activities have an additional property to store the list of its child activities. The Spring framework has been extended to accept a BPEL configuration and to instantiate and initialize the classes (using their setter methods) corresponding to the activities in the specification. The objects (Java beans) rendered act as intermediate specifications that could be transformed into a range of formal models. For the purpose of verification in this chapter, a pluggable component is employed that uses JAXB 2 APIs to render XML-based models.

To generate a formal representation, the pluggable component requires an XML-based model corresponding to each BPEL activity. Considering that the CPN models are XML based, a CPN template for each BPEL activity is utilized. A hierarchical relationship among BPEL activities is established to allow the reuse of a parent template for its child activities after any required customization. This helps to significantly reduce the number of templates required.

Compared to other techniques, the solution (1) offers a generic intermediate specification that can be transformed into a range of formal models, and (2) also offers an interface to plug in alternative components for transformation.

8.3 RELATED WORK

All solutions for formalizing a BPEL specification involve a transformation into either (1) petri nets/colored petri nets [19,25,26,32], (2) process algebras [13], (3) an abstract state machine [11,12], or (4) an automaton [4,15]. They all offer significant strides in the formal verification of a BPEL specification. However, many authors [15,19,32] do not consider BPEL's most interesting and complicated activities, such as event handlers, link, and *dead-path elimination* (DPE) associated with links. Although stahl [26] includes scenarios involving these activities, the models rendered are bulky and error-prone, owing to the plain-vanilla petri nets used. The abstract state machine–based solutions are also feature complete. However, they lack adequate tool support for simulation and verification.

To support a variety of versions of petri nets, an XML-based interchange format has been proposed known as Petri Net Markup Language (PNML) [6]. The BPEL2PNML tool [22] exploits this offering by transforming a BPEL process code into a document conforming to the PNML syntax. Thereafter the formal verification and analysis are performed using the WofBPEL [21] tool, which is built using Woflan [29]. However, due to the lack of a robust visual modeling formalism, the technique fails to render an insight into the petri net obtained (i.e., PNML). The platform-independent petri net editor (PIPE) tool used for graphical visualization of PNML models is still in its early stages of development [7].

As emphasized previously, PNML is an interchange format and can be transformed into various different versions of petri nets. The technique proposed by sloan and Khoshgoftaar [25] builds on that of Ouyang et al. [22] by transforming the PNML model yield into a CPN model. Apart from being inefficient compared to direct conversion, there is always a probability of introducing errors into the intermediate petri net model due to (1) the lack of robust visual formalism, and (2) the fact that the intermediate model is often too large for human comprehension. The importance of geometry in the understandability of a visible model has been stressed and incorporated in our work.

Table 8.1 compares related work on formalization and verification of BPEL under five different categories. These categories are listed under individual columns, and their applicability for any related work is documented using three different symbols. The criteria for constituting these categories are:

- *Tech* refers to the technique used to formalize BPEL activities. The techniques and their short codes are as follows : PA for process algebra, ASM for abstract state machines, AM for automata, PN for petri nets, and CPN for colored petri nets.
- *LN* refers to whether the links can be used to express synchronization dependency in the target model. The symbol [●] denotes "Yes," [⊗] denotes "No," and [◐] denotes cases where dead-path elimination is not covered.
- *ECF* refers to whether event, compensation, and fault handlers are covered. A [●] denotes "Yes," [⊗] denotes "No," and [◐] denotes cases where not all three handlers are covered.

TABLE 8.1 Comparative Summary of Related Work

Related Work	Tech	LN	ECF	TOOL	VIS
[13]	PA	⊗	●	⊗	⊗
[12]	ASM	●	●	⊗	⊗
[15]	AM	◐	◐	●	◐
[19]	CPN	⊗	⊗	●	●
[25]	CPN	◐	◐	●	●
[26]	PN	●	●	●	⊗
[22]	PN	●	●	●	◐
Technique presented here	CPN	●	●	●	●

- *TOOL* refers to whether a verification tool is provided for the model rendered. A [●] denotes "Yes," and [⊗] denotes "No,".
- *VIS* denotes if a robust visualization formalism exists to provide an insight into the model transformed. A [●] denotes "Yes," [⊗] denotes "No," and [◐] denotes cases where the tool is not robust.

8.4 COLORED PETRI NET SEMANTICS FOR BPEL

In this section we introduce the framework for automatic formal verification of web-service composition. As illustrated in Figure 8.1, the framework has two basic components. The first component (component A in Figure 8.1) is an extension of the Spring framework that instantiates the beans corresponding to a BPEL specification and renders the bean factory. It is also the core component of the framework. The other component (component B in Figure 8.1) transforms the Java beans into an XML-based model based on a DTD or XML schema. This component can be replaced by or supplemented by additional components required for transformation.

Figure 8.1 also highlights the four steps that are involved in transformation. The first two steps involve component A; the other two steps involve component B. The role of each step and its prominence in a component are discussed further in the following sections.

8.4.1 Component A

Component A is the core component of the framework that renders a bean factory out of a BPEL specification. It is based on the Spring framework and offers all its benefits (e.g., loose coupling and dependency injection).

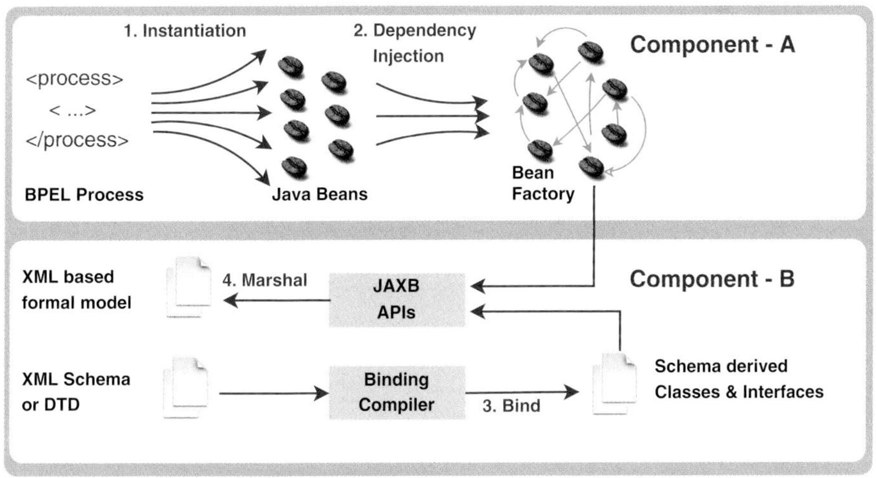

FIGURE 8.1 Architecture of the verification framework.

The similarity between a BPEL specification and a Spring configuration file forms the basis of this component. Although structurally dissimilar, they both contain the requisite information to instantiate and initialize Java beans. Consequently, the Spring framework has been extended to parse a BPEL specification (1) to recognize BPEL activities, (2) to fetch all information associated with an activity, and (3) to instantiate and initialize appropriate Java beans.

This is illustrated using Figure 8.2, wherein an equivalent Spring configuration has been formulated for a BPEL specification. The extended Spring framework operates identically with the XML files and renders identical Java beans. Figure 8.3 highlights the class that was modified to implement this feature.

The default logic for parsing an XML configuration file is implemented in the *registerBeanDefinitions* method of the *DefaultBeanDefinitionDocumentReader* class.

```
<partnerLink name="PL1"
    partnerRole="PR1"
    partnerLinkType="PLT1"/>
<variable name="V1"
    messageType="MT1"/>
<variable name="V2"
    messageType="MT2"/>
<invoke name="I1"
    partnerLink="PL1"
    portType="PT1"
    operation="OP1"
    inputVariable="V1"
    outputVariable="V2"/>
```

```
<bean id="PL1" class="PartnerLink">
<property name="partnerRole" value="PR1"/>
<property name="partnerLinkType" value="PLT1"/>
</bean>
<bean id="V1" class="Variable">
<property name="messageType" value="MT1"/>
</bean>
<bean id="V2" class="Variable">
<property name="messageType" value="MT2"/>
</bean>
<bean id="I1" class="Invoke">
<property name="partnerLink" ref="PL1"/>
<property name="portType" value="PT1"/>
<property name="operation" value="OP1"/>
<property name="inputVariable" ref="V1"/>
<property name="outputVariable" ref="V2"/>
</bean>
```

BPEL
Spring

FIGURE 8.2 Spring configuration for a BPEL specification.

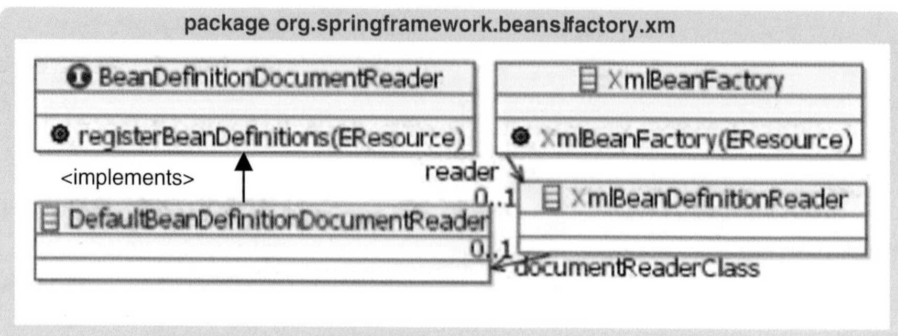

FIGURE 8.3 Class modified for underlying extension.

We extended the default logic to allow parsing of a BPEL specification. The two steps associated with this component are discussed next.

Step 1: Instantiation. The first step involves parsing a BPEL specification and instantiating the appropriate Java beans. When parsing a BPEL specification, the extended framework initially fetches all the XML elements in it. Thereafter it looks for classes corresponding to each of these elements. Considering that each BPEL activity is mapped to a Java bean, the framework should find an appropriate class for each element. The class names are essentially the same as the activity names mapped (with the exception of the first character, which is an uppercase letter). Usually, a Java bean has one property per attribute of the corresponding activity. The framework uses "setter" methods to initialize these properties with appropriate values. However, the Java beans for BPEL-structured activities have an additional property to store the references in underlying child activities. For example, as shown in Figure 8.4, the bean for the *flow* activity would store the references in all its child activities.

Instead of creating the Java beans manually, we generate them automatically using the Eclipse Modeling Framework (EMF) [1]. The framework offers a graphical interface to create an object model that is used to generate the classes. Details of this model are given in Section 8.4.3, and the model is used to create Java beans for the verification framework. Every attempt has been made to introduce hierarchy into the object model. Considering that a large number of BPEL activities have identical attributes, this allows a child class to reuse the properties of its parent class.

```
<flow name="F1">
<invoke name="I1" .../>
<invoke name="I2" .../>
<invoke name="I3" .../>
</flow>
```

```
<bean id="I1" class="Invoke">
        ....
</bean>
<bean id="I2" class="Invoke">
        ....
</bean>
<bean id="I3" class="Invoke">
        ....
</bean>
<bean id="F1" class="Flow">
<property name="contains">
  <list>
    <ref bean="I1"/>
    <ref bean="I2"/>
    <ref bean="I3"/>
  </list>
</property>
</bean>
```

BPEL
Spring

FIGURE 8.4 Bean for structured activities that store references in child activities.

Step 2: Dependency Injection. After instantiating the Java beans in step 1, their properties need to be initialized. In step 2 the framework uses the appropriate setter methods to assign these properties. Considering that this resolves any dependency between collaborating objects, the process is also known as *dependency injection*.

As illustrated in Figures 8.2 and 8.4, a property might be assigned either a value or a reference to another bean. Whereas a value is available immediately, a reference might not be available until the corresponding bean is instantiated. For example, the property *contains* of the *Flow* class, shown in Figure 8.4, can only be initialized after all three *Invoke* beans have been instantiated.

At the close of step 2, the framework renders a bean factory. This factory makes it possible to retrieve the objects contained by their names.

8.4.2 Component B

Component B yields a formal model based on the bean factory and an XML schema. As discussed previously, it has two subcomponents: a binding compiler and a binding runtime. The binding compiler requires an XML schema or a DTD that defines the structure of the XML document envisioned. It creates a set of classes that conform to this structure. These classes need to be instantiated and initialized before the binding runtime can use them to generate the XML document required. Objects from the bean factory are used to initialize these classes. The two steps associated with this component are discussed next.

Step 3: Bind. In this step, the binding compiler generates a set of annotated classes based on a schema or DTD. This schema determines the structure of the formal model produced and is different for each solution. Considering that most researchers prefer to present their solution as a set of XML models (rather than the corresponding schemas) [19,22,25,32,33], the tool *Trang* [2] can be used to obtain their XSD schemas. Usually, a schema is required per BPEL activity to transform the corresponding Java bean into a model.

Figure 8.5 illustrates an excerpt from a CPN model (which is XML based), and the corresponding schema is obtained using Trang. The autogenerated schema can be customized to further streamline the formal model rendered by the component.

Step 4: Marshal. In this step, the binding runtime actually produces the formal model from the classes generated in step 3. However, as a prerequisite, these classes must be instantiated and initialized using the objects in the bean factory. Considering that these classes have getter and setter methods for each property to be initialized, they are instantiated using a Spring configuration file, wherein their dependencies are injected to produce another bean factory. Please note that this bean factory is different from the factory generated by component A, and its beans are restricted to the classes generated in step 3. After initialization, the objects in this bean factory are used by the binding runtime to generate the formal model. The instantiation and initialization of classes are explained further using Figures 8.6 and 8.7.

```
<page id="ID1">
 <pageattr name="ID2"/>
 <place id="ID3"/>
 <place id="ID4"/>
 <trans id="ID5"/>
 <arc id="ID6"
    orientation="PtoT"/>
 <arc id="ID7"
    orientation="TtoP"/>
</page>
```

```
<xs:element name="page">
  <xs:complexType>
   <xs:sequence>
    <xs:element ref="pageattr"/>
    <xs:element maxOccurs="unbounded"
       ref="place"/>
    <xs:element ref="trans"/>
    <xs:element maxOccurs="unbounded"
       ref="arc"/>
   </xs:sequence>
   <xs:attribute name="id"
       use="required" type="xs:NCName"/>
  </xs:complexType>
 </xs:element>
 <xs:element name="pageattr">
  <xs:complexType>
   <xs:attribute name="name"
       use="required" type="xs:NCName"/>
  </xs:complexType>
 </xs:element>
       ....
</xs:schema>
```

XML
XSD

FIGURE 8.5 Schema for a fragment of a CPN model.

```
<place id="ID1003057409">
 <posattr x="-298.000000"
    y="19.000000"/>
 <text/>
 <type id="ID1003057410">
  <text tool="CPN Tools"
    version="2.2.0">
    PARTNERLINK</text>
 </type>
 <initmark id="ID1003057411">
  <text tool="CPN Tools"
    version="2.2.0">
      1`("PL1","PLT1","MR1","PR1")++
      1`("PL2","PLT2","null","PR2")
  </text>
 </initmark>
</place>
```

```
Class PartnerLink{

    String name;
    String partnerLinkType;
    String myRole;
    String partnerRole;

    //getters and setters

}
```

CPN excerpt
Java Bean
initialise from bean

FIGURE 8.6 CPN excerpt wherein the initial marking of a place is assigned from Java beans.

```
public class Place {
  protected Initmark initmark;
    ....
  //getters and setters }

public class Initmark {
  protected Text text;
  protected String id;
  //getters and setters }

public class Text {
  protected String content;
  protected String tool;
  protected String version;
  //getters and setters }

class Initialise{
  private Text text;
  public void setBf(BeanFactory bf){
    PartnerLink pl=
         bf.getBean("partnerLink");
    text.setContent(pl.getName+...);
  }
  //getters and setters }
```

```
<bean id="place" class="Place">
  <property name="initmark" ref="inim"/>
    ....
</bean>
<bean id="inim" class="Initmark">
  <property name="text" ref="text"/>
    ....
</bean>
<bean id="text" class="Text">
  <property name="tool" value=".."/>
  <property name="version" value=".."/>
</bean>
<bean id="file" class="org.springframework.
                   core.io.FileSystemResource">
  <constructor-arg value="bpel.xml"/>
</bean>
<bean id="ft" class="org.springframework.
             beans.factory.xml.XmlBeanFactory">
  <constructor-arg ref="file"/>
</bean>
<bean id="beanSecond" class="Initialise">
  <property name="bf" ref="ft"/>
  <property name="text" ref="text"/>
</bean>
```

FIGURE 8.7 Instantiation and initialization of classes for CPN excerpt in Figure 8.6.

Figure 8.6 illustrates a CPN-based solution wherein a place is initialized with all partner links in a BPEL document. Consequently, this requires copying the properties of *PartnerLink* beans into an appropriate section of the CPN excerpt (shown in brown). However, since this CPN excerpt is to be generated automatically by the JAXB bind runtime, classes used by it need to be initialized with this value.

The process of initializing the classes is explained using Figure 8.7. When the schema corresponding to the CPN excerpt is compiled (using xjc), each element of the excerpt renders a new class. Furthermore, these classes procure properties per attribute and per child node of the corresponding element. Considering that the node to be initialized is the child of a *text* element, it should be assigned using the *content* property of the *Text* class. However, the value to be assigned is stored in the bean factory generated by component A. Consequently, this bean factory is fetched (using *XmlBeanFactory*) and injected into the *Initialize* class to assign the value. As shown in Figure 8.7, each bean whose properties need to be assigned is also injected into this class. Since the bean factory from component A is injected as a property *bf*, the method *setBf* is invoked for initializing the properties of other beans. It is worth mentioning that “bpel.xml” in Figure 8.7 is the BPEL specification document.

8.4.3 Object Model for BPEL Activities

We now introduce the object model for BPEL activities. Apart from being the basis of BPEL activity classes, the XML templates are also based on it. Having a standard object model helps in customizing the templates on the fly. This is because the places to look for information in each case are known.

In this section we illustrate the semantic and syntactic relationship among BPEL activities using Figure 8.8. For example, the activities *invoke*, *receive*, and *reply* are subclasses of a parent class *InterfaceActivities*, owing to their semantic similarity. Similarly, due to their syntactic similarity, the class *Activities* has the properties *suppressJoinFailure* and *joinCondition*, which are common for its child classes. Using such relationships, a generic template can be produced for a parent class which could then be customized for each of its child classes. Each activity in Figure 8.8 is represented as a class that is related to other classes using either an "is-a" (inheritance) or a "has-a" (composition) relationship.

In the following discussion we outline the relationship among classes in Figure 8.8. These relationships are reflected in the XML templates introduced in the next section. At the top of the hierarchy is the class for *Process* which forms the root of any BPEL document. It contains a reference to *GlobalScope*, which signifies the top-level scope in a BPEL process. The class *GlobalScope*, in turn, has references to *LocalScope* for each secondary-level scope. Considering that a scope in a BPEL specification can have nested scopes of arbitrary depth, the class *LocalScope* has a self-reference in order to identify the parent scope. For example, the ternary scopes have secondary scopes as their parent.

Based on this relationship among global and local scopes, we have decided to incorporate hierarchical CPNs to model a BPEL specification wherein each additional level of hierarchy corresponds to a supplementary depth of a nested scope. This reiterates the importance of utilizing these relationships when formalizing a BPEL specification.

A scope can contain variables, compensation handlers, fault handlers, event handlers, and a primary activity. Table 8.2 lists the class for each of these activities. The class *Variable* has properties that store the name and contents of a variable. In addition, it also has an entry to store the variable type. The enumeration *VariableTypes* contains all "types" for BPEL variables. The class for primary activity and those for each of the handlers contain one or more references to "Activities". Consequently, they are discussed after introducing the classes for BPEL activities. These relationships are reflected in the templates for local and global scopes that are described in the following section.

The class *Activities* forms the superclass for all BPEL activities. It has references to *GlobalScope* and *LocalScope* that store top-level and enclosing scopes. All activities in the top-level scope have their *lScope* assigned to *null*. Considering that a BPEL specification has a single top-level scope, all activities contain the same reference in *gScope*. Also included are two properties essential to expressing synchronization dependencies using the BPEL link activity. These properties are included in the superclass, as any BPEL activity can be the source or target for a link. The references *source* and *target* in *Links* store references to these activities.

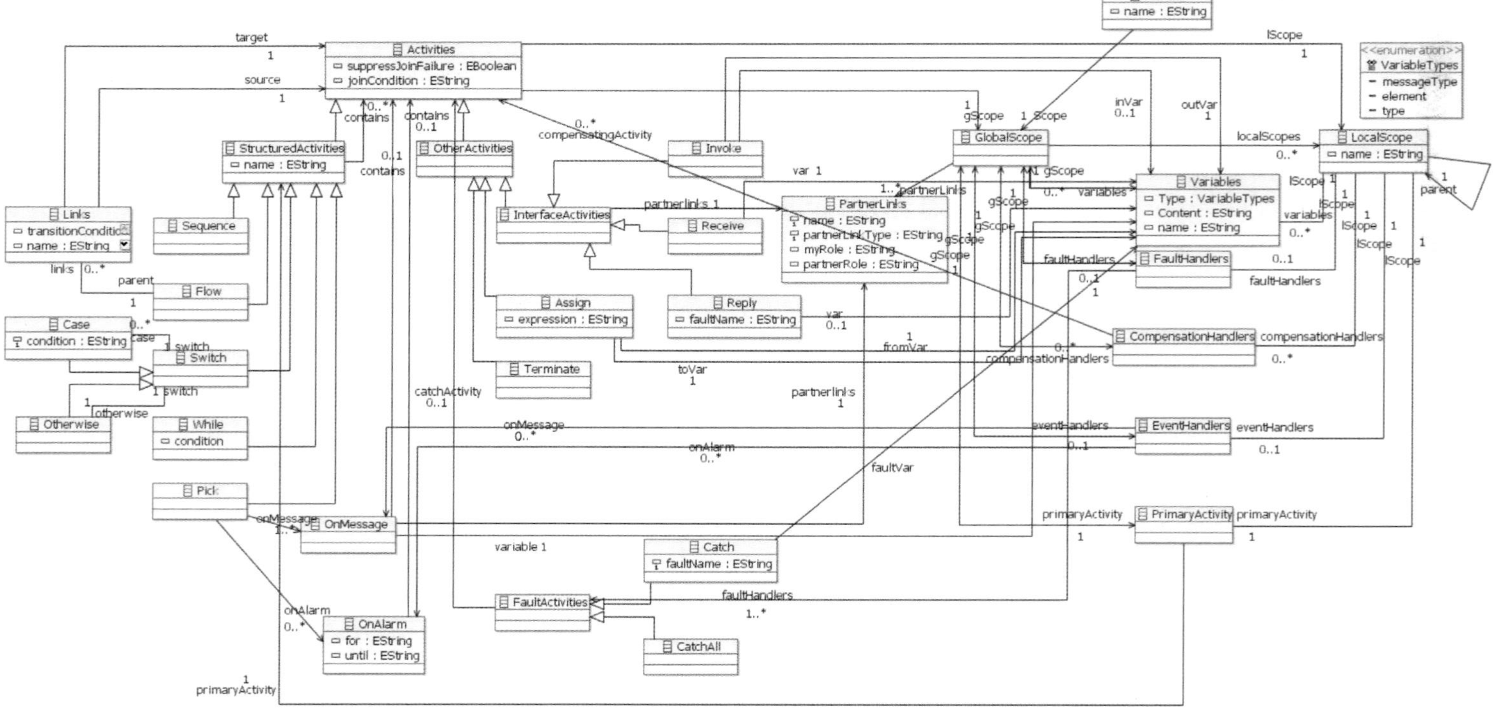

FIGURE 8.8 Object Model for BPEL Activities.

TABLE 8.2 Classes for Compensation Handlers, Fault Handlers, Event Handlers, and a Primary Activity

BPEL Activity Name	Class Name
faultHandlers	*FaultHandlers*
eventHandlers	*EventHandlers*
compensationHandlers	*CompensationHandlers*
Primary activity of a scope	*PrimaryActivity*

Based on these relationships, in the next section we describe two XML templates corresponding to an activity. While the first template is applicable for activities that are synchronized by links, the other template is used for activities that are neither the source nor the target of a link.

The class *Activities* has two subclasses, *StructuredActivities* and *OtherActivities*. As the names indicate, the former is the superclass for all structured activities in BPEL, while the remaining activities extend to the latter. The list of subactivities of a structured activity is represented by the reference *contains*. This reference to *Activities* is included in the superclass because all structured activities in BPEL can have subactivities. Table 8.3 lists the classes for structured activities.

The class *Flow* has a reference to *Links*, which stores all the links defined within a flow activity. The class *Links* also has a reference to *Flow*, which stores the enclosing *flow* activity as its parent. The class *Switch* contains references to one or more instances of *Case*, which also happens to be its subclass. The *Case* class has a property *condition* that is evaluated by *Switch* for each of its instances. The first instance encountered that satisfies the condition has its subtasks executed. Additionally, it contains a reference to its subclass *Otherwise*, whose subtasks are evaluated when none of the conditions are satisfied.

The *While* class corresponds to the BPEL *while* activity. It has a property *condition* that causes the subtasks to be executed repeatedly until it evaluates to *false*.

The class *Pick* corresponds to a BPEL *pick* activity. Considering that a pick activity can have any number of *onMessage* and *onAlarm* activities (at least one *onMessage* activity), the class *Pick* contain a reference to *OnMessage* and *OnAlarm* instances. The class *OnMessage* has a reference to *PartnerLinks*, owing to the *partnerLink* attribute of the *onMessage* activity. It also has a reference to *Variables*,

TABLE 8.3 Classes for BPEL Structured Activities

BPEL Activity Name	Class Name
sequence	*Sequence*
flow	*Flow*
switch/case/otherwise	*Switch/Case/Otherwise*
while	*While*
pick	*Pick*

corresponding to the variable attribute. The *OnAlarm* class stores the duration and deadline in its *for* and *until* attributes.

The classes *Invoke*, *Receive*, and *Reply* extend a common class *InterfaceActivities*. As the name suggests, *InterfaceActivities* is the superclass for all BPEL activities that are involved in interaction with other web services. Consequently, it contains a reference to *PartnerLinks*. The class *Invoke* has references *inVar* and *outVar*, corresponding to the *inputVariable* and *outputVariable* attributes of the *invoke* activity. Similarly, *Receive* and *Reply* contain the reference *var*, corresponding to the attribute variable. In addition, *Reply* has the property *faultName*, to store the name of the fault in case of synchronous operation.

The class *Assign* corresponds to the BPEL activity assign. It is used to copy values between variables and an expression. Consecutively, it has a property *expression* and two references, *toVar* and *fromVar*.

The handlers listed in Table 8.2 are now discussed. The class *FaultHandlers* contains references to *FaultActivities*, which in turn contains a reference to *Activities*. While the reference in *FaultHandlers* stores instances of underlying *Catch* and *CatchAll* classes, the reference in *FaultActivities* holds the subactivities of a *Catch* or *CatchAll* activity. The *Catch* class has a property *faultName* to store the fault name and a reference *faultVar* to store the fault variable. Based on the fault, a *Catch* or *CatchAll* instance is selected and its subactivities are executed.

The class *CompensationHandler* contains a reference to a set of *Activities* instances that are executed when the BPEL "compensate" activity is invoked for a particular scope. The reference *parent* in a scope is used to determine its enclosing scope and to ensure that the compensate activity is present in the compensation handler or fault handler of this enclosing scope.

The class *EventHandlers* contains a reference to the underlying *OnMessage* and *OnAlarm* instances, which in turn contain references to the list of subtasks to be executed in the event of receiving a message or a time-out. When compared to the *Pick* class, the *onMessage* reference in *EventHandlers* has a lower bound of zero. This follows from the fact that a BPEL pick activity must have at least one underlying *onMessage* activity, whereas event handlers might have none.

Each BPEL scope has a primary activity that is stored in the *primaryActivity* reference of a *PrimaryActivity* instance. Primary activities are often structured activities containing one or more underlying subactivities. Even when a primary activity is not structured, it can be wrapped with a BPEL sequence activity. Consequently, the reference *primaryActivity* contains instances of *StructuredActivities*.

The XML templates reflect the aforementioned identified relationships. Considering that

- *GlobalScope* (and *LocalScope*) "has-a" *FaultHandlers*
- *GlobalScope* (and *LocalScope*) "has-a" *EventHandlers*
- *GlobalScope* (and *LocalScope*) "has-a" *CompensationHandlers*
- *GlobalScope* (and *LocalScope*) "has-a" *Variables*
- *GlobalScope* (and *LocalScope*) "has-a" *PrimaryActivity*

these activities are included in the templates for global and local scopes in the next section. This allows each scope to have its exclusive set of handler, variable, and primary activities.

8.4.4 XML Templates

XML templates for formalizing BPEL activities are presented in this section. These templates (i.e., their schemas) are used by a JAXB 2 compiler to create a formal model using Java beans. As mentioned previously, the templates are based on an object model defined in Section 8.4.3.

Template for Global Scope. Here the template, which forms the basis of any formal model, is detailed. Additional information from the object model is used to customize this template to obtain the formal model. A CPN model could comprise either a single page or a number of pages. While the former produces a flat representation, the latter produce a hierarchical representation. Considering that the scopes in a BPEL specification could also be flat or hierarchical, we use a separate page to represent each scope. The top-level (global) scope is imperative in all BPEL specifications, and the absence of any other scope results in a flat orientation. The presence of any additional scopes results in a hierarchy.

The template (for a page corresponding to the top-level scope) is discussed. Considering that any formal model would have this page, it is used as the base in constructing the model. A template for pages corresponding to additional scopes is discussed in the next section. Figure 8.9 illustrates the XML template for a top-level scope. It also depicts the model obtained when the template is opened using CPN tools. Only the essential elements of the template are shown because of the space limitation.

The DTD for CPN tools requires the template to have *<workspaceElements>* and *<cpnet>* as its outermost elements. The element *<globbox>* contains declarations for color sets, functions, and variables. Being the base template, it contains a declaration for all other templates that might be used later. This relieves us from recording the declarations in each template and including them when the template is used.

The DTD requires the templates to have a *<page>* element for each page in a CPN model. As discussed earlier, the base template has a single page, corresponding to the top-level scope. Its child element *<pageattr>* contains an attribute that assigns the page a name. Each *<place>* element thereafter renders a place in the corresponding page of the model.

The elements that can appear more than once have an attribute "id" by which to recognize them. For example, each *<page>* has a unique id that helps in identifying and differentiating it. The DTD requires that no two elements in the template have the same id. Consequently, a counter is maintained to assign unique ids to each element as they are added. Each id should be an integer preceded by "ID".

The five *<place>* elements in the XML template correspond to the five places shown in Figure 8.9, and they appear in the same order. The *<place>* element for the topmost place is illustrated in detail to explain their relationship. The text "VA"

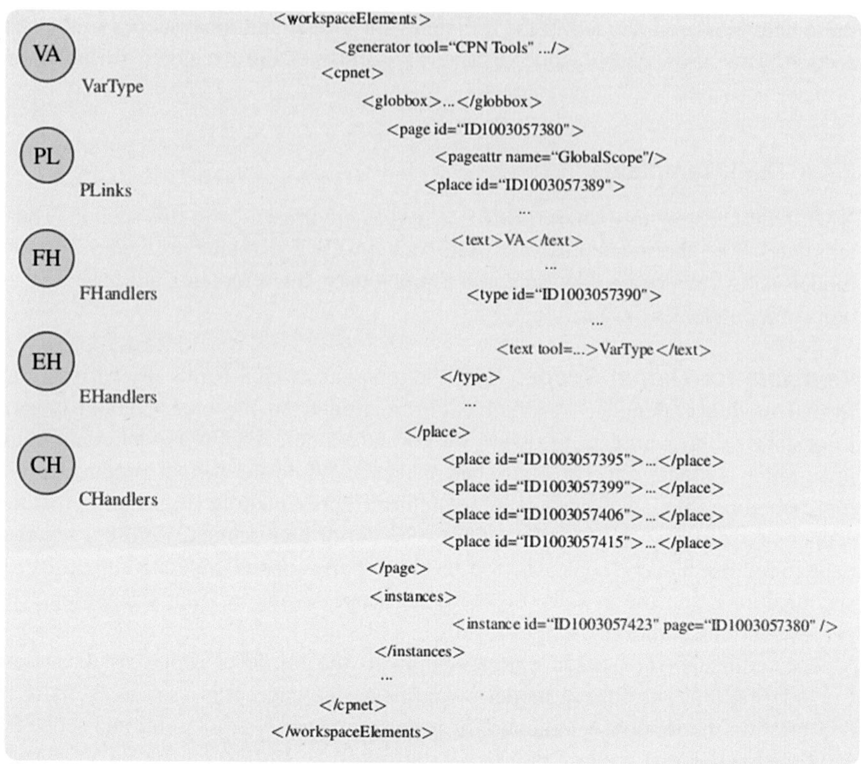

FIGURE 8.9 Template for top-level scope.

appearing inside the place comes from the subelement *<text>*, which is highlighted in red. Similarly, the color *VarType* is fetched from the subelement *<text>* of the subelement *<type>*, which is also highlighted in red. The declaration for the color set *VarType* can be found within the *<globbox>* element. Other place elements are defined similarly but are collapsed due to space constraints.

Finally, the element *<instance>* instantiates a page. Unless a page element has an *<instance>* entry within *<instances>*, the page does not appear in the model. Consequently, new entries would be added here for each new page included in the model.

Template for an Activity. The template for a basic activity is introduced. This template can be used for any basic activity with some activity-specific customizations that are discussed later. In this context, an activity is considered basic if it is neither the source nor the target of a link activity.

Figure 8.10 illustrates the XML template for a basic activity. Before an activity starts executing, it should be "ready" for execution. Similarly, once it executes, it should have "finished" execution. These two states of a BPEL activity are stored in CPN tokens as *ready* and *fin*, as shown in Figure 8.10. Some activities (e.g., invoke)

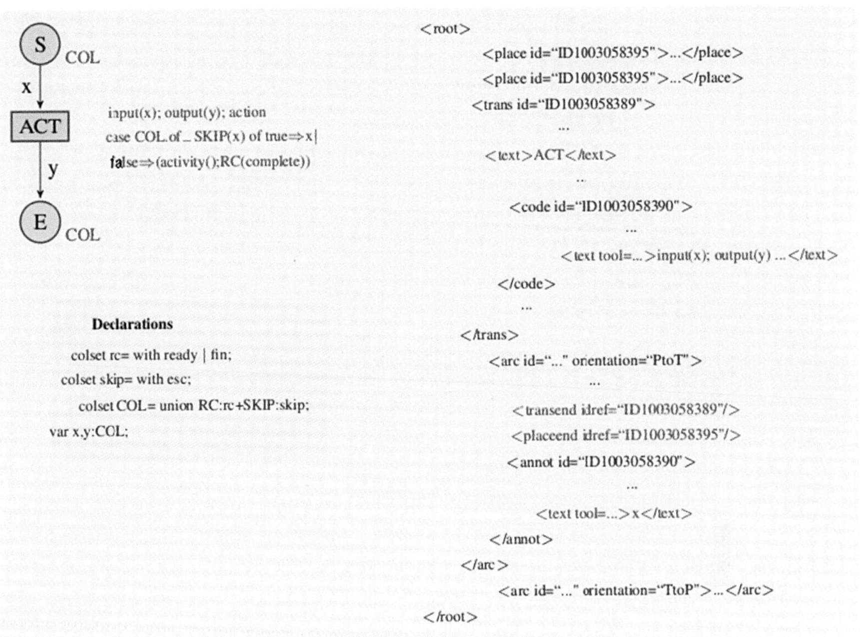

FIGURE 8.10 Template for a basic activity.

might not finish immediately and could have a waiting time. As illustrated later, such activities are modeled using *timed CPN* by adding a delay into the transition *ACT*.

Assigning a token with the aforementioned values models the normal execution of an activity. However, in case of dead-path elimination, an activity might have to be skipped entirely. To model such scenarios, the token is assigned a value "esc". The transition *ACT* examines the value in the token and behaves accordingly. Such selective behavior requires programming the *code segment* of the transition as shown in Figure 8.10.

The values that a token should have for normal execution are declared as an enumeration *rc*. Similarly, the values for skipping are defined in *skip*. To ensure that the token can be assigned values from either of these enumerations, the containing places are assigned a color set that is the union of these color sets. This union color set is assigned to places *S* and *E* in Figure 8.10. In this context, the former acts as a start place and the latter acts as a finish place. A start place contains a *ready* token when an activity is ready to execute. Similarly, a finish place contains a *fin* token after the activity finishes execution. To skip an activity, the start place is populated with a token *esc*.

Considering that an activity behaves differently based on the token in *S*, a function cs.of_col( ) is used to evaluate them dynamically. This function is defined natively for CPN Tools. For a union *u* composed of color sets *c*1 and *c*2, u.of_c2(v) returns true only if the token *v* contains a value of type *c*2. The transition *ACT* uses this function to decide on the outcome of its execution. It accepts the token in place *S* and checks its value. If the token contains a value from the *skip* color set, the activity is not executed. Otherwise, the activity is executed by calling the function activity( ), and a token with value *fin* is forwarded to place *E*.

The code segment of a transition is contained within a *<code>* element, as shown in Figure 8.10. The template also contains two *<arc>* elements, corresponding to the two arcs. The attribute *orientation* denotes if an arc is directed from a place to transition or otherwise. Its subelements *<transend>* and *<placeend>* contain the ids of transition and place that it connects. Furthermore, the arc inscriptions are contained within the subelement *<annot>*.

Template for an Activity Synchronized by Links. In this section we introduce the template for an activity that is synchronized using links. Considering that links are always defined within a *flow activity*, the actual synchronization is discussed later, when we discuss the template for the latter.

Figure 8.11 illustrates an activity whose synchronization dependencies are expressed using links. The template from the preceding section is used to model the activity. The practice of reusing templates leads to a reduction in the size of the new template. This reduction is attributed to the expulsion of any element common to several templates.

Each link has a *source* and a *target* activity. Links that have *A* as their target activity form a color set $inlinks_A$. Similarly, links that have *A* as their source activity form another color set $outlinks_A$. These color sets are subsets of $links_A$, which contains all the links associated with *A*. These sets for *ACT* are shown in Figure 8.11 (subscripts omitted).

Each incoming link has an associated boolean status that is stored in place *P* along with the link name. The place *S* initially contains an empty list of such link-name and status pairs. As the status of each link is available in place *P*, they are added to this list by transition *T*. When the statuses of all incoming links have been added to it, its length must be equal to the number of elements in the color set *inlinks*. This causes the transition *ACT* to execute and remove the list along with the ready token. To prevent the transition from executing until the status of all incoming links is available, a guard condition is attached to it.

As with a basic activity, the token is assigned a value *esc* in order to skip the activity. The transition is programmed to customize its behavior based on the contents of the token in *S*.

Considering that an activity might be the source of one or more links, the transition *ACT* needs to evaluate their *transition conditions* (if any) and determine their status. The code segment of the transition is programmed for this purpose. Initially, the *join condition* is evaluated based on the status of incoming links. The function jc( ) in Figure 8.11 performs a logical OR operation on the status of all incoming links. This is also the default behavior if no condition is specified. If this function returns *true*, the activity executes and the transition conditions of each outgoing link are evaluated. Otherwise, the activity is skipped and the status of each outgoing link is assigned *false*. In either case a token with the value *fin* is sent to place *E*. The

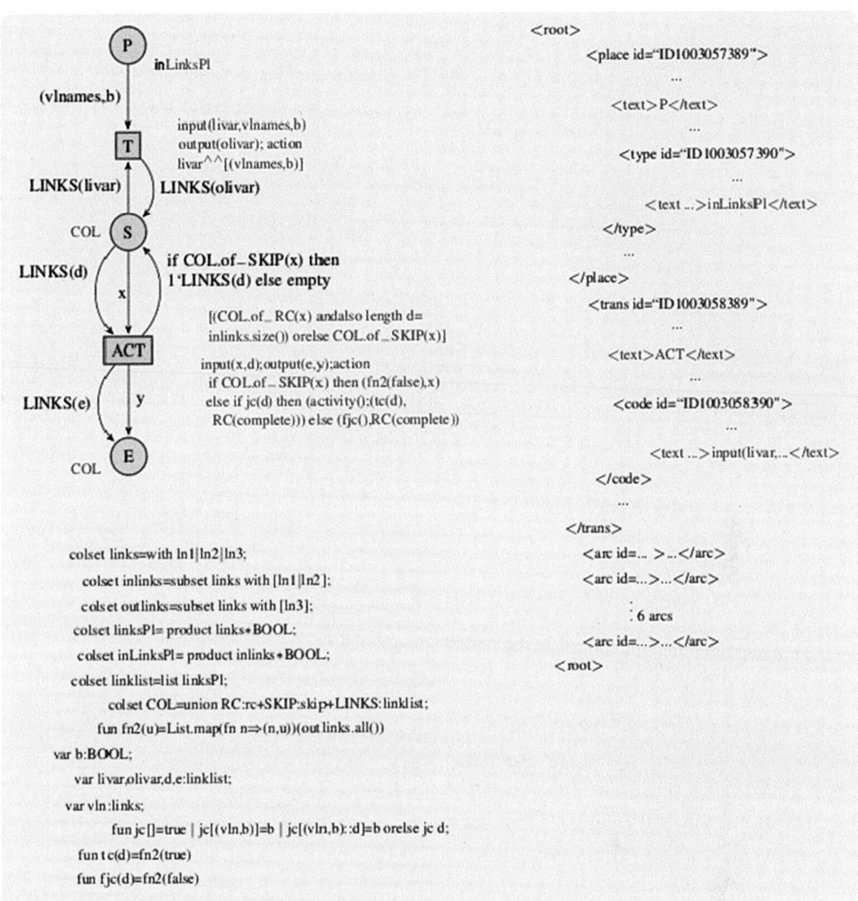

FIGURE 8.11 Template for an activity synchronized by links.

model provides dummy implementation of these functions [e.g., *tc*( ) for transition conditions] and they can be customized based on requirements.

Template for Local Scopes. In this section we describe the template for an underlying scope. As explained previously, our model represents each scope in the BPEL specification using a separate page. Consequently, the template has two subtemplates: (1) the template for substitution transition in the superpage (i.e., the page for a parent scope), and (2) the template for a page that is added for each new scope.

Figure 8.12 illustrates the template for the substitution transition that is added into the page for a parent scope for each of its child scopes. Considering that a scope might need to use the variables, fault handlers, event handlers, and partner links (if a parent is the top-level scope) of the parent scope, a bidirectional arc connects each

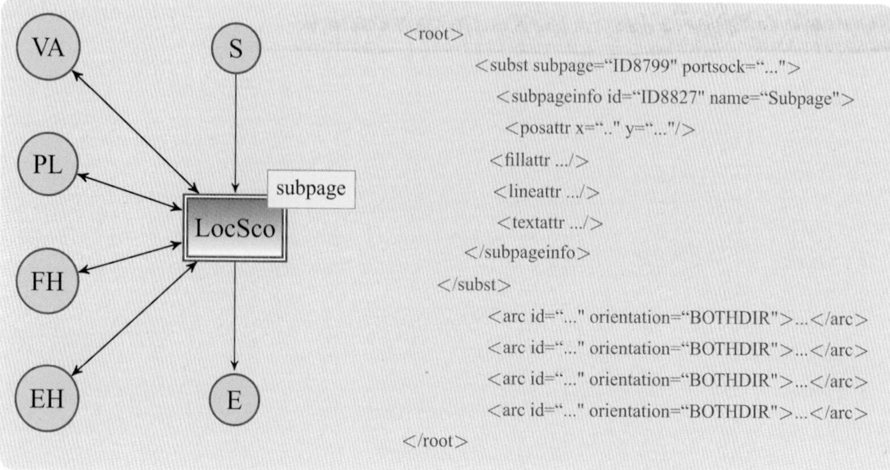

FIGURE 8.12 Template for items added to a parent page.

of the corresponding places to the substitution transition. Like any other activity, the model for the scope has the places *S* and *E*.

In addition to the elements that exist in a regular transition, a substitution transition has an element *<subst>* that contains, among other things, the *ID* of a page that it replaces and the port–socket mappings. Consequently, the XML template for the substitution transition consists of this single distinguishing element. It is appended to the template for a regular transition to obtain the complete template for the substitution transition. This is in accordance with the principle of template reusability discussed previously.

Figure 8.13 illustrates the template for a page corresponding to an underlying scope. It is similar to the template for global scope and has places to store the variables, fault handlers, and event handlers that are defined in the corresponding scope. In addition, it has port places that allow it to access the variables and handlers from overlaying scopes. This makes it possible to model a deeply nested scopes without bounds.

When the substitution transition corresponding to a scope is executed, the token from place *S* in the superpage is moved to its port place in a subpage (also termed *S* in this case). Thereafter, the activities in this scope execute and consume the tokens. Finally, the leftover token in port place *E* is copied back to its socket place.

Template for the Flow Activity. This describes the template for the *flow* activity as well as the specification of synchronization dependencies using links. Initially, the arcs, places, and transitions in red are ignored. Places *S* and *E*, along with their color set, ensure the compatibility of flow with the templates. Furthermore, like other activities it has a normal execution and a skipped execution. In case of normal execution, it simultaneously adds a *ready* token into the starting place of each subactivity, causing them to execute in parallel. It then waits until each subactivity

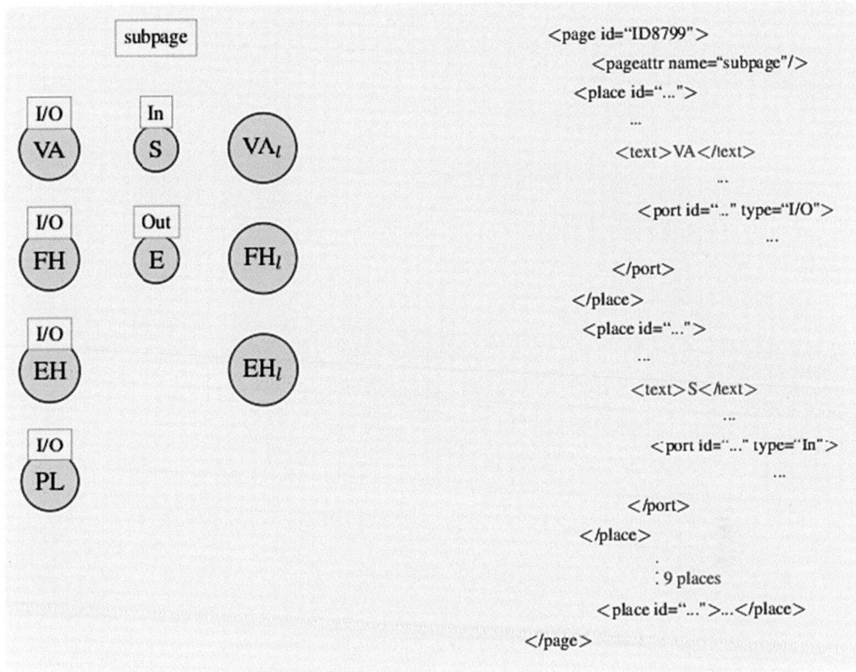

FIGURE 8.13 Template for a subpage corresponding to an underlying scope.

finishes execution by collecting the *fin* token from their *finish* places. Thereafter, it quits by populating its finish place E with an *fin* token.

The template for *flow* consists of a transition with incoming and outgoing arcs. This template is used in conjunction with the previous templates to instantiate a *flow* activity. For example, a minimal *flow* activity would contain a single subactivity (say, $A1$). To model it, the places S and E, along with a model for activity, are created using place and activity templates. Thereafter the template for *flow* is used to add a transition between S and S_1, E_1 and E, and S and E. Adding additional subactivities would require two arcs, which can be drawn using the template for arcs.

The specification of synchronization dependency is illustrated using places, transitions, and arcs in red. The template for *link* is used for this purpose. In addition, the flow template is used to connect E_3 and P using T_0. We consider a single link that has $A3$ as its source and $A2$ as its target. Consequently, the former must finish execution before the latter starts. As pointed out for *link*, the place E_3 would be populated with a list once $A3$ terminates. This list would contain a (*link* – *name*,*status*) pair for each link that has $A3$ as its source. In this case it would contain the status for the sole link considered. The transition T_0 breaks this list and populates place P with the individual elements in it. Thereafter, the status is passed to $A2$, which executes selectively based on the status of the link.

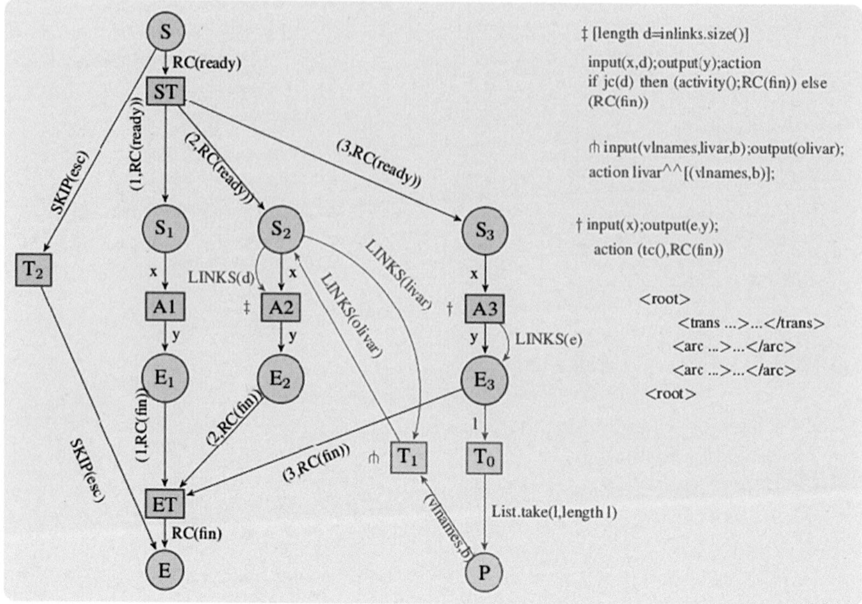

FIGURE 8.14 Template for the *flow* activity.

It should be noted that the template for *link* was introduced for an activity that had both incoming and outgoing links. However, activities *A*2 and *A*3 in Figure 8.14 have either incoming or outgoing links. Consequently, the template has been dissected into two parts for modeling these activities.

Template for the Sequence Activity. The template for the *sequence* activity is described. It is usually the primary activity of the top-level scope in a BPEL specification. Figure 8.15 illustrates the template for the *sequence* activity. At first glance it appears to be similar to the template for *flow*. However, the templates differ in the expression attached to the input and output arcs.

A *sequence* activity ensures that its subactivities execute in the sequence specified. Consequently, when modeling it, it is sufficient to populate place *S* of an activity with a *ready* token once its previous activity has an *fin* token in *E*. This would allow an activity to begin execution once its preceding activity has finished execution.

Additionally, in the case of dead-path elimination, an activity might need to skip if its preceding activity was skipped. To model such scenarios, the sequence template behaves selectively and populates the place *S* of an activity with an *esc* token when it finds a similar token in place *E* of the preceding activity.

Template for the Switch Activity. The template for the *switch* activity makes possible multiway conditional branching and is used to introduce decision points in order to control the flow of a BPEL process. Figure 8.16 illustrates a template for

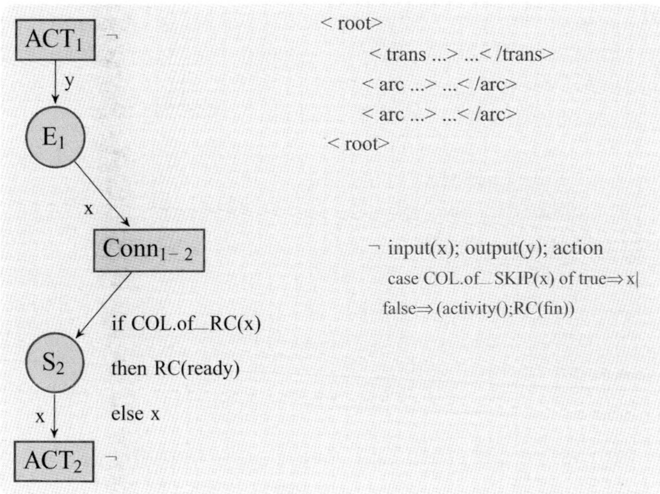

FIGURE 8.15 Template for the *sequence* activity.

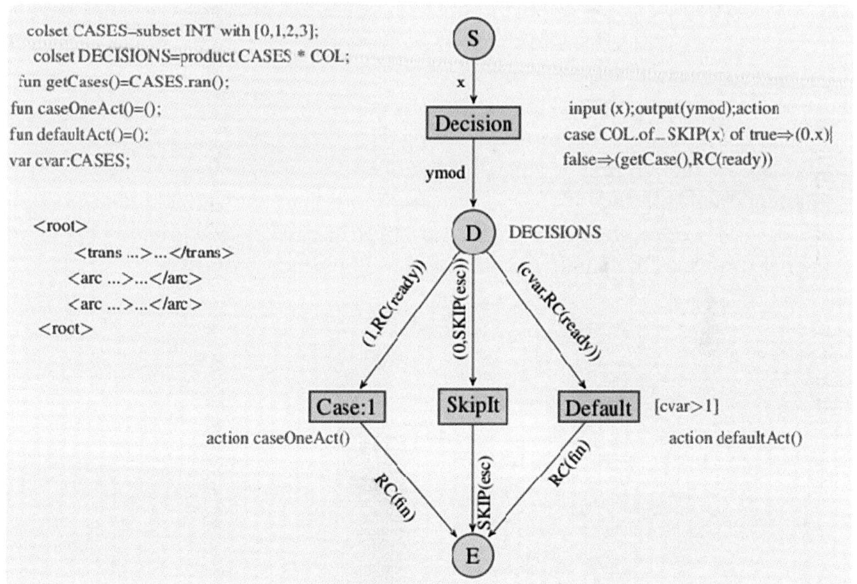

FIGURE 8.16 Template for the *switch* activity.

the *switch* activity. As with a sequence, the template for a *switch* looks similar to that for *flow*. Such a similarity is deliberate, as it enhances the re-usability of a template. However, arc expressions and code segments differ from both the *flow* and *sequence* activities.

To fit into the template for a basic activity, the template for a *switch* activity contains the required start and finish places (i.e., *S* and *E*). In addition, it has a place

D to contain the token, based on which branching decision is finalized. The transition and arcs between *S* and *D* and *D* and *E* are created using the switch template.

The transition *Decision* inspects the token in *S* to check whether it is a normal or a skipped execution. For a normal execution, the function *getCase*( ) is used to decide on the case to be executed. By default the function is implemented to select a case randomly. Each case is assigned a unique case number, and *getCase*( ) returns the case number for the case selected. However, the *default* case is assigned special case numbers. As shown in Figure 8.16, any case number greater than the number of cases would cause the default case to execute. This requires assigning the case numbers sequentially. The code segment for each case contains a function *caseXxxAct*( ) that executes the underlying activity. Skipping an activity is assigned a dummy case number of 0.

Template for the Invoke, Receive, and Reply Activities. The templates for interface activities often have a waiting time, as they are used to communicate with other web services. Each partner web service for a BPEL process is specified as a *partner link* in the specification. These are used by the interface activities (1) to call an operation (<*invoke*>), (2) to offer an operation and wait for it to be called (<*receive*>), or (3) to return the result of an operation (<*reply*>). The parameters for these operations are modeled as messages that are stored in variables. Consequently, these activities need access to the variables required.

Figure 8.17 illustrates the template for interface activities. The additional arcs are used to access the required partner links and variables. Although they always need a single partner link, they might need to use more than one variable. For example, <*invoke*> uses both input and output variables in case of synchronous operation. Table 8.4 illustrates the number of variables used by each activity.

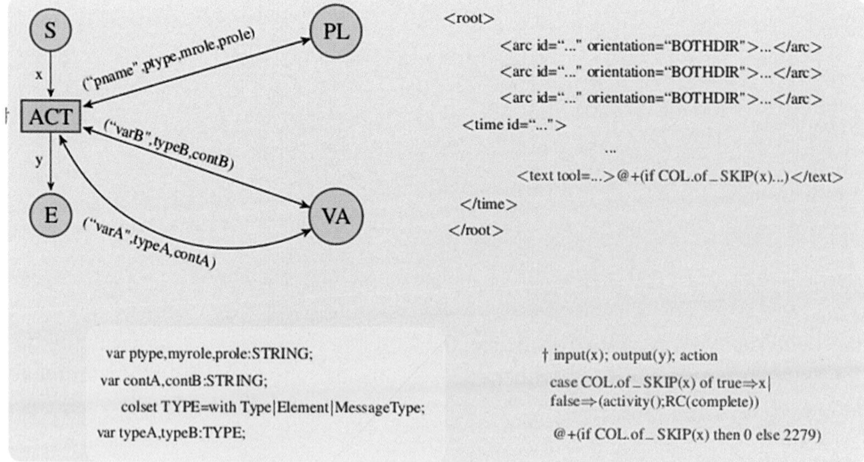

FIGURE 8.17 Template for interface activities.

TABLE 8.4 Use of Three Additional Arcs in an Interface Template

BPEL Act: Interface Act	Arc *pname*	*varA*	*varB*
invoke	Access partner-link token	Output variable	Input variable (synchronous operation)
receive	Access partner-link token	—	Input variable
reply	Access partner-link token	Output variable	

The time delay in executing an interface activity is modeled using timed CPN. This requires attaching a time delay to the transition *ACT* by adding a *<time>* element to the transition template. This element is a part of the template for interface activities.

In timed CPN, each token has an associated time stamp. When a transition fires, the time stamp is incremented by the delay specified in the transition. The model in Figure 8.17 specifies a random delay for the transition *ACT*. Specifying the delay makes it possible to account for the time incurred in interacting with a partner web service.

Template for the While Activity. Compared to the multiway conditional branching in *switch*, *while* offers two way branching with looping. Figure 8.18 illustrates the template for the *while* activity. The template consists of three arcs that need to be added to the template for a basic activity.

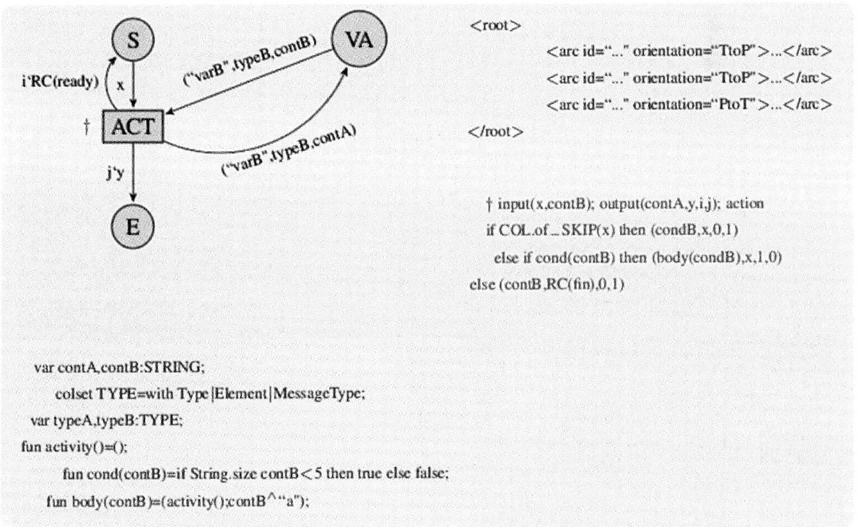

FIGURE 8.18 Template for the *while* activity.

As with any basic activity, a *ready* token in place *S* signifies that the activity is ready to execute. The transition *ACT* removes this token and uses the function *cond*( ) to determine the outcome of the condition. Usually, this function requires the content of a variable that is fetched using an arc from place *VA*. If the condition is satisfied, the function *body*( ) is called to execute the underlying activities that are specified in the function *activity*( ). Furthermore, to prevent infinite looping, this function also manipulates the content of the variable that is used by the function cond( ). Thereafter, the token *ready* is sent back to place *S* to begin the next cycle of looping.

Alternatively, if the condition is not satisfied, the underlying activities are not executed [i.e., *body*( ) is skipped] and a *fin* token is sent to *E*. By default, the function *cond*( ) checks if the content of a variable has fever than five characters. Consequently, to prevent the occurrence of an infinite loop, the function *body*( ) adds a character. These functions are customized based on the object model for the BPEL specification.

Template for Assign Activities. A template for assign activities is used to copy data between variables and expressions. This consists of arcs that are used to copy the contents of one variable into other. This template is used with the template for a basic activity to obtain a model for an assign activity. Figure 8.19 illustrates the template for an assign activity. A BPEL assign activity requires specifying a source (using *<from>*) and a destination (using *<to>*) for each copy operation (specified by *<copy>*). To ensure that the source variable is not modified, it is accessed in Figure 8.19 using a bidirectional arc. The other two arcs fetch the token for the destination variable and replace it with updated content.

Template for Handler Activities. As discussed earlier, each scope can have its own set of handlers. Figure 8.20 illustrates the model for event and fault handler activities. The XML template is similar to that of *flow* and *sequence* and therefore is not shown. Considering that an event might have an associated time delay, event handlers are represented using timed CPN. For example, a token

$$1`onAlarm(1)@IntInf\ .\ fromInt20$$

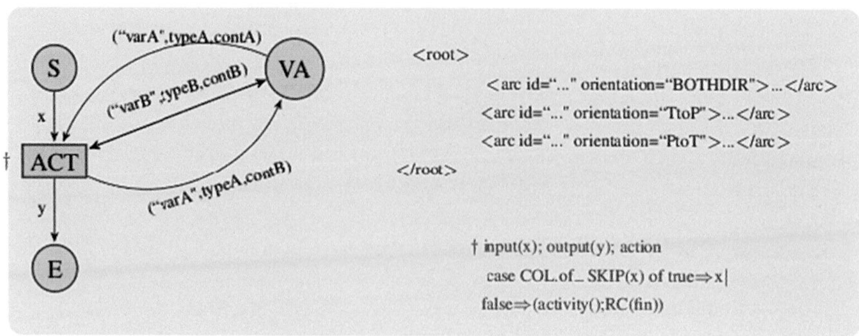

FIGURE 8.19 Template for the *assign* activity.

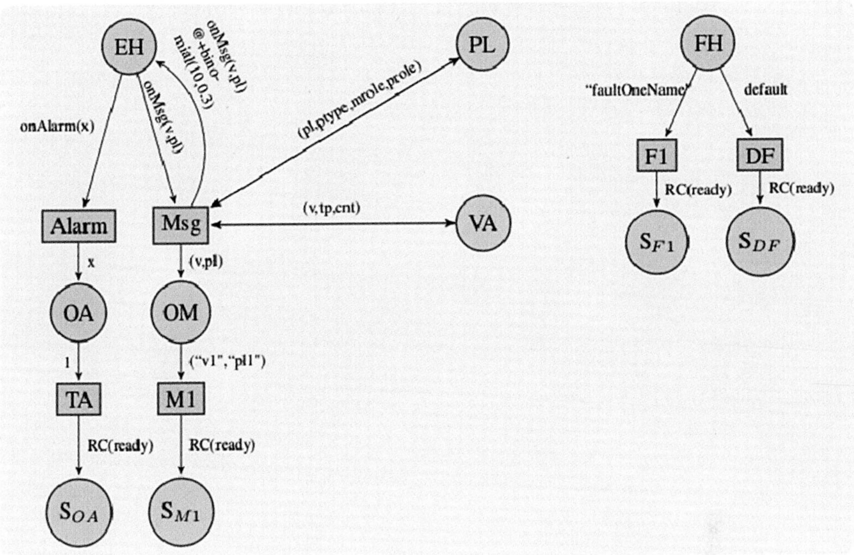

FIGURE 8.20 Template for handler activities.

has a time stamp of 20. Consequently, it will wait until all tokens with a lower time stamp enable a transition. The time stamp must be of type *Time.time* and not an integer. Therefore, an operation *IntInf.fromInt* is used to convert an integer into *Time.time* type. The color set for place *EA* is defined as

- colset ONMESSAGE = product STRING*STRING timed;
- colset ONALARM = INT timed;
- colset EHandlers = union OnMessage:ONMESSAGE+OnAlarm:ONALARM timed;

An ONALARM token is used to model a time-out, and an ONMESSAGE token offers an operation and waits for its invocation. The instant at which a time-out or operation occurs depend on the time stamp attached to these tokens. In either case, an appropriate underlying activity is triggered by adding a *ready* token into its start place. However, unlike time-outs (which can occur only once), an operation offered can be invoked any number of times. Consequently, the transition *Msg* in Figure 8.20 replaces an ONMESSAGE token after removing it from *EH*. To schedule the next operation invocation, a time delay is added to the time stamp. CPN Tools offer various *random distribution functions* that can be used to calculate this delay. Table 8.5 lists some of these functions.

Each ONALARM token is assigned a unique number in order to identify the source of a time-out. This value is bound to the variable *x* for the transition *Alarm*,

TABLE 8.5 Random Distribution Functions Offered by CPN Tools

Function	Conditions	Mean	Variance
bernoulli(p:real): int	$0.0 \leq p \leq 1.0$	p	$p(1-p)$
binomial(n:int, p:real): int	$n \geq 1, 0.0 \leq p \leq 1.0$	np	$np(1-p)$
chisq(n:int): real	$\geq n \geq 1$	n	$2n$
discrete(a:int, b:int): int	$a \leq b$	$(a+b)/2$	$[(b - a + 1)^2 - 1]/12$
erlang(n:int, r:real): real	$n \geq 1, r > 0.0$	n/r	n/r^2
exponential(r:real): real	$r > 0.0$	$1/r$	$1/r^2$
normal(n:real, v:real): real	—	n	v
poisson(m:real): int	$m > 0.0$	m	m
student(n:int): real	$n \geq 1$	0	$1/n-2$
uniform(a:real, b:real): real	$a \leq b$	$(a+b)/2$	$((b-a)^2)/12$

executes, and is copied to place *OA*. The place *OA* has an outgoing transition for each time-out that triggers the corresponding underlying activity.

Each ONMESSAGE token has a unique combination of partner link and variable names. When the transition *Msg* executes, this combination is copied to place *OM*. Similar to *OA*, *OM* has an outgoing transition for each operation that triggers the corresponding underlying activity.

In the case of fault handlers, each fault is specified using a separate *<catch>* activity. They are assigned a unique ID based on the *faultName* and/or *faultVariable* attributes specified for the corresponding catch activity. The place *FH* has an outgoing transition for each fault that triggers the underlying fault-handling activity.

The template for a basic activity is modified marginally to report faults and is shown in Figure 8.21. In addition to the two possible execution sequences discussed earlier (i.e., skipped and normal execution), an activity can also have a faulty execution. In such scenarios, a token containing the fault ID is sent to the fault handler place for local scope. Furthermore, no token is added to place *E*, as the fault prevented the activity from "finishing." The token added to *FH* allows the appropriate fault handler to execute and administer the corrective action required. A trivial fault is often handled gracefully by adding the *fin* token to *E*. However, serious faults might terminate the execution.

8.4.5 Algorithm for Cloning Templates

In this section we describe an algorithm to create the model for an activity using its templates. The algorithm is generic and can be used for any of the templates.

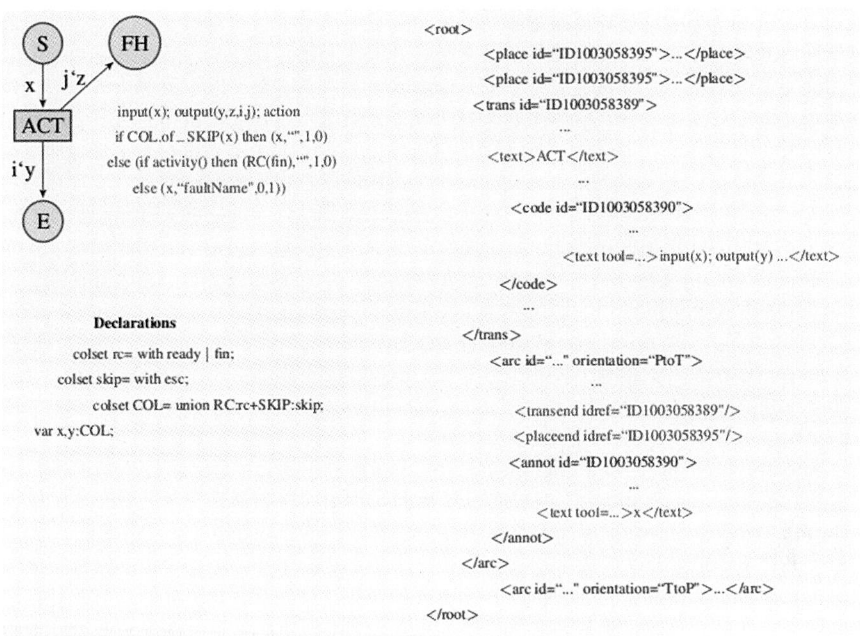

FIGURE 8.21 Modified template for basic activity that can report faults.

When creating an XML document using Java document object model (DOM) APIs, a root element is created and other elements are appended to it as child elements. Considering that the elements in an XML document can be nested up to an arbitrary depth, the element at a particular depth is appended to its enclosing element. The cloning algorithm recursively creates the element at each depth and appends it to its parent element.

In addition to cloning the template elements, the algorithm does the following:

1. Assigns a unique ID to each element of the model. The DTD for CPN Tools necessitates assigning a unique ID to each element in a CPN model.
2. Ensures that the model activities are stacked upon each other. This allows viewing and editing the model using CPN Tools.
3. Assigns a unique name to each place and transition in the model. This is a prerequisite for state-space analysis of a CPN model.

Algorithm 8.1 lists the steps for cloning a XML template. It accepts the root element of the template and recursively processes its underlying elements. In step 1, an XML element is created and assigned the name of the root element. For example, on passing the template in Figure 8.13, the element *<page/>* is created.

Thereafter, in steps 2 to 18, the newly created element is augmented with the attributes from the root element supplied. Although most of these attributes are copied along with their values, the values for certain attributes are computed based on CPN tool DTD specifications. For example, the identifier ID contains the next unique value for an "id" attribute. The DTD requires this unique value to be preceded by string "ID". Consequently, in step 5 the content of ID is concatenated with the string "ID" and assigned to the attribute "id". The identifier ID is a global variable and its value is preserved between subsequent invocations of Algorithm 8.1.

As emphasized earlier, a template has dummy ids for places and transitions that are replaced with unique values using the variable ID. However, the arcs in the template contain *<transend>* and *<placeend>* elements, which store the "id" of the transition and place that it connects. Considering that these ids are updated by Algorithm 8.1, the reference stored by the arc must also be updated. Consequently, in steps 6 to 8 the pair (dummy_ID,assigned_ID) is entered into a hash table. Thereafter the attribute *idref*(which stores the ids) for *<transend>* and *<placeend>* are assigned this new value in steps 10 and 11.

The position at which the places, transitions, and arcs in a CPN model are rendered depends on the "*x*" and "*y*" attributes of an underlying *<posattr>* element. These attributes store the displacement along the *x* and *y* axes, respectively. To shift the entire model for an activity along the *y*-axis, the appropriate value needs to be stored in the variable *depth*. Step 14 introduces a y-shift for the places, transitions, and arcs. Such a scheme makes it possible to render the activity models one upon other. Such an organized model can be viewed and edited using CPN Tools. The remaining attributes and their values are copied without changes in step 16.

Steps 19 to 21 copy the text content of the root element into the newly created element. Thereafter, the child elements of the root are fetched and processed similarly by Algorithm 8.1. The elements returned are attached to the root in step 25. Steps 28 to 30 assign unique names to places and transitions. As the value in ID is always unique, it is used to construct the name.

8.5 RESULTS

To evaluate the framework, a schema is created for each of the colored petri net templates. This was done using the tool *Trang* [2], as explained previously. Each schema defines the structure of a CPN template corresponding to a BPEL activity. They are used by a JAXB 2 compiler to transform a bean factory into a formal model. The experiment is administrated on a desktop with a 1.83-GHz Core 2 Duo processor with 2 GB of RAM running Windows XP SP2 with JRE 1.6.

Test Cases. The framework is tested on four related BPEL specifications [18]. They define a simple business process for business travel wherein the client supplies an employee name, destination, departure date, and return date when invoking the process. Thereafter the process determines the employee travel status by invoking an appropriate web service. The results from this invocation, along with those supplied by the client, are used to check the price for American and Delta airlines using their

Algorithm 8.1 Clone(Element root)

```
Data: Root
Result: The root element is rendered along with its child elements
Element e←CreateNewElement(root.getNodeName( ));
attributes←root.getAllAttributes( );
foreach attr in attributes do
    if attr.getNodeName( )="id" then
        e.setAttribute("id","ID"^ID);
        if root.getNodeName="place" or root.getNodeName="trans" then
            hashTable.put(attr.getNodeValue( ),ID);
        end
        ID←ID+1;
    else if attr.getNodeName( )="idref" then
        e.setAttribute("idref","ID"^hashTable.get(attr.getNodeValue( )));
    else if root.getNodeName()="posattr" and attr.getNodeName( )="y"
    then
        ypos←parseInteger(attr.getNodeValue( ));
        e.setAttribute("y",ypos-depth);
    else
        e.setAttribute(attr.getNodeName,attr.getNodeValue( ));
    end
end
if root.getNodeName( )="text" then
    e.setTextContent(root.getTextContent( ));
end
if root.hasChildNodes( ) then
    childNodes=root.getChildNodes( );
    foreach node in childNodes do
        e.appendChild(Clone(node));
    end
end
if e.getNodeName( )="place" or e.getNodeName="trans" then
    e.setName("Id"^ID);
end
```

exposed web services. Finally, the BPEL process selects the airline that is offering the lower price and returns the itinerary to the client. The web services required are assumed to exist.

Although all four BPEL specifications selected serve the same purpose, they use different sets of activities to achieve it. Table 8.6 illustrates the differences between these specifications.

The first row corresponds to receiving the request from the client. Based on the information attached to this request, the travel information is fetched in the second

TABLE 8.6 Difference Between BPEL Specifications Used

M1	*M2* and *M3*	*M4*
< *receive* >	< *receive* >	< *receive* >
< *invoke* >	< *scope* >	< *flow* >
	▷ < *invoke* >	▷ < *links* >
	< *scope* >	▷ < *invoke* >
	< *scope* >	
< *flow* >	▷ < *flow* >	
▷ < *invoke* >	▷▷ < *invoke* >	▷ < *invoke* >
▷ < *invoke* >	▷▷ < *invoke* >	▷ < *invoke* >
< */flow* >	▷ < */flow* >	
< *switch* >	▷ < *switch* >	▷ < *switch* >
	< */scope* >	< */flow* >
	< *scope* >	
< *invoke* >	▷ < *invoke* >	< *invoke* >
	< */scope* >	

row. Thereafter the Delta and American airline web services are invoked and the better offer is determined. Finally, the result is returned in the last row.

The specification *M*1 uses *<flow>* and *<sequence>* activities to control the business process workflow. The specifications *M*2 and *M*3 extend *M*1 by enclosing individual operations in the scope. Although *M*2 and *M*3 look similar, only *M*3 has event handlers for each scope. Considering that event handlers can increase the cost of analyzing a model (owing to simultaneous active instances), *M*2 and *M*3 are both investigated to determine additional costs. The specification *M*4 uses links for the synchronization of its activities.

Empirical Results. Figure 8.22 illustrates the total number of activities in each test case. The specifications *M*3 and *M*4 are found to have the maximum and minimum number of activities. As pointed out previously, event handlers account for the additional activities in *M*3 as compared to *M*2.

Figure 8.23 illustrates the time taken by the framework in transforming these BPEL specifications into CPN models. Except for *M*4, the transformation time increases with an increase in number of activities. However, despite having the fewest activities, the specification *M*4 defies the trend in having the maximum transformation time.

Figure 8.24 illustrates the number of places and transitions (or nodes) in the models transformed. Barring *M*4, a higher transformation time is found to produce more nodes and arcs. The model for *M*4 has the fewest nodes despite having the longest transformation time. However, a larger specification (i.e., more activities) is always found to map into a bigger model (i.e., more nodes and arcs).

Figure 8.25 illustrates the number of states (or markings) and edges in the state space for each models transformed. Despite having the minimum number of

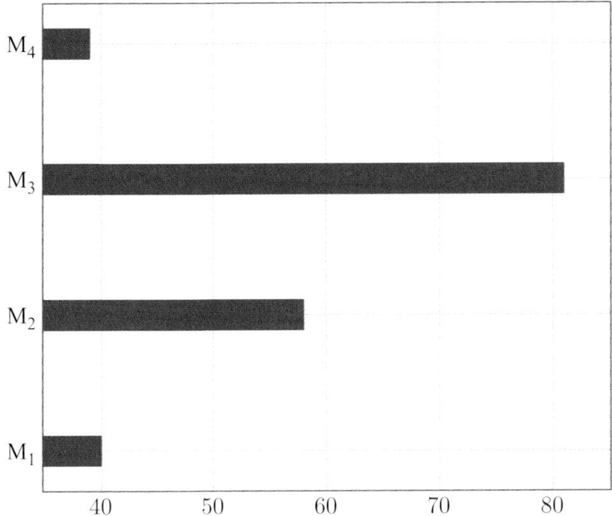

FIGURE 8.22 Number of activities in BPEL specification.

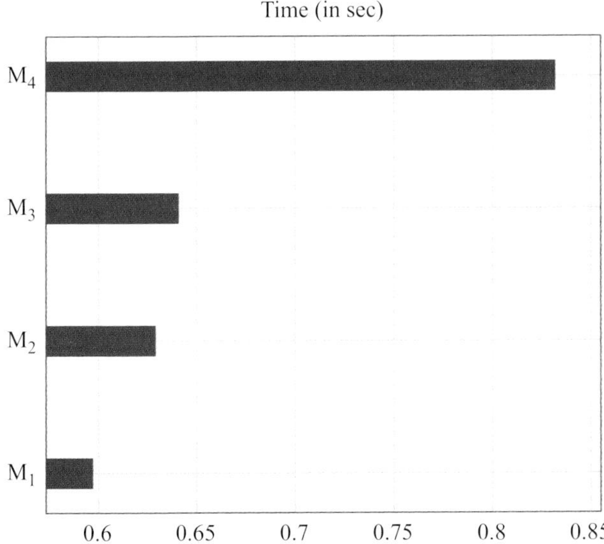

FIGURE 8.23 Time taken for BPEL-to-CPN transformation.

elements, the CPN model for *M*4 is found to produce the highest number of markings. The state space for *M*1 and *M*2 depends on the size of their models. As pointed out previously, the state space for *M*3 is infinite, owing to the presence of event handlers. Consequently, its entries are missing in Figure 8.25.

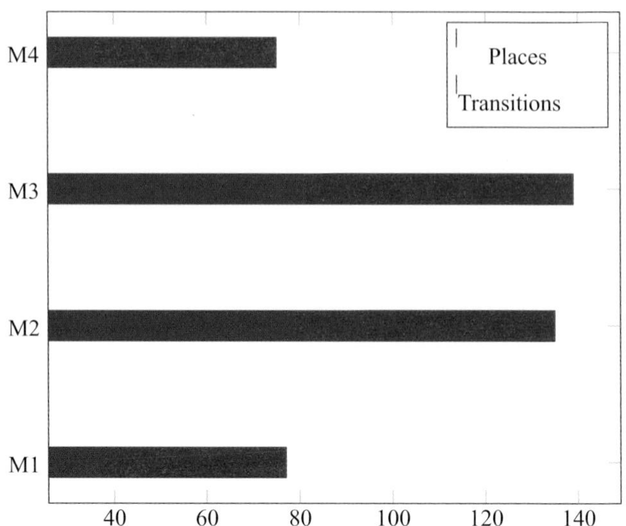

FIGURE 8.24 Number of places and transitions in the model rendered.

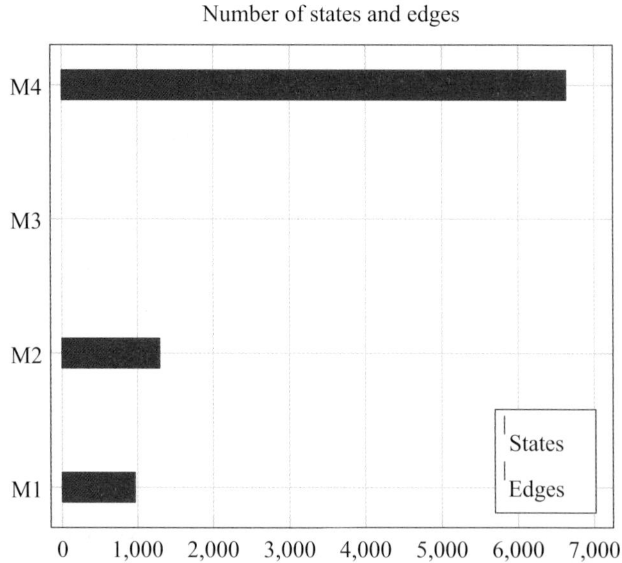

FIGURE 8.25 Number of states and edges in the state spaces of transformed models.

However, to evaluate $M3$, the time taken in generating the first 50,000 states is plotted in Figure 8.26. The plots in Figure 8.26 correspond to cases wherein the interevent time follows a *bernoulli* or *binomial* distribution. In the latter case, the plots for $n = 1000$ and $n = 10{,}000$ are manifested. Bernoulli's distribution can also

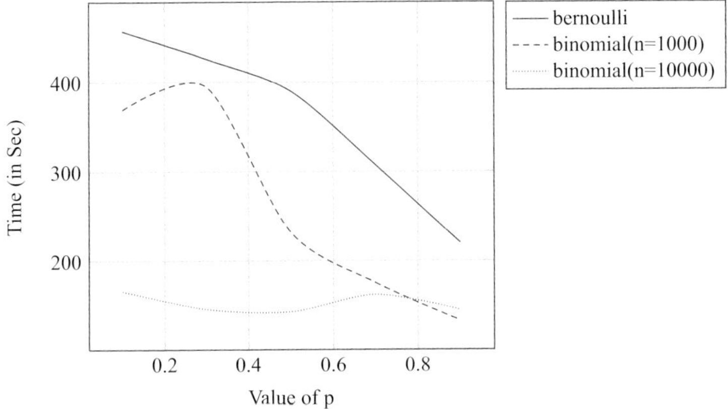

FIGURE 8.26 Time taken for generating the first 50,000 states.

be regarded as a binomial distribution with $n = 1$. Figure 8.26 illustrates that the time required to generate the first 50,000 states decreases with an increase in the value of n. It also decreases as the probability of success increases. However, the plots for $n = 10,000$ and $n = 1000$ are found to form a crest for specific probability values.

8.6 DISCUSSION

The empirical results endorse the framework implemented based on the minuscule time taken by it to transform the realistic test cases considered. The results also emphasize its importance in automated state-space analysis of BPEL specifications.

Considering that the transformation presented essentially replaces each BPEL activity with its corresponding CPN model (defined by a schema), the transformation time and the size of the model rendered are expected to depend on the size of the specification. Barring *M*4, this is reflected in Figures 8.22 to 8.24. The anomalous behavior of *M*4 is explained below.

As discussed previously the framework transforms a BPEL activity into its model based on the schemas furnished. Usually, a schema is supplied for each BPEL activity. When transforming a specification, these schemas are used sequentially in the same order as that of the corresponding activities in the specification. However, the schema for *link* does not actually produce a model. Considering that *links* are applicable for any activity, its schema requires assigning specific values to the model for the corresponding activity. The additional time can be attributed to the delay in initializing the appropriate classes with these values.

Figure 8.25 illustrates the size of the state space for each of these models. The possible combinations of status value for links and the path of execution for each of these combinations contribute to the large state space of *M*4. As pointed out previously, *M*3 has an infinite state space, owing to the presence of event handlers. Therefore, it is not plotted in Figure 8.25.

However, to evaluate $M3$, the time taken in generating the first 50,000 unique states is plotted against various random distribution functions that determine the frequency of events occurring. When events occur frequently (small n, small p), it takes a long time to generate the 50,000 states. This is because repeated execution of the part of the model corresponding to an event does not change the state. The state changes only on execution of the main flow.

8.7 SUMMARY

This chapter contributes toward enhancing the safety and reliability of a SOA-based application by verifying its underlying service composition. Issues with BPEL were identified, and techniques are described to formalize its activities to model, simulate, and verify a BPEL specification. The transformation is fully automatic and renders a CPN model. The main advantages of the approach described are:

- The object model helps to determine the relationship among BPEL activities. It forms a basis for the templates and acts as the antecedent of the CPN model obtained after transformation.
- Unlike related techniques that simply propose models for each BPEL activity, the technique described presents templates of varying granularity based on the relationship among BPEL activities.
- The templates for BPEL activities are feature-complete and conform to the DTD specified for the CPN tools.

REFERENCES

1. *Eclipse Modeling Framework*, July 2010.
2. *Trang Manual*, January 2011.
3. T. Andrews, F. Curbera, H. Dholakia, Y. Goland, J. Klein, F. Leymann, K. Liu, D. Roller, D. Smith, S. Thatte, I. Trickovic, and S. Weerawarana. *Business Process Execution Language for Web Services, Version 1.1*, May 2003.
4. J. Arias-Fisteus, L. Sánchez Fernández, and C. D. Kloos. Formal verification of BPEL4WS business collaborations. In *E-Commerce and Web Technologies*, pages 76–85, 2004.
5. A. Arkin, S. Askary, B. Bloch, F. Curbera, Y. Goland, N. Kartha, C. K. Liu, V. Mehta, S. Thatte, P. Yendluri, A. Yiu, and A. Alves. *Web Services Business Process Execution Language, Version 2.0*, December 2005.
6. J. Billington, S. Christensen, K. Van Hee, E. Kindler, O. Kummer, L. Petrucci, R. Post, C. Stehno, and M. Weber. The petri net markup language: concepts, technology, and tools. In *Proceedings of the 24th International Conference on Applications and Theory of Petri Nets*, ICATPN '03, pages 483–505. Springer-Verlag, Berlin, 2003.

7. P. Bonet, C. Lladó, R. Puigjaner, and W. J. Knottenbelt. PIPE v2.5: a petri net tool for performance modelling. In *23rd Latin American Conference on Informatics, CLEI 2007*, September 2007.
8. E. Clarke, O. Grumberg, and D. Peled. *Model Checking*. MIT Press, Cambridge, MA, 2000.
9. W. Crawford and J. Kaplan. *J2EE Design Patterns*. O'Reilly & Associates, Sebastopol, CA, 2003.
10. F. Curbera, Y. Goland, J. Klein, F. Leymann, D. Roller, S. Thatte, and S. Weerawarana. *Business Process Execution Language for Web Services, Version 1.0*. IBM, Microsoft, BEA Systems, July 2002.
11. D. Fahland, W. Reisig, and D. Fahland. ASM-based semantics for BPEL: the negative control flow. In *Proceedings of the 12th International Workshop on Abstract State Machines*, pages 131–151, 2005.
12. D. Fahland. Complete abstract operational semantics for the web service business process execution language. *Informatik-Berichte 190*. Humboldt-Universitat zu Berlin, September 2005.
13. A. Ferrara. Web services: a process algebra approach. In *Proceedings of the 2nd International Conference on Service Oriented Computing*, ICSOC '04; pages 242–251, 2004.
14. H. Foster, S. Uchitel, J. Magee, and J. Kramer. Model-based verification of web service compositions. In *Proceedings of the 18th IEEE International Conference on Automated Software Engineering, 2003*, pages 152–161, October 2003.
15. X. Fu, T. Bultan, and J. Su. Analysis of interacting BPEL web services. In *Proceedings of the 13th World Wide Web Conference*, pages 621–630. ACM, New York, 2004.
16. Y. Hao and Y. Zhang. Web services discovery based on schema matching. In *Proceedings of the 30th Australasian Conference on Computer Science*, ACSC '07, volume 62, pages 107–113. Australian Computer Society, Darlinghurst, Australia, 2007.
17. IBM. *Web Services Flow Language (WSFL 1.0)*, May 2001.
18. M. Juric. *Business Process Execution Language for Web Services*. Packt Publishing, Birmingham, UK, 2006.
19. H. Kang, X. Yang, and S. Yuan. Modeling and verification of web services composition based on CPN. In *Proceedings of the 2007 IFIP International Conference on Network and Parallel Computing Workshops*, pages 613–617. IEEE Computer Society, Washington, DC, 2007.
20. S. Merz. Model checking: a tutorial overview. In *Modeling and Verification of Parallel Processes*, pages 3–38. Springer-Verlag, Berlin, 2001.
21. C. Ouyang, E. Verbeek, W. van der Aalst, S. Breutel, M. Dumas, and A. ter Hofstede. WofBPEL: a tool for automated analysis of BPEL processes. In *Proceedings of the International Conference on Service Oriented Computing, ICSOC 2005*, volume 3826, pages 484–489. Springer-Verlag, Berlin 2005.
22. C. Ouyang, E. Verbeek, W. M. P. van der Aalst, S. Breutel, M. Dumas, and A. H. M. ter Hofstede. Formal semantics and analysis of control flow in ws-BPEL. *Science of Computer Programming*, 67:162–198, July 2007.
23. M. Paolucci, T. Kawamura, T. R. Payne, and K. P. Sycara. Semantic matching of web services capabilities. In *Proceedings of the First International Semantic Web Conference on the Semantic Web*, ISWC '02, pages 333–347. Springer-Verlag, Berlin, 2002.

24. K. Schmidt and C. Stahl. A petri net semantic for BPEL4WS validation and application. *In Proceedings of the 11th Workshop on Algorithms and Tools for Petri Nets,* AWPN '04, pages 1–6, 2004.
25. J. C. Sloan and T. M. Khoshgoftaar. From web service artifact to a readable and verifiable model. *IEEE Transactions on Services Computing*, 2:277–288, October 2009.
26. C. Stahl. A petri net semantics for BPEL. *Informatik-Berichte 188*. Humboldt-Universität zu Berlin, July 2005.
27. S. Thatte. *XLANG Web Services for Business Process Design*. Microsoft Corporation, Redmond, WA, May 2001.
28. W. M. P. van der Aalst. Don't go with the flow: web services composition standards exposed. *IEEE Intelligent Systems*, January–February 2003.
29. H. M. W. Verbeek, T. Basten, and W. M. P. van der Aalst. Diagnosing workflow processes using Woflan. *Computer Journal*, 44(4):246–279, 2001.
30. M. Westergaard, K. Jensen, S. Christensen, and L. Kristensen. *CPN Tools DTD*, December 2005.
31. P. Wohed, W. M. P. van der Aalst, M. Dumas, and A. H. M. ter Hofstede. Pattern-based analysis of BPEL4WS. *QUT Technical Report FIT-TR-2002-04*. Queensland University of Technology, Brisbane, Australia, 2002.
32. YanPing Yang, QingPing Tan, Yong Xiao, JinShan Yu, and Feng Liu. Verifying web services composition: a transformation-based approach. In *Proceedings of the 6th International Conference on Parallel and Distributed Computing Applications and Technologies*, pages 546–548. IEEE Computer Society, Washington, DC, 2005.
33. X. Yi and K. J. Kochut. A cp-nets-based design and verification framework for web services composition. In *Proceedings of the IEEE International Conference on Web Services*, ICWS '04; page 756, IEEE Computer Society, Washington, DC, 2004.

CHAPTER 9

CONCLUSIONS AND OUTLOOK

In this book we have addressed the intriguing issues related to model checking and verification of BPEL specifications. The research has been motivated by the necessity for a wider use of formal methods to enhance the safety and reliability of software systems. The research has also been driven by the lack of robustness in loosely coupled SOA-based applications.

As observed previously, model checking is a rigorous technique wherein all possible behaviors of a system are scrutinized exhaustively to determine a problem. Consequently, model checking is expected to identify all issues in a system. However, there are significant time and memory requirements in model-checking a system [6]. Therefore, the scope of model checking has hitherto been limited to critical systems where reliability is excessively important. Nevertheless, with our ever-increasing dependence on software in everyday life (e.g., traffic signals, elevators), skipping model checking amounts to risking millions of human lives.

In Chapters 5 and 6 we propose novel techniques to reduce the time and memory requirements for model checking. The reduction in memory requirements envisioned for model checking is realized by storing states as the difference from the preceding on nearest state. The time reduction is attributed to generating the reachability graph

Verification of Communication Protocols in Web Services: Model-Checking Service Compositions, First Edition. Zahir Tari, Peter Bertok, Anshuman Mukherjee.

for each module of a hierarchical model in parallel. The techniques proposed offer better results for larger models that correspond to contemporary software systems. They also have a smaller time overhead in reducing the memory requirements. Consequently, our techniques would allow model checking to acquire a larger role in the verification of a wide range of software.

In Chapter 7 we introduce a technique to install hierarchy into a flat model. Considering that a hierarchical model is often exponentially more succinct than its equivalent flat model, they are easier to analyze and maintain. Furthermore, this allows the time-reduction techniques from Chapter 6 to be applied to flat models after installing hierarchy. Compared to existing techniques, the method proposed renders an equivalent succinct model. This ensures the consistency of any analysis technique.

Finally, in Chapter 8 we propose a framework to model-check a BPEL specification. Unfortunately, the safety and reliability of SOA-based systems depend entirely on the precision of service descriptions. Consequently, any implicit assumption or unforeseen usage scenarios can lead to undesirable forms of interactions, such as a deadlock or race condition [24]. This is further exacerbated by dynamic service composition wherein services could be added, removed, or updated at runtime. The framework proposed transforms a BPEL specification into a hierarchy of data transfer objects(DTOs) that act as a generic intermediate before the actual formalization. Considering the ad hoc nature of existing solutions, the framework proposed offers significant flexibility in formalizing a BPEL specification. The framework is open and can be extended for rendering the formal model. This has been demonstrated by formalizing the intermediate Java beans into an XML-based formal model.

9.1 RESULTS

In this section we highlight our results in extending and improving the existing solutions and answering the research questions posed in Section 1.2.

Memory-Efficient State-Space Analysis Technique. A new storage technique is proposed to reduce the memory costs otherwise involved in model-checking service compositions. The technique proposed requires storing a state as the difference from one of its neighboring states. Such a setup offers several advantages over related techniques:

- The technique proposed is generic and applicable for any modeling language. Consequently, it outweighs earlier solutions, such as that of Evangelista and Pradat-Peyre [11], which are only applicable for petri net formalisms (and their extensions).
- The technique proposed is based on an exhaustive storage technique wherein each distinct state of a system is stored to identify and purge duplicate states. However, solutions based on partial storage techniques [3] often fail to identify the duplicate states.

- The difference algorithm for compressing a state is reversible and makes it possible to reinstate a condensed state. Consequently, false negatives and false positives can be prevented by expanding the stored states before comparison.
- The technique proposed provides a 95% reduction in memory requirements with only twice the processing time. Other solutions [e.g., 11,15,23] have considerably larger processing times and offer significantly less memory reduction.
- The technique proposed is flexible in allowing a choice of neighboring states to be used when calculating the difference form of a state.
- The technique proposed performs better for contemporary systems that have relatively high levels of complexity.

Time-Efficient State-Space Analysis Technique. A novel method is proposed to reduce the time requirements for model-checking a service composition. The solution necessitates that the composition be formalized as a hierarchical model, and the associated reduction is attributed to the concurrent exploration of its modules. The outcome of this exploration is stored using special data structures that act as repositories of corresponding module behavior. A module can use these data structures to determine the behavior of any other module without actually executing it. The technique proposed offers several advantages over related solutions:

- The solution proposed only necessitates a hierarchical model. This is less stringent than earlier solutions [e.g., 8,10], which necessitate the presence of stubborn sets or symmetry in the model.
- Contrary to the technique proposed, solutions based on stubborn sets and symmetry are NP-hard and use heuristic estimations [5,28].
- The technique proposed is applicable for all modeling languages that define a notion of hierarchy.
- The technique proposed offers an 86% reduction of the delay in generating the first 25,000 states. This significantly outweighs the reduction offered by related solutions [10,19].

Technique for Reducing the Size of a Model Exponentially. The technique proposed renders an exponentially more succinct representation of a service composition by embracing the notion of hierarchy. A hierarchical model consists of a set of modules wherein each module represents a system component. In such a setup, the module for a high-level component refers to its underlying components by their module names or reference. This avoids an explosion when including the actual representation of underlying components. The technique proposed outperforms the earlier solutions in several aspects:

- The technique proposed installs hierarchy to render an equivalent succinct model. However, the reduced model obtained using other techniques, [e.g., 2,9,14] is not equivalent to the original model. Furthermore, these techniques fail to preserve the properties of the original net, other than properties specifically targeted.

- The technique proposed aims to increase the analyzability and maintainability of formal models, whereas other techniques [e.g., 2,9,14], only target diminishing the state space by reducing the number of execution traces to be analyzed.
- Whereas other techniques reduce the size of a model by merging its elements (e.g., merging two or more places or transitions in petri nets) based on certain conditions, the technique proposed does the same by installing hierarchy. Hierarchical models help in identifying the overall architecture of a system, understanding its dependencies, visualizing the flow of information through it, identifying its capabilities and limitations, and calculating its complexity [4].
- The technique proposed requires finding structural similarity prior to installing hierarchy. Consequently, it is limited to graph-based formal models (e.g., petri nets).

Technique for Modeling, Simulating and Verifying a BPEL Specification. A verification framework is proposed to formalize a BPEL specification by transforming it into an XML-based formal model. This is done by extending the *Spring framework* to represent each BPEL activity using a *Java bean*. The framework instantiates the beans corresponding to activities in a BPEL specification and injects the dependencies to yield a *bean factory*. Thereafter, *Java Architecture for XML Binding (JAXB) 2* APIs are used to transform the bean factory into an XML-based formal model (e.g., colored petri nets [17]) or an interchange format (e.g., Petri Net Markup Language) for simulation and verification. Our technique offers several advantages over related solutions:

- Existing techniques [12,13,18] are adhoc and temporary in targeting specific modeling languages. The framework proposed targets all modeling languages using a generic intermediate specification.
- Contrary to most existing solutions [12,18], the solution proposed allows automatic transformation.
- The framework proposed uses DTOs as intermediates. DTOs are a commonly used design pattern in software engineering for storing and transferring data [7].
- The framework proposed makes it possible to plug a component to transform intermediate DTOs into a formal model.
- A Java Architecture for XML Binding (JAXB) 2 API-based component has been proposed to demonstrate the transformation of DTOs into an XML-based formal model.
- The framework used is the Spring framework, which offers many advantages (e.g., loosely coupled, light weight).

- An object model has been proposed to identify the hierarchical relationship among BPEL activities. This helps in mapping the BPEL activities into Java beans.
- The transformation time is significantly small (less than 0.7 s).

9.2 DISCUSSION

In this section we discuss solutions proposed in regard to the statement of the problem presented in Section 1.1. The solutions are also evaluated based on their ability to address the issues.

The reliability and robustness of a service composition is enhanced by proposing a verification framework in Chapter 8. As discussed earlier using Figure 1.3, an SOA-based application consists of a hierarchy of services, and a failure at any level could break the application. However, a service-level agreement (SLA) with the vendors providing these web services assures their reliability and quality of service. Consequently, the vulnerabilities in an SOA-based application are introduced on composing these services to create the application. To enhance the reliability and usability of an SOA-based system, the composition must be exhaustively verified for any single point of failure (SPOF). Considering that BPEL is the de facto industry standard for web-service composition, this essentially involves verifying a BPEL specification. The framework proposed verifies a composition by formalizing the corresponding BPEL specification before verifying it using a model-checking tool. This in turn makes it possible to identify the SPOFs in a composition and rectify them.

BPEL has emerged out of the Web Services Flow Language (WSFL) [16] of IBM and the XLANG [26] of Microsoft. However, WSFL is a graph-based language, whereas XLANG is a block-based language. Consequently, BPEL has both block (e.g., sequence)- and graph (e.g., flow)-based elements. The contrasting concepts in the base languages have caused many inconsistencies in BPEL that could undermine a service composition [29]. Furthermore, the textual specification of BPEL and its lack of mathematical semantics prevent formal methods from being applied directly to a BPEL specification [22,27].

Most of existing solutions directly formalize a BPEL specification using a specific modeling language before verifying it [18,25]. Despite these being legitimate solutions, they are only applicable for the modeling language targeted. Furthermore, they require scanning a BPEL specification manually and replacing each activity with its proposed formal model. Apart from being a cumbersome process, such an exercise is error-prone and time consuming. The method proposed (1) automates the transformation, and (2) is applicable to a range of modeling languages. In this pursuit it transforms the BPEL specification into intermediate DTOs before the actual formalization. DTOs are generic intermediates that could be accessed programmatically and transformed into a range of formal models. Considering that DTOs are design patterns commonly used in software engineering for storing and transferring data [7], they are used as generic intermediate specifications in the solution proposed.

The aforementioned solution is made more appealing by reducing the time and memory requirements for model checking. As discussed in Section 1.1, model-checking a contemporary software system has significant overhead owing to the huge state space of the latter. The time overhead is attributed to an analysis of the entire state space for a set of undesirable properties. Furthermore, considering that some systems repeatedly reach one or more states during execution, the model checker remembers the analyzed states by storing them in memory. Such a state of affairs accounts for the memory overhead.

In Chapter 5 we propose a technique to reduce the memory requirements by storing the states as the difference from an adjoining state. However, since this difference accounts for a *change in state* rather than of the state itself, it is possible that (1) two dissimilar states have the same difference state, and (2) two similar states have different difference states. The latter is possible because the similar states could have different adjoining states that are used in calculating the difference. This could lead to false-positive and false-negative scenarios. A false-positive scenario arises when two dissimilar states have the same difference state. Similarly, a false-negative scenario arises when two similar states have different difference states. The method proposed prevents such scenarios by devising a method to regenerate the explicit form for a difference state. The states are therefore expanded before comparison to rule out ambiguities. Asserting that the change in state is always smaller than the state itself, this technique offers up to a 95% reduction in memory requirements. The solution is based on the exhaustive storage technique discussed in Section 5.3. Furthermore, it performs better for contemporary systems that have relatively high levels of complexity.

In Chapter 6 we propose a novel method to reduce the time requirements for model-checking a service composition. The method is applicable for hierarchical models and the associated reduction is obtained by the concurrent exploration of the modules of a hierarchical model. The outcome of exploring a module is stored in special data structures that act as the repository of corresponding module behavior. A module can then use these data structures to determine the behavior of another module without actually executing it. The method offers up to an 86% reduction in time requirements.

The technique proposed also allows a human modeler to analyze and determine the SPOFs in a composition. In this pursuit, in Chapter 7 we propose a method for installing hierarchy into the formal representation of a service composition. A hierarchical model offers various levels of abstraction and expressiveness. Consequently, regardless of the size of the model for a service composition, a human modeler can analyze and determine the SPOFs. The hierarchy is installed by identifying the structurally similar components in a flat model and constituting a module for each of them.

Nevertheless, the advantages offered by the solutions proposed have some limitations. Most motably, the verification technique proposed cannot automatically formalize a BPEL specification into every existing modeling language. This is essentially because certain formal representations (e.g., process algebras) cannot be generated programmatically. However, such limitations can easily be circumvented by formalizing the specification into an intermediate formal model before obtaining the required representation. The intermediate formal model must be (1) easy to obtain from the intermediate DTOs, and (2) easy to transform into the targeted model.

Considering the additional processing time in (1) calculating the difference form for the states generated, (2) storing and retrieving the states, and (3) regenerating explicit states before comparison, the proposed memory reduction technique has an increased time overhead. Experimental results indicate that the processing time for model checking is doubled when using the solution proposed.

In addition, time-reduction techniques cannot be used in nonhierarchical models. Although this limitation is addressed by the method for installing hierarchy into a flat model, it is applicable only when the modeling language used has the semantics of hierarchy and structural similarity.

9.3 WHAT COULD BE IMPROVED?

In this section we outline the course of future research in further enhancement of the solutions proposed.

Memory Requirements for Model Checking. The technique proposed reduces the memory requirements by storing a state as the difference from its nearest or immediately preceding state. Although the results exemplify the prowess of our method, it has an associated time overhead. This overhead, in combination with the processing delay, could counter the memory reduction achieved.

Considering the significant strides in parallel and distributed computing techniques, their use in the method proposed should further reduce the time overhead. The availability of multiple computers in a distributed technique leads to (1) an increase in memory available for model checking, and (2) a decrease in delay (with an increase in processing resources). However, depending on the network latency, there could be additional time overhead in distributed model checking. Consequently, the model-checking algorithm should be optimized to require minimum network communications. Such optimizations could involve piggybacking, compression, and so on.

Time Requirements for Model Checking. The technique proposed to reduce the model-checking time is based on modular state-space generation. Such techniques generate the reachability graph for each module independently before composing them to generate the system reachability graph. However, this technique has hitherto been used sparingly. This is essentially because modular techniques are not applicable for flat models.

Considering the exquisite results obtained for the time-reduction method proposed, modular techniques should be researched further to enhance their applicability. This could be done by introducing autoformalization tools targeting hierarchical models instead of flat models. A hierarchical model could be generated by identifying the identical components of a system. In such a setup each component of the system could be represented by a module, and they would together constitute the hierarchical model. This would also enhance the analyzability and maintainability of the models.

Installing Hierarchy into Models. The technique proposed for installing hierarchy is based on identifying the structural similarities in a formal model. However, it is applicable only for graph-based models (e.g., petri nets and its extensions, automata) that define the notion of structural similarity. Consequently, the technique proposed cannot be applied for certain modeling languages (e.g., Promela [1], SMV [21]).

Considering the obvious advantages in installing hierarchy into a flat model (i.e., they can easily be analyzed and maintained, they can be subjected to the modular technique proposed in Chapter 6, etc.), the technique proposed should be extended to other modeling languages. This could be done using alternative techniques to identify the similar components of a model. Such techniques could include semantic similarity, logical similarity, and others [20].

Formalizing a BPEL Specification. The framework proposed transforms a BPEL specification into a hierarchy of DTOs before formalizing them into an XML-based formal model. The use of DTOs in software engineering as design patterns for storing and transferring data [7] legitimizes their role as generic intermediates. However, the existence of a significant number of non-XML-based modeling languages (e.g., Promela [1], SMV [21]) necessitates the transformation of DTOs into these languages. Consequently, the framework proposed should be extended with additional automatic transformations for DTOs.

This could be done by mapping BPEL activities into the alternative modeling language being used. This mapping can then be used for programmatic formalization of the DTOs into the target formal language. This transformation might require a certain degree of manual interaction, depending on the target modeling language. However, if this transformation is excessively difficult, the DTOs could be transformed into an intermediate modeling language before transforming that language into the target language.

REFERENCES

1. *Promela Manual*, January 2011.
2. G. Berthelot. Checking properties of nets using transformation. In *Advances in Petri Nets 1985, covers the 6th European Workshop on Applications and Theory in Petri Nets—Selected Papers*, pages 19–40. Springer-Verlag, London, 1986.
3. S. Christensen, L. M. Kristensen, and T. Mailund. A sweep-line method for state space exploration. In *Proceedings of the 7th International Conference on Tools and Algorithms for the Construction and Analysis of Systems, TACAS 2001,* pages 450–464, 2001.
4. G. Christopher. Software modeling introduction. *Borland White Paper*. Borland Software Corporation, Austin, TX, March 2003.

5. E. M. Clarke, E. A. Emerson, S. Jha, and A. P. Sistla. Symmetry reductions in model checking. In *Computer Aided Verification*, volume 1427 of *Lecture Notes in Computer Science*, pages 147–158. Springer-Verlag, Berlin, 1998.
6. E. Clarke, O. Grumberg, and D. Peled. *Model Checking*. MIT Press, Cambridge, MA, 2000.
7. W. Crawford and J. Kaplan. *J2EE Design Patterns*. O'Reilly & Associates, Inc., Sebastopol, CA, 2003.
8. L. Elgaard. *The Symmetry Method for Colored Petri Nets: Theory, Tools and Practical Use*. Ph.D. disestation, University of Aarhus, Denmark, 2002.
9. S. Evangelista, S. Haddad, and J.-F. Pradat-Peyre. Syntactical colored petri nets reductions. In *Proceedings of the 3rd International Symposium on Automated Technology for Verification and Analysis, ATVA 2005,* volume 3707 of *Lecture Notes in Computer Science*, pages 202–216. Springer, Verlag, Berlin, 2005.
10. S. Evangelista and J.-F. Pradat-Peyre. On the computation of stubborn sets of colored petri nets. In *Proceedings of the 27th International Conference on Application and Theory of Petri Nets, ICATPN'06*, pages 146–165. Springer-Verlag, Berlin, 2006.
11. S. Evangelista and J.-F. Pradat-Peyre. Memory efficient state space storage in explicit software model checking. In *Proceedings of the 12th International SPIN Workshop on Model Checking of Software*, volume 3639 of *Lecture Notes in Computer Science*, pages 43–57. Springer-Verlag, Berlin, 2005.
12. H. Foster, S. Uchitel, J. Magee, and J. Kramer. Model-based verification of web service compositions. In *Proceedings of the 18th IEEE International Conference on Automated Software Engineering, 2003*, pages 152–161, October 2003.
13. X. Fu, T. Bultan, and J. Su. Analysis of interacting BPEL web services. In *Proceedings of the 13th World Wide Web Conference*, pages 621–630. ACM, New York, 2004.
14. S. Haddad. A reduction theory for colored nets. In *Advances in Petri Nets 1989, covers the 9th European Workshop on Applications and Theory in Petri Nets—Selected Papers*, pages 209–235. Springer-Verlag, Berlin, 1990.
15. G. J. Holzmann. State compression in spin: recursive indexing and compression training runs. In *Proceedings of the 3rd International SPIN Workshop*, 1997.
16. F. Leyman. *Web Services Flow Language, 9 Version 0.1*, IBM, Armonk, NY, May 2001.
17. K. Jensen and L. M. Kristensen. *Colored Petri Nets: Modelling and Validation of Concurrent Systems*. Springer-Verlag, Berlin, 2009.
18. H. Kang, X. Yang, and S. Yuan. Modeling and verification of web services composition based on CPN. In *Proceedings of the 2007 IFIP International Conference on Network and Parallel Computing Workshops*, pages 613–617. IEEE Computer Society, Washington, DC, 2007.
19. L. M. Kristensen and A. Valmari. Finding stubborn sets of colored petri nets without unfolding. In *Proceedings of the 19th International Conference on Application and Theory of Petri Nets, ICATPN '98*, pages 104–123. Springer-Verlag Berlin, 1998.
20. A. G. Maguitman, F. Menczer, H. Roinestad, and A. Vespignani. Algorithmic detection of semantic similarity. In *Proceedings of the 14th International Conference on World Wide Web*, WWW '05, pages 107–116. ACM, New York, 2005.
21. K. McMillan. *SMV Manual*, November 2000.

22. K. Schmidt and C. Stahl. A petri net semantic for BPEL4WS validation and application. In *Proceedings of the 11th Workshop on Algorithms and Tools for Petri Nets, AWPN'04*, pages 1–6, 2004.
23. K. Schmidt. Using petri net invariants in state space construction. In *Proceedings of the 9th International Conference on Tools and Algorithms for the Construction and Analysis of Systems, TACAS 2003*, pages 473–488. Springer-Verlag, Berlin, 2003.
24. J. C. Sloan and T. M. Khoshgoftaar. From web service artifact to a readable and verifiable model. *IEEE Transactions on Services Computing*, 2:277–288, October 2009.
25. C. Stahl. A petri net semantics for BPEL. *Informatik-Berichte 188*. Humboldt-Universität zu Berlin, July 2005.
26. S. Thatte. *XLANG Web Services for Business Process Design*. Microsoft Corporation, Redmond, WA, May 2001.
27. W. M. P. van der Aalst. Don't go with the flow: web services composition standards exposed. *IEEE Intelligent Systems*, January–February 2003.
28. K. Varpaaniemi. Stable models for stubborn sets. *Fundamenta Informaticae*, 43:355–375, 2000.
29. P. Wohed, W. M. P. van der Aalst, M. Dumas, and A. H. M. ter Hofstede. Pattern-based analysis of BPEL4WS. *QUT Technical Report FIT-TR-2002-04*. Queensland Technical University, Brisbane, Australia, 2002.

INDEX

Verification of Communication Protocols in Web Services: Model-Checking Service Compositions, First Edition. Zahir Tari, Peter Bertok, Anshuman Mukherjee.

WILEY SERIES ON PARALLEL AND DISTRIBUTED COMPUTING

Series Editor: Albert Y. Zomaya

Parallel and Distributed Simulation Systems / Richard Fujimoto

Mobile Processing in Distributed and Open Environments / Peter Sapaty

Introduction to Parallel Algorithms / C. Xavier and S. S. Iyengar

Solutions to Parallel and Distributed Computing Problems: Lessons from Biological Sciences / Albert Y. Zomaya, Fikret Ercal, and Stephan Olariu (*Editors*)

Parallel and Distributed Computing: A Survey of Models, Paradigms, and Approaches / Claudia Leopold

Fundamentals of Distributed Object Systems: A CORBA Perspective / Zahir Tari and Omran Bukhres

Pipelined Processor Farms: Structured Design for Embedded Parallel Systems / Martin Fleury and Andrew Downton

Handbook of Wireless Networks and Mobile Computing / Ivan Stojmenović *(Editor)*

Internet-Based Workflow Management: Toward a Semantic Web / Dan C. Marinescu

Parallel Computing on Heterogeneous Networks / Alexey L. Lastovetsky

Performance Evaluation and Characteization of Parallel and Distributed Computing Tools / Salim Hariri and Manish Parashar

Distributed Computing: Fundamentals, Simulations and Advanced Topics, *Second Edition* / Hagit Attiya and Jennifer Welch

Smart Environments: Technology, Protocols, and Applications / Diane Cook and Sajal Das

Fundamentals of Computer Organization and Architecture / Mostafa Abd-El-Barr and Hesham El-Rewini

Advanced Computer Architecture and Parallel Processing / Hesham El-Rewini and Mostafa Abd-El-Barr

UPC: Distributed Shared Memory Programming / Tarek El-Ghazawi, William Carlson, Thomas Sterling, and Katherine Yelick

Handbook of Sensor Networks: Algorithms and Architectures / Ivan Stojmenović *(Editor)*

Parallel Metaheuristics: A New Class of Algorithms / Enrique Alba (*Editor*)

Design and Analysis of Distributed Algorithms / Nicola Santoro

Task Scheduling for Parallel Systems / Oliver Sinnen

Computing for Numerical Methods Using Visual C++ / Shaharuddin Salleh, Albert Y. Zomaya, and Sakhinah A. Bakar

Architecture-Independent Programming for Wireless Sensor Networks / Amol B. Bakshi and Viktor K. Prasanna

High-Performance Parallel Database Processing and Grid Databases / David Taniar, Clement Leung, Wenny Rahayu, and Sushant Goel

Algorithms and Protocols for Wireless and Mobile Ad Hoc Networks / Azzedine Boukerche (*Editor*)

Algorithms and Protocols for Wireless Sensor Networks / Azzedine Boukerche (*Editor*)

Optimization Techniques for Solving Complex Problems / Enrique Alba, Christian Blum, Pedro Isasi, Coromoto León, and Juan Antonio Gómez (*Editors*)

Emerging Wireless LANs, Wireless PANs, and Wireless MANs: IEEE 802.11, IEEE 802.15, IEEE 802.16 Wireless Standard Family / Yang Xiao and Yi Pan (*Editors*)

High-Performance Heterogeneous Computing / Alexey L. Lastovetsky and Jack Dongarra

Mobile Intelligence / Laurence T. Yang, Augustinus Borgy Waluyo, Jianhua Ma, Ling Tan, and Bala Srinivasan (*Editors*)

Advanced Computational Infrastructures for Parallel and Distributed Adaptive Applicatons / Manish Parashar and Xiaolin Li *(Editors)*

Market-Oriented Grid and Utility Computing / Rajkumar Buyya and Kris Bubendorfer *(Editors)*

Cloud Computing Principles and Paradigms / Rajkumar Buyya, James Broberg, and Andrzej Goscinski

Energy-Efficient Distributed Computing Systems / Albert Y. Zomaya and Young Choon Lee *(Editors)*

Scalable Computing and Communications: Theory and Practice / Samee U. Khan, Lizhe Wang, and Albert Y. Zomaya

The DATA Bonanza: Improving Knowledge Discovery in Science, Engineering, and Business / Malcolm Atkinson, Rob Baxter, Michelle Galea, Mark Parsons, Peter Brezany, Oscar Corcho, Jano van Hemert, and David Snelling *(Editors)*

Large Scale Network-Centric Distributed Systems / Hamid Sarbazi-Azad and Albert Y. Zomaya *(Editors)*

Verification of Communication Protocols in Web Services: Model-Checking Service Compositions / Zahir Tari, Peter Bertok, and Anshuman Mukherjee